Frances, Lady Nelson

The Life and Times of
An Admirable Wife

Other books by Sheila Hardy

The Village School

1804, That Was the Year...

The Story of Anne Candler

The Diary of a Suffolk Farmer's Wife: 1854–69

Treason's Flame

The Cretingham Murder

A Village and Its People

The House on the Hill

FRANCES, LADY NELSON

THE LIFE AND TIMES OF AN ADMIRABLE WIFE

by

Sheila Hardy

Foreword by

Colin White

SPELLMOUNT
Staplehurst

British Library Cataloguing in Publication Data:
A catalogue record for this book is available
from the British Library

Copyright © Sheila Hardy 2005
Foreword © Colin White 2005

Maps: Nevis © R A Peres;
The West Indies © The Navy Records Society;
London During the Napoleonic Wars © G M Trevelyan

ISBN 1-86227-272-7

First published in the UK in 2005 by
Spellmount Limited
The Village Centre
Staplehurst
Kent TN12 0BJ

Tel: 01580 893730
Fax: 01580 893731
E-mail: enquiries@spellmount.com
Website: www.spellmount.com

1 3 5 7 9 8 6 4 2

Printed in Great Britain by
Oaklands Book Services
Stonehouse, Gloucestershire GL10 3RQ

Contents

For Robert, who made the dream a reality

List of Maps

Foreword

by Dr Colin White

Among the Nelson papers in the British Library, there is a slim file of documents that once belonged to Frances, Lady Nelson. Most of them are mementoes of her marriage. So, for example, there is a letter of condolence written to her by the First Lord of the Admiralty, Lord Barham, in November 1805 following the death of her husband at the Battle of Trafalgar: 'It is the Death he wished for & the less to be regretted on his own Account. But the public loss is irreparable.' Or there are some notes in Nelson's bold, distinctive hand, outlining his very generous proposals for the division of his income between them at the time of their separation in 1801. As she later acknowledged, this 'far exceeded my expectation, knowing your income and had you left it to me I could not in conscience have said so much'.

Most poignant are the first two documents in the file. Both are dated 11 March – but fourteen years apart. The first is a handwritten marriage certificate, prepared by the Rector of St John's, Antigua on 11 March 1787 and bearing the signatures of the bride and groom – 'Horatio Nelson' and 'Frances Herbert Nisbet' – and of the chief witness, 'William' – Prince William Henry, later King William IV.

Filed next to it is the fragment of another letter in Nelson's handwriting, endorsed by Frances, 'This is my Lord Nelson's letter of dismissal.' Most of the body of the letter has been torn away but the 'cover' has survived and it is dated 11 March 1801. So this letter, in which Nelson told his wife brusquely 'my only wish is to be left to myself', was written on their fourteenth wedding anniversary. The cruel irony of the dating has hitherto been missed by historians – but it clearly was not lost on Frances, who carefully placed the two documents next to each other in the file. Reading them together, one suddenly becomes painfully aware of just how much she must have suffered.

Frances Nelson has not been served well by her husband's biographers, most of whom, of course, have been men. Even those most sympathetic to

9

her, have tended to portray her as colourless and timid, unable to match her husband's energy and emotional fire. Others have gone even further and, cruelly, have sought to blame the failure of her marriage on her emotional and sexual inadequacy. In particular, her role in the actual ending of the marriage, between November 1800 and January 1801, has been much misunderstood and the myth has arisen of a cold and strident woman who effectively drove her wretched husband into the arms of the more attractive and loving Emma Hamilton. This myth was memorably personified by Gladys Cooper's vivid portrayal of Frances as a stiff-backed, icy and embittered shrew in the famous Alexander Korda film, *Lady Hamilton* (1941), in which the much more attractive, and sympathetic, lovers were played by Laurence Olivier and Vivien Leigh.

One reason for this unfair portrayal of Frances is that not many of her letters to Nelson survive in the otherwise voluminous Nelson archive. This is not surprising – we know that it was his invariable custom to destroy his private correspondence before going into battle and, as a result, very few of Emma Hamilton's letters to him have survived either. The discovery, in 2001, of a significant archive of letters from Frances to Nelson's friend and prize agent, Alexander Davison, has helped historians to redress the balance a little and to show that, far from being embittered and shrewish, Frances retained very warm and loving feelings towards her husband. Here she is, writing to Davison in June 1801, more than six months after Nelson had abandoned her:

> If you do not think I have expressed My feelings My affection and My sincere desire to do every thing he wishes me I am willing to say more – if possible – Should he receive me with affection I will do every thing for him and in a gracious manner he shall have no reason to regret his goodness to me I give you my honour.

The new material also enables us to challenge some of the very unfair statements about Frances made by Nelson's apologists. So, for example, the respected editor of Nelson's letters and dispatches, Sir Nicholas Harris Nicolas, claimed in 1845 that after the couple parted in January 1801, 'Lady Nelson never made the slightest effort to recover his affection; nor was it until 23rd April that [Nelson] signified his determination to be "left to himself."' Thanks to the evidence of the 'Davison' Archive (now in the National Maritime Museum), we can show that both these statements are false. Frances made at least six separate attempts at reconciliation, each of which was rebuffed with increasing harshness. And the surviving scrap of his 'letter of dismissal' shows that Nelson was demanding to be left to himself much earlier than Nicolas supposed.

But the 11 March letter has another message for us. As mentioned earlier, part of it is missing – the upper two-thirds of the first page has been neatly torn or cut away, leaving only the last lines of the letter itself and

10

Nelson's signature. We have some idea what the rest of the letter may have said, because Nelson wrote a draft, on 4 March 1801, which has survived among his papers in the National Maritime Museum. In the opening passage, Nelson tells Frances angrily that he has heard that her son, Josiah, has expressed a wish to 'Break my Neck'. It is now clear that, anxious to preserve her husband's reputation, Frances even went so far as to destroy some of his letters to her, written at the time of their separation. 'No one shall know of these harsh and cruel letters,' she assured Davison on 2 March 1801. The torn fragment of the 'dismissal' letter in her file in the British Library shows she kept her word.

The last full-scale biography of Frances Nelson was written by EM Keate in 1939 and, since then, all Frances' surviving letters to her husband have been located and edited by Katherine Lindsay-MacDougall and George Naish in their superb, scholarly work, *Nelson's Letters to His Wife* , published by the Navy Records Society in 1958. With the discovery of the Davison Archive, the time is clearly ripe for a reassessment of the woman to whom Nelson was happily married for fourteen years and who remained faithfully and lovingly attached to him for the rest of her long life.

It is therefore a pleasure to welcome this new biography by Sheila Hardy. I hope that it will help to redress the balance a little and enable Frances to take her rightful place at Nelson's side in this bicentenary year: not as a caricature shrew but as the 'valuable wife' to whom Nelson wrote, in October 1798, 'God Almighty bless you and protect you from all harm is the constant prayer of your affectionate husband.'

Colin White
Portsmouth, May 2005

Acknowledgements

Without access to the documents held at the National Maritime Museum, Greenwich, the Nelson Museum, Monmouth, Harvard University and Naish's *The Letters of Nelson to his Wife*, this work could not have been written. I wish to record my immense gratitude to all those who gave permission for material to be quoted: Dr Colin White of the NMM for his encouragement; Daphne Knott, Librarian, the Caird Library, NMM for her unfailing enthusiasm and helpful advice; Andrew Helme in Monmouth for his generosity; Susan Halpert of the Houghton Library, Harvard for her kindness and understanding, and the Navy Records Society who gave their blessing to the work along with their kind permission to draw on Naish's work.

I hope the Lady Walpole realises how much I appreciated not only the valuable information she provided about the family at Wolterton but also her keen interest in Fanny Nelson.

My thanks too, to all the very obliging members of staff in the Local Studies Libraries of Bath, Brighton, Exmouth, Norwich, Salisbury; Suffolk Record Office and the National Archives at Kew.

In Nevis I have to thank Joan Robinson, Lornette Hanley, Vince Hubbard and Ben Carr for putting up with my many questions and frequent e-mails.

I hope that the friends I unashamedly used to help search out information will accept this token of my appreciation: Geoffrey Hamilton for Scottish material, Charles Michell who whetted my appetite for Nevis and Dr E Cockayne who answered medical queries. Ian Scrivener provided some interesting local information.

Two new 'e-mail' friends were made during the course of this research: Christine Eickelmann in Bristol shared her knowledge of John Pinney and the C18 Slave Trade and Diana Neill of the British Embassy in Paris picked up on my enthusiasm and came up with some very valuable suggestions for background reading. I hope one day to be able to thank them both personally.

I owe a tremendous debt to each of the following. Dorothy Myers, the Librarian of Capel St Mary, Suffolk Public Library Service, who worked tirelessly on my behalf to obtain the books I needed. Her cheerful smile as she handed over various tomes often helped me when the going was tough. Patricia Burnham again listened and encouraged as well as providing her genealogical expertise. Robin Wade showed his belief in my work. Sue Kerswell, as always, listened and then read what I had written. Finally, I thank my very own Captain Hardy for his naval input but most of all for having to spend the last three years in the company of Fanny Nelson.

Introduction

Different tales are told in different places but a time must come when everything will appear in a true light.

If the producers of the television programme *This Is Your Life* had ever run out of celebrities to feature, they might have considered a variation of the theme using celebrities from the past. What scope this would have provided for 'resting' actors who could have assumed the roles of not only the main subject but also all those others who were brought in to testify to the greatness, affability, kindness, generosity and all the other wonderful traits that the honoured subject was reputed to possess. Imagine the kissing and backslapping that might go on when Handel or Sir Joshua Reynolds held centre stage. And as the anecdotes of youthful indiscretions were revealed, would we learn the true story of Shakespeare's deer poaching or his shot-gun wedding to Anne Hathaway? Would there be hints to the identity of the 'Dark Lady' of the sonnets or would she be the one to make a dramatic appearance at the end of the show?

But who should occupy that all-important chair beside the celebrity? Would it have been Catherine Parr beside Henry VIII? And of the other five wives, would they have merited even a mention? I suppose Jane Seymour might warrant a seat in the rows behind Henry but one imagines there might be but glancing references to the mothers of his daughters Mary and Elizabeth.

It was who this occupant was that interested me when I watched the TV programme. Often it was the second, or even third wife, the one who had enjoyed his successful years, who accompanied the subject. Is it perverse of me to wonder how number one felt about all the adulation in which her successor basked, when she was probably the person who supported him as he was making his way to the top? How often do we hear the phrase, 'he outgrew her and she couldn't cope with his new lifestyle'? As far as the world is concerned, the current wife or partner is the only one that matters in the consideration of the subject of the big red book.

This train of thought was sparked off by the reactions I encountered whenever I mentioned that I hoped to write a biography of Lady Nelson. I can forgive the man or woman in the street for being confused but when an academic archivist sent me a list of the letters of Emma Hamilton when I had requested information about Nelson's wife, I realised it really was time that Fanny Nelson should take her rightful place in history.

When Admiral Lord Nelson returned to England in November 1800, London society was able to see for itself his ludicrous behaviour with Lady Hamilton that had been hinted at in the press and openly discussed by those who had encountered his little entourage as it travelled overland from Italy. His friends, colleagues and Admiralty officials had indicated many times during the preceding year that they believed his close friendship with Sir William Hamilton and especially his wife was inappropriate. While no one would blame a seafarer away from home for a long period taking a mistress one did expect the affair to be conducted discreetly. However much Nelson might declare that his friendship with Lady Hamilton was purely platonic and that he loved and respected his dear friend Sir William, English travellers on the continent had observed otherwise. Nelson was infatuated with the voluptuous Emma and appeared to have given little thought to how his affair with her would affect his wife. Possibly he expected her to be as complaisant as Sir William.

When Nelson went back to sea in January 1801 it seemed that his marriage was over and it was not many months before he had bought a house where he and the Hamiltons could live together. Society was appalled at the callous behaviour of the 'great naval hero'. To defend his reputation, he, Emma Hamilton and to a large extent, Nelson's brother, the Reverend William Nelson, set about a deliberate policy of maligning Fanny, blaming her for the break up of the marriage. This defamation of her character has continued for nearly two hundred years, book after book painting her as a cold, uncaring creature, starting with *The Letters of Lord Nelson to Lady Hamilton,* an anonymous work published in two volumes in 1814 at the instigation of Emma although she disclaimed any part in it.

Down the years biographers have preserved the reputation of their hero and with it have spun the story of 'one of the world's great romances'. It is only recently that some writers have begun to acknowledge that perhaps he did treat his wife rather badly but even so, they still perpetuate the same arguments against her, namely that she was cold and lacking in emotion. She has been described as a pathetic, often neurotic woman, incapable of making any decision for herself. She has been accused of being concerned only with trivia and obsessed by her own health. She is said to have lacked personal charm; her face and figure are unfavourably compared to those of Emma Hamilton and even today, the most unflattering portrait of her is reproduced on the postcards for sale at the National Maritime Museum. She is also blamed for not having a settled home ready and waiting for Nelson when he returned in 1800 and when it was acknowledged that Nelson was the father of Emma's daughter, Fanny's failure to bear him a child was cited as proof of her frigidity and the cause of his lack of physical interest in her.

Careful reading of Nelson's letters to Fanny and those from her that are still in existence reveal a very different story. It is the purpose of this book to show that Frances, Lady Nelson was a warm, affectionate, well-liked and respected woman who had at an early age learned to take responsibility for herself and others. Far from being insignificant, she could hold her own in the highest society. For fourteen years she gave Nelson her undivided love and support, bearing their time apart with great fortitude and but rarely losing her sense of humour. His cold dismissal of her almost broke her spirit but the recently discovered cache of letters that she wrote to Alexander Davison, Nelson's friend and Prize agent, shows she did not give him up without a fight. Her conduct throughout her married life was such that all who observed her agreed that she was an admirable wife.

Who Was Who

Frances Woolward (Fanny): daughter of William Woolward, Chief Justice of the island of Nevis and his wife Mary née Herbert.

Dr Josiah Nisbet: son of Walter Nisbet of the Mount Pleasant Plantation, Nevis, married Frances Woolward, died 1781.

Capt. Josiah Nisbet: son of Frances and Josiah.

John Richardson Herbert: President of Nevis, owner of the Montpelier Plantation, uncle to Fanny, father of Martha.

Martha Herbert: married Andrew Hamilton.

Sally Morton: daughter of Sally and Andrew Morton – cousin to Fanny, married Capt. Kelly.

Magnus Morton: brother to the above; inherited the Montpelier estate.

The Webbe Family: Dr Nisbet's maternal relations who lived in Salisbury.

The Pinneys: Plantation owners in Nevis who settled in Bristol. Friends of Fanny.

The Tobins: merchants in Bristol with whom Fanny often stayed.

Horatio Nelson: married Fanny Nisbet 1787.

The Revd Edmund Nelson of Burnham Thorpe, Norfolk, father of Horatio and:-

Maurice: employed in Navy Office, lived with Susannah Forde, 'blind Sukey';

William : the Rector of Hilborough, married to Sarah (Yonge), became Earl Nelson;

Edmund: died young;

Suckling : apprenticed to trade but took Holy Orders and became father's curate;

Susannah: married Thomas Bolton, a merchant, lived mainly in Norfolk had a large family that included: Susanna and Catherine, twin daughters;

Catherine: known as Kitty, married George Matcham who made his money from the East India Company. They lived at Shepherds Spring and Bath.

Charlotte Nelson: daughter of the Rector, married Samuel Hood, became Lady Bridport and, ultimately, inherited Fanny's title of Viscountess Bronte.

William Suckling: Nelson's maternal uncle; lived in Kentish Town; married (secondly) to Mary Rumsey.

The Revd William Bolton: brother of Thomas Bolton; rector of Hollesley, Suffolk; father of Mary Ann who married Lt Pierson.

CHAPTER I

The Widow Nisbet

You will have heard from my father, that I am in a fair way to changing my situation. The dear object you must like. Her sense, polite manners and to you I may say, [her] beauty, you will much admire: and although at present we may not be a rich couple, yet I have not the least doubt but we shall be a happy pair: the fault must be mine if we are not.
Nelson, December 1786

After a number of abortive attempts to find himself a suitable wife, the ambitious but almost penniless young Captain Horatio Nelson had at last found a woman who seemed just right for him. He had already sent the news home but it was in his Christmas letter to his brother William, who was also on the look out for a suitable wife, that he gave the important details. About his own age, she was neither too young, as had been the 16 year-old Miss Mary Simpson with whom he had fallen in love in Quebec in 1782, nor was she, like the most recent object of his affection, Mary Moutray, the wife of someone else. Best of all, and essential for any young man without a fortune of his own in the eighteenth century, this lady, while not rich, had the prospect of wealth, and for the present it certainly looked as if she would bring him a small but steady income.

Nelson had returned to naval service on the West India station in 1783. His brother William, a clergyman, had begged to be allowed to accompany him as his chaplain aboard the *Boreas*. The area of the Caribbean Nelson patrolled included the Leeward Islands, among them the two small colonies of St Kitts and Nevis. And it was here on the smaller of the two, Nevis, that he found the woman to whom he swore undying love and of whom he wrote: 'I could lay down my life with pleasure at this moment for her future happiness.' He was by no means the first man to anchor off these shores and find himself a beautiful, often wealthy, wife to carry back to England. Indeed, William's desire to travel with his brother may have been prompted by the possibility of meeting a husband-hungry young Creole (of European origin born in the Caribbean) heiress. Although by no means in that league, Nelson's 'dear object', the attractive young widow, Fanny Nisbet, just happened to be the niece of the most important man in Nevis.

There could not have been a greater contrast between the early childhood of Nelson and that of his future bride. Horatio Nelson was one of a large family; his father was a clergyman who came from yeoman stock rather than the landed gentry, though his mother, Catherine (née Suckling) was connected to aristocracy. Financially the family was dependent on the Reverend Edmund Nelson's clerical livings supplemented by the income from the small glebe farm that went with the living. All his children received an education but each of them, the three girls included, was brought up knowing that they would need to earn a living to support them. The family home was a remote farmhouse parsonage; an ancient building that over the years had suffered neglect through lack of money to spend on it. Situated in the flat lowlands of north Norfolk, even today this is a thinly populated, rural area. The small market towns of Kings Lynn, Fakenham and Swaffham offered some entertainment in the way of concerts and balls, but for any major event it was necessary to make the long journey to Norwich which would involve an overnight stay. Such social life as was available locally centred on visiting the homes of their neighbours and even that was dependent on the weather. And there lay the greatest contrast in background. Nelson came from the pinched, cold climate of Norfolk where even in summer biting winds can sweep across the North Sea keeping temperatures below average.

Fanny Nisbet, née Woolward, had flourished in the warmth of Nevis, an island less than a third of the size of the Isle of Wight, which on an early map bears a strong resemblance to the 'treasure island' a child might imagine. Along with its very close neighbour, St Kitts, it had been colonised by the English in the early seventeenth century, by those looking for new places to settle and to develop into trading posts. The combination of a warm equable climate, rarely hotter than 80°F, with a volcanic rich soil on the steep slopes of the central mountain, made it the ideal alternative to North America for the cultivation of cotton and tobacco. It was soon discovered that spices, in particular ginger and indigo, grew so abundantly that part of the island became known as Gingerland. However, by the middle of the century sugar had become the main crop, the production methods for which had been brought to the islands by migrant Jews from Brazil where they had settled following their expulsion from Spain and Portugal.

There was a vast difference too between the populations of Norfolk and Nevis. Most of the Nelsons' village neighbours would have been agricultural workers whose forebears were deeply rooted in the Norfolk soil, while their social equals were likely to have originated from the surrounding area too, and almost certainly they would have been of British origin. In contrast, although most of the white population had come from the British Isles, the majority of the island's people was Afro-Caribbean. The labour intensive production of sugar from planting the canes through to the fin-

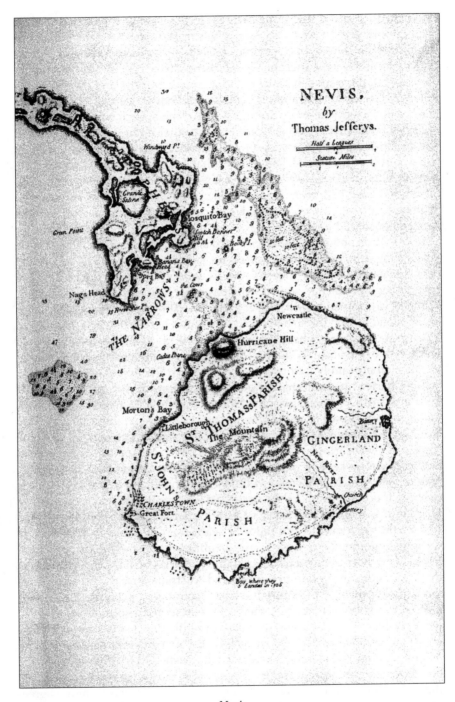

Nevis

ished product meant that quite early on in the island's history, slaves had been imported from Africa to supply the work force. Towards the end of the eighteenth century the number of slaves in Nevis had risen to around 10,000, outnumbering their masters by ten to one. Where Nelson's nurse-maid would have spoken in the broad accent of Norfolk and passed on the folklore of that county, the child Fanny would have accepted as normal the black and mixed race faces around her and the speech rhythms and leg-ends from old Africa that her nurse and the other domestic staff used. And she would have grown up accepting the concept of slavery; in fact when she was still a small child, she received her very own slave, 'a Negro man named Cato' who was left to her by a kinsman, Thomas Williams. His will stated that Cato had been 'loaned' some years earlier to Fanny's father so Williams' gift suggests that there was a close bond between child and the trusted household servant.

Information about William Woolward is scant. Unlike many islanders, he was a comparative newcomer, a second-generation settler. His father had been a seafarer who had married a Nevis widow, but rather than taking her back to England, he had stayed to help run her business. Of their two sons, William was trained to be a lawyer and in due time he became Chief Justice of the island. Given the size of Nevis, this could hardly have amounted to a full-time occupation so he was also able to engage in the family business of Herbert, Morton and Woolward, following his marriage to Mary Herbert.

The Herbert family had been among some of the first to settle in Nevis. When Charles I had granted a Royal commission for the settlement of the Leewards in 1623, emigrants joined the exodus from England for many dif-ferent reasons. Apart from those who came to escape religious persecution, there were others who wanted to evade difficult circumstances at home – the law, overbearing parents, injudicious marriages, failure of businesses – all of them seeking to make a new start in life. Others had an essential craft to offer which they knew would be in demand and might lead to their making, if not a fortune, at the very least a comfortable living; carpenters, blacksmiths, masons and farmers were obvious but the man or woman who could ply a needle as a tailor or seamstress was just as important in the new settlement. For those unable to afford the cost of the passage from England, there was a scheme comparable with that of the 'assisted passage' that operated from Britain to Canada and Australia after the Second World War. In the seventeenth century it was still common practice in England for men and women to indenture themselves as servants, promising to work for a master for a set number of years in return for a small annual wage, accommodation and food. Depending on the type of employment clothing or a livery might be included. So those who wished to try their luck abroad bound themselves to a master for five years in return for a free passage. At the end of their term of 'bondage' they would be released from the agree-ment and given five acres of land to farm, to which, with hard work and perseverance, they might add considerably.

At the opposite end of the social scale were the younger sons of the aristocracy or landed gentry who, left with but small legacies when the elder brother inherited the family estate, preferred to utilise what funds they had in the Caribbean rather than seek menial or mundane work in England. Such had been early members of the Herbert family. A cadet branch of the Earls of Pembroke they were pro-Royalists who had fled the Civil War. They bought land, established plantations and quickly rose to hold public office, several of them becoming either the President or Chief Justice of Nevis during the eighteenth century by which time the Montpelier plantation had been in the family for three generations. Diversifying into shipping and other business interests, Herbert entered into partnership with Morton and Woolward. It is difficult to know exactly which alliance came first to create this partnership, business or marriage, since both Morton and Woolward took Herbert wives. By the time Nelson visited Nevis, John Richardson Herbert was the island's President but more importantly, he was the uncle of the woman he hoped to marry.

Frances Herbert Woolward was baptised a few days after her birth in May 1761 in the parish of St George's, Nevis. Familiarly known as Fanny, she started her life in a comfortable stone-built house close to the shore in the flourishing little capital of Charlestown. Like Nelson she was a semi-orphan, her mother dying before Fanny was really able to remember her. Her father, despite his high office, seems to have left little mark on the island's record and Fanny herself never had cause to divulge anything about him in her later letters. It is only from the will of Thomas Williams of the Saddle Hill plantation that we learn that he and Woolward had engaged in some minor land deals. Although father and daughter were close, Fanny's upbringing would have depended initially upon servants and later the influence of her many relations, not just the immediate ones like the Herberts and Mortons but others like the Pinneys, Weekes, Mills, Tobins and many others who would at some time or other play a part in her life.

The smallness of the white population was such that constant intermarriage between families was inevitable and thus practically everyone was a 'cousin'. That, of course, ignored all the mixed race cousins (and half brothers and sisters) with which the island abounded. In their wills, many slave owners made provision for the black or mulatto women who had borne them children. Many granted them immediate freedom with an annuity for the rest of their life. Others left them an annual income and a plot of land on which to build a home for themselves and their offspring. Often their mixed race children were taken care of financially, marriages arranged for girls, while boys might be sent to England to be educated. The practice of taking a slave as a mistress was widespread, especially amongst those plantation owners whose wives were absent in England for months at a time. Wives may have countenanced their husbands' liaisons, accepting either that this was a normal way of life or with sheer relief in the event of a loveless, arranged match. It is probable that young women about to marry would have had this aspect of marital life explained to them. It was unlikely that any boy or girl could grow up on the islands ignorant of this particular fact of life. Since Fanny's father never remarried, he no doubt also had a mistress from amongst his slaves. Certainly her uncle John Herbert did, and possibly because he lacked legitimate sons, he acknowledged his two natural sons John and Thomas. On their father's death, John, who lived in Bristol, received a legacy of £1,000 while Thomas, who had remained in Nevis was left only £500, the difference being explained by John Herbert that he had, on a number of occasions, assisted Thomas financially. Nonetheless, his affection for John was made manifest in that he left him very personal gifts too, his gold watch with its chain and seals and all his wearing apparel. Proof enough that John junior was being treated as a gentleman.

Although an only child, Fanny was probably not as indulged as many of the cousins who provided her with companionship. With a plentiful supply of servants to do all the work, women in Nevis had the time to gratify the whims of their children, boys in particular were often thoroughly spoilt and given an inflated opinion of their own importance. Reluctantly, doting mammas would eventually have to part with their sons when they were sent back to England for school. This was especially hard as it might be several years before they saw them again. Girls, for the most part, received their education at home from governesses, though there was at least one boarding school for them on the island run by a Mrs Murray in a house on the cool, mountainous retreat that belonged to the plantation owner John Pinney. Naturally, his daughters were among the pupils. Fanny never revealed in her later correspondence what her education had been but it is likely that she shared a governess with her Herbert and Morton cousins. However, it is known that from the second half of the 1700s, girls from the islands were sent away to school, so it is feasible that in her mid teens Fanny received at least two or three years of the formal education considered suitable for a young lady, either in the Bristol area or perhaps, Edinburgh as the *Journal of a Lady of Quality* showed.

On 25 October 1774 Janet Schaw, unmarried and in her mid to late thirties, set sail from Scotland in an emigrant ship with her brother Alexander who was to take up an administrative post in St Kitts. Miss Schaw had also undertaken to accompany the three Rutherfurd children who were going out to join their father in North Carolina. Her account of the long voyage, which included some horrific storms, showed of what stern stuff the women of the eighteenth century were made. Admittedly the Schaws and Rutherfurds travelled in luxury compared with those in steerage, some of whom, having been forced into exile by the Highland clearances, had been smuggled aboard, too poor even to pay the lowest fares. Even so she had to cope with:

> ...the cabin door burst open and I was overwhelmed with an immense wave...and I found myself swimming amongst joint-stools, chests, tables

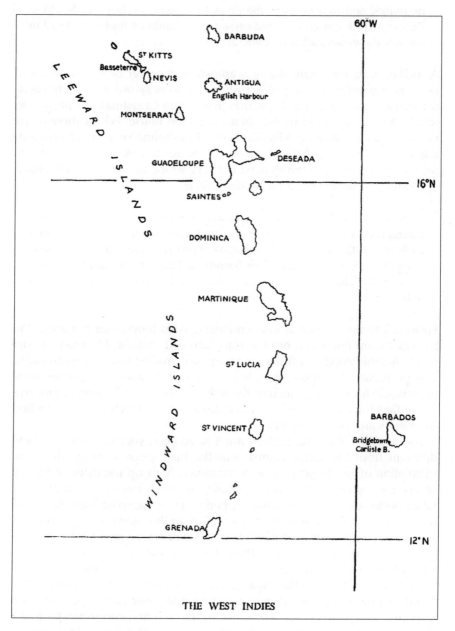

The West Indies

and all the various furniture of our parlour. [And later:]…the ship gave such a sudden and violent heel over, as everything broke from their moorings, and in a moment the great sea-chests, the boys' beds…Miss Rutherfurd's harpsichord…and myself were tumbling heels over head to the side the vessel had laid down on…

A well-educated woman, she was an astute observer of all she saw and her writings offer not only descriptions of scenery but also acute social comment. Landing in the Leewards just before Christmas the party was invited to stay with old friends in a plantation house. Whilst there many visitors came to call and: 'Miss Rutherfurd has found several of her boarding school-friends here; they have many friends to talk of, many scenes to recollect.' Miss Schaw then showed her very strong disapproval of the habit of sending expatriate children back to Britain.

This shows me how improper it is in parents to send them early from themselves and their country. They form their sentiments in Britain, their early connections there, and they leave it just when they are at an age to enjoy it most, and return to their friends and country, as banished exiles; nor can any future connection cure them of the longing they have to return to Britain.

Fortunately, the journal is also enlivened with touches of humour: 'We returned from our walk, not the least fatigued, but the Musquetoes [sic] had smelt the blood of a British man and my brother has his legs bit sadly. Our petticoats, I suppose, guarded us.' Those dreaded mosquitoes were responsible for causing much of the sickness, even death, amongst incoming settlers including the military and naval men like Nelson who patrolled the waters around the islands.

As he sailed the area, Nelson must have been very conscious of how different from his native county was the lush green scenery where the cultivation of the sugar cane was continued high up the sides of Mount Nevis, the top of which was perpetually in cloud, leading to Columbus's false conclusion that it was snow-capped when he named it Nuestra Señora de las Nieves, Our Lady of the Snows. Each of the eighty or so plantations housed not only all its field workers but also provided land for the cultivation of yams and maize to feed them. Once the canes were harvested they were brought to the mill, by no means an elaborate building, where they were ground to release the sugar juice. Depending on its location, a mill could be powered by wind, water or by cattle – one of the Pinneys even imported camels to do the job. Close to the mill and connected by pipes through which ran the extracted juice, was the boiling house. Here, under intense heat, the liquid was boiled and skimmed until it began to crystallize. At which point it was ladled into a cooler where the coarse brown sugar separated from its liquid residue known as molasses. This in turn was either reheated to extract a second grade sugar or was used for the distillation into rum in which case a still was also essential.

At certain times of the year the cloying, sickly sweet smell of boiling sugar must have hung in the air. It was to avoid this constant reminder of their business that the wealthier and more successful planters built their homes away from the mills, surrounding them with hedges of pomegranates, sweet smelling cape jasmine, lime and log-wood and orchards of at least thirty different kinds of fruit. The Norfolk boy would not have grown up eating pineapples, alligator pears and bright yellow granadilla as a matter of course as Fanny did. Nor would he have seen anything to compare with the magnificent palmetto trees with their silky white stems that grew to forty to sixty feet before spreading out twelve-foot pendulous branches that hung round the trunk like an umbrella. The palmetto, interspersed with tamarinds, flowering cedars, myrtles and lemon trees, surrounded the large and airy plantation houses. Often built to resemble the English country houses their forebears had left behind, they were not just family homes but centres of general hospitality. The colonial population cared little for the reserve or etiquette surrounding the genteel British art of visiting. Visitors came and went at all hours, thinking nothing of leaning in at open windows to talk to the occupants while they ate or even, if they felt so inclined, going in and sitting down at table with them. Strangers too were sure of a welcome as Nelson and his fellow officers were to find.

Nevis and its close neighbour St Kitts were small enough that the stratified social grouping that existed in England would have been unrealistic. Thus most of the white population was in attendance whenever a ball or a feast was held. Both were given on the slightest pretext, and apart from giving general amusement and pleasure, the balls especially offered young people a chance to weigh up a possible marriage partner. Girls 'came out' much earlier than in England and marriage at 15 or 16 was not uncommon in the islands. Young Fanny, whose upbringing had meant that she was used to being in adult company, had none of the adolescent gawkiness of many girls. With an appealing vivacity and ease of manner, her slight figure, with her dark chestnut curls setting off her small pointed face and unusually fine dark grey eyes, would have attracted more than a passing glance from the local young men. However, any potential suitor needed to be so financially secure that her lack of a substantial dowry would not be a consideration. Although no documentary proof exists, from Fanny's strong views later on the subject, her father may well have been an inveterate gambler. Cockfights, horse racing, cards and the gaming tables were all pursuits available on the islands and provided the opportunity for vast sums to be lost and won. In Woolward's case it would appear to have been the former. After a long session at the tables, accompanied by large quantities of wine and spirits, it was not surprising if tempers were lost and slanderous insults were exchanged between winners and losers. The almost inevitable way of settling the matter was for the aggrieved party to challenge the other to a duel.

Is that what happened to William Woolward? Certainly, in later life, Fanny despised this method of settling an argument. What is known is that in February 1779 Woolward somehow sustained a wound that became infected causing him to develop lockjaw or tetanus for which there was no cure. Fanny watched over him as the dreadful disease took its rapid toll, in a way preparing her for the role of nurse she would play many times in later years. Not yet 18, the girl was brought face to face with the reality of life as she watched her father writhe his way towards death despite the best efforts of the most up-to-date medical attention of young Dr Josiah Nisbet.

The second son of the owner of one of the larger Nevis plantations and from a family that claimed a noble Scottish ancestry, Josiah had returned to the island following a long spell in Scotland. From school he had gone on to Edinburgh University to study medicine; his inaugural dissertation was 'De Rheumatismo acuto', a condition that affected many in the West Indies as well as those brought up in the dampness of Great Britain. The university, which boasted some of the finest professors of the period, offered a thoroughly rounded education for the students who were drawn from different parts of the world. Nisbet was one of fifteen students who graduated from the medical school in 1768; among them was a dynamic American, Benjamin Rush, who on his return to America became a physician in Washington's army. He went on to become a delegate to congress, founder of the first anti-slavery society in America, a pioneer in the temperance movement and a co-founder of the American Philosophical Society. He and Nisbet coming from across the Atlantic may have been drawn to each other, but it is likely that the subject of slavery led them into opposing camps. While Rush was destined to return to achieve greatness, Josiah's role was more mundane. After working for a time as a locum in the Midlands, by then in his early thirties, he returned to Nevis to set up an island practice. While he waited for paying patients, he was guaranteed an income of £60 a year for taking care of the slaves that belonged to Russell's Rest plantation and he was also retained by another owner to attend the hospital he had set up for his slaves.

There must have been something immediately captivating about Fanny, for thrown together during his frequent visits to the Woolward house, Josiah had come to admire her and she in turn came to rely on his support and friendship. She was not, of course, without other support and immediately after her bereavement she was invited to make her home with her uncle, John Richardson Herbert. Since his house, Montpelier, had been almost a second home to her since childhood, this would have been an easy transition for her except that now she was no longer in charge of the household as she had been in her father's house. She continued to see Nisbet; he used his visits to plantation workers at Montpelier as an excuse to call on her. Within a month or two he had decided that she was the woman he wished to marry and so he proposed – and she accepted.

It is difficult in an age that holds such very different ideas on what constitutes a good marriage and where strong physical attraction often guides choice, to know on what basis Fanny accepted Josiah's offer. If the question is asked 'did she love him?' that immediately poses another question, how do we define 'love'? It is true that Nisbet had caught her when she was most vulnerable and needed comfort. They had shared the intimate experience of caring for her sick father. He had no illusions about her as he had seen her tired and under stress. He was, more than likely, given his profession, a gentle man, unlike the more boisterous young men of her acquaintance. But perhaps Fanny's most realistic motive for agreeing to marry him was that he would give her the independence of a married woman. She had already discovered that although she was almost the sole beneficiary of her father's estate, there was very little money to come to her which meant that she would have to rely on her uncle to provide her with a home. Although if she waited, a richer suitor might appear on the scene, without a dowry to offer her chances were limited. At least she liked Nisbet, he was a good friend and she believed they would make each other happy. So, barely four months after her father's death, on 28 June 1779, with the blessing of her uncle John Herbert, the couple exchanged their marriage vows at St John's church. The wedding feast at Montpelier brought together guests from all over Nevis and St Kitts, to witness the uniting of members from two of the most important island families.

No information exists as to where the young couple made their first home. It may have been at Mount Pleasant, the Nisbet family home especially as Josiah's elder brother Walter, who had inherited the estate was at that time living in London. This was to be but a temporary home for it was not long before Josiah revealed that he wanted to leave the island and take up the offer from a maternal uncle to start a medical practice in Salisbury. With Fanny by this time pregnant they set sail for England, most likely in one of the vessels taking its cargo of sugar to Bristol. As we know from Janet Schaw's account, the voyage would have been a testing time especially for a woman in Fanny's condition. Once landed in Bristol, home to numerous Nevisians who had settled there to run the trading end of the sugar business, there were many visits to be made, each introducing the other to all the various aunts and uncles before they moved on to Salisbury. Here they stayed first with George Webbe and his family before taking the lease on a house in the Cathedral Close from where Josiah would carry on his medical practice.

If this were Fanny's first visit to England, arriving any time during the autumn through to the spring would have been a shock to her constitution, accustomed as she was to almost constant warmth. It is likely that it was while living close to the water meadows in Salisbury that she first developed the rheumatism that was to plague her for the rest of her life. Apart from the cold and damp to contend with, when she and Josiah arrived they found the Webbes still mourning the recent loss of their 25-year-old son. With her approaching confinement and the gloom of mourning hanging over them, life for a young woman used to brightness and gaiety must have seemed perpetually grey.

Even her joy at the birth of a son, named Josiah after his father, was tainted. Fanny had discovered that her husband was not a well man. There are two versions of what caused Nisbet's ill health. One is that during his early years in Nevis, he had suffered such severe sunstroke that it had affected his brain, occasionally triggering bouts of mental instability. How much his condition was the result of over-exposure to the sun is open to question but it is worth noting that it was certainly a widely held belief at the time. Readers, who have had their blood curdled by the screams and antics of Mr Rochester's mad wife in *Jane Eyre*, will recall that the former Bertha Mason came from the West Indies. It was believed at that time that living in a cold climate would prevent the recurrence of the 'dis-ease' and that was why after returning to Nevis, Nisbet, fearing for his state of mind, had decided not to stay. It is not known what form his mental disorder took, whether it was intermittent or prolonged, violent or deeply depressive. The other belief is that he died in early October 1781 at the age of 34 from the debilitating effects of recurrent bouts of yellow fever which caused him to sink into a 'decline', a euphemism that covered many conditions.

Whatever caused his untimely death, the result was that at barely 21 Fanny had become a wife, mother and widow in just over two years. However severe her grief she had to face up to the fact that her immediate problem was money – or rather the lack of it. What little Nisbet had managed to earn as a doctor had been used during his illness and any private funds he had were tied up because of his failure to make a will. Within weeks of his death, the advertisements in the Salisbury newspaper that announced the sale of their household goods, among them Fanny's beloved harpsichord, show that not only could Fanny no longer afford to stay in the house they had rented but there were also outstanding debts to settle. The proceeds of the sale may have covered the bills and the wages due to servants. Before Nisbet's death the household would have included at the very least, the baby's nursemaid, Fanny's personal maid, Nisbet's manservant who could have doubled as groom or coachman, a general maid and perhaps a cook – a small staff compared to that to which she was accustomed in Nevis. Whoever she dispensed with Fanny would have retained the child's nurse and possibly her own attendant.

Following her husband's death Fanny had a foretaste of the peripatetic life as a guest in other people's homes that she would come to know well some years later. As was usual among families, particularly those of expatriates, her own and Nisbet's relations quickly offered her both accommodation and financial assistance. Her obvious course of action was to return to Nevis where she might justly claim support for her son from his Nisbet kin and for herself from her uncle John Herbert. At the time, however, that plan, sensible though it appeared, was not feasible. The people of Nevis were themselves under great stress. The American colonists who had been fighting for some years for their independence from Britain had finally, with the assistance of their French allies, successfully blockaded the

Leeward Islands, preventing outgoing ships leaving with cargo and mail and those incoming to land much needed supplies. The final humiliation came when the French invaded and took possession of the island in January 1782. It was hoped that by capitulating to the French the islanders would be relieved from the grim circumstances in which they found themselves. At the time John Herbert declared:

> I do not exaggerate when I most solemnly aver that to my certain knowl-edge many plantations in this island are at present without a single day's provisions for their slaves and are obliged to grind their canes before they are ripe in order to feed their Negroes with molasses.

Mercifully the French occupation was reasonably short lived, the island being returned to the British under the Treaty of Versailles in 1783.

In the meantime, still in England and unable to receive any funds from Nevis, Fanny was making the best she could of her life, dividing her time between the Tobins and others in Bristol and the Webbes and Weekeses in Salisbury. Mr Weekes was the father-in-law of John Pretor Pinney (he who had imported the camels) and guardian to his three Pinney grandsons who, years before, had been sent to school either in or near Salisbury. A prolific letter writer, J P Pinney on one occasion made a passing reference to Fanny. Having decided that after all that had happened it was time he brought his wife and younger children to England, they left Nevis in July 1783. On landing many weeks later, they had made their way to London expecting to have time to settle in before the reunion with their sons. But father-in-law spoilt everything.

> I have been much provoked at the conduct of Mr Weekes, he, on the very day of Mrs Pinney's arrival at our lodgings in London, brought up my sons from Salisbury, contrary to my desire and direction – between ten and eleven o'clock at night he reached our lodgings… As we had not the least idea of their being in town and not conceiving it possible for him to act so opposite to my wishes, after receiving my letter, we received them as strangers – we did not know them nor they us; until Mrs Josiah Nisbet, who was present, exclaimed, 'Good God! Don't you know them, they are your children?' Upon hearing that I was stupefied and should have remained so some time, had I not been roused by the situation of Mrs P – it affected her so much that she knew not what she did – she set her head-dress in a blaze by the candle – happily the boys perceived it and cried out, which enabled me to extinguish it before it had done any material damage – such a scene of distress and joy I never before experienced – we did not recover ourselves for the whole night.

While this delightfully described scene might have come straight from the pen of Fielding or Sheridan, it is not made clear exactly why Fanny was present. It could be that she was at that time staying in London and hearing of the arrival of her old friends had gone to spend the evening with them. Alternatively, since she had spent time in Salisbury with the Weekeses and knew the children, Mr Weekes may have asked her to accompany him to London with the children. In other words, she may have 'earned her keep' by undertaking such commissions for her benefactors.

It was during that year of 1783 that Nelson, who had been unemployed for some time, was at last given command of the *Boreas* and in 1784 he was sent to patrol the West Indies to enforce the new Navigation Acts that prohibited foreign ships from trading with British colonies. Later that year or possibly in January 1795 when he was anchored off St Kitts, he and his fellow officers went ashore where they were entertained to dinner by various local gentlemen and dignitaries including the president of Nevis, John Herbert. As a matter of course the visitors were invited to the local dances where the young ladies always welcomed the chance to see new faces. Not that Captain Nelson's face inspired any great longing in the hearts of most of the young women who met him. It may have been about this time that Fanny received a letter from a friend describing a dinner at which Nelson had been a guest.

> He declined drinking any wine; but after dinner, when the President, as usual gave the three following toasts, the King, the Queen and the Royal Family, and Lord Hood, this strange man regularly filled his glass and observed that those were always bumper toasts with him; which having drank, he uniformly passed the bottle and relapsed into his former taciturnity. It was impossible during this visit, for any of us to make out his real character; there was such a reserve and sternness in his behaviour, with occasional sallies, though very transient, of a superior mind. Being placed by him, I endeavoured to rouse his attention by showing him all the civilities in my power; but I drew out little more than yes or no. If you, Fanny had been there, we think you would have made something of him, you have been in the habit of attending to these odd sort of people.

When she read the letter, Fanny must have smiled at the somewhat back-handed compliment from her friend, little realising that within months her life would become entwined with that of the odd, taciturn captain.

CHAPTER II
Captain Nelson Finds a Wife

...most sincerely do I love you...my charming Fanny... most sincerely and I trust that my affection is not only founded upon the principles of reason...the more I weigh you in my mind the more reason I find to admire both your head and heart.
Nelson, August 1785

The widow Nisbet who returned to Nevis in 1784 was a very different woman to the young bride who had left the island nearly five years earlier. Then she had gone to England, full of expectation of a settled, secure life as a wife and mother. It is doubtful that she had fully appreciated that life, as a doctor's wife in the small provincial city of Salisbury, would not carry quite the same prestige as the judge's daughter in Nevis. But she had barely had the chance to understand the subtle nuances of English society before her status changed. In the years that followed, there were sharp lessons to be learned. The bride had to face up to widowhood and, what was perhaps even worse than bereavement, accept dependency on others that came from being left without financial support. Those years taught her to be both frugal and compliant with the wishes of others; she would have learnt when to hold her tongue and where she could express herself freely. Having been used to the freedom that being a beloved only child had given her, she must have had to adapt quickly to her current situation. For a woman in her position it was easy to become either a demanding creature, wallowing in self-pity, or a pathetic, self-effacing, eager-to-please figure entirely lacking in character. The evidence that Fanny was welcomed wherever she went by friends as well as relations suggests that she was neither of these, rather that she made an acceptable addition to whichever household she found herself in.

It would be a mistake to think that Fanny was consigned to living a retired life during this period. Far from it! Her time was spent moving between those relations and friends who had made their fortunes in the West Indies, those absentee landlords of large plantations and their families

35

who now lived in comfortable, often opulent surroundings, in Bristol, Bath, Salisbury and London as well as country estates in the shires. As a member of the family wherever she was, she would have shared in their social life and been introduced into the society in which they mixed. Thus she built up a wide circle of acquaintances. Poor widow with the encumbrance of a son to rear and educate, Fanny was nonetheless still an attractive young woman who must have been considered by potential suitors. As she attended balls and parties, concerts and the theatre, doubtless the gossips and matchmakers discussed the fact that she had a very wealthy uncle who would provide for her in the future and it was also believed that when the Nisbet family affairs were sorted, little Josiah's future would be taken care of. In a century when widows rarely found themselves long without an offer of a second marriage it is surprising that Fanny did not take a new husband.

With the return of Nevis to British rule came the opportunity to return to her native land and once more come under the protection of her uncle. John Richardson Herbert's offer to provide her and the child with a home was not entirely altruistic. He was in fact offering Fanny a job – the most important role in his household – that of his official hostess. As a widower, he had relied on his unmarried sister Sarah to carry out those duties. But her failing health meant she could no longer continue in that position. Her natural successor should have been the President's only child, his daughter, Martha. Legend has it that all was not well between father and daughter. It has been said that Martha had set her heart on marrying someone of whom her father disapproved. An impasse had been reached; Martha had made it perfectly plain that if she could not have her own way, then she certainly was not going to wear herself out running her father's house, presiding over stuffy dinners or entertaining dull visiting dignitaries. It has even been suggested that his daughter was not living at home. Yet there is no evidence for any of this. If she had been absent at any time, certainly she was back by the time of Fanny's return. It is much more likely that Herbert did not consider Martha mature enough to take on the position.

Had Fanny been as shy and retiring as some have suggested, Herbert certainly would not have considered her for the role either. He was not looking simply for a housekeeper to attend to the day to day running of the large house. Although this would come within her province, far more important was the ability to receive guests from all walks of life. The President's hostess would be expected to welcome the Governors of the various islands in the Caribbean, Chief Justices and lawyers, senior military and naval officers, important merchant traders as well as visiting dignitaries from Britain, even royalty on occasions. The hostess must know when it was in order to invite ladies to join the formal dinners held in the late afternoon and when it was more appropriate to invite them to take tea during the evening. Herbert's recollection of her abilities as a young girl, when she ran her father's household, must have been reinforced by good reports from those in England who had observed her more recently. No doubt too, her letters had given him the chance to assess her present capabilities. He knew that, quite apart from her ease of manner with people generally, she also possessed those additional qualities of the good hostess; she could play the harpsichord with a proficiency that could entertain guests; being well read she could converse on literature and her own talent as well as appreciation of art gave her further topics of conversation. Her recent stay in England meant that she was up-to-date on political matters as well as the current social scene and at a time when there were still the occasional French or French speaking European visitors, she was fluent enough in the language to engage them in conversation and so prevent them from feeling excluded. All in all, Herbert could not have found himself a better candidate for the post.

When she and young Josiah set sail from Bristol in one of Mr Pinney's sugar boats, Fanny knew that she was not necessarily returning to Nevis for good. In accepting her uncle's offer – almost a formal contract – he had made it clear that her duties in Nevis would end when he retired from office in 1787. At that time, he expected to return to settle in England. Having undertaken to provide for Fanny and treat Josiah as a grandson, he probably assumed that she would return with him, particularly as the boy would be educated in England.

Fanny had matured into an assured and confident woman in the years she had been away but at the same time, physically she had been affected by the climate; dampness had brought with it rheumatism and a weakness of the lungs while, without realising it, she must have reacted mentally to the oppressive grey light that predominated during the winter months. As her ship drew closer to the Leewards, where the vast expanse of often cloudless blue sky was reflected in the ocean, the warmth alone must have made her relax. Yet she was well aware that she must be prepared for the changes that the loss of the American colonies and the occupation by the French had wreaked on Nevis.

But one place at least had not changed. Herbert's Montpelier plantation was situated 600 feet above sea level on the southern slopes of the volcanic Mt Nevis where the sea breezes gently fanned the surrounding trees keeping the mosquitoes at bay. Imposing gates stood at the entrance to the driveway up to the palatial house, reckoned to be the finest on the island, that Herbert had had built for himself. The most spectacular views were to be had from its louvred windows and wide verandahs down to seas of picture postcard blueness. Here were rooms with high vaulted wooden ceilings, floors of polished hardwood and doors and window frames of mahogany. Rich floral brocades in the English fashion covered the furniture. Everything was of the finest quality; it could have been an English country house but for one thing, the close proximity of the mill that powered the machinery for the sugar extraction.

As Fanny sailed homewards, preparing herself for what lay ahead of her, it is doubtful that she entertained even the stray possibility that in picking up the threads of her old life, she might find another husband from either Nevis or St Kitts; she had no need to commit herself to anyone to provide for her.

In contrast, Nelson, who longed to have a woman on whom he could focus his devotion, had become besotted by the 30-something wife of Captain Moutray, the resident Commissioner at English Harbour in Antigua. As was customary, Capt. Moutray opened his home to any off-duty young officers who were anchored for any length of time in the harbour. Nelson and his colleague Collingwood, charmed by the elegance and friendliness of Mary Moutray, became frequent visitors. Considerably younger than her husband, Mary enjoyed their attention but probably considered her flirting with them as nothing more than harmless fun. Of the two she preferred Collingwood, allowing him the intimacy of helping to dress her hair. Nelson thought her the most perfect woman he had ever set eyes on. However, although intoxicated with love for his 'very dear friend', he demonstrated a decided lack of diplomacy by reporting her husband for a breach of naval etiquette. When he later learned that the Moutrays had been ordered home, he wallowed in his lovelorn state, confiding in a letter to brother William that the news of her leaving had left him as emotional as 'an April day'.

Mary Moutray was very different from the women who had previously provoked feelings of ardour within Nelson's breast. The two he had seriously considered asking to marry him had been very young and one can assume that they and Nelson had simply engaged in the mild flirtation of the young and inexperienced. It has been implied that the death of his mother affected him greatly, leaving him emotionally immature. In Mary, he may have seen a reflection of the woman he had lost. Although in years not that much older than he, her experience as a wife and mother, as well as that of moving in different social circles, gave her the assurance to deal with shy, unpolished young naval officers. That he mistook her kindness for a sign of a deeper interest in him is certain but even the mildest flirtation may have helped him in his later relationships. His letters show that he idealised her; according to him, she possessed all the virtues of womanhood as well as the attributes of a 'lady'. It is clear that he felt that Mary was socially superior to him for he made much of the fact that Mary had promised that if his younger sister Kitty were to be in Bath the following winter she would get to know her. At a time when it was important to be introduced into the correct level of society, Nelson believed this would be to Kitty's advantage: 'What an acquisition to any female to be acquainted with: what an example to take pattern from.'

Heartbroken though he believed himself to be, in that letter of 20 February 1785, Nelson was not above gossiping about the love affairs of his fellow officers. One of them, a Capt. Kelly, had reported that he was attached to a lady at Nevis. Nelson himself was about to sail there, taking with him a passenger, Miss Parry, the niece of the Governor of Barbados who was on her way to stay at the home of President Herbert. Jocular though he meant his remark to be, he showed his lack of confidence in his ability to attract women: 'they trust any young lady with me, being an old-fashioned fellow.'

Over the next couple of months, when he was not occupied with naval affairs, Nelson pined for Mary. In his melancholy state he brooded on the past and in replying to brother William on 3 May, he indulged yet again in poetic language to describe his feelings. William, who was also on the look-out for a wife and had paid court to several young women whose fathers might be able to advance his career, must have suggested in his reply that Nelson should try his luck with Admiral Hughes' daughter, Rosy, who during the time she had been in the Leeward Islands had so far failed to secure herself a husband. Nelson, lacking his brother's calculated approach, was not to be shaken from his pathetic state.

> This country appears now intolerable, my dear friend being absent. It is barren indeed; not all the Rosys can give a spark of joy to me...I went once up the Hill to look at the spot where I spent more happy days than in any one spot in the world. E'n the trees drooped their heads and the tamarind tree died; all was melancholy: the road is covered with thistles; let them grow.

Nine days later however, his mood was somewhat less dismal. 'I am just come from Nevis, where I have been visiting Miss Parry, Miss Herbert and a young widow.' It is odd that Nelson did not dignify 'the young widow' with a name. It suggests that he did not take much notice of her at this meeting, which would have been a fairly informal affair, and he might not have been fully aware of Fanny's position in the house. If one were uncharitable to him, one might suggest that socially conscious as he was, he thought only the niece of the Governor of Barbados and the daughter of the President of Nevis were worthy of any attention. However, he did already know Miss Parry and the lively, young Miss Martha Herbert would have demanded notice. On the other hand he may have taken more notice of Fanny then than he was willing to admit either to himself or his brother.

Had it not been for that strong sense of what was right, that same high moral stance that had been responsible for him reporting Mary Moutray's husband for an infringement of naval rules, Nelson's acquaintance with Fanny might never have gone further than that of the occasional meeting at social functions. But in an attempt to carry out the letter of the law governing foreign ships trading with a British settlement, on 25 May he sailed into the waters off Charlestown in Nevis and seized four suspect vessels he found there for: 'carrying British Registers, although they were American-built, navigated by all Americans and some of them entirely owned by Foreigners.' Unfortunately, his exploit did not achieve quite the results he had expected. For a start, with the backing of merchants and traders on shore, the four shipmasters sued him for assault and imprisonment and demanded damages of £40,000. Further it was made clear to him that if he went ashore he was likely to be arrested and imprisoned. So for some time he was a virtual prisoner in his own ship. To make matters worse, his Commander, Admiral Hughes, who had not been over scrupulous in enforcing these Navigation Acts, had failed to come to his rescue.

Many of Nelson's biographers, ignoring his reference to the young widow on 12 May, have it that he did not meet Fanny until June and then relate the touching story that demonstrates their hero's gentle nature. John Herbert, having met and liked Nelson, offered to stand surety for him during the dispute over the American ships and invited him to call at Montpelier. Nelson enjoyed an early morning uphill walk from Charlestown, but arriving before Herbert was fully dressed, he was shown into a reception room to wait. The story goes that when Herbert came down to greet him the room was empty. Somewhat puzzled he tried an adjoining room and there he discovered Nelson crawling round under the dining room table playing a make believe game with Fanny's little boy. Herbert apparently found it truly amazing that 'this great little man of whom everybody is so afraid' should demean himself to play with a child. Several days are assumed to have elapsed before Nelson visited again and it was then that Fanny met him and thanked him for his kindness and patience with her son.

The story of the encounter with the child gained much credence because it was used to show not just that Nelson was very good with children but it offered his later apologists, those who would rather believe that he never loved Fanny, a reason why he married her – she gave him a readymade family. They also point out that by his own admission, Fanny reminded him of his lost Mary; she had the same refined airs and she, too, had a son. In other words, they believe that Fanny caught him when he was most vulnerable and on the rebound. Whatever the case, it was a whirlwind courtship. Those who later painted Fanny as cold and unresponsive seem to overlook the fact that there must have been something instantly attractive about her. In the same way that Josiah Nisbet had taken little time to make up his mind that he loved Fanny, so was this no slow maturing friendship between Fanny and Nelson; if they had indeed met for the first time in mid June, it was only six or seven weeks later, by the beginning of August, that he proposed – and she accepted.

Nelson's sense of time was not always the same as other people's and he obviously did not think he had been too fast with his suit; in fact in a letter to his uncle William Suckling in London, dated 14 November 1785, he recorded: '...my present attachment is of pretty long standing.' Nelson desperately needed to convince Suckling of just how serious he was on this occasion. His uncle was only too well aware of his nephew's impetuosity of heart and would have remembered a previous occasion when he had asked for financial assistance to enable him to be in a position to propose marriage. Now the nephew described how the situation had come about, revealing that he had 'lived at [Herbert's] house, when at Nevis, since June last.' He had, he said, become a great favourite of Mr Herbert. He was quickly accepted into the wider family circle that included Herbert's sister and brother-in-law, the Mortons and their daughter Sally. He seemed to have a particular liking for 'little Sally' as he termed her; possibly she reminded him of his younger sister Kitty. Unfortunately in later years,

Nelson developed a strong antipathy towards her and tried to make Fanny sever her relations with her. But that was still far in the future, for the present with little else to occupy him, he was able to devote himself to playing with Josiah, talking to the young ladies and going for walks with them. The lovers were even able to manage time alone.

It is always difficult for an outsider to understand how other couples' marriages come about. Whatever did he/she see in the other is a question which often mystifies. In the eighteenth century, for all except the working classes, money was ultimately likely to play a greater part than physical attraction; indeed, providing the partner with the fortune was not positively repulsive, then a match could be made. The newspapers of the period abound in stories of impoverished young men who married wealthy women twice or even thrice their age, while girls still in their teens were united with husbands of a similar age to their grandfathers. As novels of the period, such as Jane Austen's *Pride and Prejudice* show, girls who lacked a good dowry or a sizeable annual income, however beautiful they might be, were unlikely to receive good offers of marriage unless their suitors were very rich. Many young men and women had to suppress their feelings of love and settle instead for an attachment based on hard economics. The best situation was the one where there was both physical attraction and enough money for the couple to live on.

Nelson had always been conscious that his family background, while it might have some good connections in it, was unable to provide him with either a private income or even the expectation of large sums of inherited money. His only income came from his naval pay and that was not sufficient to support a wife and family. As a young officer he, like millions in our own time, had hoped that he might strike lucky by winning the lottery. He and his clergyman brother regularly took shares in a ticket though neither was ever successful. Nelson's only hope of improving his financial state was with naval prize-money; a share in the value of an enemy vessel he had helped capture. But it was not sensible to rely on such gains since the amount depended on a variety of things as well as the number of people involved in the taking of the vessel. Alternatively, he could follow the example of many of his fellows and marry money.

There is no doubt that Nelson believed that Fanny would be well provided for. When he wrote to Uncle Suckling he told him of Herbert's reaction to his proposal to Fanny. He was quite willing to give his consent to the marriage on condition that Fanny fulfilled her contract to act as Herbert's hostess until 1787. Since he had an expensive lifestyle to maintain, there was not much that he could do for Fanny during his life, but he promised that on his death she would inherit twenty thousand pounds. On the other hand, should his daughter Martha die before him, Fanny would become his major beneficiary. So the distant future looked rosy but in the meantime Herbert offered him only two or three hundred pounds a year towards Fanny's maintenance. There was also the question of Josiah's future. Nelson had apparently not discovered at that time that the Nisbet family trusts were so involved that nothing had yet been resolved for the boy. So he had misled Suckling when he told him: 'her son is under her guardianship, but totally independent of her'.

It is often stated that Herbert's insistence on her staying until his retirement forced Nelson and Fanny into a long engagement. Yet a careful reading of Nelson's letter to Suckling shows that this was not necessarily the case. Nelson quoted Herbert as saying: 'I intend going to England in 1787 and remaining there my life; therefore if you two can live happily together till that event takes place, you have my consent.' This suggests that as long as Fanny remained on Nevis while Nelson continued his duties around the Caribbean, Herbert was quite happy for the marriage to take place immediately. At that time, there seemed little likelihood that Nelson's ship would be ordered back to England, and although the couple would have been apart for some of the time, Nevis was such a regular port of call that they would have seen each other at frequent intervals. So who made the decision that they should wait?

Nelson's letters to Fanny, which start on 19 August 1785, express a desire for them to be together and his longing for her grew with time. We do not have Fanny's side of the correspondence, so it is necessary to try to work out from his what her feelings were. Was she the one who decided they should wait? Had she found the little captain's overtures overwhelming? Had she, like Mary Moutray, offered him friendship, perhaps out of a sense of pity and been taken aback that he should have wanted more? Certainly he had little to recommend him. He was highly unpopular with most of Nevisian society over the episode of the American ships. He was excessively thin having had repeated bouts of fever that, in turn, had necessitated his having his head shaved which would not have been a problem had he been able to find a properly fitting wig instead of the lopsided yellowy creation he usually sported. Nor can Fanny have been drawn to him by mutual interests, for Nelson was not particularly musical; nor was he a great reader even though he did have a penchant for the poetic turn of phrase. Some would say that left only a joint interest in the child, Josiah, yet there is a strong hint that the attraction on both sides was a strong physical one.

The proposal of marriage having been made and accepted, Nelson sailed off to Antigua from where he wrote his first 'love letter' to Fanny, carefully addressing his future wife as 'Dear Mrs Nisbet'. The letter starts, not with lavish endearments but expressing his anxiety for a letter from Herbert telling him what financial provisions he was going to make. 'Most fervently do I hope his answer will be of such a tendency, as to convey real pleasure not only to myself, but also to you.' Perhaps he realised that this might sound somewhat mercenary for he continued in the same sentence – eighteenth century punctuation not being as standardised as today's:

... for most sincerely do I love you and I trust my affection is not only founded upon the principles of reason but also upon the basis of mutual attachment, indeed my charming Fanny did [I] possess a million my greatest pride and pleasure would be to share it with you; and, as I am, to live in a cottage with you I should esteem superior to living in a palace with any other I have yet met with.

He went on to tell her that he knew he had done the right thing in asking her to be his wife. 'The more I weigh you in my mind the more reason I find to admire both your head and your heart.' Teasingly immodest, he suggests that it is her good sense that made her accept him, then goes on to say that he knows that her heart ruled her choice, declaring that she must feel he: 'is the person [she] ought to expect most happiness from by return of affection.' That he was still not entirely sure of her is shown when he asked her to write to him occasionally so that separation might: 'lose some of its pangs by a mutual unreserved correspondence'. The rest of the letter is taken up with gossip which may indicate the level at which their earlier conversations had taken place. He was critical of his commander-in-chief, Admiral Sir Richard Hughes, who was making a fool of himself with a local young lady. Lady Hughes, who may have heard rumours about the affair, had travelled out in the *Boreas* with Nelson to join her husband for a spell. This had restricted the Admiral for a while but when Nelson rejoined him in Antigua, he was in high spirits for he had managed to leave his wife for a time in Barbados. Nelson showed his disapproval of the Admiral's behaviour: 'I should suppose him a bachelor instead of a married man with a family.' Fanny, who knew Hughes from his frequent visits to her uncle, was, of course, sufficiently familiar with the ways of the world, and the islands in particular, to be only too aware of the liaisons and affairs that developed between naval officers and the ladies of the place. Indeed a couple of years earlier, in 1783, the wife of her brother-in-law, Walter Nisbet, had run off with Capt. Thomas Totty, the commander of the *Sphinx* and would eventually find herself the subject of a petition to parliament for a divorce.

Continuing his gossip, Nelson regaled her with the full details of a romantic elopement which could have come straight out of an eighteenth-century novel or play. In fact the words: 'Captain Acres and Miss came out by the same ship a few weeks ago,' could have been a line from Sheridan's *The Rivals*. Young Miss Whitehead returning from school in England to her home in Antigua had indulged in a shipboard romance with young Captain Acres. On her arrival, the captain had honourably written to her father seeking permission to 'pay his addresses' to the young lady. Mr Whitehead, who probably had what he considered far better prospects in view for his daughter, ignored the letter and instructed his daughter to have nothing more to do with Acres who was by then in St Kitts. There, he met and confided in a Captain Sutherland who had made a name for himself in assisting lovelorn couples. Sutherland just happened to anchor off Antigua in time for the ball held to celebrate the birthday of the Prince of Wales. There he managed to meet Miss Whitehead and explain what she must do. Two or three days passed. Then one evening, when the dutiful daughter had entertained her mother and a visitor to several pieces on the harpsichord, she found some excuse to leave the room. Her absence was not fully noted until the visitor, on the point of leaving, wished to say goodbye. A servant was sent to find her but the young woman had gone! A search revealed that she had been carried off from the family's bathing house into a waiting boat that took her to Captain Sutherland's vessel which could just be seen leaving the harbour.

Nelson seemed to approve of this escapade, wishing the couple well and expressing the hope that the time would never come when they wished to run away from each other. From local gossip he turned to the letters that he had found on his arrival, in particular the news that his brother William had inherited a family living worth £700 a year. William, who, as befitted his new status will hereafter be referred to as the Rector, was now in a position to take a wife of his own choosing rather than one whose father might prove useful to his advancement, although that could still be very useful. With his mind still on his postbag, Nelson mentioned he had had a long letter from Mary Moutray. From this we assume that he had mentioned her to Fanny during their courtship but it was either extreme naivety or insensitivity on his part that made him continue: 'A more amiable woman can hardly exist. I wish you knew her. Your minds and manners are so congenial that you must have pleasure in the acquaintance.' How little Nelson understood the workings of a woman's mind either then or later in life.

Developing a relationship through letters can be deeply rewarding; it is often possible to reveal much more of one's true feelings than might be uttered face to face. There are, however, drawbacks and it was not long before they had to endure the frustration of waiting for an answer to what could have been a vital question. Nelson's letters had to be entrusted to whatever ship would be calling at St Kitts or Nevis. If to the former then he had to rely on someone else to take the letter on its final stage. Fanny dispatched her letters by ships going to whatever base Nelson was using. If he was sailing round the islands then it might be weeks rather than days before he received them. In addition, weather conditions could alter a ship's destination and a letter be severely delayed or not delivered at all. Reliance on a third party to act as mailman was not always satisfactory either as Nelson discovered in the early days of his courtship, when Captain Kelly failed to forward letters he had had in his possession for some time. All this meant that the correspondents at times were forced to watch what they said. Nelson knew that his letters might fall into the wrong hands, as he said in his very first letter to Fanny when hinting that he knew something about, as it happens, that same Captain Kelly: 'I could and would tell you a long history of [him] was I sure this would come safe to your hands.' To overcome this problem, Nelson devised a code for occasional use between them. It presents a delightful picture of them, once their engagement had taken place, sitting together as the naval officer, to whom ciphers were second nature, explained how it worked and Fanny wrote down the key.

Nelson's next letter written just over three weeks after the first starts with a gentle rebuke that his 'dear Fanny' had not written to him: 'I had buoyed myself up with hopes that the Admiral's schooner would have brought me a line from you.' But when he learnt from other sources that her aunt, Sarah Herbert, had died the previous week, he magnanimously allowed that this news: 'sufficiently apologises for your not thinking of an absentee.' He then assured her that he fully shared her sorrow but offered her a religious homily which concluded with his begging her to take comfort in the thought that her aunt's conduct in this world was such: 'as will insure everlasting happiness in that which is to come.' It is questionable how much comfort she received on receipt of this letter when the bulk of it was taken up with what Nelson himself called 'pecuniary considerations'. Herbert had at last replied to his letter but it appeared that he had given no definite promise as to what financial provision he would make for Fanny. However, undeterred he avowed his great love for her and was certain, he said, that she returned his love. 'I declare solemnly that did I not conceive I had the full possession of your heart no consideration should make me accept your hand.' But having said how sure he was of her, he either betrayed his insecurity or he attempted a form of emotional blackmail by adding as a postscript: 'Do I ask too much when I venture to hope for a line, or otherwise I may suppose my letters may be looked upon as troublesome.' It would have been a hard-hearted female indeed who could have resisted such a request.

A gap of three months before the next letter showed that the *Boreas* was cruising in the area of Nevis and St Kitts enabling Nelson to go ashore for several weeks at a time. In that time, the relationship between them had deepened. His 'most sincerely do I regret that I am not safe moored by thee…' suggests they were on more intimate terms. Nelson had left Nevis sometime before 13 December and en route for Antigua, his ship had been buffeted by unusually bad weather for the time of year. While he grappled with the problems that a sprung main mast and torn rigging entailed, torrential rain continued to lash the Leewards. Inevitably, his thoughts turned to the comforts he had left behind in Nevis where, it appears, a number of guests had been staying. He expressed the hope that Fanny was having a 'merry time…with your gay company.' He was, perhaps, jealous that other men might be paying her attention. He was conscious too, that because of the severe weather, many of the guests would have been unable to leave, thus Fanny's time would be further taken up with their entertainment.

His insecurity where she was concerned continued and during his next few days on shore in Nevis, he must have revealed it and precipitated an upset between them. Fanny attempted to reassure him at the time and later by letter, causing him to reply: 'you are too good and indulgent I know and feel it, but my whole life shall ever be attempting to make you completely happy, whatever whims sometimes take me.' While acknowledging that he could be moody, he excused himself: 'We are none of us perfect and myself probably much less so than you deserve.' And then, changing sud-

45

denly from the hesitant, undeserving lover, he alluded to an expression so personal to them that it need not be committed to paper: 'do rest assured my excellent ----, fill up the blank, that I am with the purest affection your Horatio Nelson.'

This intensity continued in his next letter inscribed very precisely as having been written at nine o'clock on the morning of Friday 3 March.

> Separated from my dearest what pleasure can I feel? None! Be assured all my happiness is centred with thee and where thou art not there I am not happy. Every day, hour and act convinces me of it. With my heart filled with the purest and most tender affection do I write this, for was it not so you know me well enough to be certain that even at this moment I would tell you of it. I daily thank God who ordained that I should be attached to you. He has I firmly believe intended it as a blessing to me.

However, these words of fervent love are somewhat marred by the ensuing references to money, which, he assured her, he wanted only for her sake. And just to reinforce the need for money (which he was still hoping would come in the form of an allowance from Herbert), he played on Fanny's weakest spot, her son. 'Let me repeat that my dear Josiah shall ever be considered by me as one of my own.' A noble declaration but she would have been only too aware that stepchildren were not always so readily accepted without some financial support from their natural father's family. He returned to financial matters when he continued the letter six days later. By that time he had come ashore and found letters awaiting him including one from his uncle Suckling to whom he had earlier applied for a substantial long-term loan. After telling Fanny how pleased various members of his family were that he was to marry her, he confided that in his uncle's opinion: 'Mr Herbert should consider you properly and that I should well consider my situation in life and that in my present bachelor situation I am quite an independent man with a sufficient income to keep me so.'

It was letters like this that could so easily be misunderstood and sour a relationship. Said face to face, with loving expressions, this would not have appeared half as harsh as it must have done when Fanny read it. Was he, she would have been justified in thinking, trying to get out of the engagement by emphasising that to his relations she and her child were likely to be encumbrances upon him? On the other hand when he said that he must either write or speak to Herbert on the subject, even though it was a 'disagreeable task', he may have hoped that she would pave the way for him. There was a need to settle the matter once and for all as it was rumoured that his ship might be ordered home in three months. All this would have worried Fanny even though he attempted to lessen the effect with the excuse: 'All this, my dearest, gets hold of my spirits and will not allow me to feel so pleasant as I wish.' In a long postscript to the letter he told her he had brought himself to write to Herbert. But he was obviously unhappy about matters and confessed that he wished he had not to go that day to dine with the Governor of Barbados: 'for I am miserably low spirited.' Throughout her married life Fanny would hear frequently of her husband's attacks of depression, yet he chided her if she ever mentioned her own low spirits. And low they must have been after reading thus far. However, mercurial as Nelson could be, he ended on a truly mundane note, saying that he had been unable to contact the Admiral to ask about new strings for her harpsichord.

A couple of weeks later, he was able to report that he had managed to get the strings for her but Carlisle Bay in Barbados had not proved the best of places to shop. Martha Herbert had asked him to find her a red parrot, a riding hat and some ribbon and all these seemed unobtainable. Eventually, he had to settle for a grey bird and then he discovered that since Barbadian ladies did not ride there was no need for such hats. While the shops might have little to recommend them, Admiral Hughes certainly found that the island continued to have much to hold him there. He had taken a house on shore where he had twice entertained Nelson to dinner, but on the whole he preferred the company of the local young lady who often spent the whole day with him. She was, according to Nelson, in great danger of losing her reputation; already she had been dropped by many of those who used regularly to invite her to their homes. He was careful not to name the lady but no doubt Fanny already knew it and possibly, given that the Admiral's flagship was often at Nevis, where he was entertained at Montpelier, she may have known more of the gossip than Nelson did. He was somewhat pious in his remark: 'There may be nothing criminal after all is said, but when a gentleman goes beyond what is deemed common civilities and reaches particularities the world is fond of believing any story which is current.' Just over a decade later he could have recalled these words to describe his own situation. But in 1786 Nelson still had a strict moral outlook on how married people should behave towards each other. He could not understand how Hughes could let his wife and newly married daughter sail for England without even going to say goodbye to them. 'Common decency ought to have induced such a polite man as Sir Richard to have gone down but his time is taken up here and he minds little else.'

Back in Nevis the month of March was a busy time for Fanny with visitors arriving for the festivities accompanying the wedding of her cousin, Sally Morton. Relations and friends from the other islands who were not accommodated at the Mortons' home on the Hard Times plantation filled the spare rooms at Montpelier. Fanny's time was taken up with their entertainment leaving her little time to consider when her own wedding would take place. Like her, Sally was marrying a naval officer, another member of the squadron that patrolled the islands. Capt. William Kelly was in command of the *Adamant*, Admiral Hughes' flagship and like all the other ships in the fleet, he made frequent landfalls on Nevis where he had met young Sally. If we are to believe Nelson, Kelly had a reputation for flirting with young ladies and was not above boasting of his conquests. During Nelson's early acquaintance with Fanny, he also came to know Sally – in his eyes a young girl, for whom he developed a filial affection. In letters to Fanny he would send his warmest good wishes to: 'our little Sally'. It is doubtful that in those early days he was aware that Kelly's 'young lady at Nevis' of whom he had boasted among his colleagues was Sally. Yet by the time Nelson sent his first letter to Fanny, Kelly had proposed and been accepted by the Mortons. Dismayed, Nelson hinted that he knew a great deal about Kelly adding cryptically that he hoped Kelly would prove constant. Quite what had originally caused the animosity between the two men is unclear, but Nelson made no attempt to disguise his dislike for Kelly and revealed an almost childish pettiness over the belief that on occasions Kelly had deliberately withheld his mail: 'I have no consideration for Mr Kelly nor shall I forget the civility for some time to come.' It was clear that the two men communicated only on a formal level for it was left to Fanny to break the news that the wedding had taken place in March. Writing on 17 April he told her: 'We have not even heard of Kelly's marriage or of him since he sailed.' When Kelly had sailed, the new Mrs Kelly went with him, much as Fanny hoped she would some time in the future with Nelson.

With so much going on, it was hardly surprising that Fanny had not devoted as much time as she might to teaching little Josiah his first lessons, particularly to read. Nelson may have started the process during the weeks he had spent ashore during January, for the following month he told Fanny: 'Josiah I dare say makes a wonderful progress in his book. The greatest favour you can at present grant me is to learn him to read.' His optimism was still high in April: 'I hope he [Josiah] will be able to read most charmingly to me when I come.'

This wish came in a very long letter written from Barbados on 17 April. Nelson had begun it noting that he had nothing to answer since he had not received one from her. That left him no option but to reiterate his uncertainty about when his ship was likely to be recalled and to share with her the contents of the personal letters he had received from England. Apart from those from his brother and sister he had also heard again from 'my amiable Mrs Moutray'. Shortly after her return to England, Mary had become a widow and was now in dire financial straits. 'What has this poor dear soul undergone in one twelve months. Lost father, mother, husband and part of her fortune and left with two children.' Nelson wrote at length about the misfortunes that had overtaken Mary and he expected Fanny to share his feelings. 'Indeed my dearest I can't express what I feel for her and your good heart I am sure will sympathise with mine. What is so truly affecting as a virtuous woman in distress.' That last sentence was one that should have haunted Nelson in later years but by then he had become adept at turning his blind eye.

His next letter, written on board *Boreas* on 23 April, begins abruptly:

My Dearest Fanny, – I will not begin by scolding you although you really deserve it for sending me such a letter. Had I not known the warmth of your heart, by the epistle I might have judged you had never seen me. However as I have fixed my resolve of not saying more I have done. You will not send me such another I am certain.

Since Fanny's offending letter no longer exists, it has been suggested that whatever caused this reproof was an example of her capricious nature; that she was moody and that Nelson should have heeded the signs of her future coldness towards him. This seems a very masculine reading of the situation. Was it not much more likely that when Fanny read Nelson's effusions about Mary Moutray she was doubtful of her own position? With Mary now a widow, and Nelson likely to be posted home in the next few months without having committed himself to a definite date for their marriage, was it not possible that once back in England, he might renew his relationship with Mary? The coolness of her response was an attempt to cover her hurt.

In fact, Nelson's letter should have alerted Fanny to his moodiness and bouts of ill temper. When he gave her news of her cousin Sally's arrival in Barbados, he seemed to revel in the fact that the poor girl had been seriously seasick for most of the journey. Not content with that he reported that Sally's husband, Captain Kelly, had had 'a little difference' with the Admiral. Had a woman written this description of the episode the adjective 'bitchy' would have been justified. Again one wonders what cause the Kellys had given him that he should see slights from both of them. Not for the first time, he took umbrage at what may have been an innocent oversight. In this case, so he informed Fanny, he had sent a messenger to the Governor's house where Sally was staying with Mr and Mrs Parry to ask if Sally had anything to send to Nevis. His servant had brought back: 'there was no answer, not even; "Much obliged, thank you," or any other word…I may be uncivilly treated once and then it is my misfortune, but if I put it in any person's power to be so a second time, it's my fault.' He admitted to Fanny that he felt very angry at Sally's supposedly off-hand treatment of him but did not even consider that she might not have received the message. Neither did he consider the hurt his remarks about her cousin might have on her.

He was, in fact, thoroughly taken up with his own discomfort. He complained of violent headaches brought on by having to sit for days on end during the Courts Martial that had brought the squadron together in Barbados. In addition, he and three colleagues had had some sort of contretemps with the Governor, Mr Parry. Taking the moral high ground Nelson declared: '…unless he makes a very handsome apology I never set foot in his house more'. He would later pay for this gesture for suddenly he found he was without any invitations ashore. But while he expected others to apologise profusely to him, his own were much more muted. Buried in the middle of the letter comes: '…I am sorry for what I began the letter with, therefore forgive me and I will never scold more, but trust everything to your good heart.' Quite what occasioned this change of mood is not clear but it seemed to have something to do with a letter that Fanny had given to Mr Stanley, the Solicitor of the Leeward Islands. Stanley had apparently passed it to Kelly who had waited two days after his arrival to hand it to Nelson – another reason for Nelson's anger towards Kelly.

It was almost the end of May before Nelson was able to leave Barbados and return to her: '...who it shall be business of my future life to make happy.' From 29 May until 14 June he was able to spend time with her on Nevis. The *Boreas,* lying at anchor, was kept busy firing gun salutes, seventeen on 30 May to commemorate the restoration of Charles II, and twenty-one on Sunday 4 June to celebrate the current King's birthday. This would have been marked on shore with a ball, most likely preceded by a grand dinner at Montpelier, both occasions giving Fanny and Nelson a chance to appear together in public. When *Boreas* sailed in a fresh gale on the morning of 14 June, another salute was fired, this time of thirteen guns as a mark of respect to the President, John Herbert, who sailed with Nelson to Antigua on official business. Throughout the rest of June and the whole of July, *Boreas* was patrolling the area around the islands of Antigua, St Kitts and Nevis, always on the look out for ships suspected of breaking the Navigation Acts. Nelson had not learnt his lesson despite having complained to Fanny in April that it was his seizure of a couple of Yankee ships that had kept him down in Barbados after most of the squadron had left. Now, on 8 July he arrested a schooner coming from Trinidad. Although it was flying Spanish colours he was convinced that it was an American and when she was boarded, sure enough, her papers confirmed it. The schooner with its cargo of cattle was impounded. According to the *Boreas's* log water was taken on board the schooner for the cattle but it makes no mention of what was the ultimate fate of the beasts. It may be coincidental that not long after this event, the log records that fresh beef was received on *Boreas.*

Nevis lacked a deep-water harbour, so the long boat had to be launched to bring the officers and crew ashore, and on Sunday 30 July when a storm of thunder and lightning churned up the sea, one of the sailors, John Farrell, fell overboard as the long boat was coming in. By the time he was fished out he was dead. The body was taken into Charlestown where, the following day, it found a resting place in the local churchyard. Although unhappy at the loss of one of his seamen, Nelson would have taken some comfort that he was able to bury him ashore. He himself had a fear of being buried at sea and in his will expressed the desire that in the event of his death on board his body should be taken home and interred in the churchyard at Burnham Thorpe.

After the funeral, Nelson would have gone up to Montpelier where for the last time the President was entertaining Admiral Hughes and the officers from the *Adamant* and *Latona* who were to sail for home the following day. The party would have included the Mortons who would have seized the opportunity to see their daughter Sally before she made the journey to England with her husband. It has to be hoped that Nelson and Kelly managed to control their antipathy for each other and not spoil the atmosphere which being one of leave taking must have been somewhat strained in any case. For

Fanny it must have been a time for reflection. Sally Kelly would have given her details of her newfound experience as a naval wife, no doubt embroidering the delights of life on board ship as the captain's wife and her expectations of what lay ahead of her in England. At least Sally was going to be with her husband while Fanny had only the prospect of yet another long parting from Nelson who now, in the absence of the Admiral, became the senior officer on the station and was to leave immediately for Antigua. The hurricane season was about to start and the *Boreas* would ride it out in English Harbour.

In addition, Fanny was concerned for Nelson's health. He had had intermittent bouts of fever again and the general view of the medical men who treated him was that the only course of action to effect a cure was a change of climate. While he had been at Nevis, Fanny had prescribed beef tea and a pint of goat's milk daily in an effort to build up his strength. He continued with the regime once he arrived in Antigua, telling her intimately that he wished to be strong for her sake. His letters suggest that while they may not have actually anticipated marriage, their love making had certainly progressed further than a chaste kiss. He declared he felt ardently for her, and a couple of weeks after their parting he spoke of his yearning for her. Without doubt this was a definite physical desire, which he spelt out for her in very explicit detail:

> As you begin to know something of sailors, have you not often heard that salt water and absence always wash away love? Now I am such a heretic as not to believe that faith: for behold every morning…I have had six pails of salt water at day-light poured upon my head and instead of finding what the seamen say to be true, I perceive the contrary effect: and if it goes on so contrary to prescription, you must see me before my fixed time.

He told her he could not express in words what her letters meant to him, suggesting that they contained more satisfying remarks than the mundane matters of her daily routine. He was almost euphoric in his conviction that his feelings for her were unalterable: 'it must be real affection that brings us together, not interest or compulsion which make so many unhappy.' She was his 'far better half ' and her letters continued to delight him. His sense of humour had improved too. He no longer found fault with all in Antigua's English Harbour.

Initially, he felt he had been ignored by the local inhabitants; he had not been able to rent a small house ashore away from the depredations of mosquitoes, nor had he received any invitations. The latter he put down to his reputation for doing the right thing as far as the Navigation Acts were concerned: 'I am not that jolly fellow who for a feast and plenty of wine, would sacrifice the dearest interests of his Country.' Eventually, various gentlemen did make overtures to him. Of one he wrote: 'His great attention at his house made amends for his long neglect and I forgot all anger.' Then, because Fanny had on occasions taken him to task about this failing of his he added: 'I can forgive sometimes you will allow.' However, he immediately negates that by telling her that he had no intention of being friendly with another gentleman who had previously ignored him. But the best piece of news he had for Fanny was that his health had definitely improved and that, while he had not put on much weight in spite of two pints a day of goat's milk, his lungs were now clear and he was free of chest pains.

Three weeks elapsed before his next letter but in the meantime Fanny had written to tell him there was sickness in the house. In his response he described Montpelier as an infirmary, suggesting that several of them were ill and that this was not just a case of Josiah suffering from one of the childhood diseases. It is possible that there had been an outbreak of small pox or it might have been what the islanders still call the 'creep-up' which sounds much more interesting than influenza. Although concerned for the health of all those who had suffered, Nelson was particularly anxious that Fanny would be well by the time he arrived, which he estimated would be in about another two weeks, on 9 October or thereabouts – he could hardly wait.

Sure enough he anchored off Nevis on 10 October and for the next six weeks, until 23 November, he patrolled the area, sometimes managing to stay several days at a time in Nevis. During that time, the couple found time to discuss serious matters affecting their future life together. Fanny was concerned that Josiah had not received proper maintenance from his father's share of the Nisbet estate. Nelson, who was used to having dealings with lawyers and solicitors, promised that when he was next in Antigua he would seek legal advice on what steps she could take to resolve the matter. But more pressing were the extra duties that he now had as officer in charge of the station. The most important of these was to organise the courtesy visit to the Islands by Prince William Henry, George III's sailor son, who earlier that year had been given his first command as captain of the frigate *Pegasus*. On 27 November, having left Fanny just days before, he gave the impression that he was not looking forward to it: 'This Prince hunting is but a bad sort of business. I had much rather be quiet at Montpelier.' He must have known that quiet was one thing he would not have during the Prince's tour. Four days later he wrote to say he was about to sail for Dominica where he would join up with the Prince expecting to have him back with him in Antigua about 6 December. Nevis, of course, would be included in the Prince's itinerary and it would be up to the President to provide the proper entertainment for the royal guest. Nelson promised that as soon as he could he would write to Herbert to let him know when to expect the Prince.

Although they had not been apart for more than three weeks or so, Nelson assured Fanny that it seemed an age to him and what was worse, he feared it might be some time before he would see her again. But he had little time to mope and indulge in yearnings for Fanny; his days – and nights – were fully occupied keeping up with the Prince. William Henry had all the stamina of a 20-year-old and one who had not spent years in the tropics. Although Nelson was only seven years his senior, in comparison he seemed almost middle aged. His letters over the next few weeks are full of the events that he attended with the Prince but it was apparent that the late nights and constant socialising were not entirely to his taste. However, it did provide him with a continuous source of gossip to pass to Fanny. William had charmed the younger ladies of Dominica while upsetting some of the older ones, who by their position expected to be asked to dance with him at the two balls that were held in his honour. The Prince had abandoned protocol, claiming the right of every other man to decide whom he should invite to dance. Amongst his other indiscretions, while he had been in Barbados, he had made a conquest of: 'a foolish female ready to resign herself to His Royal Highness.' Buried among this trivia, Fanny found a piece of news that must have brought her a glow of satisfaction. The Prince, who as a midshipman had held Nelson in high esteem, now told him that he was determined to be at Nelson's wedding. Not only that, he was insisting that he should give Fanny away. Nelson was gratified by this royal approval, realising that it might be very useful to him in the future. As for Fanny, she must have been flattered by the attention. William might be only the third son of the King, but how many girls of her acquaintance could claim to have royalty as a guest at their wedding, let alone one who wished to play a major part? She would have been even more impressed at the time had she realised that this Prince would one day be the King of England and remain a loyal friend to her throughout her life.

Until Christmas Nelson was caught up in the social whirl. At St John's in Antigua there had been dancing three nights in a row, which had gone on until daybreak. In the tone of a middle-aged man, Nelson commented to Fanny:

> I fancy many people were as happy to see His Royal Highness quit as they were to see him enter…for another day or two's raquet [sic] would have knocked some of the fair sex up…I could not have supposed there had been near the number of females on this island as appeared at the balls, and all being in their best clothes made them look tolerably well.

By day Nelson was riding great distances as he accompanied the Prince on inland visits. But in spite of all this exertion, he was quick to tell Fanny, his health had not suffered at all. In fact, many people had noticed how well he was looking. But by New Year's Day he was hoping that things would quieten somewhat. That, as he said himself, was a vain hope and he listed the week's forthcoming engagements.

> Today we dine with Sir Thomas [Shirley, the Governor of the Leeward Islands]; tomorrow the Prince has a party, on Wednesday he gives a dinner in St John's to the regiment, in the evening is a mulatto ball, on Thursday a cock fight dine at Col.Crosbie's brother's and a ball, on Friday somewhere but I forget, on Saturday at Mr Byam's the President.

With all the dancing that was taking place throughout the island, it was perhaps not surprising that when Nelson sent to St John's for new shoes, the shop sent him two pairs of dancing pumps by mistake.

Towards mid January 1787, this social life had begun to pall; Nelson felt he was not really cut out to spend his time waiting upon Princes when he had much rather be with Fanny. He was waiting for the new Commodore of the fleet to arrive, relieve him of his temporary duties and grant him some leave. But Sir Richard Bickerton did not seem to be in any hurry to do that – and Nelson dared not ask a favour in case it was refused. To add to the mixed feelings Nelson had at this time, most of the company of the Prince's ship was sick, probably with yellow fever, so he did not feel he could leave him to his own devices. All these thoughts and fears he poured out to Fanny:

> I believe few men before marriage or even after often say as much as I do, but I have not a thought that I wish to conceal from you. If it is possible absence increases my affection. You are never absent from my mind in any place or company.

The New Year brought with it prospects for change for John Herbert. He was due to retire and his thoughts, like those of Nelson, were on going home. At some time Nelson must have discussed how Herbert and Martha intended to return to England. Most plantation owners took passage in a merchant ship. However, Herbert had travelled short trips on board *Boreas*, and so Nelson had written offering to take them with him when he sailed for home. His letter to Fanny on the subject did not make it clear what Herbert replied though it was implied in: 'but I don't think Miss Herbert will like it, for what reason I know not. It is certainly as clean as a sugar loaded ship, although accommodation may not be so elegantly fitted up'. Justifiably, he felt keenly the implied criticism of his ship.

Nelson managed to snatch three days in Nevis at the end of January and when he sailed again, Herbert who had accompanied him may well have decided he had done the right thing in refusing the long passage home in *Boreas*. Not that the illness he developed had anything to do with the ship. Nelson reported to Fanny that her uncle had been perfectly well whilst at sea, but whenever they touched land he developed a fever. Nelson was not entirely sympathetic when Herbert expressed a desire to be at home in his own bed. 'The wish is natural but should not be indulged.' The only way to deal with fever was to let nature take its course as it did: 'Mr Herbert has dropped asleep and a most profuse perspiration has come upon him which there is no doubt will entirely carry off the fever.'

It is a pity that Nelson was not more specific about his own problems thus leaving it open to speculation as to what exactly he meant when he wrote: ' and never again do I wish to be separated from the object of my heart. ' 'Tis that separation which makes me unwell with incidents which you are acquainted with.' Although not specific in some respects, Nelson's remarks to Fanny had become more explicit and sexual in nature. A week after Mr Herbert's attack of fever, Nelson wrote jubilantly: 'We are out of English Harbour thank God, and so far on my way to be with you. I anticipate with pleasure our meeting.' He went on to say that the length of their 'acquaintance' had given him proof of the steadfastness of his own feelings for her and she had given him proof that her 'goodness increases by time'. He was aware that each of them had had the opportunity to find solace with others, yet he was convinced that in spite of it being 'difficult to be perfect' they were ideally suited to each other. He realised that words were easy: 'But one proof is worth all the protestations and when we are one I trust you will find the proof equal to your expectations.'

At last, it was Nevis's turn to welcome the royal visitor and *Boreas* and *Pegasus* lay at anchor off the island from 15 to 23 February. Again the Prince was treated to what had become almost the standard round of events: dinners with the leading gentlemen, balls to give the ladies a chance to see and be seen; a day at the races and possibly here, a chance for the Prince to sample the curative waters at the Bath House. Fanny, as the President's hostess, would have played a leading role in some of the entertainment and certainly been present at others. However, this particular royal visit demonstrated very clearly the upsets that can attend any such event. Without any warning, Fanny had been placed in a difficult position because His Royal Highness had appeared to slight President Herbert. Nelson, torn between loyalty to his Prince and his future uncle-in-law (from whom he still hoped to receive a substantial sum), found himself acting as peacemaker. As is usually the case, the upset was the result of a misunderstanding that had arisen when one of the plantation owners, George Forbes, an old friend of the Prince, let it be known that he wished to hold a dinner at his home, Bush Hill, in the Prince's honour. Invitations were issued to other gentlemen. Unfortunately, when Prince William accepted he asked that it should be a private affair without any other guests thus giving them an opportunity to reminisce about their shared experiences. Obviously Forbes had to comply with the Prince's wishes and duly informed the gentlemen of the royal request, but when he came to Mr Herbert he must have failed to explain the circumstances either fully or tactfully. So, already somewhat aggrieved, Herbert became furious when he discovered that in fact two gentlemen had been admitted to the royal presence at the dinner – one of them, by chance, being Fanny's brother-in-law Walter Nisbet. The matter rumbled on for several days with the Prince eventually assuring Nelson that he had no intention of offending anybody and certainly not Mr Herbert. Of the two who had joined Forbes and the Prince at dinner, one was a relation of Forbes and Nisbet had been asked because, having spent the day attending the Prince at the races, it was too late for him to go home.

When Nelson sailed on 22 February, he took with him a treasured piece of cargo in the shape of Fanny's pianoforte. Sometime earlier he had searched in Barbados for harpsichord strings for her. If this was for the instrument he was now carrying, then we must assume that Nevis did not number a qualified tuner amongst its craftsmen but St Kitts did and he had come on board *Boreas* to carry out the task. Nelson did not profess to have a great love of music and perhaps Fanny should have taken note of his comment: 'a man is cracking my head with tuning your pianoforte.' Then he must have realised that sounded churlish so he followed it with: 'However be assured there is nothing in this world I would not bear with to please my dearest Fanny.'

The following day he wrote to tell her he was feeling ill and as a consequence had not accompanied His Royal Highness on shore. According to him she alone was the cause of his indisposition; his overwhelming desire to be with her. He was anxious for the Prince to go, for then he could be: 'restored to you, and health and all other blessings, I doubt not would attend me.' It was clear too, that a great concern was when they would at last be married. To add to his frustration, he had asked Herbert's opinion but not received a decided answer. Herbert had assured him that the more he knew him the more he liked him and that as far as he was concerned the wedding could take place at Nelson's convenience, either in Nevis or when they arrived in England. Nelson balked at the latter suggestion, for several reasons – one of which he had already made plain to Fanny, but tellingly he gave the reason that he did not wish to wait for England was because it would give the gossips a field day: 'the ill natured part of these islands would say that I had only been playing the fool with you.' This, as they both knew, was so often the case amongst the visiting seafarers. Nelson had touched on the subject in a letter to his brother, the Rector, in May 1785 asking: 'Where is Charles Boyles? Tell him Miss – is waiting for him: Fame says she is likely to have another child. She often inquires after him.'

By the beginning of March even the Prince was beginning to feel the strain so Nelson decided to postpone a visit to Tortola until His Royal Highness was feeling better. When he began a letter to Fanny early on the morning of 6 March, Nelson was interrupted by a visit from the Prince who had, among other matters, raised one that affected Fanny. Nelson hesitantly prefaced what he had to tell her by saying: 'I am now feeling most awkward.' She, when reading, must have wondered if he was about to tell her that the wedding was postponed indefinitely. But that was far from the case. Prince William had reminded Nelson of his wish to see him married and of his promise to give the bride away. However, since it was unlikely that he would return to Nevis after the visit to Tortola and as they were anchored in Sandy Point, off St Kitts, so very close to Nevis, His Royal Highness could see no reason why the wedding should not take place immediately.

CHAPTER III

Domestic Life in Norfolk

I am married to an amiable woman, that far makes amends for everything: indeed till I married her I never knew happiness. And I am morally certain she will continue to make me a happy man for the rest of my days.
Nelson, 21 March 1787

Such is the power of princes that their commands are carried out. Nelson and the Prince arrived in Nevis on 8 March and just three days later the wedding took place. Probably neither of them gave a moment's thought to the planning and preparations that this involved. In his letter to Fanny on 6 March Nelson said only: ' I hope Mr Herbert can have no objection, especially if he considers how much it is in my interest to be well with the Prince.' Nelson had hinted more than once that he expected to benefit in some way from the Prince's patronage and he knew that Herbert would appreciate this. He went on to flatter Herbert saying that he was confident he could: 'leave it to him, persuaded that he will do everything which is right and proper on the occasion.' Herbert might well have a legion of indoor domestic servants who could attend to all the necessary details but even so, when one's guests included a member of the royal family, more than three days would normally have been required to put on the sort of celebration expected from the President. All the best English china and finest silver, glass and napery were brought out for the occasion and one of the best beef animals on the plantation was slaughtered to provide part of the wedding feast. The crew of *Boreas* was not forgotten either and they received supplies of beef the day following the wedding – and doubtless a good supply of West Indian rum was sent on board for them to drink their captain's health.

Fortunately, all the paraphernalia of a modern wedding did not exist; an eighteenth-century bride wore a fine gown that would take her through some of the social occasions she might attend during the first year of her marriage. It is likely that Fanny had had several gowns made earlier, some of which she would have worn during the Prince's royal visit to Nevis.

Given the climate and the fashion of the period, her chosen dress was made either of lace or fine white muslin cotton, trimmed with ribbons of coloured silk or of lace. Her dark hair would have been curled high upon her head and bejewelled ribbons woven into it.

Visitors to Nevis today who follow the 'Nelson trail' are shown the huge old silk cotton tree on the Montpelier estate under whose panoply Nelson and Fanny are said to have exchanged their vows on Sunday 11 March 1787. Montpelier was part of the parish of St John's but the little church in the village of Fig Tree where the marriage register can be seen, was far too small to hold all those who came to witness the wedding and join in the celebrations. These included not only most of the white population of Nevis, joined by friends and relations from the nearby islands, but also many of Nelson's naval colleagues. No details exist of the day's events. We assume since the wedding is reputed to have taken place outdoors that the weather was fine. On the marriage certificate the officiating minister stated that the ceremony had taken place at the home of the President which could, of course, include the grounds of the house. While not wishing to cast doubt on the romantic picture of the couple under the silk cotton tree, the very factual *Boreas* logbook recorded on 10 March that it had rained all day, while the report for the wedding day itself reads: 'These twenty four hours moderate' in other words, it may well have been overcast, with heavy black clouds lowering over Mount Nevis making it seem even closer to Montpelier than usual. By Monday gales were buffeting the island. It is a matter for speculation whether Josiah attended his mother as a page boy or if Martha Herbert acted as a bridesmaid to her cousin. Martha, who was to be married to the widower Andrew Hamilton within a few weeks, may have felt that Fanny's hastily prepared wedding somewhat overshadowed hers. John Herbert had by then sufficiently forgiven the Prince for excluding him from Forbes's dinner party to entertain him politely and lavishly. Deep down he must have been proud that one of His Majesty's sons had given his niece away.

Detail of what the bride wore and how she looked that day may be lacking but we do have a comment from the Prince to a correspondent. Having related that Nelson was 'head over ears in love' with a 'pretty and sensible woman' he went on to note that Nelson's health was such that: 'he is more in need of a nurse than a wife. I do not think he can live long.' Fortunately, he did not voice this opinion on the day of the wedding in Fanny's hearing. If it was a true reflection then it was hardly a promising start to her second marriage, especially when her first had been so short-lived. Later writers have described Fanny as being plain, but since the Prince was renowned for having a discriminating eye where young women were concerned, and he had met Fanny on more than one occasion, his first hand assessment of her as 'pretty' may be more valid than most.

In the same way there is no proof as to what happened at the wedding, so we do not know where Fanny and Nelson started their married life. If the Prince had to be entertained, and he had said he was looking forward to the novel idea of staying in a private home, then it is doubtful they were able to go off by themselves to have what we would term a honeymoon; it is more likely that they remained at Montpelier. From the evidence Nelson gave in a letter to a friend ten days later, his high expectations of married life had been fulfilled; Fanny was everything and more that he had hoped for. But they were not given long to enjoy the bliss of married life. Just one week and Nelson was again at sea, sailing first to St Kitts and then to Tortola for the Prince's visit there. By 21 March Nelson had received definite orders for his recall to England. As he told his old friend Captain Locker, after Tortola he would go to English Harbour in Antigua to have the *Boreas* fitted out for its return home. He was longing, he wrote, to return to his native land because he had suffered so much while he had been on the West Indian station; not only from illness but with other troubles. He was referring not only to the problems he had encountered in the enforcement of the Navigation Acts, but more recently he had become involved in supporting an action the Prince had taken that had had serious repercussions. As a result of what was considered to be arrogant and overbearing behaviour on his part, Nelson had put himself out of favour with the Admiralty. However, as he confided to Locker, he would have found all these drawbacks intolerable had they not been counterbalanced by the great happiness he had found with Fanny.

She, while making her own preparations for leaving the island for the last time, still had duties to perform for Herbert who would also take his leave of the island almost immediately after his daughter's wedding – and of course, there was that wedding to organise. A very grand affair, it would be seen as John Herbert's swansong to the island that he had served so long. At that point his intention was to retire to England for good, leaving the Montpelier estate to be managed by a Mr Huggins. Nelson returned to Nevis on 26 April for almost a month, so he was able to be present at Martha's wedding, relishing his new role as a married man, part of a couple. From his letters it is difficult to decide how Nelson felt about Martha. He had, as we know, been very fond of the other cousin, Sally, whilst she was living in Nevis though his manner changed abruptly once she married. While it was part of the eighteenth-century social etiquette to address young ladies formally unless they were very close family members, this had not applied to Sally, which suggests she may have been quite young; early teenage brides being not uncommon in the West Indies at the time. But in the case of Miss Herbert, things were different. Nelson never referred to her by her first name. Most of his letters to Fanny contained a polite message for 'Miss Herbert'; he saved his newspapers for her, he undertook shopping commissions on her behalf and he passed news and greetings to her from other naval officers who had spent time in Nevis. Yet for all his solicitous attention, the feeling remains that he did not really care for her. Maybe the feeling was mutual.

May saw the climax to all the preparations. The Prince wrote to ask Nelson to join him but he declined because there was so much going on:

Herbert is near going; and it is impossible to move a female in a few hours
– never yet having made the *Boreas* her home... Mrs Nelson returns her
thanks with Miss Herbert for your most polite remembrance of them.

How much he must have enjoyed writing the phrase 'Mrs Nelson.' The
short extract reveals much; the wedding had not yet taken place, otherwise
he would have called Martha, Mrs Hamilton; it would however be taking place shortly and almost immediately afterwards, John Herbert and
the newly-weds would leave for England. The most important part of the
letter concerns Fanny and her removal. The generally held opinion is that
after the wedding, Herbert and the Hamiltons sailed home in a merchant
ship called the *Roehampton* – and that Fanny and Josiah went with them.
No one has offered a reason why this should have been so, unless Herbert
was demanding that Fanny keep to her contract to him until he was settled
into his London house. It would seem more likely that this letter has been
overlooked or misinterpreted. Nelson stated categorically that had he been
able to sail to the Prince he would, but he was still engaged in the process
of getting all Fanny's and Josiah's belongings – which should have included
that piano – on board. There was no reason why Fanny should not have
travelled with him even though Herbert had turned down Nelson's offer to
take him and the Hamiltons in *Boreas*. The accommodation on board, which
he considered as good as any that a merchant ship could offer, had in the
past been thought good enough for Admiral Hughes' wife and daughter. It
was not unusual for wives to travel with their officer husbands and given
that this was a homeward voyage Nelson would have both wanted, and
expected, his wife and stepson with him.

In the past they had rarely had the opportunity of being alone but now
the close confines of the ship meant that they spent much time together.
This was a testing period for both of them. Fanny had the opportunity to
see her new husband against the background in which he thrived. Here,
where he was absolute master, his word obeyed without question, he grew,
metaphorically, in stature. On shore he had been a very different person;
kind and attentive to her and Josiah; sometimes almost obsequious to those
he thought his social superiors while to others he could be morose and off
hand. Fanny, often the one to smooth out the little upsets he had caused,
used to making decisions for a large household, now found that he was the
decisive one. She had made the voyage to and from England before so she
would have had a rough idea of how long it would be after they left Bermuda
before they again saw land. The last time she had travelled, she had been a
paying passenger and would have received the attention accorded to such,
but this time as the Captain's wife she would have received the very best
attention. And when Nelson invited his officers to dine, Fanny presided
as a charming hostess. It is more than likely that when necessary she also
acted as nurse to any who were in need of such ministrations. As for young
Josiah, he must have had a wonderful time being thoroughly spoilt by the

crew. The seeds of following in his stepfather's footsteps and making a career at sea were probably sown at that time.

On 26 June the *Boreas* was on course for the Scillies sailing in strong gales and generally squally weather. They passed the Lizard in Cornwall on the second day of July and finally moored at Spithead on the 5th. Lodgings were taken at Portsmouth from where, on 9 July, Nelson wrote to Captain Locker:

> My dear wife is much obliged by your kind enquiries. I have no doubt but you will like her upon acquaintance, for although I must be partial, yet she possesses great good sense and good temper.

What greater accolade could he give her! Weeks of living in very close proximity had not dulled the relationship and there was no sign that Fanny had shown any irritating feminine weaknesses. In fact it was Nelson who was ill almost immediately they landed, with what sounds like severe neuralgia. 'Indeed I have been so very unwell, with a violent cold, that I have scarcely been able to hold up my head till yesterday.' Any hopes Fanny may have had of meeting and socialising with friends and acquaintances in Portsmouth, would have been put to one side as she fulfilled the Prince's prophecy and became her husband's nurse. His head pains would have made him irritable, a condition not improved by the fact that now he was back in England, he had no idea what the future held for them. He thought he wanted a life ashore but now he was back and there was a hint of war, he wanted to be part of that. But he could make no plans until he was given a definite date for the paying off of the *Boreas.*

Then suddenly, it looked as if he might be recalled to active service. He received orders to be ready to sail at a moment's notice, so towards the end of August he took Fanny and Josiah to London, where he took lodgings for them at 10 Great Marlborough Street within walking distance of Cavendish Square where Herbert and the Hamiltons were living. Much to Nelson's chagrin, when his orders came it was to take the *Boreas* to anchor in the Thames estuary at the Great Nore and become a receiving ship for those unfortunates who had failed to avoid the marauding Press gangs. Nelson felt keenly the humiliation of such a role but worse, he confided to the Rector in a letter dated 23 September: 'We are laying here seven miles from land on the Impress service, and am as much separated from my wife as if I were in the East Indies.'

The separation was difficult for Fanny too. Quite apart from missing her husband for his own sake, she must have found it very lonely with only Josiah for company. All her life she had been accustomed to having people around her and she was used to the informal attitude to visiting that existed in the Leeward Islands. Now she was bound by the strict code of etiquette that governed the making of calls upon other ladies. Inevitably, she would have looked to her uncle and cousin for help in re-introducing her into society. That it was from Cavendish Square that Nelson wrote to the Rector on 29 October suggests that the Marlborough Street lodgings had been given up and that they were enjoying Herbert's hospitality. Nelson was still officially living aboard *Boreas* but he used his visits to the Admiralty Office as an opportunity to snatch a few hours with Fanny. When they were together there were serious matters to discuss; where they should look to make their home; what he should do if he was not immediately given another command and most pressing, the decision that would inevitably lead to more loneliness for her if or when he went back to sea, namely where Josiah should go to school.

The boy was now nearly 7 and his early education had been somewhat desultory. Nelson realised how important it was for the boy to receive a thorough education and that could only be achieved by sending him to a good school. With the uncertainty of the parents' movements, a boarding school was the obvious answer. Realising that Fanny would not relish losing daily contact with her son at such a young age, Nelson turned to the Rector for advice on suitable establishments in Norfolk, that being where he hoped they would eventually make their home. In fact the Rector had already started looking for property for them there. But choosing the right school was more important than housing and Nelson was pleased to settle the matter at the end of October: 'Many thanks for your kind enquiries about the School: it is quite the thing I wished for, and you will be pleased to tell the Master the child shall come after the Christmas holidays.' The use of the term 'school' may be misleading; it is more than likely that at this stage, Josiah would be joining a small number of boys, probably not many more than a dozen who were instructed by a clergyman in whose house some of them may have boarded.

The Rector was most anxious to meet Nelson's wife. He too had married and had recently become a father. His hopes for a son, whom he intended to name Horatio after his brother, had been dashed with the arrival of a daughter, Charlotte, but nonetheless he was looking forward to showing off his wife Sarah, the new baby and the rectory at Hilborough. Not knowing what Nelson's immediate plans were, he and Sarah offered to have Josiah live with them until such time as they could find a home in the vicinity.

On 30 November the *Boreas* that had been Nelson's home for the past four years was finally decommissioned, the Commissioner from the Admiralty coming on board to pay off both officers and crew. At last, freed from the cares of command, Nelson was able to join his wife and look forward to the Christmas festivities but as for the New Year – he had no idea how they would live on his half pay.

Christmas in Cavendish Square was celebrated as lavishly as it would have been in Nevis; there were dinners and parties, dances and musical entertainments to beguile the time but all the opulence could not compensate for the cold and damp of London. Three days into 1788, and arrangements were made for Josiah to be taken to school. The fact that Fanny had not insisted on their taking the child to Norfolk was explained by the fact that both she and Nelson were ill. Fanny's condition was exacerbated by her anxiety for her son's possible distress at being parted from his mother.

Nelson tried to temper this concern, writing in his letter to the Rector: 'Our little boy shall be at Hilborough on Tuesday or Wednesday next, escorted by Frank [Nelson's manservant at sea] who I have desired to stay two or three days till the child becomes reconciled.' However, any suggestion that Nelson was adopting a soft approach to the boy's future upbringing was dispelled in: 'I am assured of your and Mrs Nelson's goodness to him – that is, you will not allow him to do as he pleases: it's mistaken kindness where it happens.' For a moment, the reader may hear the faint echo of another stepfather, Mr Murdstone in Dickens' *David Copperfield*. Nelson was anxious that Josiah should not be allowed to feel different in any way to his fellow pupils: 'I wish him at school to have the same weekly allowance as the other boys, and whatever else may be proper for him.' Nelson may not have realised that he was indirectly passing judgement on Fanny. He obviously believed that she had been over-indulgent with Josiah and he saw it as part of his new parental duty to correct the faults that had been allowed to develop in the child before they got any worse.

Whatever feelings he might have had for Josiah – and it has to be admitted that a boy of 7 was a very different creature to an enchanting 4-year-old infant with whom he had played imaginary games under the table in Montpelier – a child did not readily fit into the Nelsons' proposed life style. As Nelson explained to the Rector, as soon as he was well enough to go out, he and Fanny intended to go to Bath in the hope that a regime that included regularly taking the waters would alleviate their various ailments. Which is where they were when, towards the end of January, in another letter to Captain Locker he shifted the emphasis on ill health on to Fanny: '...[her] lungs are so much affected by the smoke of London, that I cannot think of placing her in that situation [Locker had found them a house in London] however desirable.' The atmospheric swirling fog that features in films depicting Victorian London and the more recent smog that covered the capital in the 1950s give some indication of how smoke-ridden the capital was. In the late eighteenth century, when coal was the only fuel available for cooking and heating, every house in the capital would have had a number of chimneys belching smoke into the atmosphere. In addition to domestic chimneys, industries as varied as tanneries, dye-works, tallow chandlers and soap makers, as well as metal and tin works and those which boiled bones and whale extracts all emitted their noxious and sulphurous fumes into the thick yellow smoke that hung low like a pall. Small wonder then that those with a tendency to lung problems would find their condition aggravated by spending the winter in London.

There is no evidence that Fanny had shown any sign of throat or chest weakness until this time, but Nelson certainly had. In the months leading up to their marriage he had often complained of congestion to his lungs and had expressed the hope that once he was back in his native land, away from the searing heat of the tropics, he would recover fully. This had not happened; if anything his health had deteriorated. Fanny must have been acutely aware that it looked as if she was replaying the scenario of her first marriage. Josiah Nisbet's health had been poor while he was in the West Indies and he believed that the temperate climate of England would cure him. It had not. Instead he had gone into that state that was appropriately referred to as a decline, the body wasting away as the patient became more lethargic. The prospect of losing her second husband almost more quickly than she had the first must have led Fanny to be over careful of Nelson's health, thus earning her the reputation of being fussy. While her thoughts may have gone back to her last months with Josiah, it has to be questioned as to how much she had told Nelson about her first marriage. Perhaps he had not liked to ask her too much and therefore relied on gossip to fill in the details of her life with Nisbet. Certainly he did not get right even the basic facts about Fanny herself. He had told his uncle Suckling in November 1785, some four months after his engagement, that Fanny had lost both her parents when she was 2 and he also deducted several years from her age. Five months later, he does not seem to have a much clearer picture of her background. Writing to Suckling on the subject of John Herbert providing financially for Fanny, he made no mention of her having been in England with Nisbet, in fact he categorically stated otherwise.

When Mrs Nisbet married, Mr H promised £2000 with her, but as her husband settled in the island, [ie Nevis] where he died a few months after, it has never been paid.

He continued that Herbert had promised to give young Josiah £1,000 when he came of age, bear the expense of bringing him up and provide him with an education that would open the door to a profession. Nelson then said that Fanny was owed about £3,000 from Nisbet's family estate and for his professional services as a doctor on the island. 'But Dr Nisbet dying insane, without a Will or any Papers which were regular, has made this business rather troublesome.'

It does seem strange that during their courtship period they had not exchanged more information about each other's past. Lovers usually seek to establish a common ground, so it is hard to believe that Fanny had not mentioned that she had first hand knowledge of England; that she had lived in Salisbury and had visited relations in Bristol and London. But perhaps these revelations came slowly, just as Nelson would have revealed, piecemeal, information about his own family. Fanny knew that his father and one of his brothers were clergymen and that he had Lord Walpole for his godfather, but it is doubtful if he told her when they were first acquainted that all his sisters had worked for their livings either as milliners or shop assistants and that one, now dead, had eloped and had an illegitimate child. Fortunately, the other two sisters were now respectably married, his favourite, Kitty, to a man who had made a fortune in the East Indies. Then there was brother Suckling. Like his sisters he too had been apprenticed, in his case to learn the drapery trade. When he received a small legacy he bought a grocer's shop but he was not cut out for shop keeping; greyhound racing, hare coursing and drinking occupied most of his time and left him in debt. Brother Maurice did at least have a job, in the Customs House in London. He lived with a common law wife but he too found it hard to keep solvent. As for brother Edmund, little was said of him beyond the fact that his health was not good. Perhaps it was just as well that Fanny was introduced to this diverse family one at a time.

As politeness and duty decreed, she had begun a correspondence with her father-in-law, the Revd Edmund Nelson, as soon as she arrived in England. Her letters were not entirely successful in persuading him that he was going to get on well with her. In part this may have been due to Nelson having emphasised the grand lifestyle to which Fanny was accustomed, while she in turn had the habit of saying plainly what she thought and how she felt. Having led her to believe that once the *Boreas* arrived in England Nelson would be paid off and they would be together, she had instead found herself alone in lodgings. No wonder then that she told her father-in-law that she was feeling neither well nor happy with the situation. Edmund, who enjoyed writing letters, passed on whatever news he had to other members of the family, in particular his daughter Kitty and it was to her that he repeated that Fanny had said that the lot of a sailor's wife was a hard one. This remark has been taken to show that Fanny was ill-prepared for the life ahead of her when in fact she was merely repeating a truism. Edmund may have misinterpreted too Fanny's expressed desire to visit Norfolk. As a parent she thought she understood how anxious the father must be to see his son, so before Christmas she had written to talk about a visit to him. Edmund's reaction, which he voiced in a letter to Kitty, was couched in the slightly ironic literary style he often adopted but failed to recognise in others.

> My very polite correspondent...seems to think it will not be many weeks before she visits these Arcadian Scenes: rivers represented by a puddle, mountains by anthills, woods by bramble bushes; yet all is taste, if not hid by snow. Forbid it Fate.

Edmund need not have worried that Fanny would be disappointed in the scenery whether it was covered by snow or not for first she and Nelson must go south-westwards in search of better health. Kitty Matcham, who had hoped that during a visit to London she would meet the newly-weds, reported somewhat tersely to her father on 12 January 1788: 'Bro Horace gone to Bath.' But at least they had avoided the hail and snow that fell in Norfolk.

When it came to it, their actual departure was governed not so much by necessity of health as of expediency and future prospects. Nelson confided to Locker on 28 January:

I was rather hurried in getting down here [Bath], by Prince William having invited me to Plymouth. I was therefore glad to place Mrs Nelson here at once, which not only saved me the expense but the toil, of a journey of three hundred miles. I returned from Plymouth three days ago.

Once again the Prince had made the Nelsons act precipitately and Nelson had obeyed the royal summons without hesitation even though it might have caused him double coach fare if Fanny had not been ready to accompany him. It is said that during his stay with the Prince, Nelson dropped a hint that His Royal Highness might put Fanny's name forward as a Lady-in-Waiting at Court. As for himself, he could see no prospect at that time of returning to sea and he may have hoped that his royal friend would be able to secure him a position somewhere. Already, it had become apparent that Nelson was concerned about money and so again he hoped he might solve his problems by joining with the Rector in purchasing part of one of the expensive tickets in the Lottery.

Nelson and Fanny stayed in Bath for several weeks before going to Bristol, then Clifton and back again to Bath before going off in mid April to explore Exmouth in Devon. The stay in Exmouth was highly successful. It was probably the first time that the couple had been truly on their own without other people making demands on them. Certainly, Nelson's health improved while they were there as they enjoyed the bracing fresh air from the sea and the surrounding moors. Fanny fell in love with Exmouth and it is easy to see why. The outskirts of the little town are set on steep hills where, from the cliff top path called The Beacon, Fanny could well have imagined that she was again in the grounds of Montpelier looking down to Nevis Roads to see if Nelson's ship was lying there. On a lovely summer's day, the Atlantic at Exmouth can look almost as blue as it does in the Leewards. Even Nelson appreciated the gentle climate that blesses that part of south Devon telling his friend Hercules Ross on 6 May that his letter had:

...found me in this remote corner, where I have been this past fortnight, enjoying the benefit of a first summer to a West Indian: no bad thing. However, as usual, my health is got up again, after the Doctors telling me they could do nothing for me; Dame Nature never has failed curing me.

That he was relaxed and content at that time is apparent in the tone of the letter. He told Ross that he and Fanny were returning to London within the week but would break their journey in Bath on the Saturday night. He hoped Ross might be there too, so he said he would look for him in the Pump Room on Sunday. Ross had recently married too, an 'amiable woman' so Nelson had heard and he rejoiced that both of them had been granted: 'the greatest blessing heaven can bestow.' However, in one respect they differed: '...but in this next, my friend, you have got the start of me.' Ross must have told Nelson in his letter that Mrs Ross was pregnant. Was that something Nelson regretted, that he had been married a year but he had not yet fathered a child?

There were, however, more pressing matters than Fanny's failure to conceive. Nelson still had no idea what his future was to be or where he and Fanny would call home. From the West Country they returned to London staying in Kentish Town with Nelson's uncle, William Suckling. From there they went to Norfolk, very possibly Fanny's first experience of England north of London. But they did not go straight to Burnham Thorpe to see Edmund. To Kitty he wrote:

> When they come into Norfolk, I shall like as well if every visit is made before mine begins, and to say the truth I am not now anxious to see them. Him for a day or two I should be glad of, but to introduce a stranger to an infirm and whimsical old man, who can neither eat nor drink, nor talk, nor see, is as well let alone.

It is doubtful that Edmund really believed any of the things he said about himself here or it may be that he was indulging in self-pity, a trait his most illustrious son had inherited. The fact that he harped on the theme that he was in no hurry to meet them suggests that he was actually aggrieved that they had not come before. For this he put the blame squarely upon Fanny, she (being so grand) was keeping his Horace from him. Fanny was 'the Stranger' but eventually he unbent sufficiently to suggest to Kitty in May: '...perhaps you may introduce her by and by. I believe she will form a valuable part of our family connections and certain it is he has a claim to all my affection, having never transgressed' – which is more than could be said for the rest of his sons. But Edmund would have to wait his turn.

Their first visit in Norfolk was to the Rector and his family at Hilborough, a village about five miles south of the market town of Swaffham. For Fanny this meant a joyous reunion with her son during the school summer holiday. Although aware of how lucky she was in comparison with those West Indian mothers whose sons went to England to school as little boys and were not seen again until they were young men, she still missed Josiah. He, by all accounts, was still a reluctant scholar and reputed to have a quick temper but nonetheless, both Fanny and Nelson found him affectionate and polite. From the Rector's house they continued in Norfolk for a visit with Nelson's elder sister Susannah who lived in the city of Norwich where her husband Thomas Bolton was a merchant. Susannah was a friendly, motherly type whose life revolved around her large family of two sons and five daughters, two of which were the 7-year-old twins Susanna and Catherine. She also had her youngest brother Edmund living with them. Susannah Bolton was not pretentious; she accepted life as it came, which was just as well as her husband frequently made unwise business decisions which left them short of money and sometimes homeless when he was engaged in buying and selling property.

While they were in Norwich, Nelson took the opportunity to travel up to London to see what chance there was of getting a ship. When he wrote to Fanny on 26 August, he told her of the interview he had had with Lord Hood who had always been his friend and was now one of the Admiralty Lords. Nelson hoped that Hood would use his influence on his behalf, but from the tone of his conversation it became clear that the backing Nelson had given the Prince's actions in the Leeward Islands still counted against him, and the Admiralty were in no hurry to give him another command. Hood tried to temper Nelson's disappointment by suggesting that to someone like him there could be no satisfaction in a peacetime command but, he assured him, at the first sign of any trouble at sea he would immediately be found a good ship. Hood also made frequent enquiries about Fanny whom he had come to know during the time he had served in the West Indies.

While in London, Nelson visited Herbert and had gone with him to spend the evening with other Nevis friends at the home of Martha and her husband. Nelson could not wait until he saw Fanny to pass on the news that when the Hamiltons returned to Nevis, Herbert was going with them. The Montpelier plantation had been left in the care of an overseer who had fallen out of favour with his employer and was to be sacked. This man, Edward Huggins, had the reputation in Nevis of being the cruellest of slave masters, using the whip constantly and indiscriminately, often almost to the point of death. He was also discovered to be unreliable where other people's money was concerned. It is not clear for which of these misdemeanours Herbert had dismissed him. But he was to go, and as soon as he vacated the house, Martha and her husband would move in until their own house nearby was ready for occupation. She was also learning to ride properly so that when her 'dear father' came back in the spring she would be able to visit him daily. Nelson implied that Fanny would be as surprised by Martha's fulsome attention to her father as he had been.

This letter shed light on an item that had been referred to almost two years earlier, namely Nelson's errand to purchase a red parrot but having to settle for a grey one. This had been shipped home with other of Nelson's belongings that had been put into the Customs House where: 'I really wonder all my things are not lost, they lay in such a place.' The parrot, however, had not been consigned to the sheds but taken into the protective custody of Nelson's brother Maurice until it could be collected. 'My brother is very sorry to part with Polly.' The idea of Nelson travelling back to Norwich by stagecoach with a parrot is almost a parody.

Finally, their courtesy visits over, Nelson took Fanny 'home' to the parsonage at Burnham Thorpe. In December! 'December has visited us in all the pomp and parade of winter, wind and storm and rattling hail; clothed with frosted robes, powdered with snow, all trimmed in glittering icicles,' wrote Edmund in poetic style. Twelve months earlier, Fanny had been almost choked to death by the fogs of London, now she was in danger of hypothermia. The rambling old house, which lacking a woman's touch had suffered years of neglect, was cold and damp; Edmund had taken to living in two rooms only: 'the little dressing room and bed chamber adjoining, making the apartment somewhat like a Bath lodging.' Convenient though this may have been for him, it meant that the rest of the house, being unused became even colder and damper. The master of understatement Edmund told Kitty: 'Your very good sister-in-law finds it not so temperate as Nevis and the very robust Captain begins to feel a rumatick [sic] twinge now and then.'

If ever a marriage was to be tested, then this introduction to life at Burnham Thorpe provided the time. Apart from the sheer cold, the area itself must have proved depressing for Fanny, being so very flat. Even the slightest fall of rain was likely to cause the river to flood into the meadows in front of the house. The house itself lacked comfort, the furniture and fittings were old and worn; everything needed a thorough spring clean. It was now clear that Edmund, looking round his home, had had good reason for dreading Fanny's visit. He was suddenly aware of all its shortcomings. Not that Fanny complained. Without upsetting the small household staff of two or three, a housekeeper and Edmund's manservant and possibly a kitchen maid, all of whom had been with Edmund for years, she quietly supervised changes that made life more tolerable for all of them. Edmund quickly found that he rather liked this new daughter-in-law who did not give herself airs.

> The arrangements which have lately taken place here promise to be productive of those comforts which are adapted to my powers of enjoyment. Gentleness, quietude and good humour, neither impetuous nor insensible.

What more could one want from any woman? But he did worry that she might find life too quiet. Eventually he hoped she would be able to go out and meet people but in the meantime, he wished that he had a harpsichord or piano that she could play – not to entertain them but rather for her to: 'pass away an hour.' Edmund believed: 'Her musical powers I fancy are beyond the common sort.' The evidence is that none of the Nelsons, apart perhaps from Maurice, showed an appreciation of music. But during December Fanny would not have worried unduly that she could not play, for part of the time was taken up with Josiah joining them for the holidays.

On 31 December 1788 in the parsonage at Weston Longeville, a few miles from Norwich, the Revd James Woodforde filled in his daily diary entry:

> The coldest night I ever felt (I think) in my life and this morning also the coldest with high wind and small snow. It froze and still freezes sharply almost in every place in my house. The thermometer was the lowest I ever remember tho' it stands in my study.

A few days later his fellow clergyman, Edmund Nelson, added his comments on the weather to Kitty:

In our present cold, dreary, I had almost said uncomfortable state, the
severe season have affected both your brother and his lady. She does not
openly complain. Her attention to me demands my esteem and to her
good husband she is all he can expect…Horace has been unwell for some
days.

It would seem that the 'very robust captain' was finding that he was unable
to withstand either the cold or the rheumatism. As for Fanny, according to
Edmund writing in whimsical fashion, she was taking: '…large doses of the
bed.' He related that Fanny was only comfortable when she was tucked up
in bed with the thick woollen curtains drawn round its four posts to keep
out the draughts. This letter of Edmund's has given some the opportunity
to prove that Fanny was constantly ailing, withdrawing herself on a regular
basis. They tend to overlook the fact that Nelson's ill health was mentioned
in the same letter. If, as one would expect, Nelson and Fanny shared the bed,
then it is possible that they both retreated behind the curtains to nurse their
colds and at the same time find a little privacy.

When they had first come to Burnham Thorpe, Nelson's plan had been
that since he could not get a ship – and therefore make a decent living
– he and Fanny would go abroad to live. In one of his moments of bitter despondency when he felt that his country had treated him badly, he
had threatened to join the Russian Navy. As it was, he now turned to the
idea of going to live in France. At that time, as now, the cost of living in
France and much of Europe was considerably lower than in England and
many of the middle class and those aristocrats who were on a very limited
income found that what they had went much further abroad. Thomas
and Susannah Bolton had experimented with a year in Ostend five years
earlier. Fanny was already fluent in French so she would have no problem
settling there and Nelson was determined, after his abortive attempt some
years before, to learn to speak the language properly, it being considered
an essential part of a sailor's education to understand and speak French. In
that freezing winter, anywhere in the world would have seemed preferable
to Norfolk. But it was not long before the idea was given up. According to
Fanny many years later, the reason they stayed on in Burnham Thorpe was
that Edmund became distressed at the thought of their leaving him just
when he had become used to having them. The memorandum she wrote on
the subject was to appear in a book that would glorify Nelson so she slightly
slanted the truth of the situation.

Mr Nelson's joy at seeing this best and most affectionate of sons was so
great that he told us that we had given him a new life or some such expression, and that we had better not have come to him, than to have cheered
and then to leave him…Then we agreed to live together. A great comfort
to Mr N. and some convenience to all parties.

The last was certainly true. Living at the parsonage saved Nelson having to find the rent for a place of their own and sharing the cost of housekeeping amongst the three of them also assisted their straitened circumstances. However, the main reason for not making the move abroad was the threat posed by the French Revolution.

When Nelson agreed to stay on at Burnham Thorpe, he believed that he would find enough to keep him occupied. In the first months he had been content to wander over the fields and through the woods, often with Fanny at his side as he became re-acquainted with his childhood haunts. Then he took on the responsibility of farming the thirty acres of his father's glebe land and under the guidance of his brother-in-law, George Matcham, set about redesigning the garden, a pursuit that had become fashionable among gentlemen at that time. But he had been conditioned since boyhood for life at sea and he did not enjoy the pursuits of a country gentleman, however much he might have wished to. In early September 1789 he expressed in a letter to Capt. Locker his frustration at not being recalled to sea which he blamed, as he so often did, on the fact that he had neither independent means nor the patronage of someone important. 'I am now commencing Farmer, not a very large one, you will conceive, but enough for amusement. Shoot I cannot, therefore I have not taken out a licence.' The inability to shoot game immediately set him apart from all the farmers and gentlemen around him. Brother William, the Rector, regularly applied for the licence that enabled him to shoot over his land.

The letter to Locker returned to the theme of being neglected by those in authority: 'I see the propriety of not having built my hopes on such sandy foundations as the friendships of the Great.' Protestations that he was happy in spite of all that do not ring true and Fanny must frequently have borne the brunt of his moodiness. His strong opinions even deprived her of the opportunity of socialising at nearby Holkham Hall, the home of Thomas Coke, the Member of Parliament for that part of Norfolk. Nelson who professed to be a Tory had no intention of supporting a Whig function so when the invitation to a fete to celebrate the anniversary of the landing of William of Orange came, he sent a terse: 'Capt. Nelson's compliments to Mr & Mrs Coke & is sorry it is not in his power to accept their invitation for November 5th.' One reason why Nelson is said to have refused the invitation was that he had been made to feel socially inferior to Coke since it was to Holkham that he had to go to receive his naval pay.

Towards the end of 1789 the household at the parsonage increased when Nelson's 28-year-old brother Edmund returned from Norwich where he had been living with the Boltons. He had come home to die. He was another victim of 'the decline', that useful euphemism that covered many diseases among them tuberculosis and cancer. His father wrote: 'Poor Edmund seems to drop so gradually it is scarce to be perceived.' The further remark: 'We hope he lives in no great pain' suggests that the young man was either no longer able to communicate or he was already in a coma. He received constant attention from a Dame Smith, probably a local woman with nursing experience but Fanny too, was involved in the care of the patient. 'Poor Mrs N's trial in this instance is not a light one,' wrote her father-in-law, while after the death, when he wrote to inform his brother-in-law Thomas Bolton of the arrangements for the funeral, Nelson paid his own tribute to her 'kind offices' to his brother.

Fanny may even have welcomed the opportunity to nurse Edmund for there was little else to occupy her days beyond the traditional female pastimes of sewing and drawing. Since the parsonage lacked a piano, she could not even fill her time with music practice. Her harpsichord should have been shipped from Nevis with the rest of their belongings but had somehow gone missing. By the time it had been located the instrument had become so unglued that it was no longer worth the freight charge. For a woman who had been used to a large household, where lavish entertainment to important people from different countries had been almost a matter of daily routine, life in the Norfolk parsonage must at times have been almost beyond endurance. Since Nelson showed little interest in music, art or books, reading only newspapers and periodicals, she turned to the Revd Edmund for discussion on these subjects drawing on his small library when she needed to escape from the reality around her. Her father-in-law appreciated her intelligence and may have had her in mind when, in answer to a comment made by his daughter Kitty that she was mainly in the company of gentlemen he remarked:

> In this improved age the understanding of women are on most subjects as well cultivated, and their sentiments are generally delivered with a propriety of language equal to men, and indeed their knowledge, a few parts of learning excepted, is equally extensive and their conversation as void of trifles as their Lords...

Although the general tenor of life was monotonous, there was social life to be had. February brought the first of the year's Assemblies, that is large public dances, which were held in neighbouring towns. In King's Lynn for example, easily accessible from Burnham Thorpe, there was a special ball devoted to the dancing of the Cotillion. When Nelson took Fanny to the Assemblies, it gave him the chance to show off his new wife to the neighbours and her the opportunity to forge new acquaintance. It says much for Fanny that she settled so quickly into this very parochial background. For more entertainment it was necessary to go to Norwich. Staying for a couple or so nights with the Boltons would have allowed them to go to the Theatre Royal, perhaps to see Sheridan's *School for Scandal* or *A Trip to Scarborough*, both of which were played there in February 1789. Norwich would also have afforded Fanny the opportunity to go shopping for those items that were not available locally; on one occasion she asked Mrs Bolton where she might purchase honey water, something she had used in Nevis. When she had first come to Norfolk, the Revd Edmund had been much concerned that Fanny was not able to purchase items to the standard to which she was accustomed and had written to ask Kitty to:

> Be so good as to buy for Mrs N a plain, handsome bonnet such as she may wear at Wolterton if need be, or what you would for yourself buy for dining, visits etc. Send it down & if any covering for the neck by way of a cloak is needful, add that also.

It was to Norwich that she would have gone in September for the Grand Musical Festival devoted almost entirely to the works of Handel. Three or four days were given over to concerts that took place in the morning and the evening allowing for the late afternoon dinner in venues that varied from large halls to rooms that held no more than fifty. Nelson may have found these hard to sit through and more to his taste would have been the races at Swaffham and Fakenham or the special equestrian displays put on for public entertainment though Fanny too, would have enjoyed these outings.

They also entertained. Writing to Locker, Nelson referred to some wine that he had sent him: 'the Madeira I kept as a treat for some of my friends who are come here to see us, when behold, on examination, instead of Madeira I found as good Port wine as ever was tasted.' If they were to make a habit of entertaining, Fanny may have felt that it was a good idea to renovate some of the shabby furniture in the parsonage starting with the sofa in the sitting room. She having chosen the material and the pattern, Nelson wrote the order to Mr Scott, the upholsterer. 'A sopha [sic] cover of blue and white striped Manchester [cotton] of the pattern sent or nearly like it. The price I cannot exactly tell...A cover is sent, which fits very well except length. Let the other be 3″ deeper to hang over the legs...Mrs Nelson desires a handsome, rich blue – but not dark.' Fanny knew exactly what she wanted and left to herself could have instructed the upholsterer but Nelson, so used to giving orders whilst in command at sea, and with so little to occupy him, took it upon himself to undertake these important negotiations.

One gains the impression that Nelson saw himself very much in the role of master of the house and expected his wife to conform to the picture of the dutiful wife. This attitude places him squarely among the middle class where a woman was likely to rule the household without her husband realising it, whereas the upper class woman was frequently very much her own mistress and used to openly running affairs; such women were the hostesses whose salons wielded great political influence. Fanny's life in Nevis had prepared her for something like the latter role but she appeared to accept the former out of love for her husband. He in return tended to regard her at times as a delicate creature whose nerves had to be protected.

The story is told that one day when Nelson had gone to market to buy himself a pony, the parsonage servant announced that, in the absence of the master, a man was demanding to see her. When she confronted the visitor, he first questioned her to make sure that she was who she said, namely Mrs

Horatio Nelson, and then served her with a writ intended for her husband. Anyone, man or woman, would have been flustered by a visit from a court bailiff, especially when the writ he served was for damages assessed at £20,000. The amount today would be frightening enough; in the eighteenth century it would have been of such enormity to be almost past the average comprehension. Thus Fanny could have been forgiven if she had 'swooned' or cried or shouted and screamed. Unfortunately the only record of how she behaved was Nelson's reported anger that she had been flustered by the intrusion into their home. The term 'flustered' has led some to suggest that Fanny behaved in a particularly weak and nervous manner. That was how she was expected to behave but I suggest that it was Nelson who was really flustered, that is agitated, by the writ that referred back to the claim made by the American captains whose ships he had impounded in Nevis. Part of his agitation must have come from the fear that the Treasury was not going to settle the claim for him as had been promised. Instead of him soothing her delicate female nerves, it was more likely that Fanny had to comfort and placate her husband as he fulminated against the world in general and the Admiralty in particular.

A question much discussed no doubt by Nelson's very fecund sisters and other interested friends and relations was why, after all this time, Fanny had still not become pregnant. There are those among Fanny's detractors who cite this as proof that the marriage had already broken down and that they stayed together purely for convenience. There is no proof that this was so. As to why Fanny did not conceive, as happened even up to recent times, the failure is placed upon her. Yet Fanny had already proved that she was capable of child bearing. There is a theory that following Josiah's birth she had a gynaecological problem that prevented further conception. It is also possible that she suffered miscarriages which would not have been referred to as such in family letters but could account for some of the periods of illness from which she suffered. But it is much more likely that Nelson himself was unable to father a child at that time. His long period of ill health while in the tropics, followed by the depression caused by his disappointment at not being in favour with the Navy establishment could have contributed to his having an extremely low sperm count. While he was unlikely to say so openly in letters to his friends, there is no doubt from his covert hints that, in the first few years at least, Fanny was a satisfactory lover. Whether the lack of a child or children of their own worried either of them at that stage it is impossible to say. Fanny, being a gentle, caring and nurturing woman, would no doubt have liked more children but in many ways the care of her husband and father-in-law fulfilled her maternal needs. As for Nelson, did he really want children when he was finding it hard enough to support the family he had?

Whatever the state of the sexual side of their marriage, there was no doubt that Nelson continued to confide all his hopes and anxieties to Fanny. In 1790, when it looked as if the country might go to war with Spain, he went immediately to London to petition Lord Hood for a ship. In letters to Fanny that no longer exist he must have poured out all his distress and frustration at finding that as a result of his being implicated in the affairs of Prince William, the King himself was blocking his re-appointment. A letter from Edmund to his son on the subject illustrates the close rapport that had developed between Fanny and her father-in-law. She had told Edmund about the interview and he felt he should advise his son on what action to take:

> From the contents of those letters which your good wife has communicated to me; it seems necessary to call forth all your prudence and mature deliberation, how to act at this critical juncture so as to justify your own character and give no offence to either party.

Poor Edmund, even in his 70s, was still trying to sort out his sons' problems for them. That letter also showed that whenever Nelson and Fanny were apart, for however short a time, they wrote to each other.

'Burnham, December 11,1791...To Thomas Bolton, Merchant, Norwich... We were at Wolterton a few days and intended to have rode to Norwich last Sunday...' Once, sometimes twice a year, Nelson and Fanny were invited to stay with Nelson's godfather and namesake, Horatio, Lord Walpole at his country estate, Wolterton, a few miles north of Norwich. The Walpole family, which had been settled in Norfolk since the thirteenth century, boasted several very well known national figures amongst its members, including Sir Robert Walpole, the first British Prime Minister and Horace, the writer of Gothic novels and builder of Strawberry Hill. Nelson, who was an awful snob, enjoyed his noble connections. It says much for the depth of eighteenth-century kinship that the connection was acknowledged, since it came only through Nelson's great grandmother Mary, sister of the great Sir Robert and the diplomat, Horatio, the first Baron Walpole. Nonetheless this gave the Nelson family the right to appear on the Walpole family tree.

It was his grandmother's cousin Horatio, the second Baron, who was his godfather and occasional host. His wife, Rachel Cavendish, also came from noble stock being a daughter of the third Duke of Devonshire. At the time when Fanny was first introduced to them the Walpoles were in their 60s and even their daughters Catherine and Mary were older than Fanny. Catherine, the elder, was unmarried and approaching 40, while Mary who was married to Thomas Hussey was in her mid 30s. It has been said that the Walpoles were boring and that they treated the Nelsons' visits as a duty to poor relations. If part of the entertainment for gentlemen visitors was shooting, then no doubt Nelson would have been bored but it cannot have been too bad otherwise Nelson would have found an excuse not to go as often as he did, or stay any longer than was considered polite. Fanny seemed to enjoy her visits greatly; for her there would have been the chance to play on a good instrument as well as listen to others making music. There too, she would have appreciated the fine furniture, works of art and well stocked library as well as the carefully laid out gardens that afforded walks that did not consist of muddy lanes as at Burnham Thorpe. Fanny was accepted by the Walpoles for herself and became particularly close to Catherine, the Miss Walpole, with whom she kept up a lifelong correspondence.

In that letter to Thomas Bolton in December 1791 Nelson revealed that his friends had come to accept that he had settled to the rural way of life and could, therefore, be regarded as an authority on such matters as the purchase of Christmas turkeys. Unable to find exactly what was required in his own neighbourhood, he was forced to pass on a commission to Bolton to purchase the birds for him at Norwich market. The naval attention to detail showed in the instructions he gave Bolton telling him that Captain Locker wanted to give as presents:

> …three very fine large Norfolk turkeys also sausages sufficient to eat with them. Let the turkeys be ready for the spit sewed up in separate cloths and securely packed up in a basket. If sausage meat is more convenient let it be put into a jar and sent with them. Please to order the turkeys to be in London by Wednesday the 21st, if they are brought to you on the Saturday this weather will keep them much longer than Christmas Day.

This very domestic letter reminds the modern reader that all cooking took place over a fire and that 'spit ready' was the equivalent of today's 'oven ready' bird. In a postscript to the letter he mentioned that Fanny's son had just arrived home for the Christmas holidays,

Josiah at 11 had reached an age when serious thought had to be given to his future. It is possible that Fanny would have liked him to follow in his father's footsteps and become a doctor, but that was a vain hope unless a great deal of money could be found to support him through further schooling and then university. The Nisbet family's financial affairs were so complicated that Fanny's claim on Josiah's behalf had not been settled, neither was any promise to do so forthcoming. John Herbert provided some financial assistance but not enough to set Josiah up with a substantial future. More realistic was the idea that Josiah might train for the law as Fanny's own father had done, using some of Fanny's family connections to get him started. As for the boy himself, having spent his schooldays in the country and his holidays with a stepfather who told wonderful stories about life at sea, it was almost inevitable that the boy should choose one or the other. There was no prospect of his being able to farm his own land; so going to sea seemed the only answer. And by 1792, with war becoming more and more likely, it looked as if he would be given the opportunity of becoming a midshipman.

For Fanny, the prospect of her husband returning to sea was bad enough but to let her son go too, at so young an age, was almost unthinkable. She and Nelson discussed the matter over and over, he making it clear that the final decision must be hers. When Nelson went to London to determine his future, Josiah's was still undecided as Fanny hoped that another opening would present itself.

CHAPTER IV

Rootless

How I long to have a letter from you. Next to being with you, it is the greatest pleasure I can receive. I shall rejoice to be with you again. Indeed I look back as to the happiest period of my life the being united to such a good woman, and as I cannot show here my affection to you, I do it doubly to Josiah…
Nelson, 4 August 1793

Throughout the first three months of 1792 Nelson was up and down to London, in the words of his father: 'bowing to the High and mighty potentates,' in the hope of a new command now that it looked as if war with France was likely. However seafarers might view the situation, the Admiralty saw things differently and far from commissioning ships for service they actually decided to reduce those already established, by paying off two guard ships at Plymouth and another two at Portsmouth. Within nine months, however, the procedure was reversed; ships were commissioned, commands given out, crews mustered and bounties offered to qualified seamen and other volunteers, while the threat of impressment hung over all able bodied landsmen. Nelson's time ashore was drawing to a close.

To get to London, Nelson would have taken the coach from Norwich so he took Fanny with him as far as the city and left her for a visit with his sister Susannah. The two women took the opportunity to make short visits together to other friends and relations, in particular Susannah's sister-in-law, Miss Bolton, who was often to be found at the small seaside town of Wells. On such a visit, it was Fanny who decided they should call at Burnham to see how the Revd Edmund was. Both Kitty and Susanna wrote regularly to their father but neither visited him as often as he would have liked. While excuses might be found in their having husbands and children to look after, neither of these ever prevented them visiting other places. That Fanny cared about Edmund even when she was away from him did not go unnoticed, he knew she was: 'very attentive to me.' In fact, Fanny was well regarded by all those with whom she came into contact in Norfolk society.

It was following a dance just before Christmas that Nelson wrote to Kitty in the same gossipy terms that he had used to Fanny when cruising round the Leeward Islands. There are those who would have us believe that Nelson only gossiped in his letters to Fanny because she had little else to think about but this plainly was not so as the following showed:

> We were at the last Aylsham Assembly, where Lady Durrant made many enquiries after you...And Miss Caroline Aufrere and Miss Emily came to Mrs Nelson (they are grown extraordinary fine ladies) ...Mrs N desired me to say that Miss Durrant is grown a very fine tall young woman; Lady D is quite the old woman, lost her front teeth.

Honesty may have much to recommend it but Nelson sometimes carried it to extremes.

The year 1792 brought not only the threat of war with France but there were two other questions which occupied people's thoughts. The one, closer to home, was the fear that the revolutionary movement which had seized power in France might spread to England. Already, the Thetford-born Thomas Paine had stirred up sufficient interest in his ideas, embodied in the first edition of *The Rights of Man*, for Revolution Clubs to have been set up throughout the country. Nelson, while not actually joining such a society, was concerned enough to investigate for himself the claims of the working man to a decent standard of living. Closer to Fanny's heart and a topic that she must have discussed with some authority was the abolition of slavery. In February, the newspapers were full of horrifying accounts of the uprising of the slave population of St Domingo who managed successfully to take over the country and declare independence. Those reports had a dual effect. On the one hand the emphasis on the bloodshed and the brutality of the slaves against their former white masters made anti-abolitionists more convinced of their way of thinking, while conversely, the abolitionists used it as an argument to show how repressed the slaves were. Fanny, as a native of the West Indies would have understood, as no ordinary English person could, just how important the slaves were to the economy of the islands themselves and to Britain. No European could possibly work in the fields in the temperatures endured by those who had been born in Africa, and if the supplies from that continent ceased, then in time there would be insufficient workers to plant and harvest the canes, and sugar supplies would become more expensive than they already were. While she could argue the economics of the situation, she would perhaps have been at a loss to understand why people felt as strongly as they did. When she heard them narrating stories of excessive cruelty and inhumane behaviour, she would tell of the care her uncle and most other planters gave their slaves, relating how her first husband had actually been employed in hospitals set up specifically to nurse the sick and provide maternity care. She would have left it to her listeners to realise that apart from the Workhouse, the poor of

England could obtain medical care only if they paid for it. The slaves were part of her life and she would have known and loved many of those who worked in the house and even possibly some of those employed in other trades as well as in the fields. True, she may have witnessed a slave auction but was that really much worse than an English Michaelmas Hiring Fair?

Nelson, like most of his fellow captains and commanders who had served on the West Indian station, was an anti-abolitionist. Several of them, including Lord Rodney, Sir Peter Parker, Admirals Barrington and Hotham and Sir Joshua Rowley, were called to give evidence before a Committee of the Privy Council in the House of Commons in April 1792. Most of them agreed that in the time they had spent in the islands they had seen little cruelty and what they had was less than they had seen inflicted on British soldiers and sailors. Barrington said that in his opinion the huts in which the slaves were housed in Barbados were infinitely superior to Irish cabins and were cleaner and neater, while Lord Rodney drew attention to the fact that unlike the British agricultural peasant, who no longer had the right to a piece of land on which to grow food for his family's maintenance, every slave had a house or hut and a share in a plantation for their own use. In Jamaica on a Saturday evening he had seen between 5,000 and 6,000 Negroes taking fruit, vegetables, pigs and poultry that they had produced to sell at market. The profit was theirs and the opportunity existed for a slave to become wealthy. It was Rodney, too, who pointed out to the Commission that in an area where the sun rose around 6 am, and set at 6 pm all the year round, the working day of the slaves was often much shorter than the English agricultural labourer's in summer time. With an hour allowed for breakfast and two for dinner during the hottest part of the day, it was no wonder that the slaves were able to spend their evenings dancing. Most of the naval observers mentioned the slaves dancing and singing, the latter even while they worked.

While the moral battle for giving up the practice of dealing in slaves waged against the consequent economic effect such action would have on the country, Fanny would have read in the newspapers during August that in France the royal family had been interned; while in mid September came the horrifying revelation that between six and eight thousand people had been massacred in days of violent fighting in Paris. Norfolk was unlikely to be affected greatly by the upsurge of migrants getting out as fast as they could. However, many of the wealthier aristocrats who had fled in 1789 had left their servants behind. Now it was their turn to get out. There was little room in the new France for those who had been used to the high standard of living and effete way of life of their wealthy masters. So they flooded into London where the novelty of a French chef, valet or lady's maid appealed to the upper classes but had dire repercussions for English servants who found themselves put out of work. It was an explosive time; working people in England were very close to insurrection. So it was probably just as well that their attention should be focussed instead upon the imminent threat of war.

During November, Fanny and Nelson must have pored over the reports that regiments of marines had been mustered aboard frigates at Portsmouth, Chatham and Plymouth. They both knew that very soon his time would come to return to sea. In the meantime, the local militia had been called up and ordered to ensure they were at full strength, while throughout the country recruiting parties were enlisting men for the regular army. Vulnerable sites such as the Tower of London were fortified and troops were trained to be ready to deal with local outbreaks of trouble from revolutionary groups as well as external attack.

Then in December, Nelson read what he had been waiting for; a full Board of the Admiralty Office had commissioned around twenty captains and lieutenants. Directly Christmas was over, he made his way to London and on 7 January 1793 wrote to Fanny, who was waiting at Burnham with Josiah, the triumphant words: 'Post Nubila Phoebus – your son will explain the motto – after clouds come sunshine.' He was in fine form. Not just because he had been offered a ship but also because Lord Chatham had apologised to him for not giving him one earlier. He was back in favour! He took great pleasure in telling Fanny that he was already negotiating to have things the way he wanted them. Having been offered a choice of ships lying at Plymouth and Portsmouth, he decided it would suit him better from the point of view of travelling back and forth if he had one lying at Chatham. He could not wait to share his news with her even though he intended to be home by the end of the week. Ten days later, Edmund wrote to tell Kitty the news of Nelson's appointment and in doing so added a comment that has been open to misinterpretation. 'Poor Mrs N will, I hope, bear up with a degree of cheerfulness at the separation from so kind a Husband.' Edmund's use of the sympathetic adjective 'poor' allied with the words 'bear up with a degree of cheerfulness' has been taken by some as evidence that Fanny was already acting the part of a wilting flower and that her temper was decidedly 'uncheerful'. What has been overlooked is that in the second part of the sentence Edmund admitted to his personal feelings on the subject: '...my own loss of the constant, friendly and filial regard I have experienced, I do feel.' Edmund was an old man and concluded that Fanny would feel as bereft as he did. Thus his 'poor Mrs N' could have been substituted then, and on several other occasions, for 'poor Edmund'.

On 4 February Nelson set off for Chatham, taking with him those local boys apprenticed to him as midshipmen. In his 'great spirits' as his father described them on his departure, how much thought had been given to what was to become of Fanny once he had gone? Perhaps it was assumed that she would remain at the parsonage and that Edmund who, some time before had moved into a small cottage nearer to his church, would move back with her. It was Edmund who recounted some of the plans that Fanny had made for herself. Again labelling her 'Poor Mrs N.' and suggesting she was finding it very difficult to come to terms with Nelson's going, he told Kitty that she was going to stay on at Burnham Thorpe for a couple of weeks and then intended to visit the Rector and his family at Hilborough. While there she would go to nearby Swaffham, where she thought she might like to live, to see if she could find suitable accommodation for herself. Far from clinging to her father-in-law for comfort, Fanny appeared to be striking out for independence as far as she was able.

While he waited for his ship to be fitted out, Nelson either spent as much time with Fanny as he could or kept in touch with her by letter even when they had only recently parted, as for example when he had left her the day before and travelled to London on the night coach. All he had to impart was that for the beginning of March it had been a very fine night and that he was not feeling at all tired. But news of greater importance followed. During his stay in London at the beginning of March they exchanged several letters, one of which had included the news that Fanny's uncle, John Herbert, had died in Nevis two months earlier on 18 January. This was bound to affect them financially as Herbert had led Nelson to believe that in his will he had left him and Fanny £4,000 and £500 to Josiah.

Nelson was anxious enough about the possible legacy that he called at Herbert's London executors to see how matters stood only to be told that they had not yet opened the will but when they did they would inform him if there were anything unexpected in it. What could have upset matters was the news that the elderly Herbert had been engaged to a Miss Fraser. Had the marriage taken place and an heir been born, then all the original beneficiaries would have taken second place. However, Miss Fraser had broken the engagement, much to the relief of Herbert's daughter Martha. The prospect of the expected small fortune was tempered by the fact that it would take time before it became payable and worse, the trustees of the estate had indicated that they would not pay the £100 for that year that the Nelsons had received annually from Herbert. Nelson was most concerned. Even though he would now be receiving a full salary as a serving officer, without Herbert's £100 and with Mr Suckling unlikely to continue his contribution of a similar amount after that year: 'Our income will be lessened instead of increased.' Determined to fight for Herbert's £100, Nelson asked Fanny to find the letter from her uncle on the subject and bring it up to London with her. Considering that Fanny was just starting out on a peripatetic life, one assumes that valuable papers would have been packed securely amongst her luggage. It would be interesting to know if she travelled with all her belongings or if some of them remained at Burnham Thorpe.

Nelson had earlier suggested that Fanny should go to stay with his uncle William Suckling at Kentish Town, which at that time was on the outskirts of London. The Sucklings were currently free of family or other guests so Fanny was invited to stay with them for a month or more, if it suited her. She had also received an invitation to visit Kitty Matcham and her family at their new home near Ringwood in Hampshire. Nelson put Fanny off the idea of going to the Matchams at that time telling her that as he had had long discussions with his uncle on a variety of questions, it would be better if she came up to Kentish Town as soon as possible so that she could be a part of them. Josiah's future was one question that needed to be settled quickly. Fanny's original hope that the boy might go into law had been dashed. Mr Suckling, who knew about these things, had told Nelson that it would take their whole income to keep him as a pupil in the Temple Inns of Court. That left the Navy. In the past Nelson had shared her reluctance to the sea as a career for the boy on the grounds that to make any real progress, an officer needed a private income to supplement his naval pay. This, with the interest on his £500, Josiah would now have. So reiterating their earlier discussions, he urged Fanny to think carefully about Josiah going to sea. She was to have the final say but if she was in agreement, then of course Josiah must go with him and no one else. He suggested she bring the boy up to London with her and then when the time came he could join those other lads from their neighbourhood, many of them sons of the local clergymen, who were only too happy to be able to entrust their sons to Capt. Nelson whom they knew. From Josiah's point of view, if he had to make a career at sea, it would probably have been better for him in the long run if he had not gone with his stepfather.

Although much of that letter was devoted to serious matters, Nelson also showed concern for Fanny's well being, suggesting that she should not contemplate travelling alone from Norfolk in one day. Instead he urged her to break the journey overnight and perhaps the Rector could accompany her. He returned to his concern for her health three days later when with a touch of humour he revealed that he now knew the full contents of Herbert's will and that she would inherit her cousin Martha's share if a childless Martha should die before her. Not wishing to sound mercenary he made Josiah, who would in turn inherit from Fanny, the subject of his remarks: 'And now you will recollect that a handsome fortune for Josiah depends on your surviving Mrs Hamilton, I hope you intend a new lease of life.' This jocular comment has often been accepted at face value and used to prove Fanny's weak health, as was the following suggestion that she should, after all he had said before on the subject, go to visit the Matchams because 'a change of air will do you good.'

Fanny brought Josiah to Kentish Town some time after 15 March and during the next few days must have decided the boy should go with Nelson. While she was kept busy buying or preparing the things he would need to take with him, messages were sent back to Edmund who was charged with packing up many of Josiah's belongings and dispatching them to him. On the days when Nelson managed to get up from Chatham it must have been hard for her to have to listen while talk of the sea monopolised the conversation. As a seafarer's wife she had to learn important lore about such things as the direction of winds and their effects on shipping movements. Before sitting down to address a letter to Chatham, she would have to check first: 'If the wind is to the westward direct to me at Sheerness, if not gone by Sunday can't go for ten days.' Eventually the wind was in the right quarter and by 4 April Fanny had to say goodbye to both her husband and child as they set off for what might well prove to be dangerous times ahead. For Josiah's sake she restrained her tears. For once, Nelson was sensitive enough to realise that Fanny would worry about both of them but he tried to calm at least her maternal fears when the following day he wrote to her from his ship the *Agamemnon:* 'J & myself came down very comfortably yesterday morning and he seems quite settled, we slept on board last night and are now at home.'

Within four days of being on board, Captain Nelson had taken command and expected everything to be as it should be and was irked if it was not. So came the first of the letters which blamed Fanny for some oversight or other. Straight in, without any preamble: 'You forgot to send my things from Mr Thomas's by the Sheerness boat, but I have wrote to Mr Thomas that if not sent to go by the Chatham coach.' Having accused her of negligence he then found fault with a delivery of food supplies:

I have got a keg of tongues which I suppose you ordered, and a hamper of 3 hams, a breast of bacon and a face, not very well packed, there being no straw between them and the motion of the wagon had rubbed them very much.

Perhaps, he then realised that she would not have been responsible for the packing, so he grudgingly admitted: 'However they will do.' But there was no apology, grudging or otherwise that accompanied the note at the end of the letter to say that the things to which he had referred at the beginning had now indeed arrived. Fanny may have forgiven him when he reassured her that Josiah seemed to be very happy with life on board and that he had very little in the way of a cough. He also told her they had taken a goat on board, so she would know that he and the other boys would be getting a good daily ration of milk. For the rest of April, Fanny wrote almost daily from Kentish Town, her letters not having to go farther than Sheerness or the Nore. During that period, Josiah was often mentioned; his delight at the prospect of sailing into deep water and being far too busy to write to his mother and then his seasickness when he had his first experience of being in gale force winds. Any mother would have suffered at this piece of news but at least she had the comfort that Nelson had a good surgeon on board. Did she read between the lines that Josiah was in fact a little homesick when having told Nelson that she intended to stay with the Matchams in Hampshire, he wrote: 'Most likely I shall be able to go over to see you at Mr Matcham's for a few days, which will give your son as well as myself great pleasure.' There was even the possibility that if he remained long in Portsmouth, he would take lodgings on shore for both of them. When she came, she should: '...put up at the George. The Miss Palmers keep it still, their father you may remember is dead.' This suggests that he and Fanny had stayed at the George when they first returned to England.

Nelson was torn between seeing Fanny and getting to sea with the fleet and consequently his letters are full of niggling complaints perhaps brought on in part by the fact that he had had a bad cold which he blamed on the harsh easterly winds. Josiah had had it too but was now recovered. Had Fanny bought him towels? And where were Josiah's things? Edmund had sent them to the wrong place and being redirected they had now gone missing. And why hadn't Fanny answered the two or three letters from his sister Bolton and would she please write to Edmund for him? If she had told him that she had been involved in an accident where the coach overturned, she had made light of it because it wasn't until his brother Maurice arrived at Spithead and came aboard the *Agamemnon* that he found out that she could have been hurt.

At the beginning of May Nelson put to sea for a few days to test his ship. They experienced strong winds and poor Josiah was seasick again for a couple of days recovering in time to witness the *Agamemnon* chase two French frigates and two other armed vessels into La Hogue harbour. Lack of a pilot meant they were unable to follow up with an attack but the encounter also showed up the ship's deficiencies which had to be tackled before it sailed to the Mediterranean. When he arrived back at Spithead Nelson expected to find Fanny waiting for him. Unfortunately, she was reliant on Kitty's husband to provide her with transport and George Matcham had looked at the weather and decided that it blew too hard for Nelson to come. But eventually they were able to meet; Nelson's letter after the event suggests that the Matchams came with her and that they all stayed on board for a day or two. This would have provided Fanny the opportunity to see not only her husband but Josiah too and so settle any fears she might have had about his well-being. This visit must have been difficult for Fanny, as Nelson had received his orders to join the rest of the fleet off the Channel Isles preparatory for duty in the Mediterranean. Whatever fears she had for the future; how long she was to be parted from her husband and son; what she was to do with herself while they were gone, she managed to hide from Nelson, letting him set off happy. There is no hint in his letter that there was any coldness between them, rather the opposite: 'You shall hear from me by every opportunity.' And he carefully listed the names of the rest of his squadron so that when she read the newspapers she would know when any of them came into port. He both wanted and expected her to be involved in his activities. And as his wife he expected that she would continue to act as correspondent on his behalf to the various members of his family: 'You may write to my father to say we are gone.'

Fanny did not need reminding to write to Edmund, for not long before she had sent him a letter and a surprise present of sweet almonds knowing that he would appreciate the little treat. He, although he would not have admitted it to his family, was missing Fanny as much, if not more than his son. In a letter to George Matcham mentioning the gift, he revealed how much he missed: '...a little chat from the Ladies.' He also paid tribute to the way Fanny was handling her husband's return to sea: 'Mrs N's good sense will tell her to view everything from its fairest side.' When he wrote to Fanny he gallantly offered her his protection, couched in the formal style of an earlier era:

> My Good Madam, - At this time, I feel myself from motives of true affection and concern called upon to give every proof in my power that in the absence of your dear husband you will find in me a readiness to show those several acts of friendly attention which at any time you may have occasion to look for. From me particular I neither can or need to offer as your own prudence and understanding will suggest what is fittest, and most likely to make you happy.

The letter continued with references to Josiah's future and her 'handsome independency' as a result of Herbert's legacy. After the tortuous style he suddenly relaxed:

> If I have any chat it shall be reserved for my next…Bett Thurlow is waiting your commands with eager expectation. The boxes are still at Hilborough with all her paraphernalia.

Bett's family came from Burnham Thorpe and she had been in Fanny's service when she went to stay with the Rector's family at Hilborough. Just before Fanny left to go to Kentish Town, the girl had been taken ill and returned home on the understanding that as soon as Fanny was settled in lodgings, Bett, if she were well again, would join her as her personal maid. It is not clear if at this period Fanny travelled without a maid of her own, relying on whatever household she was in to provide her with an attendant to help her with her dress and hair. Certainly at the Matchams' new house in Ringwood, there would easily have been a spare maid to look after her needs. Fanny must have enjoyed being there for she stayed throughout the spring and early summer. George and Catherine Matcham had the advantage of a young family for Fanny to enjoy, but they also had the means for a much higher standard of living than either the Rector or the Boltons. Fanny found much more to entertain her here; among the many activities was the lavish house-warming party she helped to plan. Then as newcomers to the district, she joined the Matchams as they took advantage of the fine weather to explore the neighbourhood. Polite morning visits with neighbours were exchanged and from them came invitations to parties and balls. Ringwood was a good place to keep Fanny's mind occupied and stop her thinking too much about the war and her husband's part in it.

He, however, made sure that she was kept informed of what was in his mind. He had thought when they sailed for the Channel Islands that they would soon be engaged in some form of offensive action. That had not happened and Nelson railed against what he saw as Government manipulation of the current situation for propaganda purposes.

> We have done nothing or are intended I may venture to say. Indeed I believe we are sent out for no other purpose than to amuse the people of England by having a fleet at sea, for where we are placed the French it is not likely will have a fleet. The English are hum'd [hoaxed] and the Fleet made fools of. We can do nothing, no not even protect our trade for no privateers ever cruised in this place to intercept it. The King may be told that his fleet is at sea and the French not to be found. The Minister may stop the mouths of the opposition by saying the same thing.

This rant echoed the Nelson she had often heard in former days and she must have despaired that he had become disillusioned so soon. However, a second part to this letter written on 19 May was more cheerful, he telling her that there was a possibility he would see Torbay before finally leaving England. At the bottom of the sheet, Josiah had added a short note, one of the few letters from her son that has survived; it was the sort of letter that would make any mother gulp back the mixed tears of joy and sorrow: 'Dear Mamma – We [have] taken nothing at present nor are not likely to take anything. I am very well at present and hope you are the same.'

A gap of two weeks before the next letter suggests that Fanny travelled to Torbay to spend with Nelson whatever time he could manage ashore. But again, once he had left her and was at sea, his moods were often black as he chafed under the inactivity of the fleet. She, in contrast, was full of activity as she made plans to leave Ringwood. She was to break her journey in London, spend a few days with the Sucklings in Kentish Town, then make her way to Norfolk in time to take up the lodgings in Swaffham which she had booked from 24 June. Nelson fretted over her safety as she travelled, begging her not to trust herself again to a stage-coach after her earlier experience. Since the Nelsons were unable to afford their own carriage, Fanny had little option but to use the public coach unless the Matchams, who did have their own vehicle, took her with them as far as London.

If Fanny was excited by the prospect that by the end of June she would have somewhere she could call home for a time, two others were equally excited that she was to return to Norfolk. Edmund, dropping the formal style of his previous letter, told her again that Bett Thurlow was anxiously awaiting her summons. The reason she had been sent home from service at Hilborough was that she had been suspected of having tuberculosis, but Edmund, who during his long life had seen so many cases of the disease, assured Fanny that he could see no sign of consumption in the girl. That he himself was looking forward to having Fanny back in Norfolk even though she would still be some miles away from him was very apparent. He knew she was concerned for his welfare so confessed to her before she could hear it from another source, that the previous Sunday he had fallen off his pony outside the church. He assured her that apart from a few strains and bruises, he was now literally back on his feet.

The first letter Fanny received at her lodgings in Swaffham was a long one from her husband describing a visit he had made ashore in Spain. Those who argue that Fanny had delicate nerves and was easily upset need to explain how Nelson could send her such an account. If she really were so fragile then he was a brute to inflict some of the following upon her. It was rather the case that he knew she was robust enough to stomach it and furthermore that their relationship was so close that he simply had to share with her an experience that had affected him so deeply.

> A bull feast…was exhibited…The amphitheatre will hold 16,000 people, about 12,000 were present. 10 bulls were selected and one brought out at a time, 3 cavaliers on horseback and footmen with flags were the combatants. We had what is called a fine feast for 5 horses were killed and 2 men very much hurt…We felt for the bulls and horses and I own it would not have displeased me to have had some of the Dons tossed…How women can even sit, much more applaud such sights is astonishing. It even turned us sick and we could hardly sit it out. The dead mangled horses with their entrails tore out, the bulls covered with blood, was too much. However we have seen one and agree that nothing shall tempt us to see another.

By the beginning of August Nelson was missing Fanny greatly. Since he had left her earlier in the year he had started all his letters with a simple 'My Dear Fanny'. But on 4 August his longing for her was so great that he addressed her as 'My Dearest Fanny'. Time was hanging heavy and the lack of action against the French led him to hope that he would be home by the winter. In the meantime he would have to make do with her letters to bring him the comfort he so much desired. The problem was that her letters did not always reach him. Both of them wrote regularly yet it could be a month, sometimes much longer, before letters were received. When they did reach her, Fanny often reacted emotionally to Nelson's outpouring of his feelings about the horrors he witnessed or the battles in which he had taken part.

> Marseilles I am sure would almost be put into our hands if we acted against it. They generally wish for nothing more than our possessing it when they would get something to eat. They are now almost starving, only six days' provisions in the place.

He did not spare her either the details of numbers killed on each side in a battle.

Neither did he keep from her his wish to capture foreign ships that would bring him in a share of the prize money. This bonus to pay was welcomed by all seafarers, as young Josiah was quick to realise. In one of his rare letters to his mother he told her:

We have seized a brig valued at 10 or 12 thousand pounds and have sent
her to Leghorn but do not know if she will be condemned...We thought
we should have taken something yesterday but could not.

While the boy no doubt dreamed of what his share would bring him,
Nelson saw it only as a means to make life a little more comfortable for
Fanny and himself. He had no secrets from her but he suggested she should
keep the possibility of a windfall to herself and perhaps his father: '...for
reasons which you know as well as myself.' This was a reference to certain members of his family who were always in need of money and made
demands upon him.

Unfortunately the ship on which they had pinned their hopes was freed
and Nelson bewailed the fact that the area around Naples was unlikely
to provide him with other prizes. But following his part in defeating the
French, he had received a tremendous boost to his ego. Anchored in the bay
of Naples he had twice been sent for by the King of Naples and His Majesty
invited him to dine with him not once but twice, on the second occasion
seating him in the place of honour on his right hand. He told Fanny:

We are called by him [the King] the saviours of Italy...I have acted for my
Lord Hood in such a manner that no one could exceed and am to carry
from the King the handsomest letter in his own handwriting which could
be penned. This I got done through Sir William Hamilton and the Prime
Minister [Sir John Acton] who is also an Englishman, knowing how much
it would please the Lord.

Fanny no doubt rejoiced when she read all this but the fact that we do not
have her reply has led some to suggest that she did not give Nelson sufficient credit for his achievements. At the time, she would have asked her
husband to express her thanks to Lady Hamilton who: 'has been wonderfully kind and good to Josiah. She is a young woman of amiable manners
and who does honour to the station to which she is raised.' After all, what
mother would not have been grateful to someone who had shown kindness
to her son?

It was October before Nelson received any letters from England and
then it was one dated 26 July from Mr Suckling. Unwittingly, that gentleman stirred up matters between Nelson and Fanny by reporting that she
was making herself ill with worry. Nelson's chivvying response has again
given fuel to the idea that Fanny was a bundle of nerves. 'Why should you
fret yourself? I am well, your son is well and we are as comfortable in every
respect as the nature of our service will admit.' She was meant to be reassured by: '... we seem to feel no danger. The other day we sat at a Court
Martial... when...were firing at a battery for four hours, the shots and shells
going over us, but extraordinary as it may seem it made no difference.' And
just for good measure he told her about the *Ardent*, which had behaved with

great gallantry but had lost thirty men, either killed outright or from fatal wounds.

In August Nelson had addressed his letters to Fanny at Swaffham but at the end of September he lamented: ' 'Tis a sad thing not to know where to direct to you.' This has been taken as an indication that Fanny had left Swaffham and gone visiting. But since Nelson had not received any of her letters it is much more likely that he only thought she had. As there are no letters in existence for the period of 12 October until 1 December, it is impossible to know exactly what he was thinking during that time. But at long last, he heard from her and as he sent the letter to Swaffham, we know that was still her base. In December too, we learn from Edmund that Fanny was 'not perfectly pleased' with the town. The accepted view has been that she did not find the social life up to her expectations. It is more likely that she found it difficult to adjust to living on her own.

She had too, another problem. In spite of Edmund's assertions on the subject, it had become obvious that Bett Thurlow was ill, so Fanny consulted him on what was to be done. She always treated her servants fairly and unlike some employers, nothing would have persuaded her simply to dismiss Bett and leave her to her fate. On the other hand she needed someone capable of working but she could not afford to keep Bett and another maid. Torn between a moral responsibility to care for the girl and the practicalities that involved, she confided in Edmund. As he so often did, he put his own interpretation on her feelings and decided that she was worrying too much – and told her so. Then, making himself useful, he set about sorting it all out for her. First he talked to John Thurlow, the girl's father who immediately offered to go and bring Bett home where he hoped they would be able to nurse her back to health. However, her return would put a strain on the household budget, so, sensible man, he suggested Fanny might like to take Bett's sister Mary in her place. According to Edmund, who knew the whole family well she was: 'sixteen years of age, is a spruce girl, and knows as much as her years and education will allow of.' If Fanny were in agreement, Thurlow would come for Bett and leave Mary with her. Having lived in Burnham Thorpe for five years, Fanny probably knew most of the local families too, so she would have been able to recall this Mary as well as Bob Wilson's daughter Mary who was also available for service. The local schoolmaster also had a daughter for whom employment was required. Although the use and meaning of some eighteenth-century language has changed, Edmund's description could well mean the same now as it did then: 'Carter, the school master, has a young woman they would gladly get from home.' Then, cryptically, although no doubt it was not so to Fanny, he added: 'not the London daughter.'

The strain of Bett's health had added to Fanny's problems and Edmund commented on this. He suggested that the underlying cause for her physical symptoms was of a nervous origin. 'I am indeed vexed your health is so precarious, and your resolution not equal I fear, to the trials you meet with.'

His 'your own good understanding is a much better source of comfort, than anything that can be offered by me, or any of those who have great respect towards you' is in many ways the equivalent of 'pull yourself together'. However, he was concerned that perhaps she had been holding back in asking him for help out of respect for his own health. It then became clear that he had already tentatively suggested that she might join him in Bath for the winter. He was planning to go in early January but would delay his departure to suit her. He also dropped the hint that perhaps a shortage of money was behind Fanny's current unrest and assured her that this should not prevent her from joining him in Bath.

When Fanny had decided to make her own establishment in Swaffham, she may not have understood fully how costly this might be. True she was only renting a suite of rooms, probably a sitting room and bedroom for herself and maybe a small dressing room to accommodate her maid, but rents were high at the time, made even higher by the demands for accommodation for army officers billeted in the town. Then she had the cost of housekeeping and coals, often almost as much for one person as for two or more. Practicalities alone would have shown her that it would be sensible to give up her single living and share with Edmund. Certainly Bath had much to offer, especially in the winter months and then, as Edmund suggested, they could cut back on their living expenses in the summer months by returning to the parsonage at Burnham Thorpe which was rent free, and if he had a tenant for the winter in the shape of a curate, then the place would be kept aired and there might also be a small rent to assist towards housekeeping.

Fanny was invited to spend the Christmas period at Wolterton with the Walpoles. This was to become a regular event for her for many years and was proof that she was invited for her own sake as much as for her connection with Nelson. Had she been invited out of 'duty to a poor relation', as has been suggested, then it is unlikely that she would have maintained as close a relationship, mainly by correspondence, with the Walpoles' eldest daughter. During her stay at Wolterton, Edmund wrote again to tell her of his travel arrangements and expressed the wish that she would join him later. This particular letter referred to a practice that was very common at the time, namely the copying of letters. In fact the whole business of letter writing was very different then. It was usual to make a draft of a letter first. At a time when the cost of postage depended on the number of sheets, it was convenient to correct or amend, delete or add according to the space one had. Only when this was done, was the fair copy made. An additional advantage was that the writer then retained a copy of what had been written. Similarly, if one received a letter which contained information that would be of interest to third parties living at a distance, the recipient would often copy the letter and send it with a covering note. This Fanny often did with extracts from Nelson's letters that she thought would be of interest to his father. On this occasion she had sent him a copy of a letter from Josiah, 'your good boy' as Edmund called him, in which he had described a battle in which Nelson had taken part. The old man thanked God for guarding both their sons. On a lighter note he thanked Fanny for another letter he had just received which must have contained the information that Nelson had sent her of the prospect of prize money: 'I admire your injunction of secrecy to me who am not very loquacious and have nobody to speak to except the Widow Gab once in 5 or 6 days.' What a wonderfully descriptive nickname for the woman who acted as a cleaner at the parsonage. The letter Nelson had written on 11 September about the prize money had reached Fanny in mid December.

The delay between writing and receiving letters must have been exceptionally difficult to deal with, so it was hardly surprising that when Nelson finally received one from her on 1 December it reads as if he were talking directly to her. There was no formal opening instead he launched straight in with:

> It is impossible my dearest Fanny to say the pleasure I felt in receiving your letter of September 16th, the only one I have received from you since I left England, although you have wrote me, but now if you direct them under cover to Mr Udney at Leghorn, I shall get them to a certainty, you paying foreign postage.

His excitement at hearing from her gave him the opportunity to share with her all the frustration he felt about the conduct of the war, the lack of leadership and graft being two of his complaints. He thought it likely that future conflict would be on land rather than at sea, in which case his own future was uncertain. Having unburdened his pent up feelings, he turned to more personal matters. Again because of the time delay, his comment on her improved health was now out of date. He longed to be back home again with her. Those who have expressed the view that the Nelsons' marriage was virtually over when he went back to sea at the beginning of 1793 have overlooked such statements as:

> I assure you it cannot give you more pleasure than it will me, for us to be settled again at Burnham and I sincerely hope our father will not part with the house to anyone so as to prevent our getting into it again.

Dreaming perhaps of the domestic scene he referred to the fact that Fanny was spending time on piano practice. 'You must have a good instrument, we can afford that I am sure.' It was possible in the eighteenth century to hire a piano by the month and it may be that this was one luxury Fanny had allowed herself in Swaffham. Nelson, of course, wanted her to buy one. As he wrote of finance, he was reminded that Fanny had still not received the interest on her legacy and was concerned that she might never do so now the firm handling Herbert's affairs had gone bankrupt.

Almost as an extra Christmas present, Nelson received six letters from her. Starting from 21 August through to 2 December it was little wonder that some of his subsequent letters should refer to situations or questions long since past. Uppermost on his mind in the closing days of December were the scenes he had witnessed in the evacuation of Toulon. Again he shared his feelings on the subject with her, perhaps the only chance he had to relieve himself of the horror.

> Everything which domestic wars produce usually are multiplied at Toulon. Fathers are here without families, families without fathers. In short all is horror which we hear. The Lord [Hood] put himself at the head of the fly-ing troops and was the admiration of all but the torrent was too strong. Many of our posts were carried without resistance. At others, where the English were, everybody perished. I cannot write all, my mind is truly impressed with grief. Each teller makes the scene more horrible. Even at this moment I don't know whether fort Le Malque is blown up and the fleet left Toulon. Each is so occupied with his own misery, that no thought was given to the public. The Lord is the same collected good officer which he always was. I have wrote to Lady Hood to say he is well, she must be very uneasy.

If he had believed that Fanny was ultra sensitive he would have kept such details to himself.

Before she could receive Nelson's views on her going to Bath with the admonition that she was to call on his agents for money and not let his father pay all the bills, she had already made up her own mind and gone. It was her concern for Edmund that made her cut short her visit to Wolterton. He had written of his intention of travelling by himself to London where he would stay with Kitty Matcham's mother-in-law for a day or two before venturing off on the journey to Bath. Fanny sensed that Edmund was fear-ful about the journey but knew that he would not admit that he needed her company. So she changed her plans to fit in with his and by the end of the first week in January 1794 they were settled in lodgings at 4 Milsom Street.

Once she and Edmund were settled, it was time to make for the Pump Room and the Assembly Rooms to see who else had come for the winter. Edmund reported to Kitty: '...the place is not full yet.' The effects of the war were beginning to be felt and Edmund noted that there were many other naval wives in the city who were as anxious as Fanny and there were others who had but recently become widows as a result of the fighting. Nonetheless, the old gentleman had been ready to accompany Fanny to Tyson's Ball. Tyson held the important position of Master of Ceremonies in the Assembly Rooms and was responsible for all the arrangements for the balls that took place there. The largest of these was held in early January. According to Edmund that year there were: '1100 of Sixpences' the ticket price paid by ladies – gentlemen paid a larger fee.

For Fanny this visit to Bath was an opportunity to meet many of her old friends and relations with West Indian connections. Bristol friends like the Pinneys, Tobins and Webbes were already in residence there as were the sisters of her first husband. The former Mary Nisbet had come down from Scotland where she lived with her husband James Lockhart on a small country estate just outside Glasgow. During the previous year it had been suggested that Lockhart might find a suitable opening in business for Josiah. Now that he had the prospect of a small inheritance, Nelson thought Fanny should again tackle Lockhart on the subject.

> I wish Mr Lockhart could get Josiah a good place on shore I am sure I don't like his going to sea if he can be better provided for, and I am certain Josiah would give up the sea for anything we can wish him to do.

The Lockharts were joined in Bath by Mary's sister, the unmarried Anne Nisbet. Both women remained life-long friends of Fanny, as did her cousin Sally Kelly. She too was visiting Bath from her home in Plymouth. Although Nelson disliked Sally he recognised that she was important to Fanny: 'I am glad Mrs Kelly is coming to join the party. I know your fondness for her.' Much as was her pleasure in meeting with her old friends, Fanny also had business to complete.

It has been said that when Nelson married Fanny he believed that John Herbert intended that she would inherit his fortune should she outlive his daughter Martha. That Herbert was not as generous as Nelson had expected is often given as another of the long list of reasons why Nelson lost interest in Fanny. Herbert's will, drawn up in London in December 1788, ran to sixteen pages and mentioned Fanny only three times:

> Whereas I have hitherto allowed my niece Frances the wife of Horatio Nelson a Captain in his Majesty's Navy the yearly sum of one hundred pounds to and for her own use and benefit and may continue to allow her the same during the term of my natural life after which it is my intention that such annuity shall cease and instead thereof I give and bequeath unto my said niece Frances Nelson the sum of three thousand pounds of like lawful money of Great Britain to be paid within the space of six years next after my decease with interest for the same after the rate of five pounds per centum per annum from the day of my decease.

In other words, the interest would give Fanny an extra £150 per year. Josiah was not forgotten either, he was to receive: 'the sum of five hundred pounds…when and as soon as he shall attain his age of twenty one years.' This sum was likewise subject to an interest of 5% and the ensuing £25 a year was to be used for his maintenance and education. It was that sum which Nelson believed might be used as a premium towards any profession Josiah might enter.

The second time Fanny is mentioned comes after a long section dealing with who shall inherit after Martha. Having gone through all the possibilities of her having children who in turn have issue, he came to the point where it had to be considered that she might die childless. In that event Fanny was to receive another three thousand pounds three years after the death of Martha. Finally, in a codicil made in December 1792 after Herbert had returned to Nevis, he bequeathed a further £1,000 to Fanny. The problem that Fanny and Nelson had was that since the death of Herbert they had been worse off. The £100 annuity he had given them on marriage had stopped as he had laid down but his injunction about the payment of interest had not been followed. On several occasions Nelson had mentioned that Herbert's London agents had gone bankrupt so it was now a question of referring the matter back to the solicitor handling matters in Nevis. Nelson, as Fanny's husband, had written to Martha Hamilton, Herbert's daughter on the matter. She either ignored his letter or her reply went astray. So Nelson left it to Fanny to see what she could do with Mr Baillie, the Nevis solicitor who was also wintering in Bath. Nelson has complete faith in Fanny's competence: 'I daresay you will manage matters very well with Mr Baillie.' She had, of course, the advantage of having known him for many years.

From the centrally situated Milsom Street, Fanny and Edmund moved to New King Street at the end of February, possibly to cheaper or smaller accommodation as Fanny was intending to leave Edmund while she made a visit to Bristol where she stayed with the Pinneys. When she informed Nelson of her plans, he had wondered if on her way to Plymouth to see Sally Kelly she would call at Exmouth. He remembered their time there as fondly as she did. His letters to her while he was engaged in the siege of Bastia are full of longing for her; to be 'snug' in Burnham listening to her playing the piano but in the meantime he had her letters: 'nothing gives me a pleasure equal to them.' He usually ended his letters to her with either 'your most affectionate Horatio Nelson' or 'your most affectionate husband' but for some reason on 6 April he signed himself 'your most faithful and affectionate husband.' Was he affirming his own faithfulness because he was concerned that now Fanny was mixing in society with her old friends she might be tempted? So it was while she was staying at the Kellys' house in Plymouth that he assured her yet again how important her letters were to him:

> ...they are proofs of your affection for the many proofs of which I have reason to be thankful to that Being who has ever protected me...If it is His good pleasure nothing can rejoice me so much as being once more by your side when we shall talk over all these stories and laugh at them.

A week later he was still strongly protesting his great love for her:

> My dearest Fanny, – I need not I am sure say that all my joy is placed in you, I have none separated from you, you are present, my imagination be where I will. Every action of my life I know you must feel for, all my joys of victory are twofold to me knowing how you must partake of them...

He continued to tell her how much she, and her letters, meant to him: ' you know the pleasure they give me and before any great length of time I hope to thank you in person...How I shall rejoice to see you.' At the very end of May while she was still in Plymouth he wrote to tell her that he had received one of her letters dating from the previous December. With delays of up to five months between writing and receiving letters it would have been hardly surprising if at times, they both felt frustrated that questions were not answered or comments made on what at the time were important matters. On the other hand, when he was able, Nelson kept her fully informed as to the progress of the battles and campaigns in which he was involved. Part of his naval duty was to send official reports back to the Admiralty and these were often printed in full in the London newspapers. That he should fill his letters to his wife with naval details might seem unromantic but it was his way of sharing his experiences, making her feel that she was with him out there, as she in turn tried to make him part of what was going on at home. He took it for granted that she would be interested and understand many of the political implications behind the actions that were taking place and often he would voice to her criticism of those in authority. When he was excessively proud of his part in some action, he shared that with her too and sometimes he revealed secret information, knowing of course that by the time she received the letter, it would no longer be secret. He did, however, take a risk because he was well aware that all letters were in danger of interception and being read by others.

While Fanny was staying at Great George Street in Plymouth, the home of Captain William Kelly, his wife and small daughter, she would have met many naval men and listened to all the talk of the war against the French which at that time was still being waged mainly at sea. Her letters from Nelson with more intimate details than went into the official documents would have been widely welcomed. She would also have enjoyed the company of other naval wives and been able to share her hopes and fears with them. Some had already faced widowhood, a fate that must have been constantly at the back of Fanny's mind, especially when she heard that Nelson's squadron was at sea ready to engage the French fleet. He was exhilarated at the prospect: 'I pray God we may meet this fleet who I have no doubt we shall give a glorious account of.' But then he struck a serious note. 'If any accident should happen to me I am sure my conduct will be such as will entitle you to the Royal favour.' Pensions for widows were not automatic and were granted by the Government only in special circumstances, usually as a reward for outstanding service. Money having always been a major consideration in their marriage, Nelson was anxious that Fanny should not be in want in the event of his death but, he assured her, he was quite confident that he would survive.

Not that I have the least idea but I shall return safe to you full of honour...My name shall never be a disgrace to those who may belong to me.

> The little I have you know, except a small annuity, I have given to you. I wish it was more, but I never have got a farthing dishonestly.

As it turned out, Nelson did not get the chance to fight the French at sea but was instead sent back to Corsica where he had played a major role in the past. Now it looked as if he would again be engaged in land fighting which he did not enjoy. He returned to the subject of money in the next two or three letters. It would appear that Fanny had mentioned, perhaps only in passing, that a number of naval men in Plymouth had found themselves in possession of a small fortune as a result of the prize money they had raised from seizing foreign ships. Captain Kelly was one of these. This was a touchy subject and Nelson remarked tersely that Corsica would produce nothing for him, except honour, which he considered to be worth far more than wealth. In emphasising that he would not sacrifice his good name to obtain riches, he insinuated that those who obtained prize money had done so by unscrupulous means. He confessed that he would have liked riches but he argued, playing on Fanny's emotions: 'The only treasure to you I shall expect to bring back is Josiah and myself.'

By the time Fanny received this, she had left her cousin's home in Plymouth and moved on to Ringwood where she stayed for the next three months with the Matchams and their young family. When Nelson knew of her plans he was again concerned about her travelling alone. We learn later from Edmund that she had not been well. Since there was nothing Nelson could do, he thought his brother Maurice ought to go to Plymouth for her. Quite why he expected Maurice to travel all the way from London to do this is not clear. It may be that Maurice was staying with the Matchams but even so, why should he look after Fanny for Nelson? Unless, that is, Nelson was expecting his brother to repay in kind for the financial assistance he had received in the past. He was feeling particularly protective of Fanny at that time as well as missing her: 'I long to hear from you.' His disappointment was apparent:

> ...a post has arrived without a letter. Although I ought to thank you for so many proofs of your kindness in writing me, yet I am always wishing for letters. Therefore 'tis in letters as in money the more a person has the more he wishes for... I am so busy but I own in all my glory that except with you I would not be anywhere but where I am...

Then knowing that she scoured the newspapers for mention of him in between letters, he reassured her of his safety: '...it is possible you may have heard that a Captain of Navy got his head knocked off! To assure you it is not me I write a few lines, for if such a report should get about I well know your anxiety of mind.' Underlying this was his concern that she would read the Admiralty dispatches from Lord Hood. In these, Nelson was mentioned as playing a minor role in the surrender of Bastia in Corsica.

Nelson was aggrieved that other, less valiant and worthy officers had been given more credit than they should. He almost went as far as to accuse one of the officers of cowardice, being about to retreat but for Nelson's stern resolve. Letters such as this must have inflamed Fanny on his behalf and at times made it difficult for her not to speak her mind if she happened to be in the company of naval folk

While Fanny was in Plymouth, Edmund, his health and spirits restored by his winter stay in Bath, went to stay with the Matchams before returning home to Burnham Thorpe for the summer. Whenever they were apart, Fanny kept him informed of Nelson's movements, sending him copies of those parts of her letters that dealt with the progress of the battles. Edmund realised that he was fortunate to have a daughter-in-law who appreciated that he was very anxious about his son. Like her he was looking forward to the prospect of his coming home on leave. But he was anxious too about Fanny's health and hoped that several months at Ringwood would bring an improvement in her. He never specified what was wrong with her and it may be that he magnified her supposed ill health. The truth was he missed Fanny but he put the onus on her, suggesting that whenever she felt like returning to Bath, she had only to summon him to go with her. But it was in a postscript that he showed his true feelings. 'Indeed being much alone does not agree with me.'

Although Fanny would have noted that, she and her sister-in-law Kitty must have chuckled over most of Edmund's letter as they sat after breakfast to read it. It was full of titbits of Burnham gossip; Edmund labelled his informants of the local news as the 'Burnham Gazette'. He included marriages and deaths, told of harvest being underway; that the family at Hilborough was well and perhaps most agreeable of all to Fanny, her parrot, Poll, was flourishing. From Edmund's account it would appear that the bird had long since had its wings clipped and was tame enough to roam freely. On this occasion Poll was happily gleaning among the straw in the cornfields. All this news was duly passed on to Nelson. But the problem was he was still not getting her letters, mainly because earlier he had instructed her to have them sent to Gibraltar where he had expected to be. So he had no way of knowing if she had heard from some other source about his accident. This had occurred on either 10 or 12 July, yet when he wrote on 14 July he made no mention of it, perhaps because he did not wish to alarm her. However, on 18 August he decided she had better hear about it from him.

> You may hear, therefore as it is all past I may tell you that...a shot having struck our battery the splinters of stones from it struck me most severely in the face and breast. Although the blow was so severe as to occasion a great flow of blood from my head, yet I most fortunately escaped by only having my right eye nearly deprived of its sight. It was cut down, but is as far recovered as to be able to distinguish light from darkness, but as to all the purpose of use it is gone. However the blemish is nothing, not

to be perceived unless told. The pupil is nearly the size of the blue part, I don't know the name. At Bastia I got a sharp cut in the back…You must not think that my hurts confined me. No – nothing but the loss of a limb should have kept me from my duty…

No doubt this was meant to reassure her but his graphic description would surely only have increased her anxiety and the fact that he had not told her at the time made matters worse. As if his injury were not enough to fill her with dismay, he then related a whole chapter of other woes that had beset his company and others. Many were suffering from a climate-related sickness, among them Mary Moutray's son, a lieutenant on the *Victory*, who died a few days later. Nelson was also very concerned for the lives of Hoste and Bolton, two of his midshipmen. Furthermore at least one hundred and fifty of his men had had to take to their beds. Wounded though he had been, Nelson boasted of his own good health; 'Of 2,000 men I am the healthiest.' He also calmed any fear she might have for her son, telling her that Josiah was very well, in fact the boy was never sick. He also praised him saying that his sensible behaviour meant he now had to refer to him as a young man rather than a boy. He had earlier told Fanny that he thought Josiah was growing to be very handsome and now he reported that the boy was five feet tall. The closeness at this stage between Nelson and his stepson was reflected in the friendly banter they exchanged; on this occasion there was a minor dispute about an inch which Josiah claimed should be added to Nelson's measurement. After this light note, a more sombre tone was added; Nelson had hoped that when Lord Hood went home, he would go with him. That now looked unlikely: 'I have not nor do I build too much on my prospect of seeing you till the spring.' So the months they had been apart were to grow even longer but there was a glimmer of hope for Fanny: '…by which time I hope the war will be over and we shall get to the farm again.' Could it be possible that this time he really would give up the sea and lead a normal life at home with her?

CHAPTER V

A Peripatetic Life

Indeed my dear Fanny my love, regard and esteem for you cannot I think be exceeded by any man whatever.
Nelson, September 1794

No one could say that Fanny's life lacked variety. In the first nine months of 1794 she had experienced the social life of Bath with its great diversity of temporary population; she had visited among the wealthy merchant class of Bristol; for a time made up part of the society of naval men and their wives in Plymouth and then gone to spend the summer in the rustic gentility that surrounded the Matchams' house, Shepherd's Spring, in Ringwood. Then it was time to move again and from the peace of the countryside and a young family, Fanny went to the suburbs of London, to stay with the middle-aged Mr and Mrs Suckling. She started her visit to them in mid September 1794 and it was while she was in Kentish Town that for the first time we hear Fanny's own voice.

Asked what on earth Fanny did with herself all day, one answer would have to be that she spent a large part of her time writing letters. Quite apart from her frequent letters to her husband she maintained a regular correspondence with members of the extended Nelson family, the Walpoles and her West Indian friends and relations. Unfortunately, few of these have survived. The letters she wrote to Nelson from 1785 until the autumn of 1794 are missing, many of them destroyed by Nelson before a fierce battle, to prevent them falling into enemy hands. Compensating for this frustrating lack of earlier letters is the fact that the very first one of hers that has survived is both long and full of information.

Kentish Town, 30 September 1794. My Dearest Husband, - Yesterday was your birthday. Mr Suckling drank it with no small pleasure, gave some of his best wines and a Norfolk man deserved two geese. We were cheerful. Mr Rumsey [father of Mrs Suckling] and family were of the party. Mr Metz as usual intreated [sic] his best respects to you and said many handsome things which I received with pleasure knowing how deserving you were of them. A happy birthday for me, the next I hope we shall be together.

Fanny gave just a glimpse of the large dinner party gathered to honour nephew Horatio's birthday; and of Uncle Suckling's generosity to his guests, bringing out his best wines, possibly some that Nelson had sent him in the past, for the many toasts that were drunk round the table. References to food are scarce in Fanny's letters so the serving of two geese as part of the meal must have impressed her. These birds were traditionally associated with Michaelmas, which coincided with Nelson's birthday.

Fanny's pride in her husband shone out, but even clearer was her longing to have him home again. She told him that the news of his imminent homecoming had not only filled her with great happiness it had also made her feel better. Without dwelling on the subject, she told him that before she received word that he was safe and well she: '…had fallen into the same way I was last year.' That this refers to her having had some form of nervous debility of the type that often led women into a decline rather than a physical problem is more likely and it may have been this that earlier caused the concern about her travelling arrangements. Whatever may have caused the problem it was now in the past and not to be dwelt upon. The way in which she discussed matters, both domestic and political, showed both an acute mind and a wide knowledge. In the same way that Nelson sought to involve her in his life at sea, so she endeavoured to keep him well informed as to what was happening at home. So she told him about his brother Maurice being offered a new post at the Navy Office. He had given up his previous employment there in favour of a position that was better paid; now the new offer had raised a debate among the rest of the family as to which would be the more financially rewarding for him. She also gave him the latest news on the Matchams who had gone on an unexpected visit to Tunbridge Wells for the sake of Kitty's health. Aware of how fond her husband was of this sister she played down any fears the rest of them had, assuring him that she had nothing more than a severe cold.

Fanny's ability to empathise with others was demonstrated on a number of occasions, in particular with regard to Edmund. But in this, her first letter, she showed a sympathetic understanding of Nelson's cousin, Miss Suckling. Only a few years younger than Fanny, she was in love with an army captain, currently fighting the French in Europe. It was his intention to resign his commission, but that was a secret that had been divulged only to Fanny, who warned Nelson to whom, of course, she told everything, to be sure to make no mention of it when he replied, indicating that letters were often far from personal belongings that might be read aloud. She also showed her affection for the young woman by asking that during his travels Nelson should find a souvenir for her.

On a much more serious note, Fanny showed her great concern for the devastating effect that an outbreak of yellow fever was having on the West

Indies. This was the most virulent attack ever known; the death toll was enormous. To illustrate how quickly death came, Fanny quoted an example that would have appealed to Nelson, that of a Court Martial where the accused was practically the only one left alive before the end of the trial. To add to the already catastrophic situation, hurricanes had then swept through the area. Fanny with her knowledge of the islands realised that the winds, although causing even more anguish, would also help in stemming the fever. As she wrote about all that had been happening in her homeland and the fighting out there as well that had led to a friend being wounded and taken prisoner, her emotions got the better of her, causing her to omit a word as she told Nelson: 'Pray [take] care of yourself. How I shall rejoice to see you. You must save yourself as much as you possibly can.'

Knowing Nelson's love for gossip and the news of the day, she then filled in for him the details surrounding stories that were occupying the minds of many of the English public in September 1794.

> Lord Southampton is gone to demand the Princess of Brunswich for a wife for the Prince of Wales, everyone congratulates themselves on the change he is going to make; Mrs Fitzherbert has been long dismissed. Her violence of temper and some improprieties gave disgust.

More worrying had been the attempted assassination of George III.

> Everybody are [sic] full of the wicked design that a French watchmaker had to take away the life of our king. They were three concerned, the French man, who had made a tube, which upon blowing with his mouth a poisoned arrow was to have struck our King, a saddler and a chemist in Fleet Street. The saddler's conscience tormented him. He went and disclosed it. They were all taken up. The Playhouse was to have been the scene of wickedness, the signal for the watchmaker a call of 'riot'. I wish these French away I never liked them.

Fanny knew that she had a duty to help further Nelson's career by establishing useful contacts. So she told him that having discovered from Mr Rumsey who lived in Hampstead that Sir Andrew Hamond, a Comptroller of the Navy, lived in the neighbourhood, she planned to call on Lady Hamond. This might obtain her entrée into that lady's social circle and so an ear to the Comptroller himself. On the other hand, a risk she had to take was that Lady Hamond might not wish to take the acquaintance any further. Far less formal was her intended visit to her friend Lady Hood, who was daily awaiting her husband's arrival home from the Mediterranean and therefore might have news of exactly when Fanny might expect hers. When on 6 October she received Nelson's letter dated 12 September she was convinced that his arrival at Portsmouth was imminent. She was doubly glad that the Sucklings had invited her to stay until she went to Bath with

Edmund as this meant that she had an address where Nelson could find her so that she could go to him at once. As her plans stood at that time she was waiting for Edmund to join her at the beginning of the next month and then they would go down together, unless that is, Nelson had other plans. Edmund summed it up in a letter to Kitty.

> My movement depends upon Mrs Nelson if her residence is not at Bath, then my being there is upon a small scale, if she joins me it will be more enlarged. If your Bro wish to see Burnham, then I make no journey as yet; if he is westerly, so am I.

While longing to see him: 'My heart is full; may I see you in good health,' Fanny issued a dire warning to her husband to be especially careful about sleeping at inns when he landed in Portsmouth. Her concern harked back to the fever in the West Indies which had been spread into England. Although there had been a demand for ships coming from the Caribbean to be quarantined, it had not yet been enforced. Fanny was sensible as to how dreadful it would be if Nelson – and Josiah too – having escaped more or less unscathed in battle were to return home and catch a disease simply by stopping at a dockside inn. In the letter of 6 October there was an indication that there were letters other than the ones that have survived. Some time between 30 September and 6 October, Fanny had written to tell Nelson that his uncle Suckling had given her a present of £100. Fanny must have been so delighted and grateful for this that she needed to repeat the information. 'I wrote you how handsome your uncle had been to me. Nothing less than £100 present.' Suckling had given Nelson an annual allowance of £100 at the time of their marriage but had talked of withdrawing it following John Herbert's death believing that with their inheritance from him, the Nelsons would no longer need it. Nelson had never kept his financial affairs secret from his uncle and having been made aware that the Herbert inheritance had not been paid, the present gift suggests that Suckling realised that Fanny was short of money.

It is a misconception that it has only been in recent times that people have talked openly about intimate medical problems. Certainly the educated classes of the eighteenth century discussed such matters knowledgeably and freely and Fanny and Nelson were no exception. Having told him originally that Kitty was suffering only from a bad cold she later gave him a revised version. The waters and air of Tunbridge Wells had helped her general constitution but it had been necessary for her to go to London for specialist medical advice. Fanny had been to see her and so was able to report that Kitty was pregnant yet again: '…she breeding very contrary to his [her surgeon's] opinion.' The pregnancy was not going well and it was possible she might miscarry. Her doctor had advised: 'She is to move about till it is known whether she is bleeding or not.' That Nelson's sisters were constantly pregnant must have caused Fanny great heartache because she would have assumed that the failure to conceive was hers. As mentioned earlier, it is most likely that Nelson's health had been responsible for a low sperm count, but it is also worth noting that while his sisters were very fertile, only his brother William fathered children and then only two.

Throughout October Fanny continued to express her great excitement at the prospect of Nelson's homecoming but on 2 November she finally let her guard drop:

> My disappointment at not seeing you and my child as soon as you gave me some hope that I should is very great. The thoughts of soon seeing my affectionate husband has made me quite well, but still I flatter myself it will not be very long before you will come home. This winter will be another anxious one. What did I not suffer in my mind last? I trust in that good providence who has shown great mercies to us.

Her reaction is what one would expect from a woman who had waited so long and had her hopes raised only to have them dashed. However, it was statements like those that have given fuel to those who wish to denigrate Fanny. For her it was a no-win situation; either she was a whining, selfish woman, constantly bewailing the damage to her nerves that his absence brought, or if she kept her true feelings to herself then she laid herself open to the accusation of being cold and uncaring. A careful look at what she actually wrote shows that Edmund was correct when he wrote: '…your sister Nelson always looks upon the fairest side.'

Certainly the rest of that letter showed that Fanny did not dwell on her state, instead she was full of news that she knew he would wish to hear, such as which captains had been newly promoted. Fanny listened and read, so she was well informed about current political problems. She had a strong sense of loyalty to the Crown and condemned those who sought to foment unrest within the country. Support for the French Revolution was particularly strong in Scotland where the Government took repressive measures to prevent gatherings that might lead to the formation of private armies and the outbreak of civil war. John Horne Tooke, a long time critic of the Government had, with others, been charged with high treason. Fanny felt very strongly about those on trial:

> A wickeder set surely never lived. Many fear they have acted with so much caution they will not be hanged. Things had got to too great a height in the Scotch conventions, the terms these creatures had given to their meetings. The Dragoon Guards who in England with their line of new raised fencibles are quartered in and near London. The information that the ministry has is beyond description good. A party had met, inimical to our country, chance threw a gentleman in their way, tickets were dispersed, he put his hand out, was given one, with the name of one of the members, in he went and after he had heard all that was going forward,

how was he to get out again? He told the doorkeeper a gentleman was waiting without and that it was time for him to come in, so he had the best of his way and told it to the minister.

As to the veracity of this account, Fanny concluded with the best line that one could possibly have: 'This same person married a sister of Mrs Suckling.'

From national events, she then turned to those that affected her and Nelson. During a visit to a Mrs Mills, an old acquaintance from Nevis, she had learned what was happening on the island, especially in relation to her cousins. In his will John Herbert made his nephew Magnus Morton heir to his business after his daughter Martha. As so often happened with large estates, in order to inherit, Magnus was expected to adopt the surname Herbert. Mrs Mills' gossip was of a family rift; Magnus and Martha were not on speaking terms. She had also reported on how badly the crops had been affected by the weather and the fever. This was bad news in itself but of particular importance to them since the interest payable on the legacies for Fanny and Josiah was supposed to be drawn from the profits made on the sugar crop. They had still not received a penny of interest since the will was proved and although Fanny had written a number of times she had not received an answer. When she thought that Nelson was coming home she hoped a letter from him on the subject would have more influence but now that was something else that would have to wait.

Other news that had been exchanged with Mrs Mills concerned the promotion of various of Nelson's seafaring contacts from the West Indies. She also told of the death of Admiral Finch, who had married the daughter of Mr Stanley, the Attorney General of Nevis. Fanny disclosed that Finch, who had been ill for some time, had been living in the house of a doctor. That he had suffered from some form of mental disorder is borne out by Fanny's description of him being subject to violent passions. Fanny empathised with young Mrs Finch who had not only been left with four small children to bring up but had also to endure the mental cruelty inflicted by her mother-in-law, so perhaps the Admiral's condition had been a genetic one.

Fortunate indeed was Fanny that she had 'our good father' as she referred to Edmund. He had written to say that he would soon be leaving Burnham Thorpe for London where he would stay for a few days with Kitty's mother-in-law, who was an old friend, after which he and Fanny would journey to Bath for the winter. Although she had tried hard to keep off the subject, as she concluded her letter she returned to her disappointment at Nelson's not coming. She told him that Mr Suckling often teased her saying he knew by her face exactly what was in Nelson's letters. 'Your letter of 27 September to be sure did give me pain. I had hoped to have soon seen my dear friend and my dear young man.' Then, perhaps conscious that she might upset Nelson if she referred to it again, she turned instead to Josiah and the worries that beset a mother. 'If he is good I shall rejoice and be happy, so many turn out ill that truly parent anxiety is not to be wondered at. I feel comforted he is with [you].'

It was good for Fanny to stay with the Sucklings as life in their household was so very different to that she experienced elsewhere within the extended Nelson family. There was none of the pretentiousness of Ringwood nor the elegant refinement of Wolterton. Hilborough was dominated by the officious Rector and his rather shallow wife, while the Boltons, kind though they were, often had pressing money problems of which they made their guest aware. But in Kentish Town, Fanny found herself accepted very much as another daughter in the midst of a lively, bustling, comfortably off, upper middle class family. William Suckling held a responsible position as Collector of Customs and was financially secure enough to be able to allow Nelson £100 a year on his marriage. An affable, gregarious man, he liked to entertain his many friends. One of his closest was his colleague Thomas Rumsey, an officer of the Excise and it was his 48-year-old spinster daughter, Mary that William had married the year after the death of his wife of twenty-five years. The Rumseys were also a close-knit family and frequent visits were exchanged between the house in Kentish Town and the Rumseys' in Hampstead. Both families included Fanny in their activities thus extending her range of acquaintances.

There were other advantages to staying in Kentish Town, one of which was the close proximity to London. Since William worked in Town and had his own carriage, it was possible for Fanny to travel in with him and then have use of his vehicle until it was time for him to be collected for the homeward journey. This gave her the freedom to call on her own friends during the day or to go shopping with the Suckling ladies. It had also given her the opportunity to have some dental work carried out. Fanny rarely mentioned her personal appearance but she obviously cared very much that she should look her best for her husband. When she thought Nelson was on his way home she: '… went and had my teeth put in order.' This must have been quite radical cosmetic treatment, for she wished: ' I had done it some years back they look much better than you ever saw them.' It is possible that Fanny underwent something similar to that experienced a few years later by Harriet, Countess Granville in Paris. Writing to her sister she confided:

It is my front tooth I must lose, but we part to meet again. My dentist tells me it will not be a very painful job…It [the front tooth] is now much longer than the others, discoloured, all shaking. He will extricate it with his finger and thumb, restore its hue, file it and stick it in again, quite even with the others.

Following her visit to the dentist, Fanny became such a devotee to correct oral hygiene practices that she urged Nelson to make sure that Josiah brushed his teeth up and down not crossways.

But now, she was again to spend another winter in Bath with Edmund. It was the custom for the local newspapers to list those newly arrived in the city, presumably so that readers could quickly make contact with their friends. The issue for 24 November included among the one hundred or more names that of 'Mr & Mrs Nelson.' Those who knew them would of course realise that this was the elderly clerical gentleman and his daughter-in-law, not a married couple. They had arrived over a week before on the 16th of the month and Fanny had spent the day looking for suitable lodgings. They settled again, as they had earlier in the year in New King Street, though not in the same house. The following day, Fanny sat down to write to tell her husband of their new address and with the realisation that she was to be without him even longer, she gave in to her emotions and the ensuing letter jumped from one subject to another as they came to her mind; sometimes omitting words in her haste to write it all down.

She had received Nelson's letter dated 3 October and discovered that he had not received many of hers. This was frustrating, not least because he might construe that she had not written: 'No opportunity did I ever neglect, it has been my greatest pleasure excepting receiving one from you.' The war news had made her fearful and she prayed that he would not have an opportunity to fight the French. She tried to comfort herself: 'Could I hope for this, I should endeavour to make myself easy. My mind and poor heart are always on the rack.' Yet she tried to find solace in the fact that in his not coming home with Lord Hood, he had escaped being involved in the battle that had taken place between the French and the English squadron that had left Gibraltar. Was it any wonder that she should worry about her husband when she continually heard such news as that of Admiral Richard Bligh being captured with his ship by the French? Or that their friend Captain Weatherhead was dead as was Captain Robertson who had fallen during a land battle at Grozior where, it was said, the English had mistakenly fired upon each other. The authorities had awarded an annual pension of £100 to Mrs Robertson and £25 to each of her four small children, a very small consolation for the loss of a husband and father. And with such losses on her mind, Fanny could be excused for telling her husband: ' [my] mind is always harping upon the only friend and that the dearest we can be blest with (ie a husband)…So [when] we are together I am happy.'

After the spaciousness of the house in Kentish Town, it must have been difficult for Fanny to readjust to living with Edmund in the confines of the three or four rooms that made up their lodgings. Edmund had now reached 70 and was suffering from general debility and in the first few days in Bath, Fanny found it difficult to get him out of the house to take exercise as he complained that his feet hurt him. She was, however, full of optimism that the city would improve his general state as it had done the previous winter. Quite apart from the beneficial effects of drinking the medicinal waters and the warm baths, Edmund would gain from the social contact he so lacked in Norfolk. As far as he was concerned he was delighted to be back with

Fanny and told her to tell Nelson that wherever they finally settled, he wanted to be with them. Writing to Kitty a week or so later, Edmund told her that he was beginning to feel settled both physically and mentally. He paid tribute to Fanny's kindness to him saying she was like: '…a kind and watchful child over the infirmities and whimsies of age.' However, he was also anxious to hear from his son and had hoped Lord Hood would bring news of him. He again perhaps put some of his own feelings on to Fanny.

> His poor wife is continually in a hurry and fret about him & I find many others are the same and worse. In such a state the blessings of a marriage union are thus made a torment & most likely the Health is destroyed or the temper soured so as never to be recovered.

This very general remark has been frequently misinterpreted to apply solely to Fanny. Certainly at that time there was nothing in her behaviour to suggest that her temper had been soured.

One of the first things Fanny did on her return to Bath was to find out about sending mail to Italy. Many of her earlier letters had been sent to Gibraltar to await Nelson's arrival there but with the change of plan he advised her to send them instead care of the consul in Leghorn. She discovered there was a weekly collection for Leghorn and that a single sheet letter would cost two shillings and ten pence, a considerable sum. Not that that worried her. She was far more concerned to know which letters had reached him and suggested that in future when he wrote he put the date of her most recent letter at the bottom of his. Between them they devised a system of numbering which was almost reminiscent of the code they had used in their days of courtship.

It was not very long before Fanny and Edmund became caught up in the hectic social life that Bath offered. As Fanny went out walking, she met many old acquaintances who, in turn, told her of other new arrivals, her Bristol friends the Pinneys among them. She knew it would not be long before they visited and she hoped they might bring some news concerning the legacy. She had by that time become convinced that someone was trying to prevent them receiving their legitimate interest. She and Edmund had talked about it and he was of the opinion that Nelson had not made it clear to the executors that Fanny had his power of attorney to receive the money. In Nelson's absence, Fanny became more and more inclined to discuss personal matters with her father-in-law, respecting his opinion even if she did not always follow his advice. It was, however, a reciprocal relationship and Edmund kept nothing back from Fanny either. When he received letters from his son, it was automatic that he would pass them to Fanny to read and often he relied on her to convey his answer if he did not have time or felt unable to write. Like Fanny he was busy entertaining those who called upon him as well as making regular visits to the Pump Room to drink the water. Edmund had his own circle of acquaintances and introduced Fanny to them in the same way that he became known to her connections. So it was that with: '…some pleasant young women whose mothers are our father's acquaintance,' she had been to a concert, very possibly the third subscription concert of the season at which a Mr Vioti had played a violin concerto.

There was much for Fanny to tell her husband, and during December most of it related to Lord and Lady Hood. Fanny could not wait to share her meeting with them on 4 December and without any preamble beyond 'My Dearest Husband,' she began her letter: 'This instant left Lord and Lady Hood who received me with every mark of affection and said all that would gratify an affectionate wife, begged that I would frequently call and consider myself at home.' The words affection and affectionate perhaps now convey less strength of meaning than they did in the eighteenth century when they meant love and tenderness. So where Nelson and Fanny signed themselves as 'affectionate husband or wife', nowadays they would have used 'loving', 'affectionate' is now more likely to be reserved by grateful nieces and nephews to their generous aunts and uncles. Fanny returned to the subject of the Hoods' loving tenderness in her next letter. Lord Hood had undertaken that a letter from her would be enclosed with one from him. This was a special privilege as it meant that it would go as speedily as official correspondence could. The Lord had been: '…as affectionate as if I had been his child, assures me I shall soon see you and one of the finest colts he ever saw in his life.' This 70-year-old Admiral, who had just returned from very active service, certainly knew how to win the heart of Fanny. Not only did he continue to praise Nelson but he also gave her reassurance that he was in good health and spirits. Best of all he knew just what would please a mother by his reference to Josiah. She continued:

> I dined with them was cheerful and well dressed. Lord Hood declared he would write to you the next day and tell you I was well. He has spoke of your services and the situation you had been constantly in particularly one at Bastia to the Speaker of the House of Commons, the Lady said if justice was not done you it would not be Lord H's fault.

That the Hoods were genuinely fond of Fanny for her own sake as well as Nelson's was borne out later, and certainly at that time had she not inspired their affection they need not have bothered with her beyond a polite call or one single invitation. Instead of which, she was asked to join them at various functions including a ball. There she had the opportunity to talk at some length to Dr Harness who had been the physician to the Mediterranean fleet. Fanny liked this man very much.

> Dr Harness I am very much pleased with, he spoke so handsomely of you and did tell me many little things which to bystanders might be thought trifling, but to me highly gratifying…I wish you were in England and that

we were blessed with peace. I am glad you have got a French master, you will be able to give me instruction and I shall be happy to receive it.

Nelson was by this time living on shore in lodgings at Leghorn while his ship was being refitted. Taking French lessons would: 'with the amusements of the place fully occupy my time.' With her superior knowledge of the language, Fanny was indulging in flirtatious teasing when she said she would be happy to take lessons from Nelson. As for the other amusements of the place, we will return to those later.

Still on the subject of the Hoods, Fanny was able to report that she had heard that four ships had already sailed for the Mediterranean and others were due to follow. Once they had arrived, she had no doubt that with Hood's influence, Nelson's ship would be ordered home. Lady Hood had told her that the Lord had spoken on Nelson's behalf to those in power in London. With Lord Spencer now the First Lord, Fanny hoped that Admiralty business would be properly conducted. She felt strongly that Lord Hood himself had been neglected for further advancement blaming the press for campaigning against him. 'One of the newspapers has abused him shamefully.' Other people had also said complimentary things about Nelson. At the aforementioned ball:

> Admiral Cosby…came to Lady H he spoke of you on high terms, seemed of a communicative temper but had not an opportunity of saying much, however he did say no man in the Mediterranean had done what you had, such a conspicuous figure and supposed they would not let you stay out much longer.

In revelling in Nelson's praise, Fanny also managed to bolster Nelson's ego, persuading him that he was indeed appreciated at home.

Throughout December Fanny was almost constantly with the Hoods: 'I went to the play with them, dined and taken a long ride [with them].' However, she found that Hood liked to tease her much as Suckling had done. She knew he had had an official letter from Nelson but became slightly exasperated when he made no mention of it to her. However she dealt with the situation with her usual good humour:

> I was determined to make him smile. He had hold both my hands and said he hoped I heard from you. I told him yes and as his Lordship's letter was dated two days after mine I had an inclination to be jealous and that I should write you so.

A woman who is supposed to be of a very reserved nature seldom possesses a keen sense of humour while it is only those one feels comfortable with that one teases. And comfortable with Fanny the Hoods must have felt for they even invited her to dine with them on Christmas Day when they had other interesting guests which included a Mr Petre, one of the Corsican deputies, Fanny found: '…very pleasant and of a cheerful disposition.' The nationality of this gentleman was not made clear, Fanny noting that he: 'would not speak French on any account, said he had had enough of that.' Neither is it apparent that Edmund was included on this day but unless he had an engagement elsewhere, one cannot imagine that Fanny would have left him alone or that the Hoods would have expected her to. The only clue given is Fanny's remark to Nelson that the Hoods paid his father proper attention while Edmund himself reported to Kitty that Fanny had received a great deal of attention from Lady Hood that pleased her. Unfortunately this was another of those remarks where the nuances of eighteenth-century language have been misunderstood, creating the impression that Fanny was interested only in social climbing and cared little for those around her.

That was far from the case. Not only was her sympathy constantly engaged for the plight of others generally, she was quick to try to do whatever was in her power to help. A situation then arose that caused her great concern. For many years Nelson had had a personal servant who had been with him in the West Indies. Loyal and trustworthy Frank Lepee occupied a special place among the Nelson household. It was he who had been entrusted with the care of young Josiah when he went to Norfolk to begin his schooling. During Fanny's most recent stay in Kentish Town, she had on a number of occasions sent messages from the Sucklings to Frank showing that they too were fond of him but were worried about his health. At the end of October, Nelson wrote to tell her: '… that Frank is now continually subject to those epileptic fits, that his mind is evidently deranged…' In a letter, now lost, more detailed information had been given of Frank's condition but what is perhaps more intriguing is that following the word 'deranged' the next part of this letter is missing too, almost as if either Fanny or an earlier editor had wished it to remain unknown. Fanny's reaction was of genuine sympathy: 'Poor Frank I own I was afraid something was the matter, that he was not so good as formerly. I am so very sorry that he is in so deplorable a way.' It may be that the missing part of the letter described violence on Frank's part for she said she hoped he was never alone with Nelson. Having expressed her sympathy and concern, the practical Fanny comes to the fore. What could be done for him? To her the obvious answer was to get him home as soon as possible and treated at the Greenwich Hospital. She knew that entry to the hospital was not automatic, that a patient had to have sponsors, but since Nelson's old friend Captain Locker was the Governor of the Hospital, she assumed they would be able to count on his assistance. Nelson's own concern for Frank is marred by his apparent selfishness. 'I am sorry to tell you,' he wrote later, 'that poor Frank is better in health but that there are no hopes the surgeon tells me of his judgements returning, at least not for a certainty. I am really distressed to know what to do with him and have now no servant.' He then told Fanny how dreadful the man he had tried out as a replacement had been and that he was having to make do with 'a Norfolk ploughman.'

In the period leading up to Christmas 1794, Fanny continued in ebullient mood; after her initial disappointment, she realised she must get on with her life and make the best of things. Money continued to worry her and she was careful not to spend too much on herself, feeling that she might have overstepped the mark by spending twenty-five guineas on a piano. It is not quite clear if, while she was in Bath, she also took music lessons but she told Nelson that her learning music was an expense to him. Having been out of the country for eighteen months, he would be surprised at how much prices had risen of late. She also begged him not to spend too much on presents for her; she would appreciate some cambric lace to make ruffles and edge handkerchiefs but he was not to try to send them, rather give her the pleasure of receiving whatever he had when he did come home. On the other hand she had been more than happy to give to others and had, at Nelson's request, sent a Christmas hamper to his aged aunt in Norfolk. That news was given in a letter dated 28 December 1794. Those that followed – and there must have been a great number for Fanny had recently discovered that post was collected not once but twice weekly for Leghorn – are missing. Her next sequence started in February 1797. For what she did and what she thought during that interval of two years we are reliant on clues given in Nelson's letters and the occasional one from Edmund that contains factual evidence.

One of the reasons Edmund and Fanny went to Bath was to escape the severity of the winter, the West Country being famous for its mild climate. However, that year was different. It was so cold on Christmas Day, that Edmund insisted Fanny should not venture out to walk to the post office which was situated in one of the inns that received the mail coaches. Just how bad the weather was to become he revealed in a letter to Kitty towards the end of January: 'At present mountains of snow separate us…Colds are universal here; I have a small share; Mrs Nelson is well; we both feel the severity of the season…at Bath I never experienced such weather.' In spite of the weather and the fact that Bath was not as crowded as usual, perhaps because of the weather and/or the rising food prices about which Edmund also complained, they did continue to enjoy a social life. Edmund talked of visiting their neighbours and of a small evening party they gave which included Lady Saumarez, wife of the admiral. Many of Fanny's West Indian contacts were still in the city so she had plenty of places to visit and friends to accompany her to concerts and balls. And of course, Bath was full of women in a similar position to her own as well as the many naval captains home on leave who came to build up their strength before returning to duty.

Fanny had plenty to occupy her days. When she was forced to remain in the house there were numerous letters to write, many of them on Nelson's behalf. In her role as the Captain's wife, she wrote to Mrs Hoste, mother of one of the midshipmen who had gone from Norfolk with Nelson in 1793. Nelson was concerned when the boys did not write to their parents as frequently as he thought they should but he left it to Fanny, as a mother herself, to keep the anxious parents informed. Mrs Hoste was deeply grateful for Fanny's letter with all its information, as she had not heard from her son for many months. Fanny understood only too well what it was like waiting to hear from one's child. In her own case, even though Josiah was very tardy with his letters, he did at least have the opportunity to scratch a line at the bottom of one of his stepfather's and she did have frequent reports from Nelson.

Apart from friendly, concerned letters, Nelson sometimes asked her to write business letters, some of them not very pleasant. As it happened several of these had to be directed to Mr Hoste who had failed to remit the annual premium required for his son's training and keep at sea. Then there was the continuing correspondence over the unpaid legacy interest. To the huge extended Nelson family Fanny acted as a general post, passing the latest information of Nelson's activities and their father's state of health to each one as well as relating pieces of news that each one gave her to other members, many of whom appeared at times not to be on speaking terms. Fanny must have had either an excellent filing system for all the letters she received or an exceptionally good memory to be able to recall who had had what illness, changed house or job, given birth or died. She became the repository for a vast store of knowledge about Nelson's nephews and nieces, their education, birthdays and behaviour. Whenever Nelson mentioned someone she should write to on his behalf, she took the injunction seriously. In an age when most people rely on the telephone, e-mails and text-messages to communicate, the idea of sitting down to write two or three letters a day, every day seems inconceivable. Fanny became so proficient at it that on one occasion Nelson commented: 'Your letters, my dear Fanny, are not only affectionate but full of news. You used to say you could not write letters but very few people write so well, this without flattery.'

During the first months of 1795 the tone of Nelson's letters changed as they became more concerned with naval affairs. Yet at the same time they also appeared very loving. Almost every one begins 'My Dearest Fanny' and many of them express his desire to be with her. 'God bless you and give us a happy meeting says your most affectionate husband.'

> Much as I shall regret being so long parted from you, still we must look beyond the present day, and two or three months may have the difference of every comfort or otherwise in our income. I hope we shall have many happy years to live together.

Still there was that ever-present concern with money; if he stayed longer at sea he had more chance of prize money that would enable them to live comfortably. Whether it was intentional or otherwise Nelson seemed to be emphasising that had she received her inheritance he would not have had to stay at sea. In fact he had taken action to speed things up by writing to the executors himself. The fact that he enclosed the letters to her to deliver, suggests that he left them unsealed so that she was fully aware of their contents. Still concerned with money, at the end of January 1795, he discussed with her compensation for the loss of his eye. Strangely none of Fanny's extant letters ever made reference to his injury and Nelson himself had initially made light of it. Now he told her that Lord Hood thought his injury could produce a pension for him. But this was one of Nelson's self-pitying letters: 'Many have for much less losses handsome pensions. That I do not expect, it would be too good luck for me.' He went on to explain that if he did not get a pension then he ought to be given a rise in rank that would equal it. Had Lord Hood still been in favour with the Admiralty then he would definitely have got something.

> I ought to have the Colonel of Marines or King's Yacht, neither of which I expect, or £200 a year pension. My eye as you may conceive is now grown worse and is almost total darkness and very painful at times.

It would have been a hard-hearted wife indeed who did not react to such a letter. Fanny would have inwardly raged with indignation on Nelson's behalf while her longing to comfort him and soothe his bad eye would have been overwhelming. No good his finishing the subject with the words: 'But never mind. I can see very well with the other.' While he might have seen that as an attempt at humour, Fanny would have interpreted it as an example of his stoic resignation.

Part of Nelson's self absorption may have been induced by the lack of mail from England. By 25 February it had been over two months since he had received any, which explains why so many of the letters he sent at that time made no reference to any of Fanny's activities. One from her, dated 5 January, finally caught up with him in Leghorn just before he and the rest of the fleet put to sea ready, if required, to do battle with the French. From on board ship, on 10 March he wrote: 'I shall commence a letter at this moment to assure you, although I flatter myself that no assurance is necessary, of my constant love and affection.' What had brought on this sudden effusion? Was it that as he expected to go into battle there was, as always, the fear that he might not survive and this could be read as a farewell message to her? Or was there another reason why he should suddenly protest his love for her? While he wrote about the possibility of a glorious death and resigning himself to the will of God, was there something else underlying: 'I have no doubt in my own mind but that my conduct will be such as will not bring a blush on the face of my friends.' No one doubted that his conduct in battle at sea would be honourable but was it possible that he was just a bit concerned that rumours of his conduct on land might have been carried home?

When Nelson had written earlier to tell Fanny that he had taken lodgings on shore in Leghorn/Livorno during the refitting of his ship, he had told her of his French lessons and had mentioned there were other amusements to keep him entertained. What he did not tell her was that one of these was a lady called Adelaide Correglia who was by profession an opera singer. Nelson was not renowned for his love of music but perhaps they had other things in common. She did not speak English, he knew little Italian so conversation took place in French. No wonder Nelson was able to tell Fanny that he had made progress in the language. Little has been recorded about Adelaide except the gossip amongst seafarers that she was often present when Nelson gave dinner parties and that his behaviour with her often embarrassed his guests which hardly fits in with the suggestion that the liaison was not of a sexual nature. Others, in attempting to prove his purity have maintained that Adelaide was a spy whom he used to uncover secret information. Given the length of time he had been away and the mores of the period, no one would have been surprised – probably not even Fanny – if Nelson had taken a mistress, provided he was discreet. The problem was that Nelson had almost puritanical views on the subject as his condemnation of Admiral Hughes' behaviour in the West Indies had shown. So while he was far from discreet he was at the same time probably racked with guilt. First that he had given in to physical desire but more important, it had shown him that he was no better than other men and that was something he found hard to bear; his character and good name were everything to him, he believed he was destined to be a hero. But heroes ought not to behave badly to their wives.

The letter begun on 10 March was completed two days later when he and another ship were within four miles of the French who were trying to cut them off from the rest of the English fleet that was ten miles away. He shared his excitement with her and then signed his letter: '…ever your most faithful and affectionate husband.' And two days after that he was calling her 'his better half' and sharing with her a blow-by-blow account of the battle in which he had played a significant part: '…we killed 110 men and so cut him [the French Captain] up that he was unable to join his own fleet.' No doubt he expected Fanny to rejoice at his victory but he also expected her to write to the parents of his two young midshipmen who along with Josiah had acted as his aides-de-camp and behaved courageously. Her heart must have missed a beat when he reminded her that her young son had been in the thick of the fighting and was likely to be in more, for Nelson went on to tell her that following the refit to his ship he was then ready to sail to Corsica which would provide his last campaign and then: 'I shall have great pleasure in turning my sword into the ploughshare.'

By the end of March he had received two letters from her, one written in October 1794 six months earlier, when she had been staying in Kentish Town, and the other in mid January. Three or four days after that he received four more recent ones, three written in January and the fourth towards the end of February which means that at least two were missing in the sequence. This fourth letter Nelson described as a scolding one, Fanny having accused him of being negligent in writing. There may have been a trace of guilt behind his strong assertion: '…assure yourself, my dear Fanny, that you are never absent from my thoughts, no, not for a minute.' If Fanny had indeed heard any rumours then she must have been taken aback when she read on: 'I venture to tell you, but as a secret, that I have a Mistress given to me.' A wife with a tendency to swoon would have surely needed her smelling bottle at that point. But it was not what she feared as he proceeded to explain:

> ...no less a personage than the Goddess Bellona; so say the French verses made on me, and in them I am so covered with laurels that you will hardly find my little face. At one period I am 'the dear Nelson,' 'the amiable Nelson,' 'the fiery Nelson'.

He laughed the verses off as nonsense yet he admitted to her that he was open to flattery like everyone else.

Fanny may have chided him for not writing but she was beginning to get impatient for him to come home on leave. Every day in Bath she saw other Captains who had been sent back for a couple of months and she could not understand why he did not do the same. He offered the well worn explanation that if he were to come in the next few months he would lose prize money, and to emphasise the point he told her he had just sent £500 to his agent, his share in condemned ships and he did not wish to miss out on further gains.

> It would I assure my dear Fanny, give me infinite pleasure to return to England but it is necessary to look beyond the next moment...This would hurt me much more than staying here till October next, when I have no doubt but peace will take place and I shall look out for a peaceful cottage in Norfolk.

That was his view at the beginning of May but by the end of the month: 'I am tired of this business, however I hope peace will very soon come and send us all to our cottages again.' But peace did not come, neither did any significant naval engagement and inactivity led Nelson to introspection and occasional outbursts of pettishness in his letters. He was sure Josiah's cough was nothing more than a bad habit; he thought his sister Kitty who had not miscarried and had just had her fifth child should: '...leave off having any more' and as for that elusive interest on the legacy: 'Can it be expected we can live on air?'

Although all letters to Fanny were directed to Bath, it was clear from that of 22 June that she was either going to, or was already staying in, Bristol. There she would have been able to regale her friends with her husband's most recent exploits which included his being commissioned as a Colonel of Marines. This long hoped for promotion involved him making adjustments to his uniform and he sent Fanny a sketch of the new epaulettes he would have. The Bristol merchants with whom she stayed would have been fascinated by the description he sent of the ship his squadron had recently captured after they found it abandoned close to shore. It was believed that the master and crew had taken with them as much as they could carry but they had still left a great deal behind. When the ship had left Marseilles bound for Genoa she was said to be valued at the enormous sum of £160,000.

> However, we must expect nearly all the money is gone. I have got one large chest of silver, some lumps of gold, 7 and 8 lbs in the lump, with a great number of diamond rings, loose diamonds and other valuables on board *Agamemnon*, besides a rich cargo of silks, spices etc. However some may value her, if she gives me £100 or £500 I shall be well satisfied.

Whatever he got would be put towards their future home.

It was to this that Edmund referred when he wrote to his son in early August to congratulate him on his promotion. He told him how delighted he and Fanny were but he had hoped that Nelson would have been back by then to share the pleasure with them. Fanny, he assured him, was in very good health and had cheerful friends and neighbours to help her pass what Edmund called her 'widowhood'. He painted an intimate picture of him and Fanny sitting together: '...fixing the cottage retirement you are look-ing forward to.' As for himself: '...every month in this place of warmth, ease and quietude adds something to my strength.' A month later he wrote again and told Nelson that the bread shortages in the country to which he had referred were likely to be over soon as there had been an abundant harvest and more important, fine weather to gather it in. He also touched on political events of the time, discussing those French who had sought asylum in England and then tried to return to their native land to support the Royalists. In the country generally, the English had had enough of war but Edmund believed that: '...this Pittian Minister will not attend to the loud calls of his countrymen "Give us Peace".' The old man was in reflec-tive mood as he wrote: '...you may awhile retire from incessant fatigue and let others hear a little of the roaring cannon. I trust the fatigue of life is over with you.' This was Edmund putting his own feelings on to Nelson. He did, however, give the news that Fanny was well and as happy as could be expected and that he had, at Nelson's suggestion, taken a three-year lease on the house in New King Street.

While for Edmund that meant he would not be returning to spend the following summer in Norfolk, had Fanny realised that in spite of what Nelson said, he appeared to be in no hurry for them to find a house of their own or indeed in any hurry to come home? She had by that time become so accustomed to his mood swings that each time she opened a letter she must have wondered in what frame of mind it had been written. He constantly assured her that his health was better than it had ever been, yet in July he had written to the authorities:

I find my exertions have been beyond my strength. I have a complaint in my breast which will probably bear me down…I must, the medical people tell me, be on shore for a month or two without the thoughts of service.

In October he told her that it was rumoured that many of the fleet would go home in the spring and that he expected to be among them. For her this meant postponing their reunion for at least another six months – another winter to be got through without him. There was little comfort for her in his words: 'In short having the good opinion of my C-in-C and the friendship of my brother officers, I am as happy, separated from you, as I could wish.' Yet within two weeks of that he was bemoaning that he was tired of his ship. Such variable emotions made it very difficult at times for Fanny to know how to respond. If she sympathised when he was feeling low spirited by the time her letter reached him, he might well have forgotten what it was that he had complained of.

As it was, Nelson had little to write about except sea battles, prompting him on one occasion to exclaim: 'What a military letter' – or the lack of them – and his feeling that he was not shown proper appreciation by those in authority. In return Fanny could only try to share with him the every-day events in her life. In her effort to make him feel close to his family, she suggested some time before Christmas that when he was in Leghorn he might find presents for Mrs Bolton's twin daughters. The caring, thoughtful Fanny had realised how much it would mean to the girls to receive a present sent by their uncle from foreign shores. She knew that Nelson had bought gifts for her, so she did not feel she was asking too much of him to go shopping. His unenthusiastic reply must have disappointed her:

I will endeavour to buy something for Mr Bolton's girls but, to say the truth, when you begin in a large family you know not where to stop. Much better if you like it some time or other give them £10 and tell them to buy a couple of caps or gowns.

In other words he had pushed the responsibility on to her and her kind gesture was turned from something exciting into a mundane event.

In her letter of 25 November, Fanny had passed on a piece of Bath gossip which nearly caused Nelson to explode when he read it on Christmas Day. Since the letter itself is missing it is necessary to guess what it was exactly that was being said about Mary Moutray, the lady he had once adored.

What a scandalous report of poor Mrs Moutray. Thus all poor women who are left in the world have their characters taken away but few give credit that a civil thing is done by a man to a woman without a criminality. I do not believe a more amiable woman or a better character exists on earth. I feel quite hurt and I daresay that the reporter, if her character could be traced, is a bad woman.

It was admirable that he should defend the lady's reputation but it is interesting that he was so adamant that the relationship, whatever it was, must have been of a pure nature. While he could not possibly believe anything ill of Mary Moutray, he quite happily cast aspersions on the character of the woman who had told Fanny the gossip. This suggests he was trying to salve his own conscience while Fanny, when she received his reply, must have been surprised by his violent reaction. Most women would have felt at least a twinge of jealousy that their husbands still had such strong feelings for another woman.

For a Christmas letter, this one went from bad to worse. After his outburst over Mary, he then took Fanny to task for being too kind hearted. She had told him of a lady of her acquaintance, a Mrs F Kelly (not to be confused with her cousin) who had fallen on hard times. Nelson tersely told her that he did not know the woman, as if that really mattered when she was simply showing concern. He then moralised on the subject of those who lived beyond their income and his belief that money did not bring happiness thus skilfully bringing the theme back to his own lack of money. Still in moralistic vein, he commented next on Fanny's report that Lieutenant Allison, one of the officers sent home sick during the summer, had died soon after his arrival in England. Nelson made this an opportunity to sermonise on the subject of drink saying that since Allison had become so deranged by alcohol, his death was probably a merciful release for both him and his family. Writing the word family nudged him into commenting on another piece of news Fanny had given him, namely that after a rift, his sisters were to meet. Fanny, and no doubt Edmund too, was delighted by this. But even that did not please Nelson: 'As to Mrs M and Mrs B meeting it may be all well but the gentlemen must be unpleasant for no two people have I fancy a greater contempt for each other.' To complete this festive letter he remarked on the blockade of the West Indies fleet which had personal implications for them: '…for till we are paid I shall always have fear and trembling for our legacy. The not paying has been scandalous.' A week later he was still on the subject: 'I wish to God our legacy was safe in England.'

The clouds of depression that had descended in December were lifted with the dawn of 1796. Nelson met his new Commander-in-Chief, Sir John Jervis who had received him: '…not only with the greatest attention but with much apparent friendship.' The upshot of the meeting was that with the prospect of promotion Nelson elected to remain with the fleet for the duration of the war. Fanny was now brought face to face with the reality that will always face wives, the pull of work over family life.

> Thus, my dear Fanny, although I wish to get home, yet my fair character makes me stand forward to remain abroad, and I rather believe that Sir John writes home this day that if the fleet is kept up here, that my flag on a promotion may be sent out. The credit which I derive from all these compliments must be very satisfactory to you, and should I remain till peace, which cannot be very long, I sincerely hope, make your mind easy.

How little he understood her. Did he really believe that complimentary remarks about him from those in high places made up for the loss of his presence? He was the one who revelled in the remarks and yet he probably did not realise how cruel was the addition to this letter:

I have often heard that a postscript is better than a letter. Sir John has hinted to me that if I am not promoted I shall go home the first convoy. Keep this secret except to my father, as also the other part of the letter.

If only she had been honest enough to say to him, 'never mind the promotion, just come home', but Fanny knew that was not what her husband wanted to hear.

Neither did he wish to hear that her cousin Sally had received the interest on her legacy from Mr Baillie the solicitor in Nevis. Nelson immediately took this as a personal slight; they had been neglected because he could not put business Mr Baillie's way as could Sally's brother who had inherited the plantations. However, he took comfort from the fact that even Mr Baillie could not prevent the whole legacy being paid out eventually when six years had elapsed since Herbert's death and then: '...we shall get it all together and peace will by that time, I hope be arrived, when a cottage of our own and an income to live, if not in luxury, in comfort...we shall possess.' Sally Kelly had arrived in Bath, as had many of Fanny's Bristol friends. Together they made up what Nelson described as a pleasant party for Fanny even though he still did not care for Sally. If anything his antipathy towards her had increased and he told Fanny that one of his officers had reported to him that Sally had tried to stop Fanny from meeting people during her stay in Plymouth. He hinted that Sally was not generally liked; some even regarded her as a bit odd. In that she was becoming like Fanny's other cousin Martha, who surrounded by her thirty cats was turning into a recluse. It is to be hoped that Fanny was too busy when she received that letter to see the implication that the 'oddness' might run through the family.

January in Bath had been a busy month with the city exceptionally crowded, many drawn by the fact that the Duke and Duchess of York, who had taken a house for the winter, were expecting a visit from the Prince of Wales. At Tyson's Ball, the crush to see the young royals was almost overwhelming. It was a mercy that the exceptionally high ceilings of the Assembly Rooms allowed much of the heat engendered by so many bodies to rise upwards otherwise there would have been an even greater number of fainting ladies. Fanny liked to dance and she probably did not lack for partners, especially from among the naval officers who brought her news of her husband. While she and Sally and the younger Pinneys and Tobins danced, Edmund and the older members including her aunt Webbe would take their places at the card tables in the adjoining room.

When they were not at dances there were concerts and the theatre to attend. But it was not all amusement. Fanny had become very interested in the sermons given by Dr Randolph, a theologian who was expounding Socinian theories which, like modern Unitarianism, denied the divinity of Christ. He attracted large congregations to the Octagon chapel. This magnificent building with its eight-sided hall and balcony already drew more of the fashionable population to its services than most of the other churches including the Abbey. Apart from the many interesting ministers who took the pulpit, it also boasted a fine organ. William Herschel, the renowned astronomer, whose home was in Bath, had as a young man been organist at the Octagon. Aside from its popularity for providing spiritual stimulation, the Octagon was also a paradise for pickpockets who mingled with the servants who came to meet their employers at the end of services.

Throughout the winter months, while she received more letters from her husband telling her how much his new C-in-C thought of him, Fanny when she was not writing, reading to Edmund or going out, spent much of her time in dressmaking. She was sewing by hand the dress she intended to wear to greet her husband when he finally came home. There are no details extant of the design or material, but we can be certain that much thought went into her choice and that every stitch brought her closer to the wonderful day when she would wear it. She wrote in mid March to tell him all about it. His reply showed yet again his lack of sensitivity: 'I thank you for telling me of the gown you are working to receive me in but for fear you should not have finished it I have one, lawn I fancy, and worked the most elegantly I ever saw.' Fanny could easily have taken this as criticism that either she worked very slowly or that he doubted her ability to complete the undertaking. Having described her dress to him, his comment on the fine work on the dress he had bought might also have suggested that he did not think it as elegant as she obviously did. On the other hand he went out of his way to reassure her that he still loved her, a love that was increased: '...by that propriety of conduct which I know you are pursuing.' While he might be engaging in a liaison, he had no doubt that Fanny was completely faithful to him. Or was he? Did he suddenly realise that he had left behind him an attractive wife who might well catch the eye of another and be tempted to reciprocate. What may have occasioned such doubts was the news that his colleague, Admiral Sir Hyde Parker had had to return home on compassionate leave: 'It seems Lady Parker has behaved infamously ill and almost ruined his future peace of mind as well as his pocket.' The details of the lady's scandalous behaviour which led to a divorce have been lost.

Fanny hardly needed to be reminded on 11 May: 'It is three years this day that I sailed from Spithead.' Nelson must have realised later that month just how long the time had seemed to Fanny, for when he thanked her for her affectionate letter of 24 April, he wrote: 'I hope your patience will yet hold out.' Her letter had been full of family news, some of which had made him laugh. His brother William, the Rector, had made a long tour that had included Bath where he was able to visit his father and sister-in-law. The Rector, who had always taken himself seriously, was becoming worse and in his pursuit of promotion within the church had lately adopted the fashion for wearing gaiters. Fanny's description of him had amused Nelson greatly. But he was annoyed with other members of his family who, he believed, had taken advantage of Fanny's good nature. That involved Dolly Jaccombe who had once been a maid in Edmund's household but had moved on to the Matchams. When later Dolly had fallen ill and was unable to return to her home to be nursed, the Matchams had sent her to Bath to be looked after by Fanny and Edmund. Not literally perhaps, but they would have had to bear the expense of her keep and nursing care. Nelson accused the Matchams of being entirely selfish in that matter and others. He also could not understand why his sister had not written to him in the past three years: 'It is true I have not wrote but my sister can have little to do compared to me…'

Fashionable people did not stay in Bath during the summer months so Fanny went on a visit first during May to Kentish Town to see if she might be of help to Mr Suckling who had been ill, and then in late June to Lyme Regis in Dorset to take advantage of the sea bathing and sea air. It is not known if Edmund accompanied her there or if he returned to Norfolk for a time. Neither is it known how long she stayed or if she was with a party of friends. Nelson was not sure of her movements either during this time so when he wrote to tell her that he was sending a present for her via an officer coming on leave, he had given instructions that it should be sent to a Mr Thomas's in The Strand to await her directions. In an effort to beat import duties he had told his emissary to disperse the items into several small parcels and send them individually. One contained gentlemen's black silk stockings intended for Edmund but, he told her, if his father did not wish to keep them all then he could give two pairs to his brother Suckling. Another parcel had hams and tongues in it. These Fanny was advised not to keep until he returned in case they went off. Presents, however, were not what Fanny wanted. Her patience was being sorely tried and as often happened to her in the height of the summer her spirits sank and she became depressed for a while. Nelson tried to cheer her with the prospect of his being home to eat Christmas Dinner with her and Edmund.

The promise of coming home in the spring, the summer, in the fall or in time for Christmas had become like a mirage, always there in the distance but never to be attained. He gave yet another protestation of his devotion:

> Assure yourself, my dear Fanny, that my sincere love and affection is by no means weakened. As to coming home, who can say what tomorrow may bring forth. A few days past I wrote you it was probable we should all dine in England. Now that prospect is thrown a little forwarder. It is said we are offering to make peace.

Reminding her that a naval officer's duty was to go wherever he was sent, he played a trump card by indicating that should his squadron be withdrawn from the Mediterranean then it stood the chance of being sent out to the West Indies. She knew, only too well, that the climate there did not suit him and this time might prove fatal.

By December and back in Bath where she and Edmund had been since October, there was still no sign that he would be home for Christmas but Nelson was then encouraging Fanny to take positive steps to look for a permanent home for them. However, as always money was the problem and she was urged not to look at houses that were too expensive. She had the power to call on his agents for a statement of how much was available to spend; by now he had become resigned to not counting on the legacy to assist them in the purchase. In the news from home Fanny had told him about his brother Suckling who, although now a clergyman and acting as his father's curate at Burnham Thorpe, had not entirely given up his old ways. There were times when Nelson despaired of his brothers.

> Poor Suckling will drink, he is too late to reform in that respect and we must make the best of it. I wish he could get a living of £100 a year but that I own I see no prospect of. As to his expenses, my father cannot nor ought not to go too far.

Fanny had already heard much of this from Edmund who was very concerned for his son. He had thought when he had financed Suckling through his years at Cambridge that that would be an end to his problems, as it was, he was now paying him to be his curate as well as supplying him with a home to live in. It was too much to have to settle his debts too. Nelson's views on drinking were almost as strong as those on extra-marital affairs. 'As to wine he nor those of much larger incomes can afford to drink it and a man can live very happy without sight of it.' As with many other things, the time would come when Nelson would change his opinion.

Christmas passed and 1797 began. Nelson's squadron moved out of the Mediterranean and into the Atlantic off the coast of Spain where he managed to capture a number of ships that would prove valuable prizes. On St Valentine's Day he was engaged in the highly successful battle off Cape St Vincent. He sent home to Fanny a copy of his official report on his part in the battle enclosed in a short note written on 16 February which told her: 'I am mostly perfectly well and rich in honour.' By the beginning of March her letters of December and January that had been sent to Gibraltar and then to Lisbon finally reached him. As for those written in February through to June, they have survived, so Fanny may again speak for herself.

CHAPTER VI

Settled in Bath

Yours of the 18 December I have received. I can only say God bless you.
Nelson, 13 February 1797

If the sequence of letters from Fanny that starts in early February 1797 is indicative of those written in the two years preceding, then Nelson had been kept well supplied with information on any number of topics. What is apparent is that in the two years since her own voice had been heard, Fanny had changed. It may be simply that she was now two years older; that at 36 she was approaching middle age. But there seems more to it than that; she had become more assured, more capable of dealing with difficulties whatever they were. This should not come as a surprise, because had she not learned to cope with whatever everyday problems had come her way she would have buckled under the weight of them. She had learned too to live with disappointment; it is hard to imagine what it must have been like for her to have her hopes of her husband's return raised and then dashed when month after month, year after year he remained at sea. Inevitably, the only way she could survive this long period of separation was to make a life for herself. Nonetheless, however busy about the home or socially active she was, she could not disguise the fact that she missed his physical presence dreadfully as that letter of 8 February told him: 'I long for to be with you.'

She was unable to stop her anxiety at not having heard from him bubbling to the surface. From newspapers and general conversation she was aware that he was probably involved in fighting the Spanish. She had tried to maintain patience and wait until a letter came from him but finally, she had given in and written to her old friend Lord Hood to ask if he had any inside information. This had resulted in her receiving a copy of Admiral Young's letter which told her that Nelson was indeed safe but that she must not expect to hear from him for a bit. Lord Hood thought highly enough of Fanny's character and integrity to trust her to keep secret some of the naval information he had passed on to her. Had she been known to be a gossip or a woman of limited intelligence, he certainly would not have confided in her.

Once she had been reassured, she was able to congratulate her husband on his great successes. Then it was time to tell him what was happening at home. Uppermost in her mind was Edmund's health. What Fanny described as cold and fever, probably influenza, had been widespread but Edmund's attack must have been very severe for she told Nelson that she had never before seen him so ill. She gave only sketchy details but enough to give a brief glimpse of their domestic life. It would seem that Edmund had symptoms that had frightened Will, his manservant, so much that he had fetched Fanny during the night. Unfortunately, in doing so, it became clear the man had been drinking; in Fanny's version of the story he was 'dead drunk'. The shock, whether of Edmund's illness or Will's drunkenness had, she thought, given her a cold just when she had got over the last one. However, she assured Nelson that his father was now recovered and she had managed to get him out to take exercise.

Servants were proving to be a problem at that time. Apart from Will's drinking Fanny had to put up with a bad tempered and disgruntled maid. This was that same Bett Thurlow who some years before had been sent home suffering from suspected tuberculosis. Whether or not her sister had taken her place was never mentioned but Bett had returned to Fanny in October 1795. It had not been the smoothest of relationships: 'Bett Thurlow who has long thought Bath did not agree with her left me in the midst of it [Edmund's illness] and without my having a servant. I am better without her, she was dissatisfied and never contented and a most wretched temper.' Having said she was better off without the girl, Fanny was then faced with finding a replacement, not an easy task in Bath where:

> The characters of servants …is I am sorry to say very bad and of the two evils I preferred her, knowing her temper and only wished her to stay till we returned into Norfolk or my dear husband was in England.

Fanny eventually settled for a 'nice young woman …from Torbay' who did not mind the prospect of travelling with her employer.

Turning from the purely domestic Fanny had several other pieces of family news to impart. The Matchams had put their Hampshire home up for sale and were thinking of buying somewhere close to Bath. Edmund, who thought his son-in-law something of a dilettante, was of the opinion that he would quickly tire of that location as he had done others. All the Bolton family were well but brother Suckling was back to his old ways gambling as well as drinking according to his brother Maurice. Fanny decided it would be best to keep that piece of information away from Edmund so as not to make him even more worried about him than he already was. Of all the brothers, Maurice was the one of whom Fanny was most fond. They corresponded regularly and their mutual regard grew with time.

Maurice had neither the pretentious ambition of the Rector nor the vices of Suckling.

Another cause of Fanny's more confident approach to life was that her social circle had widened considerably. Apart from public functions, she had extended the number of acquaintances on whom she could call or who would visit her. In a lively letter dated 15 February she gives a glimpse of how ladies brought together by the common bond of husbands or sons serving in the Army or Navy exchanged the latest news that their letters contained. Her new friend, Mrs Twigge had received: 'a very cheerful witty letter' from her husband, the General, which reported a conversation he had had with Nelson. Apparently Nelson had thought the other looked too old to have a mother still living. Fanny teased Nelson by recounting that the General, who was an astute man, had said of him: '…you are a most excellent commander but no courtier.' Also present at this gathering had been the General's brother, Capt. Twigge, who had assured Fanny that the General was a very good looking man. Had Nelson been inclined to jealousy he might have noticed that Capt. Twigge's name cropped up later in her letter as having been present at a dinner party given by Admiral Dickson. While Edmund had been so ill she had not liked to leave him alone in the evening, but when he felt better he had insisted she go to what turned out to be quite an intimate affair; only two tables set up for cards and no one leaving before supper was served. Fanny had talked for some time with Capt.Twigge. She told Nelson she had asked if he had any up to date news of the action at sea but she did not relate to her husband if there had been any further conversation between them.

From such idle talk Fanny then turned to the question that was engaging most of the population at that time, namely would the French try to invade? She herself appeared quite unruffled by the idea, as apparently were most people. The French might be foolish enough to try but everyone agreed they would be unsuccessful. At least that was the opinion in Bath. However, of interest to Nelson were the eastern counties and so Fanny reported that Norfolk and Suffolk were preparing to have men in camp there by the spring ready to repulse any invasion attempt along that coast. Fanny was more concerned with the human misery that the invasion scare was causing individuals, many of whom were selling up their homes and estates, just in case. From this concern she passed on to a subject very close to her heart and one that made her quite angry with the government of the day:

> The accounts from all parts of the West Indies are truly afflicting. The deaths of the unfortunate men who are sent out there are not noticed. Government suppresses the accounts reaching the public as much as possible.

In her eyes not only had the government much to answer for, even worse were those who were profiteering from the misfortunes of war, specifically those in what we would now term the pharmaceutical industry.

> I think the contractors for medicines have much to answer. Mr Searle called on our father and said he was intimately acquainted with one of the Directors of Apothecaries Hall, and that day the directors had received an order to pack up fourteen thousand pounds (£14,000) worth of medicine for the West Indies. The bark [of the cinchona tree from which quinine was produced] which had been sent out had grown in this country, and even the James's powders were so adulterated that no quantity remained. I think their act is truly wicked.

Fanny could not believe that such contractors could possibly be Englishmen. In her opinion they must be French: '...for they do not allow there is a Supreme Being.'

Light hearted or angry, Fanny was unable to hide in the latter part of her letter her great longing for Nelson. Poetically she told him: 'The sunshine I want must come from the Mediterranean' and then she let him know without a doubt that her longing was a strongly physical one. She referred to suppressing her own needs while he has been away: 'A feeling temper was certainly a great inconvenience' but they will certainly make up for it: '...what will be the pleasure when I see my dear husband.' She ends with a prayer: 'God bless and protect my dearest,' before closing with her usual, 'your affectionate wife'.

Then came the big news. Fanny had been taking her usual morning walk in the centre of Bath when a gentleman of her acquaintance, Capt. Frame, who was sitting in the Coffee House reading the newspaper looked up and saw her pass. Normally this captain's behaviour was excessively polite so Fanny was a little taken aback when he almost ran down the street from the Coffee House in pursuit of her. Had she seen the paper or indeed had she heard the news? Her husband had been promoted to the rank of Rear Admiral. Fanny could hardly wait to tell Edmund who, according to Fanny, became more elated than she had ever seen him. Over and over Edmund retold the story of how when the young Nelson first went to sea, his brother-in-law, Capt. Maurice Suckling, had told him that he would live to see his son become an admiral. Naturally, Fanny too was full of congratulations on her husband's success and she tactfully let him think that his promotion had had an immediate effect on her status.

One of the highlights of the Bath social calendar was the Ladies' Night given by the members of the Catch Club. There was always a scramble for tickets for this event, as much as twenty guineas being offered for one, so, much as Fanny wanted to go she feared there was little chance she would secure a precious ticket. But, sensible woman, she used one of her West Indian contacts, Sir Thomas Shirley, to see what he could do on her behalf. He said he would try but when it had reached almost ten o'clock on the night in question, she had resigned herself to not going to the concert. Then, there was Sir Thomas's servant at her front door with a ticket. What was she to do? Edmund had settled the question for her; she must go. So she dressed in her best and away she went laughing to Edmund as she left: 'The Admiral's wife has got a ticket.' She knew her husband, as much as her father-in-law, would appreciate the credit she had given to him.

There was even more exciting news for her to impart in this letter of 23 February. At long last some money had been released from Herbert's legacy. Fanny had written to Mr Baillie asking for explanations about the delay in payments. Although Nelson had said he would write and deal with the matter, it appears that Fanny's letter had been sufficiently strong and business-like for Baillie to take immediate notice of it. Within a week he had brought her £450. There were still some matters concerning the legacy to be settled but at least she had something. Ever practical, she had thought of sending part of the sum she had received to Nelson's agents to bank for the future, but the climate of opinion in Bath was that with the fear of invasion it was better to keep one's cash to hand.

Although she received news from other people the last letter Fanny had from Nelson had been sent from Gibraltar on 14 December. She carried this around with her in her pocket and had read it so often it had become almost worn out. Despite the lack of letters from him, she continued to write regularly, often with additional ones penned on the spur of the moment when the wife of an important admiral or general was sending mail. Finally on 10 March Fanny received the very brief letter Nelson had written on 16 February telling her that he and Josiah were safe and well – and rich in honour. When she wrote the following day she told him just how much she had worried about him at that time but paid tribute to the great kindness she had received from his brother Maurice and Capt.Locker who had written immediately to reassure her that the press reports that he had been wounded were not true. Nelson must have been delighted when she told him he was:

> universally the subject of conversation... Lord, Lady and Lady Mary Howe amongst others sent to know how you were...The letters that I have had from common acquaintances will take me at least a week to answer them.

This was added to such remarks as Lady Saumarez had quoted from her admiral husband's letter: 'Com.Nelson's conduct was above praise.' Some years later an observer wrote that Nelson snuffed up the incense of praise that Lady Hamilton puffed up for him. Fanny had been quite adept at the process herself. She quoted from a letter she had received from Mr Sutherland: 'I have this instant heard of Sir J Jervis's battle in which Admiral Nelson bore a most conspicuous part, as he has in every service he was engaged in.' And if that was not enough praise for him, she then added that of Lord Hood who had asked that she would send him whatever details of the battle Nelson sent to her.

Fanny was amused by the attention she received as a result of her husband's valour. She related how on the day after she had received Nelson's letter she went to a morning concert given by Colonel Glover who had some time before sailed with his regiment on board Nelson's ship the *Agamemnon*. On her arrival at the concert Baron Dillon, an Irish Member of Parliament, who also held the title of free baron of the Holy Roman Empire, had greeted her effusively. According to Fanny:

> I thought Baron Dillon would have kissed me he said 'Madam, I have seen you at Mr Glass's therefore I will speak and sincerely do I wish you joy.' In short he announced who I was, they all made their bow…

Modestly Fanny went on: 'I was very glad when they had taken their seats and the misses taken their seats at the pianoforte.'

After discussing how well Edmund had withstood all the congratulations he had received on his son's behalf, Fanny went on to playfully chide Nelson about attempting to board ships during battle. He was not to tempt Providence further and reminding him of his new rank she begged that in future he would: 'Leave it for Captains.' Then in reflective mood she reminded him: 'Tomorrow is our wedding day, when it gave me a dear husband, and my child the best of fathers.' This remark has led to some confusion. It has always been assumed, and the marriage certificate corroborates it, that their wedding had taken place on 11 March, but if Fanny was correct when she wrote '11 March' on her letter then she celebrated on the 12th. Not that she would have celebrated; that would wait until he came home. She did not belabour the point, merely asking: 'Do come home this summer or in the autumn.'

When Nelson had written his fairly short letter from Lagos Bay on 22 February, he had included a long account of his part in the battle. Compared with the official report he sent to the Admiralty, this was a very personal description intended for the eyes of Fanny and Edmund and possibly a few close friends and relations. On board Nelson's ship were the officers and men of the 69th Regiment, among them a young Lieutenant Pierson. Nelson gave graphic details of how Pierson and his men along with Capt. Berry had boarded the Spanish ship. What must Fanny and Edmund have thought as they read: '…a soldier of the 69th regiment having broke the upper quarter gallery window jumped in followed by myself and others as fast as possible, I found the cabin doors fastened, and some Spanish officers fired their pistols…' For a woman of delicate nerves, this would have been too much, especially when there were bodies falling all around. But Fanny was made of sterner stuff. She read to the end: '…the Spanish captain with a bow presented me his sword and said the Admiral was dying of his wounds below…' and beyond to the little anecdotes Nelson had written which included a recipe for making an Olla Podrida. This began:

> Take a Spanish first rate and an 80 gunship and after well *battering* and *basting* them for an hour keep throwing in your *force balls* and be sure to let these be well *seasoned*. Your *fire* must never *slacken* for a moment, but

1. View of Nevis – Nicholas Pocock, 1790. © Bristol Museums and Art Gallery. Reproduced courtesy of Eickelmann & Small.

2. The old sugar mill in the grounds of the Montpelier Hotel, Nevis. © The author.

3. The memorial tablet to Fanny's first husband, Dr Josiah Nisbet, in the church of Stratford-sub-Castle, Salisbury, Wiltshire. Reproduced courtesy of A Henderson.

4. A miniature of Fanny painted by Daniel Orme. Ref. A0094 © National Maritime Museum, London – with special thanks to Lucy Waitt.

5. Capt Horatio Nelson, painted by John Francis Rigaud. Ref. BHC2901 ©
National Maritime Museum, London.

6. The church in the village of Fig Tree, Nevis where the Nelsons' marriage certificate is kept. © The author.

7. The lace overskirt which formed part of Fanny's wedding dress. Ref. D7648-1 © National Maritime Museum, London.

8. The Rectory, Burnham Thorpe, Norfolk by Francis Pocock. Ref. BHC1772 ©
National Maritime Museum, London.

9. The Revd Edmund Nelson
painted by Sir William
Beechey. Ref. BHC2881
© National Maritime Museum,
London.

10. Wolterton Hall, Norfolk, home of Lord and Lady Walpole. Reproduced courtesy of Lord and Lady Walpole.

11. The quay, Ipswich, Suffolk from an engraving by George Frost. Reproduced courtesy of the Suffolk Record Office.

12. The Rotunda, Ipswich, Suffolk from an engraving by George Frost. Reproduced courtesy of the Suffolk Record Office.

13. Burgess' London shop. Taken from a facsimile of an advertisement from 1788.

14. A black lace parasol lined with silk reputed to have belonged to Fanny. Reproduced courtesy of The Norfolk Nelson Museum, Great Yarmouth.

Sir
    I have received a letter from the
Post Office Exmouth Devonshire informing me that a letter directed to
The Viscountess Nelson has been
forwarded Sept 7th to the Post Office
Zurich Switzerland, Which letter I
request may be forwarded to me
at Dieppe
        I am
            your Humble Servant
        Frances H Nelson & Bronte

Hotel Roi d'Angleterre
Oct 8th 1822 –

15. A letter written by Fanny from Dieppe in 1822. © The Nelson Museum and Local History Centre, Monmouth.

16. The vault in Littleham churchyard, Exmouth, Devon where Fanny, her son and grandchildren are buried. © The author.

must be kept up as brisk as possible during the whole time so soon as you perceive your Spaniards to be well *stewed*...

and so it continued in culinary vein ending with the words 'Nelson his art of cooking Spaniards'.

Fanny not only read this account over a number of times, she also made at least one copy of it which she sent, at his request, to Lord Hood. She was not entirely sure whether she should have done so but Edmund had advised her that there could be no harm in it. Lord Hood in his comments said: 'The glorious share Adm. Nelson had in the action will immortalize his name in the pages of the history of England.' Furthermore, Fanny was able to tell Nelson that Lord Hood had shown the account in circles where it might prove to his advantage. What music that must have been to the ears of the man who longed to be a hero! As must have been the letter from Lord Walpole to Edmund telling him that nothing was talked of in London except *Nelson* [sic] and enclosing an extract from a letter from Capt. Collingwood to Sir Edward Blackett giving further plaudits. The list of correspondents grew while the little parlour at New King Street was daily filled with important people anxious to convey their congratulations to the great man's wife and father. General Tarleton's brother and his wife came as did Admiral Dickson and then came Governor Bruce and Mr Daniel the Attorney General from Dominique both of whom had known Nelson in his days of service in the West Indies. Governor Bruce had told her about his attendance at a recent Court Levee where he had spoken to Prince William who was loud in his praise of Nelson and his good sense.

As a postscript to this letter and perhaps as her answer to Nelson's Olla Podrida, she sent him:

Love apple catch up in necked narrow bottomed jars. Semolina a root of a tree grounded very good for puddings, orange flower water – citron port wine.

Perhaps there was some code in this message about tomato ketchup and semolina! On the other hand it did bring them both down to earth and continuing in the domestic vein we learn that Fanny was not averse to chatting with her maid. The young woman had lived in Lisbon as a maid to a wealthy merchant whose trade was in Portugal and she had told Fanny enough about the place for Fanny to write light heartedly to her husband '...I am willing that you should partake of the good things, I hear that place abounds with.'

Family matters were now occupying the minds of both Edmund and Fanny. She was able to report that much to their relief Maurice had been reinstated to his former position at the Navy Board at a salary of £300 a year. A little less enjoyable was the news that the Rector, who had written them a very affectionate letter, was threatening to make a visit to them as soon as Nelson arrived home. He was determined on this and to underline just what she thought about it, Fanny repeated the word 'determined'. Neither was she particularly enthusiastic about the Rector's invitation for her to spend the summer with him and his family at Hilborough. Edmund had talked of going back to Burnham but his movements were hampered by the fact that he had promised to accommodate his daughter, Mrs Bolton and her twin girls for six months. It was not made clear why, or where Mr Bolton was to be during this period but presumably their younger children were left in the care of servants. For part of the time the twins and their mother were to visit their aunt Matcham.

But all this was trivial in comparison with the depressing economic news that swept the country. Partly inspired by the fear of invasion, as Fanny had mentioned earlier, more and more people were withdrawing their cash deposits from the various small private banks which abounded throughout the country. This great demand for cash meant that many banks found themselves unable to honour the bank notes issued in their name. This led to the banks crashing with the subsequent great financial losses incurred by many. Fanny told Nelson about the situation and of its effects on people they knew:

> The Bury bank has stopped payment. Lord Cornwallis has lost thousands, Sir Charles Davis is a great sufferer. Mr Maynard who is here from Suffolk has lost five hundred, which he says is a serious inconvenience. The Cambridge bank is broke. Bridport bank totters, Bristol bank is not thought to stand very firm.

This last was of serious concern to Fanny:

> Mr Baillie gave me two bank notes of Bristol, each twenty pounds, I got rid of one as soon as I received it, the other stuck fast, I sent it to Mr Tobin last week and requested him to get a Bank of England note for me. I hope he will succeed, scarcity of money is very great.

Edmund considered that Fanny worried too much about such matters: 'Our father tells me the old women get hold of me and make me look grave.' Certainly, Fanny spent a great deal of her time with other women but they were not all, by any means, old. Fanny got on extremely well with most women; those who had their husbands with them, obviously did not see her as a threat, while others saw her as a kind confidante and amusing companion. She was often loud in her praise of her friends; of Mrs Napier she wrote: 'she is without exception one of the most charming women I have ever had the pleasure of knowing', and Miss Athill she called her great favourite. She told Nelson she had come to know a Mrs Rickets, the sister of Nelson's C-in-C, Sir John Jervis. She was a pleasant, well-bred woman in Fanny's opinion and her daughter Lady Northesk was equally pleasant. However, Fanny did not like the current fashion of speech which the ladies of quality had adopted of laughing or smiling at every word they said.

Having told Nelson about this new mode, she suddenly realised how much female fashion had changed in the years he had been away:

> Now our waists are lengthened, heads dressed *flat* at the *sides*, very high in front and low upon the forehead, short sleeves, some ladies showing their elbows, short petticoats, nay above the ankle with the fashionable, and little or no heels to the shoes. Gloves almost beyond the pocket of anyone, none but the long ones are of use. None less than 3/- a pair. Coloured and white the same price.

The woman who could write about the trivia of fashion, who sometimes felt that her letters were full of nothing, could, just occasionally, write passionately of her feelings as she did on 10 April when she had received a particularly loving letter from Nelson. She was almost overcome that he had said how much pleasure he gained from hearing from her and his loving concern for her health was like a healing balm. 'The heartfelt satisfaction at your expression of returning to me "laughing-back", gives me a pleasure, a something which I am certain none can feel but those who are sincerely attached to a husband.' Fanny was not only astute in many of her judgements at a practical level but she also had an acute understanding of what love involved: 'They are fine feelings but exquisitely painful.' However, she could not fill up her letters that cost one shilling and eight pence for postage each time with emotional outpouring, her husband needed to be kept informed as to what was happening within the family. Most of this revolved around plans for the summer. Edmund had announced that he would not, after all, go back to Norfolk but would instead accompany Fanny to Clifton. Ever amenable, Fanny fell in with his ideas even though she had not intended to go to Clifton that year:

> but indeed a little country air will do me good. Bath is so hot in the summer and so stinking that very few remain in it. I have often been told this situation was too low. It is very near the river, but when I considered, after making enquiries as to the rent of houses in good situations and found the rent differed so materially I was determined to remain… This house £90 a year: Gay St. £160, the higher you go the dearer.

While she was writing this letter Fanny received one from her old friend, Mrs Pinney, inviting her to Bristol for the Sheriff's ball, a grand occasion at any time but that year of particular importance as one of the Pinneys was about to take on that office. Fanny told Nelson she would decline the invitation, as she did not like being in overcrowded rooms. She also confessed then that she had of recent months become much quieter than he had ever known her; Edmund, she said, teased her that he had more spirit than she had. Fanny may not have been feeling well at the time of writing but her social engagements of the previous few weeks certainly do not give the impression that she was leading a secluded life. Her remark: 'I mean to grow quite gay when I see my dearest husband and Josiah' was merely her way of reassuring her husband that without him she could not sparkle as she had done previously. That suggests that he had thought of her as bright and lively before he went to sea. In which case that refutes the argument of those who would have us believe that in the six years they lived ashore in Norfolk, Fanny had developed into a whining hypochondriac.

Edmund wavered yet again about where he would spend the summer. Mrs Bolton having decided she would not come to Bath after all that year, Edmund had no reason to stay, so he dithered between going to Norfolk or accompanying Fanny to Clifton. She confided to Nelson that he had changed his plans many times but she was trying hard to keep him to the Clifton plan as she was concerned that he would find the long journey into Norfolk too strenuous, especially as he still suffered from a violent cough and cold. So she would go to Bristol for a few days and while there she would look for suitable accommodation in Clifton, preferably a small house or rooms in a house where they would be the only lodgers. Edmund had heard very good reports of the efficacy of a newly discovered spring at Clifton that was thought to be as good as the old one and so he had set his heart on trying it.

Over-cautious about his own health, Edmund was given to magnifying any little ailment Fanny might have and although she had had a cold and had been a bit miserable as one often is with a cold, her letter of 17 April was a mixture of sensible remarks about looking for property and light-hearted banter about the latest Bath gossip. It was another of those instances when the contents of a private letter, in this case to the Ansteys, had become public knowledge. It concerned what Sir John Jervis, Nelson's C-in-C had said in a letter to the Admiralty about one of his fellow officers. When she had told Nelson what the letter was purported to have said, she laughingly backed up its veracity: 'I give you word for word. It was first told me by his cousin Western and this day my hairdresser told it me.' This intimate disclosure is followed by another tiny glimpse into the domestic life of Fanny and Edmund, namely that they have the parrot Poll, or as Fanny called her on this occasion, Polly, with them which conjures up a delightful picture of the bird's cage forming part of their luggage when they travelled to Bath. Fanny told Nelson that the bird was well and talking. No doubt its main vocabulary provided by Fanny and Edmund would have centred on Nelson. At that time they were in all probability trying to teach it to say 'Admiral'.

Bristol was hardly the best place for getting away from talk of the economy but they did also talk of Nelson which made Fanny proud and pleased for his sake that he was finally getting the recognition he deserved. While she gladly accepted all the praise that was heaped upon him, she could not resist poking fun at some of it as she did after the visit to her old friends, the Pinneys: 'Mrs Pinney declares Mr P. talked in his sleep of you.' By this time Fanny had experienced so much in the way of congratulation that she had learned to distinguish what was genuine. In this category she placed that of Mr Pinney whose: '…heart was so full when he saw me, that he could not speak, his congratulations were pleasant they were from his heart.'

During that week in Bristol spent at the home of James Tobin in Berkeley Square, Fanny also learnt what was going on in Nevis as regards the settlement of her uncle's estate. As in all families, disagreements had broken out between the cousins Martha Hamilton and Magnus Morton over the entail of the estate which Martha, or her husband and solicitors, had endeavoured to break by buying off Morton. It all became very involved with who said what to whom and as far as Fanny was concerned: '…as experience has taught me not to believe one half of what I heard I gave little credit.' Fanny felt herself sufficiently removed from the in-fighting of her cousins to take any part in it but she was delighted to hear that Morton expected to ship four hundred hogsheads of sugar to England that year, the sale of which was expected to raise enough to pay off all the estate debts and finally, the legacies. Fanny regretted that the money that would have been so helpful to Nelson had been so long coming. Fanny never appeared envious of those who possessed great wealth; her experience of life had shown her that it did not necessarily bring happiness, but with a generosity of spirit she wished well to those who had large fortunes, hoping they would live to enjoy it and be as happy as they thought the money would make them.

Fanny imparted all the news from Bristol on her return to Bath on 2 May. Awaiting her was the letter her husband had written on 3 April. This had had a profound effect on her: 'We are generally open to flattery and your telling me "my heart is entirely with you" is too pleasing not to notice it, particularly as I feel every affectionate and sincere attachment for my dear husband.' She had obviously read the letter through many times before she sat down to answer it and that may account for why she copied his date on her letter, writing 3 April instead of 3 May thus inadvertently causing Nelson scholars to place this letter out of sequence. In her next one she told of how happy Edmund had been, shedding tears of joy, when they heard that Nelson had been presented with the freedom of Norwich on the same day as Prince Henry of Gloucester.

But Fanny was not obsessed purely with news of her husband. She took a wider view and some of her remarks on current politics showed that she not only listened carefully but she also understood the conversations to which she was a party. The names she mentions were important political figures. 'Mr Burke is still here. He tells Mr Tarleton that Mr Windham's abilities are great that he had for some time back disapproved of measure and that Mr W. knew it and that Mr W had for some time back been in the minority in the Council, that if other measures are not pursued our finances are ruined.' Burke was the Edmund Burke who had been a major force in English politics but was now not far off death; in her account Fanny observed that he looked very ill. General Sir Banastre Tarleton had fought in the American wars before entering Parliament to represent Liverpool, while William

Windham, a great friend of Burke's was MP for Norwich and had held office as Secretary for War since 1794. Having looked at the wider picture, Fanny remarked on the fact that the Government had introduced even more taxes to help pay for the war. The one that was causing most outrage among the public was the turnpike tax. Travellers expected to pay the toll for using the privately owned gated roads but resented the additional levy placed on this charge by a Government that had earned itself the title of 'Public Robber'. Much of the rest of her news was Norfolk related including the slight iciness there had been when the Revd Mr Hoste had called upon them one evening. Fanny had written to him earlier on Nelson's behalf to remind him that he had not settled his account for his son's keep at sea. Although he made pretty remarks about Nelson's success, Fanny, the perfect hostess, sensed that he was a little ill at ease so: 'I was very polite and took care not to be a bit stiff' and invited him to take tea with her and Edmund.

One of Fanny's strengths, or perhaps it was a weakness, was her ability to empathise with others but her sympathy was not reserved just for those she knew. Nor did she follow the belief that those who strayed from the path of strict morality should necessarily be punished. For no other reason than that her heart had been touched, she wrote to Nelson about the case of the estranged wife of Lord Derby. What she found so very sad was that when the lady died, no one was prepared to take responsibility for her burial. Her husband refused point blank to have anything to do with the matter and her brother, the Duke of Hamilton, initially did the same. However after the body had lain neglected for some days, he eventually relented: '... a spark of natural feeling being left...She was still his sister, let her conduct been ever so bad.' Lady Derby may have succumbed to the temptations of the flesh but that Fanny could forgive. But despite her early reputation of being able to mix with everyone, Fanny could not tolerate those, usually women, who gave themselves airs. One such who came in for harsh criticism was Lady Elliott whom Nelson had met in Corsica where her husband had been Viceroy. Nelson had told Fanny that on her return to England, Lady Elliott would be visiting Bath and had suggested that Fanny should call on her. Fanny had done so but she had not liked the lady at all.

> The day I returned her visit I thought she received me as if I was honoured. I told our father on my return that Lady E. had forgotten she was not the person she was at Corsica, however she is mistaken, it is not in her power by her acquaintance to honour your wife.

As Nelson had been quite impressed by the lady, he probably was not pleased that his wife had adopted this attitude especially when she had also told him that she had heard that Lady Elliott had not been at all popular in Corsica because of her failure to mix with the local population.

By the end of May most of the notables had left Bath but one newcomer had recently brought much delight to Fanny and Edmund. Captain Berry, who had served with Nelson before he was given his own ship, had called on them to give them all the news he could of Nelson and Josiah too, for the boy had served with Berry to gain additional experience before he was promoted to lieutenant. Berry was a favourite of Fanny, she had recommended him to Nelson and her trust in him had been well founded. Fanny's excitement at the young man's visit shone through her description to Nelson. 'He dined with us and was not out of my sight [except] when he went to dress for dinner, still I had more questions to ask, was sorry when he took his leave.' Berry had answered all he could, telling her little details about Josiah such as his eyes being darker than she remembered. He had also looked at the miniature of Nelson which she wore but he had declared it looked nothing like the man he knew. This had the effect of underlining the fact that in the four years he had been away her husband too had changed. She hoped that when Nelson came home, which their visitor had indicated would be soon, he might have another portrait done for her. Not only did Berry bring them intimate and up-to-date information, he had also brought gifts. From Nelson himself there were two paintings, sea-scapes which she had put up on the wall in her own little sitting room so that she could often gaze at them. Capt. Fremantle's new wife Betsey had sent her a silk handkerchief and: 'a bunch of Roman pearls.' Honest Fanny relayed to her husband what she had found out about these pearls: 'I thought [they] had been real and I took them to a jeweller to have them dressed, they were composed of rice, therefore they were not to be touched.' But she was not unduly upset: 'They look well in bandeaux round the head which is now the fashion.' Capt. Berry had also brought a gift for her, a pretty workbag in which to keep her sewing. She had been unsure of the propriety of accepting it but once he had assured her it was not expensive she had been happy to do so.

Berry's visit was so important to her that it took precedence over the news that she had read in the official *Gazette* on 27 May, namely that Nelson had been knighted. While proud for him, believing it was his due for which he had long toiled, she felt he deserved more from his country. As for her, tongue in cheek, she said her new form of address sat as easily as if she was born to it. She was going to enjoy being Lady Nelson. She would have had several letters from various sources with the new inscription but Nelson did not use it until 15 June by which time he had received three of Fanny's letters written in May. In a previous one he told her that he bought a gown for her and some sashes as well as more paintings. He did not say so, but they must both have seen the acquisition of paintings as being the start of the furnishing of their future home, the purchase of which was occupying both their thoughts. It may have been in response to Fanny's mention that she had bought a printed copy of the account of the battle of 14 February that led him to send her the last three verses of a poem about him. He had already copied out for her a piece of laudatory praise which he had found dropped on the quarter deck of his ship but he was confident that she and his father would appreciate both pieces. This composed by 'an old sailor' ended:

True British valour has appalled / The proud insulting foe
What late was Nelson's Olio called / Has laid the Dons full low.
This hero brave old England's boast / Grappled two ships along
Forced them to strike on their own coast / And lasting laurels won.
Long will this fact in history shine / Give me the fair sex say
A Nelson for my valentine / On the auspicious day.

When Nelson wrote on 29 June he referred to the most recent letters he had received from her, one exactly one month earlier and the other written on 5 June. That one is no longer extant but must have contained some of her deepest longings and fears: 'Rest assured my dear Fanny, of my most perfect love affection and esteem for your person and character, which the more I see of the world the more I must admire.' It was, he said, only his honourable desire to serve his country that kept him from her, that plus the hope that he might take more prizes that would give them the chance for a few more luxuries. 'I pray God it may soon be peace and that we may get into the cottage. Nothing but a thorough conviction that I should do wrong (which you would not I am sure wish me to do) shall induce me to stay here beyond 1 October.' This was the date he was now holding out for. Dare she believe him or was she again destined for disappointment?

Fanny wrote the last extant letter in this sequence on 19 June. In it she excused herself for having so little to comment upon, as she had not had the great pleasure of hearing from him. Instead she filled her page with family news. It was clear that her brother-in-law George Matcham had upset Edmund and this in turn made life difficult for Fanny. Matcham, despite being told earlier by Edmund that house rents in Bath were very high as was the general cost of living, had nevertheless come looking for himself. Finding that what he had been told was true, he thought he might accept the offer Edmund had made to let them have the house in which he and Fanny lived. The Rector's wife decided to have her say on the subject too and told Kitty Matcham that Edmund and Fanny would move out so that she could be installed in New King Street before her next lying-in in September. Quite where Edmund and Fanny would go depended on whether or not Nelson had arrived home by then.

Not dwelling too much on that subject, she gave other news. All the Matcham children, apart from one had what she described as 'scorbutic humour', a form of vitamin deficiency that brought them out in spots, but apart from that they had good health. Although pregnant yet again, Kitty Matcham remained well – or at least, so her husband said. From the prospect of a birth, Fanny moved to its forerunner, an announcement of an engagement to marry. Lieutenant Pierson, who had been with Nelson in the battle on St Valentine's Day, had proposed to Mary Ann the daughter of the Revd William Bolton, a brother of Edmund's Norfolk son-in-law. Mentioning Thomas, Fanny said she was pleased to hear how well things were going for him and she was sure that Nelson would feel the same way. This may have been a veiled reference to the fact that Nelson had earlier sent home a sum of money to be distributed amongst his relations. Bolton often found it difficult to make ends meet and Edmund, who always discussed these things with Fanny, was convinced that in his latest move he had taken on a farm far too large for him to manage. Alternatively Fanny may have been suggesting that if Bolton's crops were abundant that was a good sign generally which might lead to a fall in the cost of living. She had heard, she said, from a number of people how cheap everything was in Paris compared with England; meat as low as 2d for half a pound and bread a mere 1½ d a loaf. Half in fun she remarked that if that really was the case, then by the time Nelson came home there would hardly be anyone left in England.

The rest of the letter was taken up with all the callers they had had and how the conversation had always revolved around Nelson; one had talked of him as 'our Norfolk hero' while another's 'mode of speaking of you was couched in the handsomest manner.' In between these items and the news that when the Bolton twins and their mother had stayed in London with brother Maurice, he had taught Susanna music, probably the basics of playing the piano, and talked French with the girls, Fanny was fighting off giving way to her anxiety that she had not heard from Nelson. She excused her feelings by saying that it was nearing the time when he had originally thought he would be on his way home. She was in fact bracing herself for this being delayed again. She said: 'I can't write you a cheerful letter because I have not had a letter from you.' That sentence is another of those quoted by her critics to show her despondent nature, yet the letter, taken as a whole, is a brave attempt to present an interesting, informative and often humorous narrative.

When he did write, Nelson did his best to reassure her he was safe: 'I fancy you may rely that I shall bring my head back.' While teasing her, at the same time he expected that by that time she would have already bought a house for them. His lackadaisical attitude to so important a purchase was quite different to how he would have approached anything to do with a ship. 'I do not see the necessity of your taking the trouble of seeing it. We must rely on some person's judgement.' Taking lodgings for a short time without first viewing them is one thing but to buy a house unseen is altogether different. But perhaps Nelson's attitude was that it did not really matter what it was like as long as they were together. So, having chivvied Fanny into getting on with the house buying, he then gave her another commission, to find a suitable supplier of blankets because, with her approval, that was what he intended his Christmas gift to the poor of Burnham to be that year. Having taken it for granted that she would approve, he then gave his instructions. He had obviously done his homework as he told her he thought the supplier was at Frome in Somerset. From there she was to order fifty large blankets of the best quality, each of which was to have the letter N woven in its centre. That, he said would ensure that they would be instantly recognisable and therefore the recipients would be unable to sell them. Little did he under-stand the workings of the human mind and no doubt, even when the blan-kets had passed the seven years of wear he thought they might have, they would have become valuable relics after his death.

On 4 July he sent her the briefest of notes that told her all she really wanted to know: 'My Dearest Fanny…I am most perfectly well and ever believe me my dearest love, your most affectionate Horatio Nelson'. By the 12th he was explaining that when he was sent off on detachment from the fleet he was not always able to find a way of getting his letters to her but that did not mean he had not written. She would in time receive them all. 'Never fancy for a moment you are absent from my thoughts or that I neglect writ-ing.' He then commented on the news Fanny had written on 19 June.

> You surprise me about Lt Pierson I never heard a syllable about it. However they know their own concerns best but I should not have approved of him as a son-in-law, although I believe him to be a very good young man, but I don't think he will make a pleasant husband. He is too nice [fastidious] in his dress and fidgety and has not the knack of being contented with his situation.

Thus was Nelson's assessment of the young man and as if to back up his case, he quoted Josiah's opinion. 'He does not believe Mr P will marry anyone who has not a great deal of money and he believes Mr P will turn merchant.' Fanny would make up her own mind when she got to know Pierson better in the future.

As a tailpiece to that letter and in the next he told her he was going on a little cruise and she must not worry if she did not hear from him. At the same time he sent her a list of the prize money due to him with the names of the agents in London who were holding the money. It was not expected to amount to more than £800 but he wanted her to collect it as soon as pos-sible. What he did not tell her, though perhaps she understood from 'a little cruise', was that an attack was planned on Tenerife with the object of cap-turing Spanish treasure ships. She would eventually read in the newspapers all about the lack of success of the venture and the varying reports of her husband's injuries. He made light of these when he wrote on 5 August:

> I am so confident of your affection that I feel the pleasure you will receive will be equal whether my letter is wrote by my right hand or left, it was the chance of war and I have great reason to be thankful, and I know it will add much to your pleasure in finding that Josiah under God's providence was principally instrumental in saving my life.

Nelson had promised he would be home in October but fate brought him back to Spithead on 1 September and as he had said in his letters of 5 and 16 August: ' [I] shall be with you perhaps as soon as this letter' and 'The cottage is now more necessary than ever.'

CHAPTER VII

Search for a Home

Happy, happy shall I be to return to a little but neat cottage.
Nelson, 1795

It was during his first year back at sea that Nelson realised that he and Fanny needed somewhere permanent that they could truly call home. When he had hoisted his flag in January 1793 he seemed quite happy she should make her home wherever she felt inclined, leaving her free to come and stay in whichever English port he found himself. The drawback to this peripatetic lifestyle she adopted meant that often her husband was not sure where she was. 'I wish much to hear you are fixed at some place to your satisfaction,' he wrote on 20 August 1793. While in late September he bemoaned, ' 'Tis a sad thing not to know where to direct [letters] to you.' His concern was sufficient that a month later he confided in a letter to a family member who had commented on Fanny's health: 'I cannot but feel uneasy at the accounts you give me of Mrs Nelson. I wish she was comfortably set-tled in a house or good lodgings, in a place she liked.'

By November of that year when Fanny had returned briefly to the lodg-ings in Swaffham, it is possible that in one of her letters, no longer extant, she too mentioned the idea of having a fixed base. Her heart must have sunk when she read Nelson's reply. 'I assure you it cannot give you more pleasure than it will me, for us to be settled again at Burnham and I sincerely hope our father will not part with the house to any one so as to prevent our get-ting into it again.' Having endured five years of bitter winters at the parson-age and being only too well acquainted with the drawbacks of the old house and the money needed to make it truly comfortable, this was probably the last place she wanted to settle. Wisely, the topic was dropped in favour of her going to join her father-in-law in Bath where they would share a house to their mutual benefit. Perhaps relieved that he need not worry for a bit, Nelson wrote on 27 December: 'As you desire my opinion about Bath…. I have only to *order* that you do what you like and give you full power, to give my assent to your own wishes – that is settled.' So she and Edmund had taken a long lease on the house in Bath and it had become a matter of expectation that when Nelson came home he would join them there unless she had managed to find them a permanent home elsewhere. Edmund and she discussed where this might be, and on 17 December Fanny said that he had found just the place for them advertised in the Norfolk newspapers which Fanny was in the habit of reading aloud to him. The old gentleman was not serious of course, a house with three hundred acres near Cromer was not at all what Nelson had in mind, or indeed could afford.

However, the thought of the two of them in their own rural retreat had not faded from Nelson's thoughts and when answering a letter from Fanny in which she had told him she was practising hard with her music, he expressed the hope of 'hearing you play on the pianoforte when we are snug at Burnham.' By the autumn he had realised that his old home might not be available when it suited him; they might have to look farther afield, that in fact they might have to buy 'some snug cottage whenever we may be obliged to quit the Parsonage.' This was a theme he returned to in October: 'Before spring I hope we shall have peace when we must look out for some little cottage. I shall return to the plough with redoubled glee I assure you.' Did Fanny allow herself a wry smile at this, as she recalled how 'following the plough' had palled in the past? Nevertheless, the idea of returning to a life ashore was taking a stronger hold on Nelson. It was only the lack of sufficient money upon which to live that was holding him back, so:

> ...much as I shall regret being so long parted from you, still we must look beyond the present day, and two or three months may have the difference of every comfort or otherwise in our income. I hope we have many happy years to live together and if we can bring £2000 round I am determined to purchase some neat cottage where we shall never have occasion to change.

That was in January 1795. Two or three months passed and it was May before he returned to the subject, again assuring Fanny that when peace came he would look out for a peaceful cottage in Norfolk. A few weeks later he told her: 'I hope to save my pay which with a little addition will buy us a very little cottage where I shall be as happy as in a house as large as Holkham.' The very mention of Holkham Hall, not far from Burnham Thorpe, owned by the Coke family showed that Nelson still dreamed of returning to his native Norfolk. And for a man as ambitious as he proved to be, the very fact that he chose Holkham as his comparison, showed that his later remark: 'a little farm and my good name is all my want or wishes,' was part of the delusion he built about himself.

As the months turned into years, Fanny settled into a routine, spending the winter months in Bath and the summer visiting friends in Bristol, Lyme Regis or Plymouth. Each time she visited someone else's house, she must have experienced at the least a twinge of envy of those who had a settled home. She would have been unnatural had she not dreamed of the day when she was able to choose the furniture and decorations for a house she had selected rather than having to make the best of what was offered in the furnished accommodation in which she lived. She had never had a home she could truly call her own. Since the death of her father she had always been either a guest or a tenant in someone else's property. While her husband dreamed his idyll of the country cottage what did Fanny want? And more to the point when was she likely to have a say in the matter?

In February 1796, perhaps after some prodding by Fanny, Nelson returned to the subject, though he made it plain that there was as yet no chance of his coming home for some time. He showed a decided lack of sensitivity when he wrote that she must be patient. She can have derived little comfort from:

> However the years will soon wear away and then we shall get it all together and peace will by that time, I hope be arrived, when a cottage of our own and an income to live, if not in luxury, in comfort.

During March and April he returned to the theme but then saying that it would not be long before he was home and they would get to their cottage.

By this time it was obvious that the question of buying a house had become a source of conversation between Fanny and Edmund and consequently with other members of the family. Brother William, the Rector, took it upon himself to start scouting for them in Norfolk and wrote to tell Nelson that a very nice property called Tofts was coming on the market. Nelson replied somewhat roundly that he certainly was not in the financial position to afford such a place. But for both Nelson and Fanny the project gave them something on which to centre their thoughts. It was almost as if it were an affirmation that he would survive to return to her and they would have a future together while on a mundane level it gave him something to save for. Perhaps goaded by his brother, just after receiving the Rector's letter, he wrote to Fanny to tell her that there was some money to draw on:

> You will not find it much but if any place in Norfolk is to be come at which may suit us I wish you would buy it. We can always sell again if it does not answer our expectations, a little land and we can improve the cottage. Do not be afraid, I shall most certainly like your choice.

The rather sentimental picture of the 'neat little country cottage' for which he yearned is not quite what it seems. 'Little' is a relative term and Nelson was certainly not looking to set up home in a wattle and daub thatched 'two up, two down' or, if his sights were still set on Norfolk, a brick and flint version of that. He was looking for something much more substantial. Jane Austen provided a contemporary definition of the term 'cottage' in her novel *Sense and Sensibilty*.

As a house, Barton Cottage, though small, was comfortable and compact; but as a cottage it was defective, for the building was regular, the roof was tiled, the window-shutters were not painted green, nor were the walls covered with honeysuckles. A narrow passage led directly through the house into the garden behind. On each side of the entrance was a sitting room, about sixteen feet square; and beyond them were the offices and the stairs. Four bedrooms and two garrets formed the rest of the house.

Presented with this basis, Mrs Dashwood had plans for the future.

These parlours are both too small ...and I have some thoughts of throwing the passage into one of them, with perhaps a part of the other, and so leave the remainder of that other for an entrance; this with a new drawing-room, which may be easily added and a bedchamber and garret above, will make it a very snug little cottage. I could wish the stairs were handsome. But one must not expect everything; though I suppose it would be no difficult matter to widen them.

Nelson warming to the idea of ownership told Fanny in December to find out how much money Marsh and Creed, his agents, had in hand for him and urged her to buy somewhere in Norfolk, again assuring her: 'I believe it impossible I shall not follow the plough with much greater satisfaction than viewing all the magnificent scenes of Italy.' There spoke a man who, tired of his lengthy duty at sea, longed for a sight of his homeland and the prospect of a life that in reality was unlikely to live up to his expectations. But for the moment he believed that was what he really wanted; as he told Fanny in February of 1797 with an air of almost weary desperation: 'Do as you like about the house near Norwich or elsewhere I shall like it if you do. We want a real fixed home.'

To those who have experienced the vagaries of the modern housing market, where it is often necessary to make a decision to buy on first viewing or risk losing the house of one's choice, it is hard to imagine what it must have been like for the Nelsons. Fanny would hear of a house, discuss its possibilities with Edmund and then write to her husband, because although he had passed the responsibility of the decision and purchase to her, understandably she wished for his approval or comments at least. That does not mean that Fanny felt herself incapable of making decisions, indeed she was to prove that she had a good understanding of both human nature and the late eighteenth-century property market. It was certain too, that at this stage of their marriage, Nelson did not regard his wife as an insignificant female incapable of taking decisive action. Rather <u>he</u> was the indecisive one for having stated that they needed a real fixed home one month, the next he was writing: 'If my Father wishes for any part of it [the money] I beg he will take it that would give me more pleasure than buying house or land.' Fortunately by the time this letter reached her she had already started her search in earnest.

Like Mrs Dashwood, Fanny was not daunted by the prospect of having to adapt a house to make it suit. In March of 1797 she wrote to her husband about Mile End House, a property near Norwich that was for sale with thirty-eight acres of land. It must have been in one of the missing letters that she had first mentioned this property for she refers to it as being 'not yet disposed of'. She promised she would make further enquiries though clearly she and Edmund had already discussed what they knew of it at some length. 'Our Father thinks it too small, the eating room may be, but if it answers in all respects but that, a window may be thrown out.' She ended, however, with the plaintive plea: 'I wish you would say something more positive about it.'

Nelson wrote to confide to her exactly what their financial situation was, listing how much was deposited with the agents, what his marine pay was, what bills he had outstanding, finally arriving at a total of £2,304.

> I hope instead of drawing to considerably increase my fortune. It is said and I believe it cannot be much less or anything that £5000 will be my share of prize money to 1 March. This you will keep to yourself but from you I can have no wish to keep any secret, therefore you will know how far you can go and that £2000 can be spared for a home. We must not be vagabonds any longer.

At times her frustration at being given the task of finding them a home and not being able to discuss things with him apart from in letters must have been difficult to contain. Having expressed her thoughts in writing, she could never be certain that the letter would reach him. And if it did, there was no knowing how long it would be before his reply came. Small wonder that at times they appeared to be at cross purposes, he making reference to a topic that was, by the time Fanny read it, long over and done with.

On this occasion, she followed the earlier letter nine days later with another still on the subject of houses. She reminded him that a Mr Edwin of Norwich had promised to keep: 'a good look out for a cottage and land for you.' So much for promises: 'We never heard from him.' She was still waiting for the details of Mile End House but she said, very sensibly: '...buying a house without either of us seeing it I don't like.' The question of house purchase was dominating the household conversation. 'Indeed I am sure our Father will never think any [house] large enough that I shall.' This was one of the very rare occasions when Fanny showed her irritation with the old man. However, by the time the letter was ready for posting, things had changed. The long-awaited details had finally arrived and Mile End House was no longer an issue. In her postscript, Fanny reported that it was not suitable being: 'very much out of repair' and 'lacking a wash house.' In a subsequent letter she revealed that the phrase 'out of repair' meant that the roof of the house had caved in.

While Fanny concerned herself with practicalities like the structural condition of houses and the size of rooms, Nelson simply responded with remarks such as: '... as to fortune we must be content with a little [income] and the cottage. Near Norwich or any other place you like better, will I assure you content me.' No wonder she asked him to be more positive, though to be fair to him there was really very little contribution he could make at that time.

But before that airy comment arrived she was already on the track of another house, the details of which give a small insight into the social life of Bath. While Fanny was at an evening function, she met a Mr Lucas who came from Norfolk. As they had the county in common, their host had introduced them and it was not long before the conversation had turned to properties for sale there. Mr Lucas told her that he thought it very likely that Sir Barney Bargrave's house with twenty acres of land would soon be on the market. The house was apparently some eight miles from Norwich but Fanny could not remember if he had said it was situated on the road to Bungay or that to Bury St Edmunds. Mr Lucas had indicated that there were at that time a number of large, rundown houses available in the county, a sign of the depression that was hitting property owners. But at the same time the price of land was increasing rapidly.

Several of Fanny's letters reached Nelson during May and when he came to answer them he did not have them all to hand so he commented on what he could remember. Having earlier told her that £2,000 was her limit he then told her she could:

> build upon £5000 in addition to my half pay, it may be more, but this you
> are sure of besides your money from Mr Herbert and if Lord Hugh does
> not waylay us it will I doubt not be much more. I recollect the house in the
> Upper Close Norwich. Do I desire as you like.

His next letter however told her that the prize money might not be as much as he hoped. What was Fanny to do? She was instructed to buy a house yet could never be quite certain how much money was at her disposal; all she could really rely on was the £2,000 and the interest she received from John Herbert's estate.

Norfolk was still the preferred location, for Nelson at least, and dutifully Fanny was concentrating on that county, so it was only in passing that she mentioned Ipswich where Nelson's sister Susannah Bolton and her family were going to spend the winter with her husband's brother, the Revd William Bolton. He, like many other eighteenth-century clergymen, was often absent from his parish, the small coastal village of Hollesley in Suffolk, leaving parochial duties to the care of a curate. Even when he was not taking the waters in Bath or visiting London, he and his family lived, not in his parish but in a house in the centre of Ipswich. And, as Fanny was to discover later, his behaviour in that town was not always what was expected from a churchman. For Nelson, Ipswich was the town that had asked him in 1795 to stand for election as one of its two members of

Parliament. He had considered the request carefully since had he been elected – and it was considered that he would be – it would have provided the ideal opportunity to leave the sea. However, he was forced to turn it down on the grounds that not having a private income he could not afford a career that at that time was unpaid.

Replying when it came to her husband's comment on their straitened means, Fanny robustly told him that the sum he had in mind would be quite sufficient for their needs. Prudent, practical woman that she was, she dismissed the idea of having an overlarge house; she could see no point in unnecessary space. Aware of how many visitors they were likely to have at a time, she sensibly asserted, 'we must have nothing to do with more spare bedrooms than one or two.' By that time she was on the track of a house that was reputed to be quite modern, having been built by a Mr Sanby: 'intended for the use of Mrs Sanby who is now dead.' She does not make clear if this referred to a son who had built a house for his ageing mother thus releasing the family home to him, or if Mr Sanby had become a widower before he and his wife were able to move in.

By now, everyone seemed to be aware of the Nelsons' desire to find a property and the ever helpful (or meddlesome) Rector of Hilborough having had his earlier suggestion of Tofts rejected by his brother, wrote to Fanny to tell her of his latest find, a farm of about a hundred acres near Pickenham, quite close to his own parish. Fanny was not impressed. Both the farmhouse and the outbuildings were in a poor state of repair. However, it seemed that the Rector had thought his brother might like to acquire the property in order to knock down the house and build something more to his liking. He further suggested that with so much land he could make money by letting off the portion he didn't want for his own use.

In her response, Fanny revealed not only her commonsense but also a better understanding of the economic situation of the period than her brother-in-law. The woman who has been accused of being an insignificant nonentity showed her mettle, telling her husband: 'I have said nay: that will never do these times. Building is so very expensive.' And just in case her husband should think that she was perhaps being too adamant, she softened her decision slightly by adding: '... besides our Father says the situation is a very bad one.' However, the search went on and she had heard of somewhere else. In another brief snapshot of Bath life she reported that when Mr Hoste, he who had not settled his account with Nelson, had called to see her and Edmund, he had passed on the gossip that a Mr Hogges of Aylsham was about to dispose of his house. And gossip was indeed involved, for the reason that Mr Hogges was leaving was that: 'Mr H's female attachment lives in London.' Then, illustrating the way that business was often conducted in those days, Mr Hoste had offered to act as go-between on their behalf, as he had a friend who was acquainted with Mr Hogges. The property in question was in the small town of Aylsham and therefore did not have much land with it but the house itself was in very good condition, and although there were not many, the rooms were large and well fitted out.

Not deterred by her rejection of his last proposition, within a fortnight the Rector was recommending a house at Carlton belonging to a Mr Partridge. This one had only thirty acres with it but again Fanny declined to consider it on the grounds that the house was far too big with its three parlours and a drawing room. Although by the end of May, she was beginning to despair of ever finding the right property, she tried to remain cheerful and told Nelson that she now had both Mr Moss and Mr Edwin, who hadn't forgotten his promise after all, to let her know if they heard of anything suitable.

In another of her letters that has not survived she must have mentioned that the Matchams had put their house in Ringwood up for sale. Fanny, of course, knew the house well and since she preferred the gentler air of Hampshire to that of Norfolk, she mentioned the house to Nelson. For some reason, although he had never seen it, Nelson had taken against it. Perhaps he did not like the idea of his brother-in-law's cast offs:

> … nor do I fancy if it was within our purse it would suit us. A cottage is absolutely all we can look to and £2,000 is the fullest extent which we can afford for it, and if you do not object I should like Norfolk in preference to any other part of the kingdom but do as you please and I have no doubt but I shall be satisfied. I should be glad if the house was bought.

A sentiment Fanny endorsed wholeheartedly. However, by the time the news had reached Nelson that Mr Moss and Mr Edwin were scouring Norfolk on his behalf, he had other, more important things on his mind. In the fierce battle off Tenerife he had been injured seriously enough to warrant his removal home.

As soon as he had struck his flag at Portsmouth, Nelson went straight to join Fanny and his father. There are at least two versions of his arrival in Bath, one that on a Sunday evening at the beginning of September Fanny was sitting quietly when she heard a carriage stop in the road below her window and a few seconds later she recognised the voice of her husband talking to the coachman as he alighted from the vehicle. The second account is very similar except that in that one, Fanny was disturbed by the cheers of a small crowd when the carriage stopped. Either way, she must have rushed down to the front door to greet him. It is hard to imagine what her reaction must have been when she saw him. He had been away for almost four and a half years and although during his time in the West Indies, she had seen him looking ill she could not have been prepared for what she now saw. At their last meeting in the spring of 1793, she had said goodbye to a man who had built up his strength after five years of country living. But the man who stood before her now had aged far more than he should have done, he was blind in one eye and still bore the scratches and bruises he had acquired in the recent battle that had cruelly deprived him of his right arm. Fanny's natural instinct would have been to throw herself into his arms and it is likely that unthinkingly she did so, clasping him to her only to be reminded when he winced, how much he was suffering from his injuries.

Perhaps it was just as well that a new home had not been found for Bath was probably the best place for Nelson at that time. Had Fanny been but recently moved into the Norfolk cottage of his dreams, the weak and disabled hero might have found that the drawbacks to living in a house that had yet to have Fanny's decorative and domestic stamp placed upon it, added a further irritant to a temper that must necessarily already have been stretched by the acute pain he was in. But at least in Bath he could take the waters and, if he chose, take part in the social scene. Even if he professed not to court popularity and fame, the newly created Admiral Lord Nelson enjoyed being the hero of the hour and even more being given the opportunity to renew acquaintance with fellow seafarers. For a week or two Nelson availed himself of the therapeutic and medical treatments available in Bath but he was still in such severe pain that he needed to take opium daily to gain relief from it. Fulfilling the prophecy Prince William had made on her wedding day, Fanny, who had so looked forward to having her husband back beside her, not least in her bed, found that instead of being her husband's lover she became his nurse, tending him carefully, changing his dressings and comforting him when the pain became unbearable. Yet in retrospect the next few months were to prove to be amongst the happiest the couple spent together.

The medical resources in Bath were not equipped to deal with the fearful complications to the stump of the arm that had been amputated, so it became necessary for Nelson to go to London for further consultation and treatment. He and Fanny left Edmund in Bath and by 19 September had taken lodgings at 141 New Bond Street for the duration of their stay. Here they were able to have the semblance of a normal life together. Between medical consultations and treatments, there was the opportunity for Nelson to visit not only old friends like Captain Locker and relations like his uncle Suckling and brother Maurice but also important naval contacts. One of the first to call on them was brother William, the Rector. With his brother's elevation to the peerage, the Rector saw how this might prove advantageous to him. He was intensely ambitious and hoped that he might be given a stall in one of the cathedrals, opening the way to his eventually becoming a dean, archdeacon or best of all, a bishop. In a letter to Nelson after his visit he joked about this but the insinuation is there that his brother could and should use his influence on the Rector's behalf.

The Rector had also busied himself with helping to design Nelson's coat of arms. This was not as altruistic as it might seem at first glance, he had a vested interest in the heraldic arms for should Nelson die without an heir, as seemed very likely, then the Rector, or his son, would inherit the title. At that time the Rector went out of his way to make himself excessively pleasant to Fanny, something he would not have done had he believed that the relationship between Nelson and Fanny was anything other than happy. When writing to Nelson, the Rector having mentioned something personal to him, begged Nelson not to tell anyone except of course, Fanny, what he had revealed. This assumed that he knew Nelson had no secrets from his wife.

During this period we have to rely on the letters written by them to other people or by members of the family to get a picture of how they passed the time. The end of September brought Nelson's thirty-ninth birthday, the first one he had celebrated at home for years. Two days before that he attended court where the King invested him with the Order of the Bath and afterwards had talked to him at some length. This was a proud moment not only for Nelson but the Rector too who had the honour of being presented for the first time, thus firing his imagination of future grandeur. Several days later, Fanny and Nelson dined at Greenwich with Lord Hood taking with them in their hired carriage Sir Gilbert Elliot whom Nelson had met in Italy. He wrote: 'Nelson looks better and much fresher than I ever remember him' – another indication that Fanny and her husband were happy and relaxed with each other. Fanny was aware that as soon as the doctors were satisfied that Nelson was fit, he would have to return to sea, but while they had time together, they were able to give serious thought to the question of their home. It is not difficult to imagine them sitting discussing exactly what they would like to have and, more importantly, where it should be situated. So, knowing Nelson's preference for Norfolk, how did they end up buying a property in Suffolk?

The Revd William Bolton may have sent them the newspaper containing details of a property to be auctioned in Ipswich or, as it was one of a number of lots of a large estate, it may have been advertised in the London papers. According to the *Ipswich Journal*, amongst the nine lots formerly the property of the late John Kirby to be offered for sale at the White Horse Inn in Ipswich on Tuesday 26 September at 11am was Round Wood Farm:

a modern built messuage; consisting of a small hall, 2 genteel parlours, a dressing room, kitchen, back kitchen, dairy, cellar, three wine vaults, 4 good bedchambers, 2 dressing rooms and 2 servants' chambers. Also a large barn, stables, cow house and other offices; well planted garden and 50 acres, 1 rod, 35 perches by survey of exceedingly rich arable land situate in the parishes of St Margaret's, Rushmere and Wix Ufford.

It could almost have served as the model for Mrs Dashwood's cottage in *Sense and Sensibility*.

Many believe that Nelson bought the property at that auction with an agent acting on his behalf. Had this been the case, given how well known the Admiral was, one would have assumed it would have been reported in the *Ipswich Journal* during the week following the sale. That did not happen and the first mention of the property came when Edmund wrote to Kitty on 30 October:

By a letter yesterday from Lady Nelson I learn they are gone to look at a house very near Ipswich which they mean to purchase if no great obstacle prevents.

This suggests that the house failed to sell at auction and the Nelsons bought by private treaty. Whatever the case, the farm, set on high ground just under a mile from the centre of Ipswich on the road leading to Woodbridge, obviously met with their approval. And on 4 November the *Ipswich Journal* was able to announce proudly: 'the gallant Admiral Lord Nelson has purchased the Round Wood Place near this town.' Nelson must have been highly delighted that he got the property for the price he had always quoted, namely £2,000. The legal documents were signed three weeks later on 18 November with Captain Berry acting as one of the witnesses. At last they had achieved their 'neat cottage'. However, it was to be some time before they would be able to settle in and play happy families. The property had a sitting tenant, a Captain Edgar and he had six months still to run on his lease.

Just before Christmas, Nelson was passed by the medical officers as being fit to return to active service, though at that stage he did not know when a ship would be ready for him. He told his Captain, Edward Berry that if he intended to marry his fiancée, Miss Foster from Norwich, then he had better do so as quickly as possible before the call came. Then he and Fanny went to Bath to spend the holidays with Edmund and other members of the family before returning in February to the lodgings in New Bond Street. During that time Nelson visited Lord Spencer, the First Lord of the Admiralty, almost daily to discuss naval matters connected with the Mediterranean fleet. Lady Spencer who took very seriously her role as hostess recalled her first impression of Nelson, describing him as 'a most uncouth creature', sickly looking and one whose general appearance was 'that of an idiot' but when he spoke 'his wonderful mind broke forth' riveting her attention. During one conversation he had with her he told her all about Fanny, saying how beautiful and accomplished she was; comparing her to an angel in her tenderness to him, not only in dressing his awful wounds, in fact, he believed she had saved his life. Lady Spencer had been somewhat taken aback by such an outspoken tribute and might have taken it as an exaggeration had she herself not witnessed the Nelsons together. The First Lord's wife had an absolute rule that naval wives were not invited to her dinner parties. Nelson had received such an invitation for his last night in town before returning to sea. He pleaded his case with Lady Spencer and she broke the rule and Fanny was invited too. 'His attentions to her were those of a lover. He handed her to dinner and sat by her; apologizing to me, by saying he was so little with her, that he would not, voluntarily lose an instant of her society.' Lady Spencer had seen enough of human nature to be able to recognise genuine feelings. Her description of the couple certainly does not fit in with that of those who would have us believe that the marriage had died before 1793.

Nelson hoisted his flag on board the *Vanguard* at Portsmouth on 29 March 1798, after almost seven months of living ashore with Fanny. For both of them it must have been very difficult to readjust to their former ways of life and until Nelson was under sail and fully occupied, it is possible to read in his almost daily letters to Fanny just how much he missed her. Perhaps that is why his first letter was a bad tempered one: he had arrived in Portsmouth after a tiring journey and discovered on opening his trunk that he had only one pair of black silk stockings and hardly any shirts. Over the next week, once he had gone on board, there were further complaints about missing articles of clothing and other essentials. There are those who have seized upon this little episode as an example of Fanny's negligence, or even laziness over what should have been the careful packing of her lord and master's trunks. They do not take into account that she would not have done the packing herself but would have supervised the servant who had a list of what was to be placed within the trunks. In addition, the critics seem to have overlooked the fact that Nelson was not the only one leaving the house in London. Fanny, Kitty Bolton, who had been staying with them, and the servants were to return to Bath on the same day. So there was a general packing up which is how, in the confusion, Fanny's little blue pillow ended up among Nelson's things.

Part of the problem stemmed from their having had a change of servant during the last few days they were in London. Ryson, the maid, was questioned and maintained that much of what was said to be missing, including some coins, had indeed been packed. Fanny believed that Nelson's man, Tom Allen, had been careless in leaving the trunks unlocked when they had stayed in the inn, something she had specifically warned him about. She did not wish to hint that Allen was untrustworthy but neither was she going to take the blame for the missing objects until she was certain that he, and Nelson too, had carried out a thorough search. Although Fanny described the whole episode as mortifying she did not let herself become cowed by it, in fact having said she wished to leave the subject, she returned to it after she had questioned Nelson's niece, Kitty, who for some reason had now adopted the name of Kate: 'Kate has been out this morning I have just been asking her whose memory is better than mine and she says the money was sent in the trunk. I think we can't all be mistaken.'

While Nelson was understandably annoyed – and showed it – his letters are still full of love: 'I can only repeat, what I hope you know, that you are uppermost in my thoughts.' However, also uppermost was the fact that in his trunk he had found the weights of her scales! These were most likely to have been from a set used for weighing out medicinal powders and pills rather than ingredients in the kitchen. Just as he was getting under sail he wrote: 'Nothing in this world can exceed the pleasure I shall have in returning to you,' and the following day: 'From my heart, I wish it was peace, then not a moment would I lose in getting to my cottage.'

If it was hard for Nelson to readjust to being at sea again, it must have been even harder for Fanny to return to her former way of life. In the first few days after their parting, her letters were bright and cheerful, full of activity in preparing for the move but also brimming over with her love for him:

> I feel that I have a great deal to say. My mind feels composed and quiet when I consider how very lately I have seen you. God grant that we may not be very long before we meet and then I shall hope we may live for some years together without being so very often separated.

The following day, 5 April, she replied to his letter, described as kind and affectionate.

> Indeed I have always felt your sincere attachment and at no one period could I feel it more strongly than I do at this moment and I hope as some few years are past, time enough to know our dispositions, we may flatter ourselves it will last.

Then, like all seafarers' wives, she confided that when the wind had blown strongly the night before she had worried about his safety and longed for him to be home with her. The wind unsettled her and made her depressed. And there was much else to depress the population as a whole at the time. Fear of invasion by the French was again rife and many families, particularly those who had homes near to the coast, had moved to Bath, believing it to be a safe inland haven. In Ireland, where discontent had been brewing for some time, rebellion had finally broken out and English troops who should have been guarding their native shores against invasion were being dispatched there instead. The bloodshed was horrific. Fanny summed it up: 'The news is melancholy from Ireland.' And hitting everybody too was the high level of taxation; Fanny was scathing about those citizens who tried to evade paying their share.

> Conceive of Mr Braithwaite keeping 16 horses and says he uses but four, [has] 9 men servants and enters four. Mr Sherston it seems told him it was shame that everybody was throwing the load off their shoulders.

On a personal, family level, Fanny reported that Nelson's brother-in-law, George Matcham, had fallen off his horse. The accident had occurred at three o'clock in the morning when Matcham was riding home very drunk after an evening out. Fanny had little sympathy for him since he was unhurt, remarking that the sensible horse had taken itself home where Matcham's son Tom had found it and then sent a groom back with it to look for his father.

Although Fanny found herself slipping back into the routine of life in Bath, she was very anxious to move to her new home, but until such time as their tenant's lease ran out and he vacated Round Wood, she must wait patiently. Edmund, too, had his problems with a lease: he had taken a long one on the house in King Street and now had to find someone willing to take the rest of the tenure off his hands. Since he and Fanny had lived comfortably together for so long, it had been taken for granted, particularly by his own children, that he would continue to do so. However, had he decided to stay in Bath, he would still have needed to give up this particular tenancy, the house being far too big for him on his own.

Until she had an actual date for occupation Fanny could neither begin packing up her personal possessions in Bath nor, more importantly, go shopping in London to furnish the house. She was in a quandary over what immediate plans to make. Then having settled what she would do, on 6 April she:

> ...received a letter from Mr W.Bolton telling me Captain Edgar had called to give him notice that he would quit the house this week. Had he written three weeks back, it might have made some difference to our plans. I will write immediately to Mr Bolton requesting him to get a proper person to take charge of the house – coals to be found and board wages. I shall be very anxious to get down.

Nelson had more important things to think about than furniture or domestic help. He had decided that as he was now to live in his own home like a gentleman he should set about taking advantage of those three wine vaults it possessed. On the same day that Fanny had written to him about Captain Edgar, he wrote to tell her:

> I have paid the duties for my wines and Mr Campbell is gone ashore to enquire what the land carriage will be to Ipswich. If your cellar will not take the pipe (a cask holding 105 gallons), I am sure you may put it in the back pantry. On the other side [of the paper] I send you a perfect list [of the wines]. Mr Bolton or Admiral Reeve will give houseroom, if Captain Edgar cannot receive it. The Collector of the Customs here thinks it very dangerous sending it by water from its being necessary to change vessels so often.

The delivery charge for one pipe of port, one hogshead (52 ½ gallons) of Busellis, a quarter cask of Ponte and another of old Malaga with four cases of Panchoretta Tent and two dozen of Tenerife (sent him by the Governor) turned out to be £17.14. 0d. Fanny's years at Montpelier and her visits to her wealthy friends and relations would have made her knowledgeable about wines.

Having dealt with what to him was the most important detail, he went on to other matters for her to attend to. Again he was having problems with the father of a newly joined midshipman who had not paid his son's bill. Would Fanny write to the gentleman and tell him how much Nelson had been inconvenienced? He trusted her implicitly to write the correct sort of letter just as he expected her to know the details of the contract for the sale of the house that dealt with the land taxes. And rather belatedly, bearing in mind the length of time his letters sometimes took to arrive, he cautioned her not to sign any papers that had to do with Captain Edgar without sending them to be scrutinised either by Mr Notcutt the solicitor or Mr Bolton.

Had Fanny always waited for her husband's advice or approval, little would have been achieved. As it was, it suddenly became essential that the house, now left vacant, should be occupied as soon as possible. In Bath, a Mr Baddley took it upon himself to inform her that he had heard that the Government had ordered that all empty houses in Suffolk should be requisitioned for use as barracks. Fanny took decisive action. She wrote to Graham's warehouse in London where the furniture she had bought was being stored, giving orders that it should be dispatched to Round Wood as soon as possible. More immediately, she sensibly requested Mr Bolton to have a bed put up in the house, thus establishing that the property was lived in and asked him to let it be widely known in the town that she was coming very soon. When Nelson heard about this he lovingly teased her:

> I do not believe government will by force take your house and if they did by a proper letter, I am sure it would be instantly resigned again for if they kept you in the street I would instantly strike my flag and come home to protect you.

Within a few days she had sorted all her pictures and they, with her pianoforte, were packed ready to leave Bath. She told Nelson that she would not feel very comfortable until she had followed but before she could leave, the problem of Edmund and the other house had to be resolved. This became imperative when Edmund announced his intention of going to Ipswich with her rather than waiting until she was settled. Fanny had been invited to stay with the Sucklings in Kentish Town while she finished buying furniture and fittings. She had intended this to be a fairly leisurely visit but now she would have to cut it short to accommodate Edmund's plan that he would come to London for a night and then they would travel together to Ipswich. So plans had to be made as to the occupancy of the house they were leaving until such time as a tenant could be found. Under normal circumstances they would have left one of the servants to care-take but Edmund's man Will, who would have been the obvious candidate, had become totally unreliable. The family always felt tremendous responsibility for their servants so although he was no longer useful to them, Edmund arranged that Will should return to Norfolk to join Suckling Nelson at the parsonage. It is doubtful if this was a wise move given that both Suckling and Will drank heavily, but Fanny and Nelson must have ignored that aspect concentrating rather on a shared private joke that Will was going on condition that he never worked in the garden. Perhaps resentful that he was to leave Edmund, Fanny later confided that'his [Will's] behaviour is so exceedingly bad that it is not to be borne with: in short we run no little risk either to be robbed or to have the house burned.' The servants they had at that time in addition to Will and Ryson consisted of: 'An old Catholic cook near 60 years of age and a girl of fourteen.'

Just before she left at the beginning of May, the gossip ran like wildfire around Bath that Lord St Vincent and his fleet had been engaged in battle against the Spanish fleet. The reports varied from day to day sending all the naval wives whose husbands might be involved into a panic. Fanny was not alone in suffering the now recognised symptoms of a panic attack:

> I was almost done up, seized with violent perspirations from which I took cold, but I daresay I shall soon be well. Poor Mrs Godfrey burning with heat, quite in a fever; but in the midst of her own anxiety she said she felt most sincerely for me, for that she had never seen any poor creature so affected.

But Fanny did not dwell on her 'nasty turn', instead she looked for verification of the details and was pleased when one of the admirals told them that he thought the whole episode was a pack of lies. True, Fanny could succumb to weakness but she could just as quickly pull herself together and get on with life as she knew she must. So having told her dearest husband about it, she immediately related that she had: 'all my treasures in your absence well packed by Champness and safely lodged at Wiltshire's Warehouse before I left Bath, with a proper direction to be forwarded to Round Wood.' She left for London on 3 May, spending a night en route. She stayed with the Sucklings in Kentish Town while she undertook errands such as calling at a carpet showroom and Graham's warehouse. These visits were not always as straightforward as she would have wished. Since, at that stage she had no vehicle of her own, she had to rely on the use of Mr Suckling's carriage, but one day she was only half way through her business transactions when the coachman interrupted her to say he had received a message to go and fetch his master from his work at the Custom House. This put Fanny under pressure; she had a great deal to accomplish in a very short time. Had she had only herself to consider she could have stayed in Town longer, but Edmund had written to announce which day he would be arriving and of his intention to stay but the one night. Amenable although the old gentleman appeared, once Edmund had made up his mind to a course of action, it had to be followed.

Having totalled up the costs of all she had bought, Fanny felt guilty that she had spent so much. Throughout most of their married life, Nelson had preached economy. However much he said that he did not care about money and however generous he appeared to be, particularly to members of his family, he constantly reminded Fanny of how limited their income was, that he had not reaped the financial rewards that others had. Conditioned by this, Fanny had always spent as wisely as she could. There are even suggestions that in the early years of Nelson's return to sea, she almost starved herself in order to save on the housekeeping. Certainly while she lived with Edmund whose dietary needs were few, they would not have had a lavish table. So, just before she set out for Round Wood she wrote to her husband: 'when I have paid every bill I [will] send you exactly the expenses of the furniture.' Perhaps to soften the blow as to how much that might be, she added she had collected a few little things for him. Among them – showing her own economical streak – were: '...two very good silver plates, bought them second hand, had them cleaned and your crest engraved upon them.' Now that Nelson had a title it would be expected that when he came home and they entertained, he should not be disgraced by a lack of decent silver.

In this letter dated 15 May, Fanny also imparted some gossip, which with hindsight was to prove horribly ironic. During a call she had made on Lady St Vincent she had learned of the breakdown of a naval marriage. Lady St Vincent:

> ...a good woman, spoke very humanely and tenderly of the unfortunate Lady Elizabeth Rickets. She is generally pitied. If Lord St Vincent should ever say anything on the subject do lean on the poor woman's side; Lady Elizabeth has written to him [Lord St Vincent, who was her brother] begging that he would intercede with her husband to grant her one interview. I could write a great deal.

Unfortunately, by refraining from writing more on the subject, Fanny did not disclose what had caused the breach between Lady Elizabeth and her husband. Some men appeared to adopt a very callous attitude when separating from their wives because almost immediately after she had mentioned the plea to Ricketts to meet and talk with his wife, she related another marital rift, that of Captain Peard 'who is determined to be divorced. Mrs Thomas tells me poor Mrs Peard won't live long. He won't see her.'

Fanny often took the pain of others upon herself and her sympathy for these two women was very real. However, she could not allow herself to dwell too long on their sadness as her main preoccupation was to make sure that she was ready to leave for Ipswich by the time Edmund arrived. He had come up to London in the Bath coach, accompanied, as was customary, by the manservant they had recently hired to take the place of Will. Ever the perfect gentleman, Edmund had taken a fellow passenger, a young lady, under his protection and on arrival in London he had hired a cab for them both and insisted that he should deliver her safely to her mother's house in Kensington. He had just been shown into the parlour to meet the young lady's mother when, upon looking out of the window, he saw his new manservant running down the road. Telling Fanny about it later, Edmund described the man's gait as the most extraordinary he had ever seen. Although chase was given, there was no sign of him and they never heard of him again. When Edmund examined the man's belongings ready to have them sent back to Bath to where it was presumed he had returned it was discovered that his clothing was in such an appalling state that it was fit only to be burnt. From what he also found, Edmund believed there was evidence that the man had been taking 'violent medicines improperly'. Fanny was upset when she heard as she had helped interview the man and believed him to be a thoroughly good servant, but instead they had exchanged a drunken servant for a drug addict. Not only was she disappointed that her judgement of character was not as sound as she thought, they now had only one footman so perhaps it was just as well that they got to their new home as soon as possible.

They set off on Saturday, spending the night at an inn on the way, so it was Sunday before they saw the house. Fanny had seen it only once and that in the late autumn so she was quite impressed to see it now with its five-year-old trees in full leaf. To Edmund it was summation of months of talk and according to Fanny: 'Our father was for staying…he viewed everything attentively and I never saw him so thoroughly satisfied as he was and he says the more he examines everything the better he is pleased.' As for Fanny, she felt very emotional, thanking God that at last she was under 'your own roof'. She examined the thickness of the walls, discussed with Mr Fuller, the farm tenant how high the trees might be in another five years and promptly started planning to plant even more trees to add to the beauty of the place. Having met her housekeeper and given orders for their reception on the following day, they returned to Ipswich for the night.

Next day, Edmund was like an impatient child. He chafed at Fanny's having to make a courtesy call on Mrs Bolton to thank her husband for all he had done on her behalf. Rather than wait for Fanny to finish her call and order a chaise to take them, he decided he and the footman should walk to the house and so, according to Fanny: '…he set off …and walked up a high Suffolk hill.' While nowhere near as flat as Norfolk, Suffolk is not renowned for its hills, but because the town of Ipswich lies in a hollow surrounding its river, a number of short steep hills do lead out from the town to the surrounding area. The road to Woodbridge was one of these; it rises quite steeply at the town's end, flattens out for a spell and then has another steep rise before levelling out. The nursery rhyme *The Grand Old Duke of York* is said to commemorate this hill. Ipswich being a garrison town soldiers regularly marched between their barracks in the town and another along this road to an area known as Rushmere Heath for manoeuvres and, on occasions, inspections by the commander-in-chief, the Duke of York.

In the 1790s Ipswich was only just beginning to extend beyond the medieval boundaries set when the borough received its charter in 1203. At that time its importance depended mainly on its sheltered port set some twelve miles up-river from the sea. Great was the trade that passed between the town and continental ports, and local inhabitants were as used to hearing foreign voices as they were the accents of merchants from Norfolk or the Midlands. Here, in the fourteenth century, Geoffrey Chaucer's grandfather had had a flourishing business importing wine from Europe. The town's wealth can be judged by the fact that by the Middle Ages it boasted twelve large parish churches, a number of them surrounding the highly populated dock area. Here, too, came monks to set up monasteries and convents, and friars to work among the sick and the poor. Cardinal Wolsey, who was born in the town, intended to build a first-rate college to give local poor but bright boys the same opportunities he had had, a project that lost out to Hampton Court, leaving it to other wealthy sons of the town to endow the free grammar school, almshouses and a hospital.

Foreigners found refuge in the town; Huguenots brought their silk weaving skills, Jews expelled from Holland at the beginning of the eighteenth century settled and built a synagogue in the rope-making area. Employment was plentiful in the shipyards that lined both sides of the Orwell, craftsmen fashioning the plentiful supply of local timber, especially oak, into vessels that were used both for trade and war. Ipswich ships carried foreign coals to Newcastle, wool to the continent, local produce to London and travelled up to Greenland to catch whales. Naval ships were not only built and repaired there, in winter months when campaigns were halted or during the lull of peacetime, the river provided secure anchorage; on occasions as many as two hundred ships could be seen lying in the Orwell. No wonder then that the town proved a popular place for resting or retired admirals or captains to put down their anchors. The town was awash with them in the late eighteenth century. Those who had made a fortune from prize money set about becoming landed gentlemen and the shores of both the Orwell and its neighbour the Stour were lined with the elegant country houses of the Admirals Vernon, Broke and Harland.

The less affluent stayed in the town itself where large family houses rubbed shoulders with those of merchants or traders where the ground floor had become a shop or manufactory. Towards the end of the 1700s, as house prices in London grew making rents beyond the means of many, the town experienced an influx of families who found it a cheaper place to live. With London accessible by coach within twelve hours, many businessmen would travel by the overnight coach on Sunday which would have them in Town by 6 a.m. on Monday ready to start work. Staying in cheap lodgings during the week, they returned to their families at the weekend.

These people plus the Army and Navy officers were accustomed to a high standard of goods in the shops and the provision of varied entertainment. So the local people endeavoured to provide it. By the time Fanny and Edmund came to Ipswich it was a lively, if somewhat overcrowded town, that throbbed with life. Not as genteel as Bath, of course, but almost as interesting in the characters that were to be found there and Ipswich had attempted to aspire to be a spa town. Medicinal springs had been uncovered and their therapeutic value attested to. The following advertisement from the *Ipswich Journal*, may provide a clue as to why Fanny had looked favourably on the town.

The Salt Water Baths:- The Proprietor thinks it his duty to inform his friends, that agreeable to their requests, he has (at a considerable expense) fitted up the Gentlemen and Ladies Baths in such a stile [sic] as he flatters himself will meet with their approbation. The favors [sic] of the Ladies and Gentlemen who please to make use of the Baths will be thankfully acknowledged. Terms from the Bathkeeper.

Unfortunately, too many places were trying to climb onto that particular bandwagon – close to Ipswich itself the ports of Mistley and Harwich had speculative building work in progress but they lacked the social cachet of Bath or Brighton.

The Frenchman, de la Rochefoucauld, visiting Ipswich in 1784 may inadvertently have given another reason for the Nelsons' move there. After describing the narrow streets and poor road surfaces which were uncomfortable for both pedestrian and vehicular traffic, he commented:

The town gives the impression of being empty: one sees hardly anyone in the streets and this impression derives a little from the spread of the town which is much increased by the large number of gardens within its bounds. They boast this makes the air very salubrious.

Added to salt water baths and good air, he found that the town was: 'very well inhabited, many gentlefolk living there and besides that, tradespeople. All gather every evening in a coffee house, where one can play cards and eat which is very convenient for strangers.'

Had he returned in 1798, he would have found that even the garden areas could not disguise the number of troops in the town. The very week Fanny arrived a report appeared in the local paper that the sound of beating drums accompanying the troops marching through Tavern Street, one of the main thoroughfares, had caused frightened horses to charge against the window of an upholsterer's shop. The impact was such that the frame and twenty-five panes of glass were completely smashed. Neither had Fanny been misled when she was told that every empty house, warehouse or other suitable building had been commandeered for temporary barracks. Even the large mansion house, most recently occupied by John Kirby who had also owned Round Wood, had been requisitioned for the use of General Balfour, the Area Commander. But then, de la Rochefoucauld would not have been in the country in any case; in May all emigrants were given ten days' notice to leave.

So it was in rather nervous times that Fanny and Edmund took up residence. Now they were able to examine exactly what they had and what needed to be done. Fanny revealed to Nelson that there had been some concern over the water supply to the house, which was provided by a well and a pump. Nelson's brother-in-law, Thomas Bolton and his brother William had cast doubt on the efficacy of both well and pump. They had opined that since Round Wood stood on high ground, there was little likelihood of finding any other water source. However, Fanny had sensibly consulted Mr Fuller, her farm tenant, and on his advice had the well thoroughly cleaned out and deepened by several feet. This had been expensive but since it now produced 'particularly good' water it was obviously well worthwhile. Similarly she had had the pump looked at by an expert and been told that once various parts had been renewed it would be in good working order.

Left to themselves, the builders and others would have got on with their jobs but they, and Fanny, had to endure the interference, no doubt well intentioned, of the Bolton brothers. The Revd William Bolton took it upon himself to oversee the well project and disagreeing violently with one of the workmen over what needed to be done to the pump, very nearly caused a strike. The fact that he then declared that 'there must be a court martial held and I will sit upon it' incensed the builders and even worse, upset Edmund. Fanny found herself having to act as mediator amongst all parties. Although she advised Edmund to try and mask his dislike of Bolton, she admitted to Nelson that she found him 'an officious man' but she was canny enough to recognise that there were times when he could be useful to her and she intended to make the most of that.

In the first few weeks of her occupation of the house, Fanny showed herself to be a woman thoroughly in command and furthermore one who was enjoying what she was doing. She intended to have the builders in to make a few internal changes; in the eating parlour, too small perhaps to bear the formal designation dining room, a closet or large cupboard was to be knocked out in order to accommodate a sideboard. She had also discovered damp in a dressing room attached to one of the main bedrooms and decided that one of the ways to cure it would be to block up a north facing window and insert another to the east. She believed that these minor adjustments would be sufficient for them: 'until I have the happiness of seeing you.'

Edmund was just as carried away with the house as she was, though his plans were somewhat grander, rather in the manner of Mrs Dashwood in *Sense and Sensibility*. 'Our Father thinks you must throw out a good dining room next to the present eating room and a bedroom over it, then you will have a good room to yourself and a very good house good enough for anybody.' It was Edmund, too, who made the decision that he had no use for a dressing room so it might as well be fitted out to accommodate visitors such as his granddaughters. It was not long before one or other of the Bolton twin sisters came to stay regularly.

Having been on the receiving end of hospitality for so long, Fanny now found that she was to be the provider. Nelson's older sister Mrs Thomas Bolton was at that time living in lodgings in Ipswich, so she and various members of her family were frequently at Round Wood. Visits usually took the form of coming to dinner and spending the night but Kitty and Susanna took it in turns to stay for longer periods. On one occasion Fanny related that the Boltons, with two of their sons and two daughters had made a visit.

When they left, they took the girl who had been staying at Round Wood with them and left the other. The Thomas Boltons were again somewhat financially straitened so it was left to Edmund to bear the cost of a post chaise to transport them home. Edmund, much as he loved his daughters, was not blind to either their faults or those of his sons-in-law. After the visitors had left he complained to Fanny that Bolton never once thought to thank either him or Fanny for the expenses they had incurred on his grand-daughter Kitty's behalf. For herself, Fanny decided that they were all ' cunning people'. She said that a series of little things showed what they could be like and quoted as an example:

> Last Sunday Susanna came from Ipswich early in the morning to spend the day with Kitty. When I was ready for church I called for the girls, Kitty answered: 'Susanna can't go to church.' Upon which I said, 'Why?' 'She has no gloves.' 'And did she come from Ipswich without gloves?' 'No, but they are not good enough.'

What Fanny did not tell Nelson was whether she took the broad hint and provided the girl with better ones.

CHAPTER VIII
Mistress of Round Wood

...believe me nothing in this world can exceed the pleasure I shall have in returning to you.
Nelson, April 1798

Starting life in a new town is never easy; for Fanny and Edmund it was the first time they had lived where they did not have long-established roots and a large circle of acquaintances. So how difficult was it for Fanny to find her place in Ipswich society? She knew the Boltons, of course, but as middle ranking society they were not in a position to introduce her to those who could offer entrée to the better houses and ensure that she was invited to the right occasions. She had taken up residence in the town, not as plain Mrs Nelson but as the wife of a naval hero who had been rewarded with a baronetcy. As Lady Nelson she could expect to be received in places where Mrs Nelson would have been excluded. Word had gone out via the local newspaper that she and Edmund had arrived and it was not long before they received the requisite courtesy calls and invitations to visit from some of the population, among them retired seafarers like Admiral Reeve who had known Nelson at sea.

Among the first to make her acquaintance were Captain and Mrs Boucher. His was a military rank and he was commander of the troops who were quartered at 'the top of the hill' – not the 'ten thousand men' of the rhyme but the seven or eight thousand who were housed in a large range of temporary buildings either side of the Woodbridge Road on land belonging to the Cold Hall estate, just down the road from Round Wood. The Bouchers occupied a large house in the centre of Ipswich but the couple lived simply, reflecting the difficult times the country was experiencing, thus, Fanny related: 'they give no dinners' by which she meant that they did not entertain on a grand scale. When they invited her to dine with them for the first time on 4 June, included among the guests were the two Misses Lloyd, daughters of the owner of Hintlesham Hall, a large estate a few miles out

161

of Ipswich in the opposite direction to Round Wood. Although Fanny liked these women and met them again on other occasions, the ladies did not seem inclined to deepen the acquaintance. Their excuse, which may well have been the truth, was that they were unable to venture far afield; their little ponies which drew their carriage could just about manage to take them as far as Ipswich but anything farther overtaxed the animals and then they were forced to stay home the following day.

Transport had never been a problem in Bath. There, Fanny had been able to walk to most of the places she wished to visit or take a sedan chair if the weather was inclement or the night was dark. But one of the drawbacks to living at Round Wood was that she could not just step out to do the odd bit of shopping, make a morning call or stroll to the hot baths. If she wanted to go anywhere she had to rely either on being taken in someone else's carriage or she had to hire a chaise which, as she told Nelson in a letter, was far too expensive to do often. The problem was compounded by the fact that the government had imposed such swingeing taxes on the number of horses used for private transport that a great many people who had been accustomed to keeping large carriages had switched to using the smaller chaises or traps that required one or at the most two horses to pull them. Others among Fanny's new acquaintances, like Major Heron and his wife who lived in the town, had actually given up their horses entirely.

She had been in the town barely a fortnight when the annual celebrations for the King's Birthday were held. Fanny had been accustomed to the festivities held in Bath for this occasion and no doubt expected, when she was invited to make up a party to go to the Ball at Alderton's Coffee House on Monday 4 June after dining with the Bouchers, that this would be something similar. It did not, however, live up to expectations, partly because there was a very poor attendance, 'thinness itself' in her words. Nonetheless, she was not deterred and appeared to enjoy herself. As she did a few days later when Admiral Reeve gave a very fine dinner in her honour, thus introducing her to even more people. However, there were drawbacks to accepting some invitations as she discovered when she agreed to accompany the Admiral to watch the weekly training meeting of the local militia. When he first put the request to her, she had taken the precaution of making sure that this was not the outdoor event that regularly took place on Westerfield Green when all the regiments quartered within the town assembled for review and where the noise from officers shouting orders, the tramp of horses' hooves and the smell of gunpowder as volleys of fire were exchanged must have been unbearable. Instead they went at nine o'clock in the evening to the Assembly Rooms where members of the public paid a shilling for the privilege of watching for two hours how their Loyal Volunteers were preparing to defend them. The evening also provided an opportunity to meet and exchange news with other members of the town and immediate neighbourhood. Perhaps because her sympathies were with naval rather than military manoeuvring, Fanny found the spectacle rather boring and left after an hour 'having had quite enough for my shilling'. But she did not attempt to spoil the enjoyment of the Bolton twin who had accompanied her and was no doubt enjoying looking at the part time soldiers in their uniforms. She hurriedly made arrangements for the girl to remain with her aunt Bolton who was also present and go home with her for the night.

Much more to her taste if she had another shilling to spare, would have been the 'Panorama with Motion' that was on display at Mr Norton's establishment on the Cornhill. Here she could see a re-enactment of Admiral Duncan's victory the previous October over the Dutch fleet. In the past displays of this kind had always been flat but this one, using the very latest in technical advances, had been able to overcome that defect and according to the newspaper advertisement:

> vessels are made to appear as large as real, as well as the sea, and are in constant motion and impress the mind of every beholder with respect and admiration for the British navy on which we so much depend.

Admiral Reeve took it upon himself to become Fanny's protector. As time passed both Fanny and Edmund came to rely on him for companionship, advice and local gossip. Although slightly deaf, the 65-year-old loved nothing better than idle chitchat about his friends and neighbours, which at times slightly irritated Fanny. Nonetheless, a sincere and long-lasting affection developed between her and the retired seafarer. They had at bottom a common interest, he spoke a language she understood and his tales of life at sea would have enthralled her and Edmund. A native of Ipswich where his father had been the minister of St Nicholas parish, he knew and was known to most people. One of Reeve's sisters, Clara, a novelist of some repute, also lived in the town but since Fanny never mentioned her it must be concluded that her literary circle did not overlap the naval one. The old bachelor Admiral may have enjoyed escorting an attractive younger woman whom he knew to be happily married and therefore posed no threat to either of them or it may be he looked upon Fanny as a surrogate daughter. Whatever the case he was determined she should go out and about as much as possible.

To this end he quite often arranged little local excursions for Fanny that included other friends. One such was to the large nursery garden situated halfway up the Woodbridge Road which specialised in many of the exotic plants that were so popular at the time. Eighteenth-century landowners, even those with very small estates, were not content to wait years for plants and trees to grow to an agreeable size so specialist gardeners provided them with almost fully-grown trees and mature plants to create an instant garden. Glasshouses nurtured the vines, orange trees and pineapple plants that would fill the orangeries of larger country houses. To these nurseries came keen gardeners to buy and visitors to admire. In fact it was a perfect venue for a pleasant late morning or afternoon excursion for a group of friends. And so it was that one day still in early June, the Admiral, Major and Mrs Heron, Mrs Susannah Bolton and one of her daughters and several others took Fanny to the nursery in order that she might buy plants for Round Wood.

Amongst all the many glories her eye was captured by a display of carnations, her favourite flower. She especially admired the blooms of two that were new to her and then she was struck by the particularly fine shade of green of one that was still in bud. Fanny turned to ask the gardener what colour it would eventually be. Unfortunately the man was very deaf and thought she had asked its name so he replied: 'Admiral Nelson, a curious plant named last year.' Everyone was so surprised at this response that they all stared at the poor man and some even laughed. Not comprehending what was going on the man leapt to the conclusion that they were mocking what was a very rare plant and he told them in no uncertain terms that he only had the one root stock and that was worth a guinea to him and that he would not accept two if it were offered. Reeve, always a peacemaker, calmed the man and presented him to Fanny telling him who she was. The nurseryman was beside himself with delight and went round the rest of the party to tell them about this exciting turn of affairs. The outcome was that Fanny was to receive two layers or cuttings from the 'Admiral Nelson' for which she had only to pay half a guinea. In relating the episode to her husband, she acknowledged that this was still expensive but in the circumstances surely she could be excused a little extravagance? She knew that her husband would be delighted that his name had been given to a flower that would give pleasure to thousands.

Having spent most of her married life in rented accommodation where the garden was the responsibility of others, now that she had her own, Fanny was becoming very interested in gardening. She had obviously discussed the subject with the Admiral who had brought back from a visit to Italy some hardy plants for his own garden. Realising that she could hardly ask Nelson to think of doing the same when he returned, she suggested that Josiah might select a few carnation and geranium plants for her; later she asked for a few hardy shrubs and some seeds. It may have been wishful thinking on her part when she recalled that Josiah was fond of gardening. The 12-year-old boy might have been but he can scarcely have had much opportunity to indulge his fondness during the past five years. However, she had given the hint.

More immediate was the need to get the garden itself into shape. The previous tenant, Captain Edgar, obviously had no interest in horticulture so not only had the grounds been neglected but he had also allowed the surrounding walls to fall into disrepair. Round Wood already had five-year-old trees planted around it and Fanny had asked the tenant farmer, Mr Fuller, to estimate how long it would be before the trees were grown sufficiently to afford good shade. His reply of another five years satisfied her being part of her long-term plan for the property. In July she went ahead and had a small plantation laid down. Unconsciously perhaps, Fanny was trying to recreate the tree-filled landscape of Nevis. In the meantime, there were immediate pleasures to be enjoyed: '…we have a great many larks and plenty of blackbirds', while among the trees she had discovered a very fine morello cherry. Full of energy and enthusiasm Fanny talked knowledgeably about having the tree covered with a net, to preserve the fruit from the depredations of those blackbirds. Her imagination had already leapt forward as she saw herself picking the cherries and preserving them in brandy for her husband's pleasure.

But before she could start on her plans for the garden there were necessary and basic repairs to be made to the house. These were put in hand immediately and by the middle of June, less than a month after she had moved in, builders had bricked up two windows and opened up a third. That, she believed, would greatly improve the look of the house but more importantly the alterations had allowed the walls to dry out thus curing the problem of dampness. But the structural work had left several of the interior walls in need of repapering and the woodwork to be painted. Fanny was not sure if Edmund would be able to stand the upheaval of living in the house with decorators and decided it would be better to wait and have the work done while they were away. This was probably a wise decision. She had already suffered a severe shock to her nerves when the lad who was painting the troughs round the edge of the roof had slipped and fallen. Mercifully he had escaped unhurt, but she did not wish to put herself under further pressure.

Strangely, she was much less affected by the rumour of imminent invasion. The alarm had been raised when, through a thick sea mist, a fleet had been detected lying off the coast at Aldeburgh. Messages were immediately sent to General Balfour and the troops were put on alert. Living so close to the barracks, Fanny and Edmund were only too aware of troop movements. While Edmund fretted that they should leave at once and return to Bath where he still had the house, Fanny was resolute that unless things got really bad, it was her duty to remain at the cottage. She related the event to Nelson quite calmly, telling him that the scare had been caused by a convoy of becalmed merchant ships. Rather than dwelling on how fearful it all was, she told her husband how well the local troops had responded to the emergency.

From such important news she then passed on the local gossip. First was that she had received a courtesy call from 'one of the great of Ipswich, Mrs Trotman,' wife of one of the town's two elected Bailiffs. Basking in reflected glory, the lady had talked at great length about her acquaintance with the town's two members of parliament. Sir Andrew Hamond was 'pronounced a charming man' who, according to Fanny, Mrs Trotman appeared to be 'half in love with' and Mr Crickitt too was very much liked. This emphasis on the two members of parliament was either tactless on the lady's part or it may be that she was unaware of the fact that she was slightly rubbing salt into old wounds, Nelson having been earlier offered the opportunity to represent the borough. Hamond was an old adversary of Nelson. Honoured though Fanny should have been by this visit from Mrs Trotman, it became clear that she did not intend to pursue the acquaintance. Although Fanny had been quite ruthless in an earlier letter of her intention to make use of Mr Bolton, she was not by nature a user and even though it would have been most convenient, she declined Mrs Trotman's offer to call for her and take her wherever she wanted to go in her open carriage. Fanny made her excuses as kindly and politely as she could citing her fear of the current situation as her reason for not going out. As it happened it was just as well she did refuse for Mrs Trotman's driver was somewhat unreliable and a few weeks later succeeded in overturning the carriage in an accident that caused his mistress quite severe injury.

Fanny's second piece of gossip concerned the Revd William Bolton for whom she had little respect. He had kept his distance from her ever since she had asked him, on Nelson's behalf, for the overdue premium for his cadet son. In relating that as the money had not been forthcoming, she was of the opinion that Bolton was either very poor or 'a very sad character'. Fanny then confessed to her husband that she had listened to the chatter of her maid who had told her: 'they say at Ipswich his family is supported from the gaming table. True it is he is always there, so his family says, but they call it the coffee house.'

But while Fanny like most normal human beings was not averse to hearing gossip, she also proved herself to be a ready and sympathetic listener. Perhaps it was because she was the mother of an absent son that she attracted the confidences of young men. Had she been either an insipid character or an overbearing, arrogant woman then certainly young men like Lieutenant Pierson would not have poured out their hearts to her. It had come as a surprise to both Nelson and Josiah, neither of whom held a very high opinion of him, that Pierson had proposed to and been accepted by William Bolton's daughter Mary Ann. Just as Nelson had been when Fanny met him, the young army officer was not financially secure enough to consider marriage without some sort of assistance from his future wife's father. This he confided to Fanny who knew only too well, from her own recent experience, that any help from that quarter was highly unlikely.

'Poor Pierson', as Fanny often referred to him, came to discuss matters with her and ask how he might honourably extricate himself from the engagement without running the risk of a breach of promise action. Fanny advised him to talk frankly to Mary Ann in the hope that the girl would understand and release him from the engagement. With Fanny's words to spur him he went on a visit to his fiancée who was spending the summer in her father's parish at Hollesley. On his return, Pierson called again on Fanny who was very worried at how grave and serious he had become. She also became quite angry on his behalf that Bolton had not responded to the young man's anxiety as to where he would find the money to support a wife; Bolton of all people should have appreciated that when Pierson had proposed he had gambled on future promotion that had not come. Pierson had been less direct with Mary Ann telling her only that if there was anything about him to which she objected, then it was not too late for her to withdraw from the engagement. All that succeeded in doing was to endear him further to her. In a dramatic gesture the desperate young man told Fanny he intended to apply to the Duke of York himself to send him on duty anywhere in the world. Pierson, no doubt, left feeling better once he had told Fanny his troubles but she then took them upon her own shoulders.

Visitors continued to come; Nelson's twin nieces Kitty, sometimes referred to as Kate, and Susanna had from the very beginning taken it in turns to get away from domestic duties at home and enjoy the social life their aunt could offer. It is difficult to know how much Fanny enjoyed having these young women with her. In part she had them out of a sense of duty to her husband but they did provide her with young company to balance that of Edmund. Their grandfather liked the idea of having them in the house; it had been his idea to turn his dressing room into a bedroom for them, but he was forced to admit that sometimes he found them difficult to bear, especially Kate who was extremely argumentative and liked to have the last word in any discussion. While Fanny was prepared to tolerate youthful forthrightness, she found it harder to accept the lackadaisical attitude of both girls to their personal appearance which made her confide: 'I wish I could make them cleaner and nicer in their person.'

Much more enjoyable was the visit from Captain Berry's new bride who arrived towards the end of June. The former Miss Louisa Foster was a daughter of a Norwich cleric and it is likely that she and her family had known Fanny from her days at Burnham Thorpe. As Fanny had done, Mrs Berry was embarking on a peripatetic life-style. She had been married for six months, only three of which had been spent with her husband before he had embarked with Nelson at the end of March. Apart from her immediate family, Fanny was probably the ideal person to cheer her. With her own experience of long separations, she would have provided both comfort when the newlywed was depressed and an example of how to behave when the waiting and anxiety became oppressive. She would learn much from Fanny who was a willing teacher and in turn found her good mannered guest very pleasant company. Fanny described her to Nelson as a very mild young woman, so unlike his nieces and therefore a welcome addition to the daily life of the household.

One of the accomplishments considered vital for any eighteenth- century woman was the ability to sew. This could vary from the purely decorative piece of embroidery, regarded as a leisure activity to occupy the time, to the more practical that encompassed dressmaking. Fanny, we know, was both competent and confident enough to undertake the making of a special dress to wear when her husband came home. But what she and Louisa Berry embarked upon was a far from trivial project.

Tell Captain B. I set her to work upon the sofa cover and the numberless cushions you had in the *Captain*, and by the time we have completely finished what we have taken in hand, she will be fully qualified to make furniture for the bedstead.

That would have included making the heavy curtains to surround the bed as well as stitching sheets and pillow-covers and possibly a quilt too. Although Fanny wrote half in fun, one senses that both women enjoyed the project. Sewing in company with another provided an excellent opportunity to talk on a range of subjects when the mood took them without their feeling they were wasting time. It gave them pleasure but it also taxed their minds: '…it serves to amuse just now. It requires a great deal of contriving.' But her next remark showed that occupation of the hands was not really enough for them. 'How very fortunate your time is so much taken up, that it must prevent you from thinking. We have little else to do.'

She had reason to be somewhat plaintive. She wrote as regularly and as cheerfully as she could but it was 25 June and she had heard nothing from Nelson since 4 May. There had been no intelligence either from the Navy Office beyond the basic information that Lord St Vincent had taken the Fleet on an expedition in the Mediterranean. It must have been difficult for the two women to stop themselves wondering continually about the fate of their respective husbands. Distraction came however, in the form of courtesy calls from the ladies of the district or as Fanny disparagingly noted: 'a few what are called ladies'. These, for whatever reason, she did not like. Mrs Boucher she liked very much and she was pleased to receive a visit from Lady Harland; to both of these she accorded the accolade that they were gentlewomen, that is they lived up to their good breeding.

Lady Harland, although considerably older than Fanny, being in her mid 60s, would have had much in common with Fanny as her late husband, Admiral Sir Robert, had been at sea for most of his life until ill health had forced him ashore. Some years into her widowhood, she had also lost at least two of her daughters in their 20s through childbirth but her son had bought a property at Wherstead, a mile or so from Ipswich to the south, set on high ground with magnificent views overlooking the Orwell. Talk of different properties had formed part of the conversation and Lady Harland told Fanny that it had been generally rumoured that the Nelsons had bought Round Wood merely as a stopgap for the summer and had no intention of settling. That explained why Fanny had not been 'noticed' by several of the 'better' families. Amongst her earliest visitors had been Sir William and Lady Middleton who regularly entertained members of the royal family, particularly Prince William, at their home, Shrubland Hall at Coddenham on the main road to Norwich. Whenever they came to visit they arrived in their coach drawn by four horses thus giving Fanny the chance to report to Nelson that the carriage drive at Round Wood was well able to take such a vehicle. Admiral Reeve, anxious that Fanny should not feel slighted by those who had failed to call, assured her that before the 'country' families – defined as those who drove four horses and lived in style – made any overtures of acquaintance, they always wanted to know how long newcomers intended staying. He asked if she would like him to spread the word that on his return Nelson intended to spend some months each year at Round Wood and that Fanny would like to be acquainted. She gave an affirmative to the former but declined the latter.

Fanny found it hard to tolerate snobbishness, especially among women who held a position in society by dint of marriage rather than upbringing. She was well used to mixing with 'good society' and could hold her own with Lords and Ladies, those who had inherited titles as well as those who had received them as a reward for political or naval service. She was, perhaps, more at ease with the 'great ones' than Nelson himself, who tended to be blinded by titles and position. Her introduction to the cream of Ipswich society came during the highlight of the social calendar, Race Week. Held at the beginning of July, the town filled to overflowing and the county families entertained many visitors in their country mansions. The races occupied the middle of the day, often following a late formal breakfast to which many guests were invited, while after dinner, the evenings were taken up with entertainment provided by plays at the theatre and public balls. Fanny took Mrs Berry and Susanna to two balls and a breakfast during the week. Of the latter she said little. However:

> The balls were well attended by the county families. Lord and Lady
> Broom, Lord and Lady Rouse, the Rowleys, Sir Harry and Lady Parker.
> Admiral Reeve introduced them to me. I found Lady P. a very proud
> woman and Sir Harry a very great man.

This was Fanny's way of describing people who, in her opinion, were putting on airs. Sir Harry, who as brother of Admiral Sir Hyde Parker obviously thought himself to have a far greater understanding of naval matters than a mere woman, cross questioned her about Nelson's whereabouts. Fanny held her own but she was not impressed by the 'great' who were staying with Admiral Reeve. He had invited her to dine with them but she declined one invitation revealing that she had: 'neither inclination nor strength to hold out, particularly as we were not to go to the ball till 9 o'clock.' Since dinner would have started mid afternoon it is understandable that she might find the long period in such company more than she could bear. However she was asked to join the county families at the supper interval of the ball; again she declined and took her tea instead with a 'cheerful party, the Bouchers etc.' These were people to whom she could relate, people who were relaxed with each other. The formality of the period was nicely defined in Fanny's comment: 'Lady Broom stood by me some time. She looked as if she wished to speak to me.' For the second ball, Fanny and Mrs Berry dined first with the Bouchers whose party included a

Mr Harry Bunbury. This young army officer who later inherited his family estates in Suffolk proved invaluable, since as he knew most people in the ballroom he was able to give them a running commentary on who was who and with whom. He was also a useful dancing partner.

So for a few days at the beginning of July, Fanny was in high spirits but then she was plunged into depression with her concern for Nelson from whom she still had not heard. Such war news as she could glean from the newspapers and conversations had increased her anxiety for his safety and that of Josiah. The fact that she did not know if her son was with Nelson, because he too did not write, added to her fears. 'A line from him would do me good.' She confessed in a letter of 16 July that there had never before been a period during the war when she had been so fearful. However, having told him how low spirited she felt, she almost immediately tried to make light of her feelings by saying that she was sure that all would turn out well for him.

Then her brother-in-law, Suckling Nelson, came to stay. He was in poor health, probably from his excessive drinking, and low-spirited too and made them all more depressed as he gave the gloomy news from Edmund's part of Norfolk. It was a dreary tale of sickness, people being forced to sell up and others moving into much smaller properties. Even the Cokes of Holkham had been forced to give up their set of horses and were reduced to using only two. On the domestic front, Fanny had an unexpected problem to contend with when a case of Nelson's wine was opened. An eighteenth-century case contained more than the present dozen bottles so Fanny was horrified to discover that many of the bottles of rum, claret and other liquors had leaked because of poor corks. Some bottles were now only half full leaving the remaining contents in danger of contamination. Fortunately Capt. Boucher, who had given invaluable advice about the storage of the wine initially and had given Edmund instruction on how to set up the wine racks in the cellars, was on hand. He had examined all the bottles thoroughly and then recommended that all the faulty corks should be drawn and the wine rebottled. Amongst the consignment there was a sweet wine which, Fanny told Nelson, was of such rare quality that nowadays it was hardly ever served. This had been carefully decanted into pint bottles. In the event that Nelson should consider buying further wine for his cellar, the practical Fanny decided she would make it a priority to look around for a supply of good corks to send him.

That was a concern she could do something about. More worrying was Edmund who had begun to complain that weak eyesight prevented his reading or writing as much as he had and so relied on her to do it for him. Fanny was astute enough to recognise that his real problem was lack of stimulation or 'amusement' as she termed it. The house was proving to be too far away from the centre of activity for casual callers to drop in, and for him to hire a chaise every time he wanted to go out was expensive. Edmund craved company. Fortunately, Captain Boucher and his wife were often able to provide this. Their house in Ipswich had become the one where Fanny felt she might call without invitation. She described to Nelson how after church they called at the Bouchers and persuaded them to return with them to Round Wood for dinner 'which cheered us all. Our father was glad to have someone to talk to.'

And then she exploded, letting out all her pent-up frustration: 'How any creature could possibly tell us this was a good neighbourhood! We talked of it to Capt. Boucher, he said by no means.' The cause of this outburst appears to be the lack of attention to her from the county families. She had been in the area for barely two months yet seemed to think that by that time she should have met all the important people. She did admit that Boucher had told her:

The Berners never mixed with anybody. Sir W.Rowley was full 17 miles from us. Sir R Harland was a very gay [off hand or dissolute] young man and no gentlewoman ever went to his house; once a year at the Races he either gave a breakfast or a dinner. General Dalrimple, Sir Robert's brother-in-law lives with him. The world thinks Sir R H is fond of gaming and has lost very much at play, he will soon be fleeced by his relation.

Dissolute Sir Robert might be but that did not prevent Fanny, Nelson's sister Mrs Bolton and young Mrs Berry taking a tour round the gentleman's property, a custom much indulged in at that time. The house was set at the top of a hill to the south of Ipswich, overlooking the wide sweep of the Orwell down towards the sea and across to the wooded banks on the far side. Although the house was not completely finished – gossip said that shortage of cash was the problem – Fanny thought it every bit as beautiful as she had been led to believe. As was customary, a servant showed the ladies over the house. Often this duty was the privilege of the housekeeper but in this case their guide was a very polite manservant. When they reached the bedrooms, the man opened the door for them but discreetly remained outside in the corridor. Once they were inside the room the ladies saw the reason for his discretion: according to Fanny the room was filled with the: 'indecent ornaments of a gay young man'. These included fine, naked statues of both sexes and very handsome looking glasses at the bottom of the bedstead. Fanny was not unduly shocked, indeed in a different setting these were objects to be admired but positioned as they were the women were: 'not much impressed with favourable sentiments of the owner.' Fanny was genuinely upset that such a lovely house in one of the most beautiful settings she had ever seen should have been marred by its interior decoration.

Someone else who came in for condemnation was referred to as 'the Queen of a certain town.' This lady, an acquaintance of Nelson, had apparently made all sorts of promises to him to invite Fanny into her social circle. Having met her, Fanny knew that they were unlikely to become friends.

She did not mince her words to Nelson; in her view the woman was an arrant social climber with a glib tongue and dissolute morals. Her house had become a venue for serious card playing where the stakes were high.

Money was proving a constant worry. Bills had come in for the carpenters' repairs and there was yet more work to be done. She was aware that it would cost a great deal to put the house in thoroughly good order and that at present they were simply patching up. Almost a necessity had been the provision of new shutters for some of the windows but she was trying to make do with the existing ones in the parlour while they were still in the house even though as she humorously suggested: '…they admit wind enough when they are done up to make it a matter of some moment where to place the candlesticks.' With draughts like that it was hardly surprising that Fanny complained of ear problems although she was willing to put them down to nerves. However, on the plus side, she was able to report that some money had come in. Marsh and Creed, his agents, had written to say that they were holding £385.12.8d on Nelson's behalf. This represented his share in prize money and when she asked them to send it to her she requested details of how much related to each ship. She had either observed Nelson's methods of accounting or he had trained her but either way, she promised that she would list it all out exactly as he did. And at long last, perhaps having been lucky either at cards or the gaming tables, William Bolton had given her £60 on account towards the sum he owed for his son's expenses at sea.

From the newspapers Fanny gleaned that Nelson had been to Naples and then to Malta but she still had not received a letter from him to verify this. But at least she had had a recent opportunity to talk about her husband to someone new. She had had a surprise visit from John Thompson, one of the sailors who had served with Nelson in the *Agamemnon*. He had been taken prisoner in France and managed to escape with five other men. He had been making his way to London from the coast when he heard that Fanny was in Ipswich so he had stopped off to see her. Her compassion was aroused when she saw how thin he was and she had immediately provided a meal for him. She herself enjoyed 'a long dish of chat' with him and when he left she made sure that he had sufficient funds for his journey to London. That Thompson felt he could call on Fanny without invitation showed that he must have heard good reports of her. Had her reputation for being cold hearted already been established, then he would not have taken such a liberty. Little did she know and certainly he did not, that in a year or two, Nelson would be using Thompson's name to cover his illicit dealings.

Thompson no doubt was asked for his opinion on the latest acquisition in the parlour. Finally the long awaited portrait of Nelson had arrived and been placed on the wall opposite the east window above Fanny's writing table where she could gaze at it. It had already become 'her companion, her sincere friend in his absence'. Edmund too was delighted with the portrait, considering it a very good likeness.

At the end of July Fanny lost the company of Mrs Berry. She had proved the perfect antidote to the Bolton girls who still came to stay periodically. However, they did have the prospect of a visit from the Sucklings of Kentish Town to look forward to in mid August and Fanny felt that would provide Edmund with the company and conversation he craved. But she was less anxious to entertain the Rector and his wife. Conscious again of the expense she might be causing her husband she lamented that extra people in the house meant that she had to employ a third woman servant. She had tried to make do with two but found there was too much for them to do. And with the constant rise in prices it had been impossible to cut her housekeeping expenses. Certainly she did not keep a lavish table for even had she either the wish or the means to do so, commodities such as fish and fowl were impossible to come by.

The end of July finally brought: 'brightness to her mind and ideas' when she received, courtesy of Mr Nepean, the Secretary to the Admiralty, two letters from Nelson dated 18 May and 15 June. She was overwhelmed with emotion yet when she came to write her reply she found it hard to tell him how much these letters meant to her beyond: '…[the letters] both of which I thank you for and need not tell you how truly welcome they were.' The closest she came to revealing her feelings was when she told him that Boucher had superintended the bottling of a pipe of Madeira which had produced forty-one dozen bottles but that she had no intention of touching: '…any of these good things till you come to the cottage.' She longed to share everything with him but in his absence she sent him a parcel containing 'various good things'. In her letter of 28 May Fanny listed the contents of the parcel she was sending as '2 silver plated plates, knife, seal, prayer book and a hussey [mending kit], 2 pairs of buckles, tape and bobbins. Italian paste.' Some years later Miss Ellis Cornelia Knights revealed that Fanny was also in the habit of sending Nelson the latest books, most of which, it appeared, remained unread. The brightness of Fanny's mind and ideas did not last long. While the letters proved almost the sole topic of conversation between her and Edmund, Fanny's thoughts were taken up with the news of the return to England of Sir Richard Calder and Capt. Gray. If they could come, why could not Nelson?

Further news contained in this letter of 13 August dealt with Edmund's failing eyesight that prevented him writing his usual long letter to his son. One of his greatest amusements was to listen to Fanny reading the London newspapers that were sent down to them which contained more naval news than the *Ipswich Journal*. Fanny's own postbag was quite full that week. Lord Hood wrote to tell her he had been seriously ill with shingles; he did not spare her any of the details, telling of the great blotches round his body that for four nights would not allow him any rest in bed. However, he had now recovered sufficiently that he had been out once on his horse and he thought it would not be long before he was getting out and about again. Her sister-in-law, Anne Nisbet, was another of her correspondents, as was her friend from Bath, Mrs Sherston who, amongst other news, imparted the information that Admiral Cornwall had adopted Capt.Whitby as his son and therefore his heir. There may have been more to this casual piece of information than is at first apparent. It is possible that Whitby was Admiral Cornwall's stepson just as Josiah was Nelson's. Fanny may have been giving her husband a hint that it would please her if he made Josiah his heir. On the other hand it may have been that, since all these people were known to Nelson, Fanny simply assumed their activities would interest him. She herself was still deeply concerned for the plight of young Capt.Pierson.

Towards the end of August Fanny was again busy and consequently had less time to worry that the last letter she had received from Nelson dated 15 June was very short and had told her little beyond the fact that having been to Sardinia he was then lying off Naples and was in excellent health. The fine, warm weather that had led to an early and bountiful harvest had helped to raise her spirits. Fanny was able to appreciate, as artists have down the years, the beauty of the clear, wide Suffolk sky. Despite the newspaper reports of the activities of the Mediterranean fleet, she had to concentrate her mind on the visit of London friends, Nelson's uncle Suckling and his wife. It had been touch and go as to whether this visit would actually take place as ill health had overshadowed it. Mrs Suckling's father, Mr Rumsey, had been seriously ill and had begged his daughter not to go away and leave him and then Mr Suckling himself had been very sick.

Perhaps it was because they lived surrounded by ill health that made both men and women in the late eighteenth century acutely interested in the vital details of a medical condition, in particular anything to do with the bowels. In Mr Suckling's case we learn that having suffered severe constipation for two days and a night this had been followed by a serious and debilitating bout of 'severe scouring', that is acute diarrhoea. Mr Suckling was not alone in his suffering; the complaint, whatever it was, must have been widespread judging from the piece in the *Ipswich Journal* in September:

> Remedy for prevalent Bowel Complaint:- Take 2 ounces of mutton suet near the kidney, cut very small, simmer in 1 pint Milk till it comes to half a pint. Strain off and take a coffee cup full warm, frequently if the stomach can bear it.

If such remedies did not work then it was better to follow the advice Suckling's doctors had given him and seek a change of air. So he had come to spend two quite hectic days at Round Wood. On the first of these, the Bouchers, the Revd Bolton and Pierson were invited to meet him. The following day two Army majors who were staying with the Berners and Mr and Mrs Heron were asked to dine with the party which also included Edmund's daughter, Mrs Bolton, who had been staying for the week. Nelson's good wine was brought out for them to drink to his good health and speedy return. Everyone seemed in high spirits and even Edmund was beginning to overcome his dislike of Bolton. It is possible that this change may have been encouraged by the fact that Bolton had contributed some fine lobsters and a hare for the dinner table. To cap this pleasant time, Fanny received a letter from Miss Walpole, telling her that her great friends, the family of Admiral Broke, who had a large estate on the banks of the Orwell at Nacton, were very anxious to meet her. Gradually, Fanny was being drawn into the elite social circle of the county families.

But however many slight distractions there were – and that included a week's visit from the Rector – Fanny and Edmund were constantly aware that Nelson was in danger. The second week in September brought them some relief when finally they received a letter written over three months earlier while Nelson had been cruising off Sardinia. More reassuring was the note written on the back by his agent informing her that 'Sir Horatio was well on the 19th July.' But even this was not sufficient to calm Fanny's fears. With only the newspapers to rely on she castigated them:

[they] have tormented and almost killed me in regard to the desperate action you have fought with the French fleet. How human faculties can be brought to make others intentionally miserable I cannot conceive. In my opinion a newspaper writer, or a fabricator for them, is a despicable creature bearing a human shape.

She tried hard to keep her feelings in check, committing Nelson to God's protection but she did so long for her husband's return. In the absence of his letters to answer, she is aware that while telling him of her feelings, she must not overburden him with her woes: 'I feel most sensibly how much you have to do and must beg you will let your mind and body rest as much as possible.'

She was only too aware that her accounts of life must seem very mundane with nothing more to report than who had visited and how well or otherwise people appeared to be. When she had driven her sister-in-law Bolton home after her visit she returned with two of her children, Kitty and 11-year-old George who was in need of medical advice. That Mrs Bolton left Fanny to seek this for her showed that she knew her sister-in-law was eminently capable of dealing with the situation but more important would probably also pay the medical bill. George was suffering from a 'scalt [scald] head,' a childhood disease of the scalp for which mercury was the recommended treatment. Quite apart from the disease of the head, Fanny quickly assessed that George was very backward for his age. He was intended for a career at sea but she guessed he would not be ready to go for two or three years as he could barely read. However, like most young boys he was excited by the sight of soldiers, as was his older sister Kitty for different reasons, so Fanny was able to give them some amusement by sending them off down the road to watch the troops exercising.

While young George stayed for six weeks, his sisters took it in turns to come for a week or so at a time. They, with the constant stream of visitors, helped keep the housekeeping bills high. Although Nelson had assured Fanny she should indulge herself, she was conscious that he had added the proviso, if he could afford it. So she continued in the same careful way she had begun. Living, as she was, for the day he returned, everything was to be stored up for then. Except, that is, the fruits from their own garden that she had bottled for him. With love and great pleasure she carefully filled nine small stone jars of cherries in brandy and five each of currant and apricot jelly. Carried away by her domesticity, as she packed the box that was to carry these gifts to Nelson, she told of the awful rain that had bruised much of the fruit and worse that the price of sugar had risen beyond belief. ' We now drink sugar at 1/6 per pound.'

At the beginning of September, Edmund began to talk of leaving some time in November to spend the winter in Bath. On 17 September he wrote to Kitty Matcham about his future plans:

Lady N. is apprehensive this place may be too cold for the winter, & moreover the house wants paint etc, therefore, no accident preventing, intends to remove to Bath about the end of November or early December. Must therefore request you to look at your leisure for a house for 4 or 5 months certain, in a good situation, that is in Bladud's Buildings or Axford, Fountain Buildings, Edgar or Belmont as far as No.5 or 6, the field side of Gay Street. A small house about 4 guineas per week...Your sister will spend a week or 2 with us before she removes to Cranwich [Norfolk]. Bro Will [the Rector] & wife intend to be at Bath for the improvement of Charlotte.

This was another of those occasions when Edmund put his own wishes into the mouth of Fanny. He was restless and wanted to return to Bath as soon as possible. Fanny had planned to wait until after her Christmas visit to the Walpoles, before going to Bath, if she went at all, especially that now that all the window shutters had been finished the cottage was quite cosy. But Edmund had found that the clear air at Round Wood could be biting; he tried to convince Fanny that it was the keenest air she had breathed for years and that it would affect her health. Telling Nelson of Edmund's concern for her she noted that surprisingly she had had fewer colds there than anywhere. But Edmund wanted very much to see his daughter Kitty Matcham and he knew that if he presented Fanny with a fait accompli as regards a house, then she would fall in with his arrangements. But before they left there were yet more visitors to entertain including Captain Berry's sister Patty, who came for several weeks. She was a lively young woman who provided Fanny with just the kind of companionship she needed at that time, bringing as she did her news of activities in other parts of the country and conversation which did not revolve around the different members of the Nelson family. Then there was just the Boltons' visit before the season at Round Wood wound down.

When in 1798 Fanny sat down to write her usual letter to her husband on 1 October, she was able to refer to the most recent letter she had received. Dated 20 July it had told her that:

> I have been sent after the French fleet but have not been able to find them… Since I wrote you a line from off Naples we have been to Malta, to Alexandria in Egypt, Syria into Asia and are returned here (in Sicily) without success.

To what he had told her – information that was two and a half months out of date – she added what she had already learned:

> The newspapers let me rest a week, then began again with their conjectures and this last week have positively asserted you have gained some advantages over the French fleet assuring the public you arrived safely with your prizes at Naples…A letter of one line will rejoice my heart, and I think I shall soon be gratified.

The rest of the letter was full of domestic news and messages for Capt. Berry from his sister including a fashion note that one of Berry's old girl friends had taken to wearing her hair without powder which: 'makes her look particularly amiable.' She would not have written so frivolously had she known that on that very day, news had been received in London that would set alight the imagination of the country and start a train of events that would alter Fanny's life irrevocably.

Had she received Nelson's letter (now missing) written after 1 August, she would have known just how much of a part he had played in the tremendous Battle of the Nile. That of 11 August told her that he was: '…as much better as could be expected', referring to the near fatal wound he had received on his forehead. When Fanny did finally get this letter she would have clung to the promise: 'I shall most probably be in England in November.' But her reaction to this and the letters that followed have to be guessed at because there are none extant from her until June 1799, almost nine months later. So, again, for the events that occurred during that period it is necessary to seek them in Nelson's letters to Fanny, other correspondence and the press. And it was the newspapers which now reported details of the battle taken from the naval dispatches sent to the Admiralty. Eighteenth-century newspapers, although limited in size compared with those of the present day, were just as anxious to find human stories to enliven their columns and frequently resorted to regurgitating items from each other. The *Ipswich Journal* had a scoop insofar as the town could now claim to be Nelson's home.

6 October 1798: On arrival here on Wednesday last, [3 Oct] of the news of the glorious victory over the French fleet by Admiral Nelson flags were hoisted upon several steeples & at private houses; the bells rang & guns were fired in various parts of the town all day. But in the evening the inhabitants were gratified with a sight quite new in its kind. Orders having been previously given by Gen. Balfour, about 5 o'clock, the different regiments quartered here began to assemble and move towards Stoke-hills, where they were placed in the following manner: The Loyal First Volunteer Infantry on the right, 1st Regiment of Dragoon Guards, the East Norfolk, East Essex, Oxfordshire Regiments of Militia & Loyal Ipswich Light Cavalry on the left & Generals Balfour & Manners passing the line occasionally on horseback, attended by aides de camp. About 6, signals were given by 3 rockets from the centre line – a royal salute fired 21 guns from the field pieces, after which a feu-de-joy from one end of the line to the other, which reached upwards of a mile. Repeated 3 times & the evening being fine the extent of fire had a pleasing effect.

Similar displays took place up and down the country but only Ipswich had the wife and father of Admiral Nelson at their display. Although the paper did not report it, Generals Balfour and Manner would have reserved a special place for her at the event and it was most likely Admiral Reeve who fetched her and Edmund and Miss Patty and who ever else was staying and carried them off to watch the display, held not at the usual training ground but in fields that had the backdrop of the Orwell to give extra dramatic effect. Whatever Fanny may have thought about the Volunteers' practice night at the Assembly Rooms she could not fail to be impressed by this tribute to her husband especially when the massed bands struck up Rule Britannia, for at that moment the British Navy's supremacy was in no doubt.

The following day Fanny received so many visitors wishing to offer their congratulations that she and Edmund were glad to escape the house and ride into the town centre to see the decorations and impromptu illuminations that decorated the shops and streets. According to the *Ipswich Journal* most of the decoration was second rate but what it lacked in good taste it made up for in its spontaneous show of good will; picking out one 'device' as an example: 'One we must mention as truly appropriate in a barber's shop, which was "May the enemies of Great Britain be shaved with a blunt razor." ' If Fanny read these accounts then she would have smiled at the comment about herself and Edmund that appeared in the same edition: 'Lady Nelson & the father of the Admiral reside at the Round Wood Farm, near this town, where from their conciliatory manners they are generally beloved of all classes.' Well, as far as she knew, they had not upset anyone in the not quite five months they had been there. But she would not have been pleased by the report in *The Times* of 8 October, obviously picked up from the local newspaper, which read: 'Mr Nelson, the father of the gallant admiral, has long resided at Round Wood Farm near Ipswich, beloved and respected by his neighbours. Lady Nelson, since the absence of her husband, has lived with him.' Edmund would have chuckled that Ipswich was claiming him, a true born Norfolk man, as a long term resident while Fanny would have been justifiably annoyed that the reporter had not acknowledged that Round Wood belonged to Nelson and was her home.

The festivities continued. The regiments in the barracks had a public Grand Field Day culminating in a ball given in Nelson's honour. There is no record of Fanny attending but given her friendship with Capt. and Mrs Boucher and other members of the military it would be unlikely that she would have missed the occasion, especially as she enjoyed dancing. After the months of not knowing exactly where her husband was, hearing very little, even from official sources, of the danger he was in, her euphoria at learning that he was safe and a hero to boot must have carried her through the next few days. She could rejoice at last and what better way to show her exhilaration than by being among friends and dancing? On Tuesday 16 October she was guest of honour at a Ball and supper at the Assembly Rooms, both of which according to the *Ipswich Journal* were: '…in a high degree brilliant & worthy of that great & important occasion.' The streets, illuminated with variegated lights leading to the Assembly Rooms, were lined with spectators eager to see the arrival of the three hundred notable and important guests who had been invited from the principal families in the neighbourhood. Carriages started arriving from seven o'clock, giving those in the street a free show of all the beautiful dresses and hairstyles of the ladies of the gentry. By eight most had arrived and the way was left clear for the guests of honour. Then the bells of the nearby Tower church rang out and the streets echoed with the tremendous cheers of the bystanders that went on and on. Those waiting inside knew that Fanny and her party had arrived. Fanny was led into the ballroom by Admiral Sir Richard Hughes, Nelson's commander-in-chief in the Leeward Islands and an old friend of Fanny's. Admiral Reeve walked beside Edmund and they progressed to the top of the room followed by Miss Patty who was accorded her own applause as sister of Capt. Berry of the *Vanguard*. Capt. Boucher was her escort. After the official welcome the dancing began and continued until midnight when supper was served. During the 'elegant supper' a great many toasts were drunk to absent heroes as well as present company. After that dancing continued until morning. For one night, Fanny had been the centre of attraction and she enjoyed every moment. Now all she wanted to make her completely happy was her husband home with her, preferably for good.

CHAPTER IX

Lady Nelson

My pride is being your husband, the son of my dear father and in having Sir William and Lady Hamilton for my friends.
Nelson, October 1798

One of the first letters Fanny received about Nelson's action at the Battle of the Nile came from her brother-in-law Maurice who worked at the Navy Office. Over the years she and Maurice were to become close not least because he was often able to pass on to her the accounts of Nelson's activities when they arrived in the Office. He was quick to reassure her on 4 October that Nelson had not been severely wounded during the battle: '…my brother was wounded over the right eye and he was in perfect health and spirits and there was not the least danger in the wound and it would be quite well in the course of a week or ten days.' In that letter he also broke the news to Fanny that Nelson was to be rewarded with a peerage as a reward for his services. He asked that at present she keep to herself that Lord Spencer had discussed with him the title Nelson might take. Maurice had not liked to ask what degree of peerage was to be conferred on his brother but asked if Fanny had ever heard him voice an opinion as to what title he would take should it be offered. In fact Maurice was not telling Fanny anything new; she had already been asked the same question by Lord Hood to whom she replied on 4 October: 'His Father and myself thinks he will like Baron Nelson. His unbounded affection for his father would make him wish to have it Baron Nelson.' She also revealed that although she was not at all well, probably from excitement, she had arranged for a brace of pheasants and a hare to be sent by the night coach to London for him and Lady Hood.

Two days later Maurice, who now knew that Nelson had been created Baron Nelson of the Nile, wrote expressing his dissatisfaction that his brother should be so shabbily treated in comparison with St Vincent who had become an earl and Duncan a viscount. The disgruntled reaction was caused in part by one of the frequent Nelson family squabbles. That Nelson had been granted a hereditary peerage brought home to Fanny that she had failed to provide an heir. Although Nelson had always declared that he regarded Josiah as his son, he had not taken any legal steps to adopt him as his official heir. From Maurice's letter it appeared that the Rector considered himself to be the next in line: 'William may have all the honours to himself. It will be my wish and request to my brother not to put my name in the patent...I move in too humble a sphere to think of such a thing.' As Maurice was the older brother, one might have presumed him to be the natural successor but it may be that since he was childless, the succession moved to those who had children.

The argument over the title rumbled on. In another letter to Lord Hood on 18 October, Fanny confided that: '...the honours which have been conferred on Lord Nelson is I am told the subject of conversation every where.' Whether she had been listening to general comments or was referring to articles in the press, she told him that public opinion held that Nelson had not been sufficiently rewarded. In a much stronger tone than she was accustomed to use she said she felt 'mortified in the extreme' on Nelson's behalf. So much so that when she wrote to Nelson, she had intended to ignore the new title and address the letter as she would have done earlier. Her anger rings through this statement but the voice of reason, namely Edmund, calmed her: 'Mr Nelson requested I would give him every mark of distinction which his own title would allow.'

While Maurice's humility might be a bit excessive, his concern for Fanny's health and well-being was very real. He seemed to understand better than her husband how nerve racking it was for her to have to wait for news. Conscious that her anxiety was stretched to the limit with the additional worry about Josiah's safety, he tried to keep her informed about his movements too. He knew Fanny well enough to realise that she would rather have the truth, even if it were unpalatable:

> I have been fearful you were not well as I had not heard from you for some time. As I know unpleasant news flies fast enough, I forbore saying anything respecting Captain Nisbet, however I will tell you all I know of the matter, which is contained in a letter from the Consul at Tunis to the Navy Board. I don't recollect the date, some time the latter end of June I think. After mentioning the loss of *L'Aigle,* he says 'I have hired a vessel for the use of Capt. Nisbet who is going in search of Admiral Nelson's fleet, with one hundred men.' From which circumstances we conjecture Capt.Nisbet and his men were passengers in *L'Aigle.*

Having reassured her that her son was safe, he then gave her news of Captain Berry. Reports received at the beginning of October had been conflicting, either his ship had been taken by the French or it had been so badly damaged in the action it had sunk. Fanny would have been deeply affected by this report for she regarded Berry, who had been one of her protégés, and his wife as very dear friends. However she would have tried hard not to show how deeply she was concerned for the sake of his sister Patty who was still staying with her.

In the way of such personal letters good news is mixed with bad and idle chit-chat blended with more serious topics. Maurice commented on the account she had given of the grand ball in Ipswich. Light heartedly, he told her he could match that. He had received an invitation from the Prime Minister, Mr Pitt himself, to a grand celebratory dinner. Unfortunately, on the day the great man had been unwell and unable to attend, but plenty of other 'great men' had been present. Sir Andrew Hamond (comptroller of the Navy and MP for Ipswich) had introduced Maurice – as Nelson's representative – to all the important gentlemen. Lord Hood had made a point of seeking him out and had asked especially after Fanny. Hood had also referred to the vexed question of who was to be heir to Nelson's title. And on that subject, Maurice confided to Fanny: 'I suspect my letter have offended William [the Rector] as I have not heard from him but I wrote my mind.' Pursuing the subject of heirs, Maurice reported that he had been to see Uncle Suckling who was very ill. Mr Rumsey, fearing that his old friend might be near to death, had informed Maurice, whom he believed to be Suckling's legal heir, of his condition. Although Suckling had a son and a daughter who bore his name they had both been born out of wedlock. It is believed that the former Miss Rumsey had been Suckling's mistress for many years. However, what mattered to Maurice was that Suckling had become very feeble and believed he would not get any better: '...he attributed his present complaint to his journey into Suffolk.'

Throughout October letters of congratulation on Nelson's success continued to arrive at Round Wood. Nelson's old friend Capt. Locker wrote to say how happy he was to hear that Nelson had escaped relatively unscathed. He also expressed the wish that it would not be long before Fanny saw her husband: '...the happiest meeting is my most hearty wish.' With his letter he enclosed a copy of one he had received from Lady St Vincent asking for Fanny's address. To Locker she had written:

> I beg you will accept my sincere congratulations on the important victory obtained by our friend Nelson over the French fleet. The becoming sense of piety he shews on the occasion crowns all...By the last dispatches from Lord St Vincent [C-in-C of the Mediterranean] he [Nelson] was well, but he will be in infinitely better spirits when I hear again. The happiness he will derive from the high credit done to his judgement on this occasion will almost exceed description.

This was high praise indeed, which would have delighted both Fanny and Edmund and no doubt yet another copy of it was made to send to Nelson.

Amongst the more personal correspondence was the letter from Mrs Lockhart, Fanny's sister-in-law from her first marriage. She had retained contact with her Nisbet relations, not least for her son's sake and it is evident from the few letters that have survived that they corresponded on a regular basis. Mrs Lockart said all the right things in the way of congratulations and concern for 'Nelson's health and happiness'. Her letter was accompanied by a gift of two white satin screens embroidered by her daughters, Mary and Isabella. She hoped Fanny would accept them as the girls would be so honoured if they could be found a place in 'Sir Horatio Nelson's house'. She then gave a lively account of the bonfire that had been held in her Scottish village near Glasgow and of the illuminations in the city itself, all in honour of the great victory. It was, Mrs Lockart felt, a very exciting time for everyone but for Fanny in particular. One sentence in her letter stands out in being almost prophetic:

> You was always steady and not apt to be led away with the vanities of this world, but you really will now require more than common principles to withstand all that I hope in God await you.

In addition to the many letters she received, Fanny found that many of the Suffolk families who had previously ignored her now wished to be acquainted. However, she was not to be seduced by this sudden attention and felt strongly that if she was worth knowing it should be for herself rather than for what her husband had achieved. As she told Lord Hood:

> Since my dear Lord, my husband, has gained this victory I have been honoured with the notice of the great in this neighbourhood – truly I don't thank them: they ought to have found their way to the cottage before – that is my way of thinking.

Her antipathy was reserved mainly for the ladies who had neglected her. She did however accept with no small pleasure the honour paid to her by Lord Chatham, the First Lord of the Admiralty (and older brother of the Prime Minister) who, during a visit to Ipswich, asked the Generals Manners and Balfour to take him to call on her at Round Wood. She then met all these generals and others at a military review on Westerfield Green. With a touch of humour she mentioned that the troublesome cough she had might have been exacerbated by that visit where: '…the window of the chaise being frequently down, gave me rather more fresh air than was necessary.' She made light of it hoping that: 'a little ass's milk will … set all to rights again.'

An outburst of coughing at the wrong moment was the last thing she needed as November came because she had a very important engagement to fill. Nelson had told her in a letter written on 16 September: 'Should the King give me a peerage I believe I scarcely need state the propriety of your going to court. Don't mind the expense.' The first opportunity to attend the Queen's Drawing Room was on 22 November. Before she could leave she had to close down Round Wood for the winter. She had also to make sure that everything they would need for the next few months was packed and the necessary travelling arrangements made for Edmund to get to Bath. Finally she packed what she needed for her stay in London. Then accompanied by her maid and one of the Bolton twins, on Friday 16 November as the *Ipswich Journal* reliably informed its readers: '...Lady Nelson set off from home to London.' This gave her a week before the big day to do all that had to be done, such as finding a suitable gown in which to appear before Her Majesty, have her hair dressed and meet her friends. She took accommodation at the small hotel in new Bond Street run by Mr Jones. That this was not an opulent or very fashionable hotel worried Fanny not a jot. She did not need trappings to bolster either her confidence or position. She had been most amused when she was approached by someone who actually believed, that since Nelson's elevation to the peerage, she had the ear of those at the top. One supplicant, who had asked her to drop a word on his behalf to Lord Spencer, was fully convinced that a request from her would receive immediate attention.

Such was her close relationship with the elderly Lord Hood that she could share with him these little incidents that amused her – or in this particular case, amazed her. The etiquette of attending a royal Drawing Room required that a newcomer should be introduced by someone who had already been presented to the Queen, so Fanny asked Lady Hood if she might accompany her. Anyone in Fanny's position might have been so wrapped up in her own presentation that she would not consider another's feelings but Fanny remembered that Lady Hood had not been well, and realising that the occasion might be fatiguing for her, begged Lady Hood not to feel under any obligation to her. In an effort not to seem too enthusiastic, she confessed that she was not that anxious to go but considered it to be her duty for her husband's sake. When the day came, Fanny was presented to the Queen, not by Lady Hood but by the much more socially superior Countess of Chatham. *The Times* listed Fanny amongst the 'principal female nobility and gentry'.

While Fanny was in London Nelson's letter of 1 October was redirected from Ipswich. It was a particularly poignant letter as along with all the heady details he gave of the adulation he was receiving, he talked of his birthday. Since 1793 he had been at home for this occasion only once and that had been the previous year when they had happily celebrated together quietly in Bath. How very different had been this year's occasion, his 40th:

> On my birthday night 80 people dined at Sir William's, 1740 came to a ball, 800 supped conducted on such a style of elegance as I never saw or shall again probably. A rostral column is erected under a magnificent canopy never Lady Hamilton says to come down while they remain in Naples. My father will tell you all about it, in the front Nelson, on the pedestal 'veni, vidi, vici,' anchors inscriptions having [part missing] were numerous.

As a finishing touch he added words written by Ellis Cornelia Knight. 'The British Nelson rivals Caesar's fame / Like him he came, he saw, he overcame, / In conquest modest as in action brave / To God the glory pious Nelson gave.' Fanny and the family would never be able to compete with that.

Alexander Davison, Nelson's close friend and agent, was another of Fanny's correspondents. Only recently have many of her letters to him come to light. These are now in the safe keeping of the National Maritime Museum Library at Greenwich. From the tone of the letters it is clear that Fanny regarded both the Davisons as friends rather than mere business acquaintances. They had a London home in St James's Square, just off Pall Mall where Fanny was a frequent visitor whenever she was in town. With access to information coming from the Navy Office, Davison, who worked closely with Maurice Nelson, was often in a position to give Fanny the very latest reports of the whereabouts of her husband. Following her brief stay in London during November, Fanny had gone to join Edmund in Bath and it was from there she wrote on 18 December to say since she had left London she had heard nothing from Nelson except that letter of 1 October. Ten days later she wrote again that she still had: 'No letter from my dear Lord.' She had not been well, she told Davison, which was hardly surprising given that the weather, which before Christmas had been mild, damp and foggy, had suddenly become excessively cold. Had Fanny still been in Ipswich she would have experienced temperatures of around 10°F.

From the only recent letter she had, she knew that Nelson continued on duty in the Mediterranean, spending much of his time in the Naples area. In the eleven years of their marriage Fanny had come to recognise just how much her husband longed, needed even, to be highly regarded not just by his peers but the world in general. Many times during their long correspondence while he was at sea, he complained to her when he thought those in authority had slighted him or he believed he had been passed over for promotion. But how very different things were now! Regardless of opinion at home, in Italy he was a great hero; the King and Queen of Naples held him in the very highest esteem as did the British Government's representative, Sir William Hamilton who with his wife had offered him such splendid hospitality. Nelson wanted to share his triumph with Fanny. That letter, dated coincidentally on the day that the news of his victory had reached England, told her:

> ... the Grand Signior has ordered me a rich jewel: if it was worth a million my pleasure will be to see it in your possession. My pride is being your husband, the son of my dear Father and in having Sir William and Lady Hamilton for my friends.

If her heart had swelled with overwhelming love for him at this tribute to her, when did her head start hearing the warning bells? At that stage Nelson always referred to the Hamiltons as a couple:

186

…it is impossible for me to express the affectionate kindness both Sir William and her Ladyship has shown me. I had not a wish which was not anticipated and all their study was how to please me best. Never, never shall I forget them. Except from you my dearest Fanny, did I ever before experience friendship?

In an age when couples often married for economic, social or dynastic reasons rather than romantic love, friendship, as defined in 'one joined to another in intimacy and mutual benevolence independent of sexual or family love', was also a strong basis for a happy marriage. Nelson often called Fanny his friend intending it as a tribute to her. He also accorded the term to his father, again showing the depth of his love for him. But now he was widening his circle of those very dear to him to include the Hamiltons.

He seemed guilelessly to anticipate that Fanny too could be included in this new friendship. Lady Hamilton had volunteered to write Fanny: '…a line of what passed on the day of my sailing.' It must have been well into the New Year before Fanny received this letter of 11 December. Nelson had returned to Naples where the Queen herself had made him promise not to leave until matters had improved within the kingdom. Aware that he had not written as often as he should to her and his father, he blamed the excessive amount of naval correspondence that had to take precedence. He played on Fanny's anxiety that he was making himself ill with overwork:

…but Lady Hamilton's goodness forces me out at noon for an hour. What can I say of her and Sir William's goodness to me. They are in fact with the exception of you and my dear father the dearest friends I have in this world. I live as Sir William's son in the house and my glory is as dear to them as their own. In short I am under such obligations that I can never repay them but with my eternal gratitude.

Knowing that Fanny would read this letter to Edmund, he was a trifle naïve in suggesting that the Hamiltons were now as dear to him as his wife and father. Edmund might have been delighted that his son was forming such a close attachment to Hamilton, a man in a very high position, but both he and Fanny were made to feel guilty that they had not responded as rapturously to his 'glory' as he felt they should. In writing about Lady Hamilton Nelson exhibited a lack of both tact and sensitivity to his wife. If he saw his role in the Hamilton household as that of a son, was Fanny to understand that Nelson regarded Lady Hamilton as a mother figure? Hardly. Fanny had listened to enough gossip in the past to know all about that lady's previous dubious history that included how when the Hon. Charles Greville found it expedient to get rid of her as mistress he had passed her on to his uncle Sir William Hamilton who after some years had married her. Nelson had made an oblique reference to her earlier reputation on the first occasion he met her in 1793: 'She is a young woman of amiable manners who does honour to the station to which she is raised.' Five years on she was unlikely to have matured into a mother figure for him but in his desire to praise Lady Hamilton he suggested she might be so to Josiah. Insensitively he wrote to his wife:

> The improvement made in Josiah by Lady Hamilton is wonderful. She seems the only person he minds and his faults are not omitted to be told him but in such a way as pleases him, and his, your and my obligation are infinite on that score.

This must have touched a raw nerve in Fanny who was fiercely protective of the son she had not seen for so long. She desperately wanted him to do well and earn Nelson's regard for him as an individual as much as a stepson. She knew, for Nelson continually told her so: '...his manners are so rough.' Since he had spent the last six years at sea, Fanny had been denied the opportunity to shape her son's behaviour yet she undoubtedly felt the implied criticism. What mother would not have been upset to be told that another woman was having a refining influence on her only son? And even worse, to be told that she should feel under an obligation to that other woman. In writing of Josiah at this time Nelson went out of his way to reassure his wife:

> ...dear Josiah's heart is as good and as humane as ever was covered by human breast, but his manners are so rough, but God bless him I love him dearly with all his roughness.

Lady Hamilton meanwhile, carried out her 'dear friend's' request and wrote to Fanny in late October or early November and again on 2 December. Just in case her first letter had not reached Fanny she reiterated its contents:

> I hope your Ladyship received my former letter with an account of Lord Nelson's arrival and his reception from their Sicilian Majesties and also the congratulations and compliments from this amiable and adorable Queen to your Ladyship.

If Fanny was amused or flabbergasted by the flamboyant language, whichever reaction it was must have increased as she read on.

> Lord Nelson is adored here and looked on as the deliverer of this country. He was not well when he first arrived, but by nursing [she was implying an intimacy here] and asses' milk he went from Naples quite recovered. The King and Queen adore him and if he had been their brother they could not have shewn him more respect and attention. I need not tell your Ladyship how happy Sir William and myself are at having an opportunity of seeing our dear, respectable, brave friend return here with so much honour to himself and glory for his country.

Before telling her that Nelson's wound was quite well, Lady Hamilton either realised that she had perhaps exceeded the bounds of propriety or she was completely artless when she wrote: 'We only wanted you [with us] to be completely happy.' Then she again caused Fanny annoyance or possibly anger by writing about Josiah.

> Josiah is so much improved in every respect. We are all delighted with him. He is an excellent officer and very steady and one of the best hearts in the world. I love him much and although we quarrel sometimes, he loves me and does as I would have him. He is in the way of being rich, for he has taken many prizes. He is indefatigable in his line, never sleeps out of his ship and I am sure will make a great officer.

It is feasible that Lady Hamilton honestly thought that these kind remarks about Josiah would please his mother. All they did, however, was to emphasise the degree of intimacy between the lady and Nelson, for how else could she have known about Josiah's qualities as an officer if she had not discussed them with Nelson? Understandably, Fanny would have been irritated by the influence that Lady Hamilton professed to have with Josiah. And understandable too was any jealousy Fanny might have felt at the postscript to this letter that contained a message from her son: 'J. desired his duty to your Ladyship and says he will write as soon as he has time but he has been very busy for some time past.' It would not have taken much imagination for Fanny to see her son dancing attendance on the other lady yet not being able to find time for his mother.

Whatever misgivings Fanny had on the receipt of this letter were dispelled by the news that Nelson intended, if all was well, to leave Naples in March. On his arrival in England at the end of May or beginning of June, he hoped for four months' leave. If that letter, whenever it arrived, filled her with happiness and longing, the next one must have made her realise how much in some respects her husband had changed. It also highlighted the long delay in the receipt of letters, for when Nelson wrote on 2 January 1799 he had received nothing from Fanny since 8 October. In this letter he reiterated his intention to apply for leave to come home in March. He also revealed that he felt disgruntled, having had a disagreement with his new commander-in-chief, Sir Sidney Smith.

> As a piece of my command is lopped off by the great S. S. S. there can be no occasion for a Nelson. However my mind is satisfied with myself and although I shall return much poorer than when I set out, yet my heart is at ease.

Leaving aside the high opinion he held of himself he could not resist threatening Fanny with the possibility of a lack of money for the future. Yet in the next sentence, the man who a few years earlier had longed for a return to farming and life in a small house in the country now declared:

> I must have a house in London if possible…The rooms must be light and
> airy, but this is supposing my pension is handsome…if we have money a
> neat ['of elegant simplicity' – nicely made or proportioned – OED] house
> in London near Hyde Park, but on no account on the other side of Portman
> Square. I detest Baker Street. In short do as you please you know my
> wishes and income. A neat carriage I desire you will order and if possible
> get good servants. You will take care I am not let down.

The reason a good address in London was so important to him lies in a later
sentence: 'The King has elevated me and I must support my station, in short
whether I am at home a month sooner or later a house in London must be
had furnished and ready for us.' Nelson had received notification of his peerage on 18 November and thereafter signed all his correspondence simply
'Nelson'. Presumably he believed that on his return he would be expected
to entertain – hence the need for good servants – and would be entertained
in return thus requiring his own carriage. Status was all-important to him; if
one had a position in life then one must show that one could support it. It is
debatable how much of this attitude was the product of Nelson's previous
observation of other members of his profession when they were ennobled or
the influence of the Hamiltons and the style of life they led.

More unsettling for Fanny was Nelson's request that she should think
very carefully about Round Wood. Did it really suit her? If not, she was to
look for somewhere else – and this time she was to take into consideration
that: '…we must have a good dining room and bed chambers, a kitchen
must be thought of and room for servants with coach house and stables.'
Fanny must surely have reflected on how different this was to his previous
attitude to house purchase. In one breath he appeared to be specifying what
he required and then shelving the responsibility on to her to make the decision as to whether it were better to alter and extend a place they did not like
or have somewhere built to their own specification. It began to appear that
Round Wood and Ipswich were no longer grand enough for Baron Nelson.
In his next letter he decided that Bath was the better place for his father
and Fanny: ' [it] will not only agree better with our dear Father than Round
Wood but be more pleasant and cheerful for you.'

That phrase 'pleasant and cheerful' has often been used by her detractors
to suggest that Fanny lacked spirit, was constantly bemoaning her lot in life
and ever in need of diversion. No doubt in comparison with the ebullient
Lady Hamilton, with her flair for artistic and dramatic poses and powerful
singing voice, Fanny's quieter temperament would have seemed in need
of pleasant and cheerful diversion. Even if Nelson intended his remark to
show his loving concern, it suggests that he had forgotten the realities of
her life and that far from seeking amusement to pass the time, he had for
years taken it for granted that she would deal with any problem that arose.

In many ways he used her to undertake commissions on his behalf that he would not ask of his agents. She was the one expected to write asking for overdue payments for cadets, or to put off politely those who sought Nelson's assistance in getting a post at sea. Far from being the 'little woman who shouldn't worry her pretty little head about such matters', Fanny was the one who was faced with the responsibility for filling in the Government forms for the latest revenue-raising scheme. Pitt's administration had tried various ingenious methods to finance the wars of the day from taxing such things as the number of wheels on a wagon to the powder used for wigs, but in 1799 it had introduced an Income Tax of two shillings in the pound.

On the afternoon of the day she was to go to Clifton, Fanny received a visit from a Clerk to the Income Commission. For a moment she must have recalled that occasion years before when the bailiffs had arrived at the Norfolk parsonage to serve Nelson with the writ for damages. This visit was entirely unexpected as she had already been in correspondence with Davison who, she thought, would handle the questions she could not answer about certain aspects of Nelson's income: 'The statement of my Lord's riches in money [her underlining] is to the best of my knowledge perfectly correct.' In order to answer the question about the amount of Land Tax they paid on Round Wood, she had written to Mr Fuller, the tenant. The law-abiding daughter of the former chief justice of Nevis was very conscious of the importance of making an accurate and speedy declaration, so she had asked Fuller to send the information direct to Davison by return of post. As for the amount of pension Nelson had been granted following the loss of his arm, Fanny had to rely on her memory: 'Now I recollect, Mr Monk told me, the Nett of the Pension was £900 and odd shillings' and then showing her keen sense of what was right as well as the importance of accounting for every penny: 'it is best to be exact.'

That as far as she was concerned was that; everything that should be done had been. Thus she was somewhat taken aback by her visitor from the Income Commission. Fanny was extremely good at describing conversations and making a scene come alive and her description of Mr Else, the Clerk, is almost that of the stereotypical bureaucrat. He began by telling her that the Commission had been extremely indulgent towards her…but…she had not filled out correctly the Schedule she had been sent; items of Lord Nelson's income were missing. She replied that she had put on the printed form that Mr Davison would give them all the information they needed to complete the form. However, that apparently was not sufficient for the official, the form had to be filled in by her. Thus, he desired that she would write the following to Davison:

> Mr Davison will please to state the income of Lord Nelson and that Lady Nelson may make a return agreeable to the Act in Bath – producing a certificate that the Tax is paid elsewhere will of course be discharged from the charge in Bath.

Fanny no doubt dealt with the Clerk with her usual courtesy even though she must have been annoyed that his request meant more letters to be written immediately thus causing her to have to cancel her travel arrangements to Clifton that evening and make an alternative booking for the following day. There was almost a tone of exasperation in her request to Davison: 'Will you have the goodness to write to the Commissioner or the proper person on this subject.'

Certainly there were occasions when Fanny seemed less able to withstand the pressures put upon her. When she first received the news in January that Nelson intended to come home, she told Davison that she had confessed to her brother-in-law Maurice that she was 'nervous beyond description'. She did not give him the reason she was in such an emotional state. True, she was looking forward to being reunited with the husband she loved deeply but why such apprehension? They had endured four years apart while this time he had been gone less than a year. Although she did not admit it, perhaps even to herself, she feared that Nelson had become a changed man. The only way she could account for the changes in attitude that were revealed in his letters was that he was a sick man. A few days later she wrote to Davison to tell him of Nelson's requirements for a London house: 'My dear Lord's letter assure me he only waits for leave to return to England… he has desired me to take a ready furnished house immediately.' No wonder with this injunction that Fanny needed to have some idea when his leave was likely to start. Was she to drop any plans she might have made and rush off to London to wait – for who knew how long? That she felt under emotional pressure showed clearly: her normal well-formed, controlled handwriting was all over the place and the page, which was usually filled almost to the edge, had extra wide margins. She was, however, much more controlled when she wrote in April that she had had a visit from an officer, just back in England, who had brought the news that Nelson had not been granted leave. If ever there was an occasion for Fanny to be angry or have 'an attack of nerves' this was it. And she now revealed what had caused much of her anxiety as she passed on to Davison the views of Lord Hood who: 'always expressed his fears that Sir and Lady H would use their influence to keep Lord Nelson with them'. Fanny's only comment was the terse: 'they have succeeded.' Controlled she might appear but in the same letter she confessed that: 'I am sadly hurt and out of humour.' As well she might be, for she could not have failed to notice that from 21 March, Nelson's usual address to her as 'My Dearest Fanny,' had changed to 'Dear Fanny.' Realising that she was powerless to change matters she added with resignation: 'I trust in God and hope my husband's successes will continue.'

In the meantime, however reluctant she felt, her life had to continue as normal. On the advice of Edmund, who had declared that for her husband's sake she must show herself in the right circles, she planned to go to London in the middle of May in order to attend the Queen's Birthday celebrations. In addition to all her other concerns was that wretched Income Tax return.

She realised that she had not declared Nelson's carriage that he had had in London. She had asked her tenant at Round Wood to do it for her: 'I hope I have not done anything wrong – the Government I would not cheat for the world.' But at least she did receive some good news; Josiah's ship the *Thalia* had captured an enemy ship that was likely to bring the captors a good bounty. The report had come to her at least third hand. One of the serving officers in *Thalia*, Lieutenant Whitley, had written to tell his father all about it. As was the custom among the close knit society of Bath, the non intimate parts of the letter had been read aloud in a company that included Lady Bowyer. This lady, described by Fanny as 'a mother and a good woman', knowing Fanny's interest in the *Thalia* had hurried to call on her and impart the good tidings. Since she understood that Lt Whitley's share was to be £1,200, Lady Bowyer thought that Capt. Josiah Nisbet's would be even greater. For Fanny this was a double blessing; her son was safe and he was managing to accrue some independent means. It had become apparent to her from the few letters she did receive from Nelson that Josiah was no longer in his stepfather's good graces. Nelson did not give her any detail, merely:

> I wish I could say much to your and my satisfaction about J but I am sorry to say and with real grief, that he has nothing good about him, he must sooner or later be broke, but I am sure neither you or I can help it – I have done with the subject it is an ungrateful one.

The reason for Nelson's change in attitude is not entirely explained by the complaint that the young man lacked polish in his manners and had a quick temper. The root of the problem lay with Lady Hamilton. It has been suggested that Josiah disapproved of his stepfather's close relationship with her; that at Nelson's birthday party, Josiah had drunk too much and accused his stepfather of putting Lady Hamilton before his mother. It was also possible that the young man was himself attracted to her, as Nelson had been to Mary Moutray and was jealous that Nelson received more attention than he did. Having been infatuated on a number of occasions when he was young, Nelson must have recognised the signs in Josiah. It is feasible that Lady Hamilton played one off against the other. Whatever the case, something drastic had occurred. 'J has got a commission for *Thalia*. I wish he may deserve it. However he has had more done for him than any young man in the service and made I fear the worst use of his advantages.' That may have been Nelson's honest opinion but he must have known how deeply his remarks would wound Fanny.

Apart from inwardly grieving there was little she could do to alter the situation so she carried on with the routine of daily life, accepting that this now included being sought out by those who had previously ignored her, or being able to take her place at Court for splendid occasions like the Royal birthdays. There were other benefits to be had from being the wife of a national hero. One that pleased her particularly was the dedication of music to Nelson. Nelson's niece Charlotte wrote to tell her uncle that new songs celebrating the Battle of the Nile appeared in print daily. She was learning to play many of them, in particular the grand march and a piece for dancing called 'Lady Nelson's Fancy'. Fanny, the accomplished pianist, would also have been quick to learn those pieces so that she, like Charlotte might: 'have the pleasure of playing them to you [Nelson].' She had been delighted to receive from the composer himself in St Petersburgh a presentation copy of a martial piece written in honour of the victory and was present at the concert in Bath when it was performed there for the first time.

Almost from the moment she became part of the Nelson family, Fanny was looked to by one or other of them for advice or money – sometimes both. Her brother-in-law, the Rector, now very conscious of his new position in relation to his famous brother, determined that his daughter Charlotte should have the benefit of a London boarding school education. The fact that he consulted Fanny for her opinion on the establishment he had in mind showed that he considered that she would know about such things and even though she had no direct experience, having no daughters of her own, he must have believed that amongst her acquaintances there would be some who would. There were two further considerations; when Lady Nelson had her own house in Town, Charlotte would be able to make visits there from school and thus gain entrée into a social life that was not available to her in Norfolk. While on a more mercenary level, since the Rector was expecting his brother to make a major contribution to the educational costs, it was politic of him to get Fanny's support and interest. In a lengthy letter written on 1 April, the Rector reported that during a recent stay in Brecon he had met a Mrs Thomas Berney who had offered him her advice on:

> a school at Chelsea, called White-lands House, the conduct and manage-
> ment of which she said she knew to be exceptionable and the attention
> paid to the health and morals of the young ladies unequalled by any other
> school in or near London. I told her that at present the business was in
> your Ladyship's hands…but…if you were not fixed, we should be happy
> to pay attention to her recommendation. Mrs Berney further added that
> Mrs [Misses] Clarke and Thomas the governesses of the school were well
> behaved good tempered accomplished people and that she looked upon
> them more as sisters, than anything else.

With a fulsomeness that Fanny must have come eventually to loathe, he continued: '…we must all allow Mrs Berney is a good judge, being so accomplished herself.' However, the decision was to be Fanny's and only if she agreed would he get his wife to write to the school to arrange for Charlotte to attend after the Whitsun holidays.

Another matter arising from Nelson's elevation to the peerage to be dealt with was what uniform was now appropriate to be worn by the male staff of their household for special occasions. On this somewhat tricky question

Fanny apparently turned the tables and asked for the Rector's advice. With unaccustomed modesty the Rector had to admit:

> ... with regard to the full dress livery, I cannot say that I am a competent judge, I should think a London tailor who is used to make them for the nobility who frequent St James's will immediately know from seeing the undress [the everyday livery].

Having admitted a lack of knowledge, most people would have stopped there but not the Rector; he still had to voice an opinion:

> However, my idea is this. The coat lined with yellow and yellow button holes, the collar and cuffs black velvet the same as at present, only it should have a standing collar, the waistcoat yellow, and I think there should be shag [a long-napped rough cloth] breeches the colour of the waistcoat, the coat and waistcoat pockets and collar should be embroidered with a worsted lace composed of the colours of the livery with the cross which comprises part of the crest worked upon it, one or two gold epaulets as you please on the coat and a gold laced hat is my general idea.

The Rector admitted that he had based his ideas on what he had seen of Lord Walpole's full dress livery. Without doubt he had paid close attention to detail as he ended by mentioning that the buttons should have: 'either the aigrette [white heron] or *San Josef* crests upon them.'

In closing the Rector mentioned that his sister, Mrs Bolton, was staying with him and his family at Hilborough. Earlier in the year, Thomas Bolton had bought a large farm at Cranwich, a few miles from Hilborough so at last it looked as if the Boltons would have a settled home. Most of the Nelson family believed that Thomas had overstretched himself with this purchase and so it turned out and it was not long before he found himself in financial difficulties. Like the rest of the family, he turned to Nelson for help – or rather to Fanny to draw upon Nelson's reserves. Fanny had to ask Davison for the cash in a letter of 19 April that showed her frustration with her brother-in-law.

> I have this day received so pressing a letter from Mr B for £200 that it must be sent to him (which I am afraid is like a drop of water in the sea.) Therefore I beg you will lend me £200 – Bank Post Bills of that value (taking the numbers) to be enclosed in a blank cover on Monday – I shall write this day to Mr B to send to the Post Office on Tuesday for it.

Here was a competent woman. However strongly she may have felt about Bolton's improvidence, it was her duty as Nelson's wife to help his family, as her husband had wished her to do. Although it was necessary to apply to Davison for the money, she was sensible of the need at a time of so many forgeries, for the precaution of recording the numbers of the bank bills. She also wasted no time in dealing with the request and organised the details of when and how the delivery should take place. It says much for the speed and reliability of the mail coach service that Fanny's letter of the 19th brought her the £200 the next day. She then endorsed both bills making them payable to Bolton, and put them on that day's coach ready for Bolton to collect on the following day.

Other matters too were pressing in on her. Writing to thank Davison for handling the bank bills, she reminded him that she and Edmund would shortly be visiting London and that she would then take the opportunity to discuss with him the question of a house, although earlier she had asked him not to do anything about it. But she had recently received some disturbing news from Mr Fuller who was keeping an eye on Round Wood. While she had thought she had left the house in reasonably good order it now transpired: '…the roof very leaky, the walls in a bad state, in short not fit for me to inhabit – therefore if you can persuade the proprietor of the House you have seen to wait I will thank you.' Deep down Fanny was reluctant to commit to a London home for she ended by saying: 'Mr N [Edmund] desires me to say all this to you.'

The strain was beginning to affect her health and when she wrote next to Davison on 29 April it was to tell him that she had been: '…very much indisposed.' Whatever her condition it was serious enough for her physician to bleed her. She had, she said, with that exactness for detail, had: '…upwards of eight oz [ounces] of blood taken from me.' She was left feeling that the air in Bath was no longer doing her any good so she intended to move immediately to Clifton and sent her personal maid to find a suitable house to rent for her and Edmund. However, Clifton did not have the desired effect of improving either her health or that of Edmund. Both seem to have suffered from the stress of not knowing when Nelson was likely to return. Fanny told Davison she believed that anxiety: '…will shake the strongest' and she did not think she could boast of being one of them. Apart from her own concern she had the additional worry of Edmund. Although he had recovered sufficiently to get up for breakfast and remain in his chair for part of the day, he had been very ill. Fanny always approached illness, both her own and that of others in a sensible, practical manner so she rather thought that Edmund was not quite as bad as the attendant apothecary did. It was clear that Edmund's illness was of mental rather than physical origin and Fanny found it both distressing to have to witness: '…his extreme agitation upon hearing a carriage or a knock.' Edmund remembered that the last time Nelson returned he had arrived at the house unannounced and anticipated this would happen again.

There were still no letters from Nelson. In early May Fanny, who was trying to find out when the ten thousand pounds that had been voted by the East India Company to Nelson as a reward for his victory would be paid into Davison's hands, revealed that although she had mentioned this in her letters to her husband, she had not received any reaction from him because: 'you know we have had so little communication, for some months.' As usual she was not prepared to believe that this was in any way Nelson's fault, rather she blamed the erratic nature of mail reaching ships in the Mediterranean. Touchingly, she pleaded with Davison to tell her of anything that he heard relative to Nelson.

At the beginning of June Fanny and Edmund moved into 92 Sloane Street in London. On 4 June she attended a Drawing Room in honour of the King's Birthday. For this occasion according to *The Morning Herald*, Fanny:

>...was most magnificently attired in a superb embroidery of silver, in drapery of stripes, with a robe of silver, ornamented to correspond...a beautiful head dress with an elegant plumage of ostrich feathers.

She had been conveyed to the Drawing Room in the sedan chair belonging to her friends, Lord and Lady Walpole who, as always, were genuinely pleased to see Fanny and make her part of their social circle.

With her innate good manners, Fanny was widely accepted. The same cannot be said for the Rector. This bombastic man frequently caused her embarrassment. As she told Nelson on 7 June, in what amounted to an addition to the long letter she had already written that day: 'I cannot say his manners are better. The roughest mortal surely that ever lived.' She quoted as an example the time when she had been about to leave the house for a carriage ride with her friend Mrs Buckley when the Rector had demanded that she take his wife and children with them. 'He frightened Mrs Buckley...however I assured [her] it was only an odd method he had acquired in speaking.' The problem with the Rector was that he was a constant thorn in the flesh of his father as well as the rest of the family. It was bad enough to have to endure the man himself occasionally but after each of his visits she had to listen while Edmund discussed his son.

While Edmund was blinkered as far as the absent Horatio was concerned, he held no illusions about his elder son whom he regarded as being ambitious, proud and selfish. On this occasion he came to vent his spleen against the Boltons who were responsible for the Rector's latest feeling of wounded pride. He felt it reflected badly on him that they had become the topic of local Norfolk gossip with their high spending and ever increasing debts. Worse still, the Rector had heard that Bolton was still obtaining credit from tradesmen and others on the strength of having a brother-in-law who was a great Lord who was going to pay all his debts. This did not suit the Rector who had his own designs on any spare money Nelson might have. He had already decided that his son and heir, Horatio, must receive the education that would fit him to be a gentleman. But he realised, as he believed Fanny could not, just how expensive this would be. Fanny and Edmund had let him run his course without making any comment. Their silence did not deter him one bit. For Fanny there had been further embarrassment, not for herself but for young Kitty Bolton who was also present and must have been distressed by the remarks about her father. Having endured the evening in the Rector's company, his conversation was resurrected the following day as Edmund went over it and gave Fanny his opinion of his son's behaviour. With great reluctance, not least because there was some problem over their sleeping arrangements. Edmund and Fanny had agreed to visit the Rectory on their way to Burnham.

> Our Father was speaking of the accommodation. I said, 'They have three good bedrooms, Horatio can sleep in his sister's for she will be at school.'
> … [Edmund replied] 'Horatio is never to be turned out of his bed again for anyone, so his father says.'

Obviously the Rector did not consider that a young 'gentleman' should ever have to consider the wishes or needs of others. Fanny who was normally very indulgent of young people was adamant: 'I never saw a child stand a fairer chance of being spoiled than he does, his ideas will be great indeed.' She may have held her tongue on some occasions but when the Rector commented that she had done very little entertaining during her stay in London except for members of the family but that when: 'My Lord comes home, things will be in better style, ' she very firmly reminded him that she was keeping two houses going and the London one was very expensive. She was indeed finding that the cost of living in London was very high even though she lived as economically as possible. She pointed out to Nelson, as she had done in earlier years, that he had been away so long, he had no true comprehension of just how expensive everything had become. Apart from rent and housekeeping bills she had also recently given Edmund £100 to help pay outstanding bills he expected to find when he reached Burnham. His son Suckling had died at the end of April and Edmund had to sort out his affairs including the debts that he had left. Edmund had not asked her for the money but had confided that he knew of at least one bill for £50. Sensitive to his need Fanny had quietly passed over the hundred pounds.

Towards the end of June, Edmund went to Burnham Thorpe for a few weeks. Apart from clearing up Suckling's affairs he had to arrange for a new curate for the parish who would also become the tenant of the parsonage. Fanny returned to Round Wood where almost immediately she was taken ill with what she described as 'a slow fever'. This condition, although not reckoned dangerous, she found tiresome, mainly because it caused a skin irritation. The frightening report she had received earlier about the state of Round Wood proved to be exaggerated and when she saw it for herself she found that not only was it in fairly good order it was still very pleasant. Although the house had withstood its depredations the very severe winter had taken its toll on a number of the inhabitants of Ipswich.

While she and Edmund were apart, they corresponded regularly and much of the news from Norfolk was duly passed from him to Fanny who forwarded it to Nelson. Some snippets would have specially pleased him; for example, that his former captain, Berry, now Sir Edward had recovered from his wounds and was about to return to service, taking with him Nelson's young nephew, George Bolton. Full of genuine compassion, Fanny told him: 'You will be truly concerned to hear Mr Barnard is dead, he drank himself mad and died raving. Mrs B with five sons in great distress.' Barnard was a clergyman who had married the daughter of the wealthy landowner in Burnham Thorpe, Sir Mordant. Fanny added that the Rector, who as always had to voice his opinion, believed that Barnard had taken to drink to cover his disappointment that his wife's rich relations had not found him a good living – a perhaps not very subtle way for the Rector to pave the way for his own ambitions. Fanny's concern was for the widow and her five sons left penniless. 'Our Father thinks all the great connections will raise something comfortable for Mrs B, I wish it may be so. God protect her.' Fanny could still remember her own early widowhood and how dependent she had been on the financial assistance of wealthy relations. On a happier note, she reported that there was now another Frances Herbert Nelson. Outram, the purser from the *Enterprise*, one of Nelson's earlier commands, had written to beg the liberty of naming his ninth child after her. This amused Fanny greatly especially as she had had two letters from him which had been full of: ' –the honour – your goodness. I won't forget joking – "but Miss Frances must not be at your honour's service." I will send her something.'

Another recipient of a christening gift from Fanny was Davison's latest child who was to be named Horatio. Nelson and Fanny were asked to be godparents but the date for the service was not fixed in advance, so although Fanny had gone up to London again for a few days to stay in Sloane Street in order to go with Davison to view the house he had in mind for Nelson's homecoming, she did not hear about the christening until Maurice Nelson told her of it on 8 July. In a light-hearted letter to Davison she wrote that she had been told: '…the little hero is to be made a Christian tomorrow.' She joked that this had left her insufficient time to get a new gown for the occasion and:

I would not for the world pay him so little respect. Therefore if this said personage is to be christened tomorrow Mrs D must stand for me – Maurice stands for his brother.

She then casually added that again she had not been well, her doctor advising her against going out. Far from making a great thing of her indisposition, whatever it was, she asserted: 'I shall be well in a few days.' She made no mention of her actual gift to her godson but, in a thoughtful and caring gesture, she enclosed a monetary gift for the baby's nurse.

Some time before 18 July she was back in Ipswich and again entertaining her in-laws, the Boltons, who came for Race Week. Edmund was there too, having returned from Norfolk in such a debilitated state that Fanny had doubts as to how much longer he could survive: '...his cough is painful to hear and he spits terribly.' In this feeble state his only pleasure was to take a daily carriage ride in the early afternoon, a practice that did not have Fanny's entire approval, as the weather was hot and the dusty roads likely to aggravate his bronchial condition. Edmund seemed to be happy only in Fanny's company: '...he won't have any of his children with him.' The constant bickering of the siblings and their demands for money disturbed him and it was he who advised Fanny to send the Boltons home, telling her to use the excuse that Josiah was expected home on leave at any time. Sadly, Edmund was beginning to doubt if he would live to see his own son come home. In his fondness for her he told Fanny that if he did survive to witness Nelson's homecoming, then the first thing he would tell Horatio was that he was to take care of her: 'I am sure he will do everything he can to make you happy.' The old man had convinced himself that Nelson's desire for wealth was only for Fanny's benefit. He was also resolute in his belief that it was because his son was indispensable that he was not given leave. Both he and Fanny clung to the belief that the lack of letters was due to some mishap: 'I am sure he writes, who can be so wicked as to take away my letters.' So yet again, she had to rely on Davison for the latest report on her husband's health and movements.

Her relationship with Davison was very important to her. Being Nelson's confidant and business manager he offered Fanny a vital link with her husband. What must have started out as a purely business arrangement between him and Fanny had over the years developed into a close family friendship. He was important to her, too, in providing an outlet for the thoughts and feelings she could not express to others. She could, and did, discuss her health matters with him. In return he confided his own medical problems to her. On occasions she was able to disclose to him some of the burden she felt from looking after Edmund, something that she could not do either to Nelson or other members of the family. Davison was, as Edmund had said: 'a very feeling good man.' And it was to this aspect of his nature that she appealed in that letter of 18 July which also revealed her as a good and feeling woman.

At a time when medical care was almost beyond the reach of the lower paid and entry to such free hospitals that existed was open only to those who could find a sponsor, Fanny asked Davison:

> Can you get a housemaid of mine in the Middlesex Hospital or any other. She is a good woman, very ill, very honest and very poor – if she had health, a capital servant. She stays here till her strength will allow her to get to London by the day coach. She is a Devonshire woman – her disorder Scorbutic Rheumatism.

It is a pity that the Nelson biographers who describe Fanny as cold and unfeeling did not have access to this particular letter. Not only did she pay tribute to the servant's qualities but she also showed immense concern for her welfare. She did not simply dismiss the woman who was no longer capable of work and leave her to fend for herself. In her ailing state, the obvious place for the woman would have been the Workhouse. Significantly Fanny mentioned the maid's place of birth as Devonshire. Under the Poor Law, the woman would be expected to return to her native parish to gain admittance to the local Workhouse. It was doubtful if the woman could have made such a long journey. Instead, Fanny kept her and provided nursing care, hoping that when she was able to travel the shorter distance to London in the comfort of the day coach rather than the cheaper carrier's wagon, the woman would be admitted to hospital for proper medical treatment.

On the whole Fanny's servants caused her little trouble. Edmund had had the drug-crazed man who had run away the year before when he had come from Bath to London en route to Ipswich, and now they were faced with another man in whom they had placed trust, letting them down badly. Fanny's account of the event that led to her having to dismiss the coachman was not entirely straightforward but it appeared that the stables at Round Wood were burgled. The stable window had been prised open and the coachman's greatcoats and other articles had been taken. At the time builders were carrying out repairs to the stables so naturally suspicion fell upon them. Investigations were carried out by Mr Ripshaw, the Ipswich jailer, described by Fanny as a man: '...whose judgement is thought very good.' He questioned the builders first and then the servants before reaching the conclusion that all the evidence, such as it was, pointed to the coachman. They did not press charges but she and Edmund felt that it was impossible to keep him on. Edmund had taken it upon himself to speak to the man, pointing out that it was his keeping company with bad women that had led to his downfall and that if he did not give up this way of life then inevitably he would end up on the gallows. Fanny had her doubts that the little lecture would have any long lasting effect, especially when she later discovered that amongst his peers the man had a bad reputation and worse: '...his treatment of his wife was shocking.'

Fanny felt comfortable in her correspondence with Davison. She gave him the trivia of her life as well as the important details. Thus in early August she told him that she was expecting Sir Edward and Lady Berry to stay for a couple of days with her, breaking their journey from Norwich to London. She proudly stated that now the Cottage had been papered it looked much better: '...quite ready to receive my Lord.' With this remark, Fanny, in effect answered the question Nelson had posed earlier. Yes, she was quite happy to remain at Round Wood. In fact she was considering the purchase of extra land. Their tenant farmer Mr Fuller was most anxious that an adjoining farm which was for sale should be added to their holding. Fuller had brought the plans and every detail appertaining to the farm for her to scrutinise. Fanny was not sure what advantage such a purchase would have for them but Edmund was extremely keen on the idea of

enlarging the property. As for Fuller, he was so anxious to increase his acre-
age that he was willing to pay almost any rent to Fanny rather than see the
farm pass into other hands. Edmund decided that he would consult someone who knew about land values and so the bombastic Revd Bolton was
asked his opinion. Revealing the high prices of the period, he had advised,
as Fanny wrote to Nelson: '...you must pay £500 more than it is worth in
order to make your little farm complete.'

Financial matters were again a topic of conversation between husband
and wife. In the middle of August, Fanny had received a letter written by
Nelson just a month before. He referred right back to April when Fanny had
given Thomas Bolton £200. Now he wished her to make other gifts on his
behalf from the money he was due from the East India Company. Edmund,
Maurice and the Rector were to have £500 apiece and another £500 was to
be offered to his sister Kitty Matcham at Fanny's discretion: 'if you think my
sister desires it.' As for Bolton, Nelson was extremely pleased that Fanny
had so promptly dealt with his request for the £200, now he was to be given
another £300 and she was to: '... let it be a God send without any restric-
tion.' Nelson's open-handed generosity is tempered by the comment: 'If I
was rich I would do more but it will very soon be known how poor I am
except my yearly income.' In her reply to this, Fanny gave the impression
that she felt Nelson was criticising her for not distributing his gifts sooner:
'The disposal of £2,500 to your brothers and sisters I should certainly have
complied with.' But, she pointed out, he had specified that the money was
to come from the East India Company's gift and this had not yet been paid
into his accounts. In fact, she understood that it was the intention of the
Company to wait until such time as they could make a presentation to him
in person. Almost defensively, she stated that the decision not to mention
the gifts to anyone in the family had not been hers alone; Edmund had
advised her to remain silent on the subject. Still with an edge to her tone, she
said that if Nelson wanted it paid immediately, she had no doubt Davison
would lend her the money.

It is possible that her edginess might have been caused by the fact that
she and Edmund had left Round Wood for a visit to Norfolk. They were
staying in the parsonage at Burnham Thorpe where they had been joined
by the Rector and his wife and Mrs Bolton. Thinking that Edmund's stay
would be no longer than a fortnight, Fanny had declined an invitation to
stay at Wolterton, only to find that Edmund had so much business that
needed his attention that they would be staying longer. However, some
of the monotony of life at the parsonage was relieved when Fanny twice
dined at Holkham Hall. One occasion was a public dinner to celebrate the
anniversary of the Nile. Fanny, who was accompanied by the Rector, was
received very graciously by the Cokes. Mr Coke made a point of sending his
compliments to Nelson; no doubt he had forgotten Nelson's terse refusal to
attend a similar gathering years before. Other guests included her friends
the Walpoles and the Revd Mr Hoste and his family. Strangely, it was only

in a letter to Davison that Fanny mentioned the second dinner party at Holkham. Perhaps she feared that Nelson would not have approved of her becoming too friendly with the Cokes. And it was to Davison that she confided that she could not wait to leave Norfolk. The weather was the sort she hated, cold and damp. At the very end of August, there had been so much rain the harvest still had not been brought in.

However, a ray of sunshine had brightened her life before she left Burnham in the second week of September with the arrival of an early August letter from her husband. Just how desperately she treasured these letters was shown when in her reply she told Nelson that it had been delivered to Round Wood first: 'which deprived me of great pleasure for two days.' This particular letter must have been read over and over as it described the celebrations held for the first anniversary of the Battle of the Nile:

> The King (of Naples) dined with me and when HM drank my health a royal salute of 21 guns was fired from all His Majesty's ships of war and from all the castles. In the evening there was a general illumination. Amongst others a large vessel was fitted out like a Roman galley. On the oars were fixed lamps and in the centre was erected a rostral column with my name, at the stern elevated were two angels supporting my picture. In short the beauty of the thing was beyond my powers of description. More than 2000 variegated lamps were fixed round the vessel, an orchestra was fitted up and filled with the very best musicians and singers. The piece of music was in a great measure my praises, describing their distress, but Nelson comes, the invincible Nelson and we are safe and happy again. This must not make you think me vain so very far from it and I relate it more from gratitude than vanity.

Fanny made no comment beyond the hope that the King of Naples would remember Nelson's great service. He had already done so but Fanny had yet to hear that she was now the Duchess of Bronte. Instead, with the approach of winter, she voiced the thought: 'I should like very much to spend a few months in a warm climate.' Then almost wistfully she added: I sometimes think you will be home before long.'

Back once more at Round Wood, Fanny was full of news. She asked after young George Bolton who had accompanied Sir Edward Berry to the Mediterranean. Berry had taken letters for her that she hoped would bring Nelson more up-to-date news than those which had travelled through the usual routes. The weather, which she described as melancholy, was still causing general concern mainly because of its dire effect on the crops. October was almost over and: 'Harvest very backward.' The implications of this meant a vast increase in the price of bread and the resultant rise in the numbers claiming Poor Relief. But all was not gloom; Fanny had: 'one piece of news to tell you which causes a few "is it possible?" ' Admiral Dickson, whose wife had died some few months earlier, was about to marry a girl of 18. It had been a whirlwind courtship of only three weeks. The Admiral whose ship was in Yarmouth, had fallen desperately in love the moment he had set eyes on young Miss Willings, the daughter of a minor canon of Norwich cathedral. He had given balls both on board the ship and ashore in order that he might be near her. The friends with whom she was staying were about to remove the young woman from harm's way when the elderly, besotted Admiral sent a late night messenger with the offer of his hand and a generous settlement. The marriage was to take place almost immediately. Fanny commented: 'Surely he has lost his senses.' But of the future bride she observed: 'I have seen her, she looks a gentlewoman and is very much liked.'

Continuing the matrimonial theme, Fanny reported that she had heard that Admiral Nugent and his wife had separated, apparently from a failure to agree, or as Fanny called it 'a difference of temper.' Fanny showed great sympathy for all those concerned, the wife because she had but recently given birth and would now face bringing up the child on her own and equally for the husband who, it was said, had been overjoyed at the birth of his baby daughter. Furthermore she felt the hurt that her friend Lady Parker was suffering from the collapse of her daughter's marriage.

Another match pending was a local one. The parties concerned were unknown to Nelson and Fanny had probably not met them either but she had observed them. Somewhat caustically she commented:

Miss Susanna I took to the concert last Thursday. We were entertained by seeing an old nabob make love to a very rich porter brewer's [John Cobbold] daughter. The world says her father can give her £20,000 and still she must marry one of the most unpleasant looking men in the world for the sake of driving four horses.

On a happier note she wrote that the former Mary Ann Bolton, Mrs Pierson, had just given birth to a daughter a few days earlier, as had Nelson's sister, Kitty Matcham.

Unusually, when noting that she had Susanna staying, she wrote: 'I gratified your good father very much in bringing [her] home with me.' That suggested Edmund had put some pressure upon her to do so as normally she referred to Edmund as 'our' father. Fanny hinted that Susanna had an uncontrollable temper that was likely to flare up if she did not have her own way. For the sake of a calm household, Fanny vowed she would do nothing to provoke her in the hope that the girl would be able to restrain herself.

By the middle of October, Fanny was still writing regularly to her husband but getting little in return: 'I long to hear from you. My latest date was 4 August.' She was conscious that often she filled her letters with trivia: 'truly my chit chat is hardly worth your reading' as she told him of courtesy visits made and exchanged with people like the wife of the current army chief in Ipswich, and the fact that Edmund derived great pleasure from the garden even though the air was damp from the constant rain. At least the fact that Round Wood was on high ground was a distinct advantage as there was no fear of flooding as happened in several areas of the town.

At the same time, she often expressed firmly held opinions about the affairs of the day. One such was the custom of duelling. Some months earlier even Prime Minister Pitt had been engaged in a duel. On this particular occasion it was Earl St Vincent who was the subject of a challenge by Admiral Sir John Orde who was serving as his third-in-command. Orde's grievance was that he had been superseded by Nelson and Curtiss. St Vincent, who in any case had been very ill, refused to accept the challenge, thus winning Fanny's approval: 'Every man who refuses a challenge exalts himself in my opinion.' Perhaps it was because she was taking a moral stance that Fanny was reminded of what to her was a serious lapse in good manners:

> I wonder Lady Hamilton never acknowledge all the prints I requested Mr Davison to send her. I packed them up myself and Mr Davison told me he would send them by the first good opportunity. This is 10 or 11 months back.

And then, maybe thinking she might have offended her husband: 'Make my best regards to her and ask if they are received.' If there was a hint of jealousy here it is doubtful that Nelson would have noticed it. Fanny must have found it a strain to keep up the tone of a dutiful wife, especially when there were things going on relating to her husband that she knew nothing of, which left her feeling slightly embarrassed. There was more than a touch of acid in the remark: 'Mr W Bolton come bowing to congratulate me on your being created Duke de Bronte and was surprised I had not heard it.' Most of the newspapers had carried the item but not one that Fanny had seen. Her comment to Nelson: 'I hope if this news is true you have money given to support the rank', has been taken by some to indicate Fanny's cold refusal to accord Nelson the praise he deserved. Rather it was her concern that with his constant emphasis on his lack of wealth that he would be unable to live up to his new status. She reiterated that she spent carefully but: 'every article of life is so dear. Beef 9s.4d a stone. Coals very dear.'

In her next letter on 21 October, Fanny told how at ten o'clock the previous night a chaise had pulled up at the front door at Round Wood and a Lt Parker, one of Nelson's protégés came into the house for a few minutes to report that when he had left him on 8 September Nelson was well and safe. Parker had been entrusted with dispatches from the King of Naples to Vienna and thence to England. He and another official messenger had crossed the German Sea to Yarmouth and were making their way with their intelligence to London. However, Parker took the not unprecedented step of making the late night detour to see Fanny. She had a week before had a visit from a Capt. Oswald who was also en route from Yarmouth. It was advantageous that Round Wood lay on the main road from the port. This evening, however, she was so overcome with joy to see someone who could bring her such recent news of Nelson's health and also that of Josiah that she: '…could not hear or see and was obliged to call in our good father, who made enquiries and amongst the rest, if you were Duke of Bronte.' The visit was over in a matter of minutes but: 'The young man's extreme gratitude [to Nelson] and modesty will never be obliterated from your good father's and my memory.'

Parker confirmed the details that Josiah had sent his mother that the place from which Nelson had taken his dukedom was in Sicily, an island, Fanny considered, where it might well be preferable to have a country property rather than one near Naples. Filled with elation after her late night visit, Fanny longed: 'to hear of the arrival of Sir William and Lady Hamilton.' Obviously, Parker had indicated that the Hamiltons were on their way to England and would be arriving very shortly. As Fanny was also thinking of going to London it would be: 'such a good opportunity of acknowledging and thanking Sir William and Lady Hamilton for their attention and kindness to you and my son.' In the midst of her pleasure that the Hamiltons would no longer be around to distract her husband, Fanny got bogged down with one of the reasons she needed to go to London. When she had ordered a carriage to be made for Nelson, the coach-maker had loaned her a carriage to use in the meantime but this was now past its best and according to her coachman the wheels would not last much longer. Thus her plan was to return it to Lukin, the coach-builder in London, and take delivery of the new one.

Edmund was to remain at Round Wood but the irascible Susanna would accompany Fanny. Despite it being Edmund's desire to have the girl stay, he found her very difficult. When Fanny excused the girl as still being young, Edmund said she was a true Bolton and he pitied any man who dared to marry either Susanna or Catherine, her twin. It was his opinion that no man would be so foolhardy as to dare to take either of them on. In fact, only one of the sisters did marry. While on the subject of the Boltons, Fanny again enquired after the health and progress of young George who unlike his sisters had: 'a very affectionate temper.' Laughing at herself, she continued: 'He speaks of Lady Nelson as a very superior creature [after] only six weeks attention to him.' It was to be some weeks before Nelson broke the news to her that young George had died on the voyage out to the Mediterranean.

While waiting to hear that Sir William and Lady Hamilton had landed, the plain but very much wealthier Mr and Mrs Andrew Hamilton had already arrived in London. Mrs Hamilton was of course, Fanny's cousin, the former Martha Herbert. The closeness that existed between Fanny and her other relations had not been maintained with Martha. In part this stemmed from the fact that Martha had inherited a great deal from her father while Fanny had had great difficulty in wresting the interest on her legacy out of the Trustees. However, Fanny had written politely to her cousin and in return received a most fulsome letter. Fanny as a mere captain's wife was one thing, as her Ladyship and now a Viscountess she would be worth cultivating, so her praise of Nelson and his generosity in looking after Josiah was very great. She brought Fanny up-to-date news from Nevis but it was her intention now to settle in England provided the crops did well enough to bring her a good return.

Before Fanny left for London, Nelson sent her a copy of the King of Naples' letter praising his bravery and giving details of the dukedom of Bronte. He revelled in his new honour and from the moment the King had conferred it upon him, he signed all his correspondence, even to Fanny and his family, as 'Bronte Nelson'. Fanny made some comment on the copy but she had a more immediate worry, one that had led to lengthy discussions with Edmund. At long last, Marsh, who handled the collection of money due to Nelson, had managed to secure the £10,000 from the East India Company. Sensibly, he had used £2,000 to buy stock in the company and had then written to ask Fanny what was to be done with the balance; should he perhaps buy more stock?

Clearly Fanny always shared business as well as personal letters with Edmund and this one was no exception. Edmund pondered on the subject all night: '…our Father the following day asked me what I intended doing in regard to the sum you desired me to give your family out of the donation from the East India Company.' For some reason that has not been made clear, this did not please Fanny but to appease Edmund she said she would instruct Marsh to distribute the money but: '…candidly I did not intend noticing your letter of 14 July which contained your desire till I had wrote to you upon this subject.' She had mentioned this subject in other letters but because of the delay in receiving Nelson's reply she had been left unsure if his previous generous gesture had been a mere whim of the moment. Possibly she was concerned that he was giving away a large sum that they themselves might need. It would have been understandable if she were slightly annoyed that she who was so careful to live within their means should have to subsidise those who were profligate. Whatever her own strong feelings on the subject she listened to the sensible advice Edmund gave.

> Our Father gave me his opinion in these words 'if his brothers and sisters ever hear that you had a letter desiring a portion of the East India Company gift to be given them and you withhold it, I think it will make an irreparable breach between you and them and Horace may say I knew very well what I was about.'

While accepting the advice but still slightly aggrieved, Fanny told Marsh of Nelson's desire to give £2,500 to his family. The rest he could invest as he thought fit: ' was no judge nor did I wish to interfere in money matters.' Perhaps because she wished to avoid the role of Lady Bountiful she left it to Edmund to inform each member of the family of their gift. Having got that unpleasant matter out of the way and possibly feeling that she had not given as much attention to the letter concerning Bronte as she ought, she returned to it as a postscript. Obliquely showing that she was mixing on a regular basis with the 'county' set, she reported that Mr Berners, a very wealthy landowner with a splendid property overlooking the Orwell had visited Bronte in the past and was able to give her a very pleasing account of the place. So much so that: 'with great difficulty I refrain from making you a visit [instead] I hope you will consent to my going out [there], particularly as my health is really indifferent.' Fanny's critics cite this as an example of her pathetic emphasis on her health but her next sentence belied this as, tongue in cheek, she said Edmund would go with her and her friend Patty Berry had volunteered to come as her personal maid.

Davison had been charged with finding a house for Fanny's stay in London. This he had done, but he omitted to let her know when the tenancy began so that she could send the servants up to prepare for her and Edmund who had now decided he had had enough of Ipswich and wanted the stimulus of Town. Even more remiss, Davison had failed to give her the number of the house so she had to write twice to ask for it. She realised that Davison was a busy man but: 'the number is a very necessary thing to know, therefore if you have not time to desire one of your People to give me a line for I cannot send any servants or packages till I hear.' The packages may well have been both heavy and bulky because she intended to send them from Ipswich by hoy, a small sailing vessel that plied between the Orwell and the Thames. While gently reminding him of his lapse, she gave him another commission, that of purchasing two hats for Nelson from Butler's his hatter, one of gold lace the other a round one. As for the rest of 'My Dear Lord's' shopping list she would undertake those when she was settled in Town.

CHAPTER X

The Long Wait

...even the shrubs are trimmed up and smiling all ready to receive my Lord...
Fanny Nelson, 1799

Fanny's trip to London at the beginning of November1799 was a short one, into which she managed to pack a great deal. Nelson had entrusted to her a letter for delivery to Lady Spencer, the wife of the First Lord of the Admiralty. Bearing in mind the etiquette of the time, Fanny felt very honoured that she was actually received by her Ladyship. This was much more than a mere formal visit for Lady Spencer, who seemed to be privy to all the latest naval intelligence, not only let her into the secret that Nelson was expected at Minorca but was also able to reassure Fanny that the very latest reports indicated that Nelson was well. This and much more Fanny imparted to her husband in a letter dated 13 November. After telling him that his wishes had been carried out and his siblings had each received their monetary gift, she talked again, this time rather more seriously about her going abroad, preferably to join him on his voyage home. One of the visits she had made in London was to consult a doctor.

> I was ordered to Lisbon by the physician who attends me, he fears the winter will be too severe for me. Not knowing whether you would like my going out of the kingdom I have declined doing it till I have received your positive consent.

This was the third time that Fanny had hinted that she wished to go out and meet him. She had already received a number of offers from different naval officers to take her to the Mediterranean to her husband. It may be that her reluctance to accept them until she had Nelson's approval to do so was that she hoped his sending for her would offer strong proof that the rumours she had heard were not true. Already there was speculation in some quarters that he was deliberately delaying his return. As for the doctor's recommendation of Lisbon, he should have perhaps consulted with those who had been there recently. The 21-year-old Mary Nisbet, Countess of Elgin was forthright in her assessment of the city:

> The filth and stink of this place you can form no idea. All I have ever heard falls short of the reality. In walking from the boat to the hotel the smell was so intolerable I could hardly bear it. They fling everything out of the windows like Auld Reaky [sic] but without any notice. We had no less than three escapes. Then, my alarm for Boxer [her dog] for the town swarms with dogs who are kept to eat up the dirt in the streets…I drove all over the Town this morning and I absolutely came home quite sick with the dirt and nastiness of the people and things…I am so shockingly bit by the Miss-Kitties [mosquitoes] that it is enough to put anyone in a fever.

It was just as well that Fanny did not have access to Mary Nisbet's next letter, dated 23 September from Gibraltar. To her mother in Scotland she gave the news that Nelson had been made Duke d'Albrate (a phonetic rendering of Bronte) with £4,000 a year. 'They say there never was a man turned so *vain glorious* (that's the phrase) in the world as Lord Nelson – he is now completely managed by Lady Hamilton.' A week later the Countess posed the question:

> How shall I make up to the Duke de Bronte when I arrive at Palermo. Now I will lay a bet you do not know who that is – Why no other than Lord N! I saw an Officer at Gibraltar who assured me he had seen a letter signed by Lord N 'de Bronte & Nelson', in which letter he told his friends this was his title & £3,000 a year with it.

Gossips were as inaccurate in those days as they are now. As she suffered acutely from rheumatism, it was as well that Fanny did not venture to the Mediterranean because, again according to Mary Nisbet:

> …every creature on board who ever had the slightest rheumatism, has had a pretty severe attack and they say it is always the case…I never had it so bad in my life as I have had it in my head this week past, indeed Capt. Morris tells me he never has the rheumatism but here.

The young Countess's letters offer a clear-sighted view of Nelson and Lady Hamilton about whom she had much to say, most of it uncomplimentary. She found her overpowering and too effusive. According to her, Emma's great friendship with the Queen of Naples was very one sided, the Neapolitans were said to laugh at her behind her back but she was tolerated as she had such a strong influence over Nelson. However,

I must acknowledge she is pleasant [and] makes up amazingly…as my Father would say, 'There is a fine Woman for you, good flesh and blood.' She is indeed a Whapper! [sic] And I think her manner very vulgar. It is really humiliating to see Lord N he seems quite dying and yet as if he had no other thought than her. He told Elgin privately that he had lived a year in the house with her and that her beauty was nothing in comparison to the goodness of her heart…Is it not a pity a man who gained so much credit should fling himself away in this shameful manner?

While Mary was passing on her impressions to her mother in Scotland, her husband writing to his mother described Nelson's appearance:

He looks very old, has lost his upper teeth, sees ill of one eye and has a film coming over both of them. He has pains pretty constantly from his late wound in the head. His figure is mean and in general, his countenance is without animation.

Given the custom of interesting letters being read aloud in company or copied and sent on to friends and relations, it can not have been long before the gossipmongers were having a field day. The question is, how much of it did Fanny hear?

It is said that the wife is always the last to hear, having been protected from the gossip by her friends. Lady Spencer must have been aware of the situation and that may account for her extra kindness to Fanny who clung desperately to the idea that her husband would soon be home and they would be able to resume their life together. Having talked of her need for a warmer climate she told Nelson that Round Wood in the winter was too cold for both her and Edmund. Her rheumatism was bad and she had developed a lingering cough. The doctor had ordered her to spend some months in London which, because of the high concentration of chimney smoke in the atmosphere, was considered warmer than the east coast. Medical advice was that as early as possible in the year she should bathe in the sea air. 'I am to go and brace my nerves'. Sea air is still regarded as bracing and it is likely that Fanny used the term 'bracing her nerves' to describe a general invigoration of the body, rather than that she was suffering from depression.

On a lighter note she regaled Nelson with a description of a visit she had made to her cousin Martha, now settled back in England and about to move to a house on Harley Street. Fanny looked at her cousin's marriage with a critical eye:

Poor Hamilton much good may [it] do him the prospect of my cousin's great fortune. She was truly glad to see me, made kind enquiries after you and Josiah, declares Mr H has never been in his sober senses since he heard of the Battle of the Nile. Mr H absolutely cries with joy when he mentions it. Everybody in the W[est] I[ndies] claimed you as their acquaintance who (Mr H says) has seen the hem of your garment.

Fanny's pride in her husband was great, but she was level headed enough to find some of the public adulation excessive.

One of the main reasons for this visit to London, had been to take delivery of Nelson's carriage. '[It] is finished, it is really elegantly neat.' However, as she had heard a very strong rumour that Nelson would shortly be on his way home, since he had not been given the command of the Mediterranean fleet as he hoped, she decided: 'I will not use the chariot, that I may have the pleasure of seeing you get into it.' She did not say how she was to return to Round Wood or how she and Edmund were to travel back to London to stay in the house Davison was finding for them. A final piece of family gossip was that Maurice and his brother the Rector had reconciled their differences over the title and were now on good terms. The Rector was seriously considering taking lodgings in London for the Christmas period especially if the news that Nelson would be home by then was true.

By 25 November Fanny and Susanna were back at Round Wood where preparations were being made for the imminent removal to No. 54 St James's Street, London for the winter. Even at that busy time, Fanny was not clear of the Nelson family. Mrs Bolton and Susanna's twin, Kitty, arrived from Norfolk en route for a month's visit to their Bolton relations on the Suffolk coast with the intention of staying until the day before Fanny and Edmund set off for London. Mrs Bolton discussed Nelson's gift to them, saying it had made them happy; a euphemistic way of saying it had helped with their debts. One of the ways the Boltons cut their housekeeping bills was to make long visits to other family members. On the other hand, the Rector, who with his thank you had sent one of his long and obsequious letters, marred his gratitude by suggesting that he expected Fanny to give Mr Windham, the Secretary of State for War and the MP for Norwich, a gentle hint that the State had so far done nothing for the members of Nelson's family. The Rector, whose only interest was himself, was angling for some lucrative preferment within the Church. This letter aroused Fanny's anger, while Edmund was saddened that his son: 'was so pressing and dissatisfied.' Edmund supported Fanny in her decision not to even consider mentioning the subject to Mr Windham when their paths happened to cross. 'Some women can say or do anything. I cannot and feel happy – it is my disposition by which I never get myself into any scrapes.'

Despite the problems of the family, the atrocious weather which allowed them few other visitors and the daily tramp past their door of the soldiers brought back from an unsuccessful campaign against Napoleon in Holland, Fanny was endeavouring to keep calm and optimistic for: 'I hear from all quarters that you are expected home.' Lord Hood was a constant correspondent as was the wife of Lord St Vincent and both passed on whatever relevant naval news they had.

The Sun etc. positively say that Lord Keith is to have command in the Mediterranean. From all these things I really begin to flatter myself I shall see my dear husband and son before long…You see by the date of my letter [3.12.1799] we are safely arrived in town – a small furnished house at 7 guineas per week, consisting of two rooms and a light closet on [each] floor. Quite large enough for you and my Josiah should you think it right for him to come home.

Fanny undoubtedly thought this house, probably of three storeys and a basement, though small in comparison with the grander London houses, would suit Nelson situated as it was on the edge of Green Park connecting Piccadilly with Pall Mall. Rumours were still flying that Nelson was at Gibraltar and would make his return from there. Fanny hoped that it was true not just for her own sake but also for Edmund who had taken a turn for the worse since reaching London. He had aged rapidly, become very frail and had little appetite. His doctor had given him medicine to help his digestion but even so all he ate was a little fish and game. Fanny had given him the back drawing room for a bedroom so that he could have quiet at night, which suggests that the front of the house may have been noisy. Once again Fanny found herself in the role of nurse trying hard to do everything she could for his comfort. Edmund was a reasonably undemanding patient who assured her that he could not ask for more attention than she gave.

If she was tied to the house because of Edmund, this did not stem the flow of those who called on her. Mr and Mrs George Mills, friends from Nevis, came to say goodbye before leaving for the West Indies. As often happened with those who had been sugar-rich, their lavish lifestyle in England had led them to bankruptcy, forcing them back home to salvage what they could from their already heavily mortgaged plantations. Lady Hamond, the wife of Sir Andrew Hamond, the Comptroller of the Navy, was another visitor. She must have regarded Fanny as a sympathetic listener whom she could trust or she was exceedingly indiscreet in her conversation, for she regaled Fanny with stories about her husband's constant complaining. A more welcome caller was Capt. Hood with his news that Nelson had reached Minorca and was half way home.

Sir Peter Parker who had served out on the Jamaica station and had been one of Nelson's earliest patrons called with his daughter deputising for Lady Parker who was ill. Fanny returned the visit a day or two later when she found:

her spirits was [sic] so agitated when she talked of you, that I found it necessary to make my visit short. She tells me she has written two long letters to you endeavouring to point out the necessity of your coming home.

On the strength of their long acquaintance it appears that Lady Parker had cast herself in the role of concerned parent in writing to Nelson. Did she write to reprimand him for flouting navy orders to proceed home or did she caution him that his lengthy stay in the Hamiltons' house and his spending so much time in Lady Hamilton's company was causing tongues to wag and more importantly, making those in authority question both his reliability and ability to command? Fanny followed up this account with a sentence that showed that not only did she fully understand Nelson's frustration that he felt he was not appreciated by the authorities in England, but also that her acute common sense enabled her to weigh up the situation accurately.

I am fully persuaded many are jealous of your character and your countrymen in general will allow you are deserving of all that had been done, but for all the world to acknowledge your great abilities is another thing.

A week later and Edmund was upset yet again by his son the Rector who was still harping on the same tune of the lack of dignities granted to the Nelson family. This annoyed Fanny, not just because of her brother-in-law's avaricious attitude but because she spent all her time nursing Edmund, doing all in her power to keep him comfortable in body and calm in mind and then it was all undone by the upset the Rector's letters caused. She told Nelson: 'I must write…and beg him not to be so tiresome.'

Many of Fanny's visitors were men of the sea who knew each other and passed information to her when they could. Although she had written three days earlier, when Admiral Young called just before he was due to sail and promised to take a letter to her husband, she had to sit down and think what was new. In typical English fashion her first comment was on the weather; it had turned cold and dry which she had been told would do them all good. She had also seen Capt. Locker who spent all his time talking about his good friend Nelson. Admiral Barrington had passed on gossip about Admiral Pringle, the funniest bit of which was that he looked very odd in his new wig which was so small it did not cover his ears at all. She also related that hair powder had gone out of fashion. The reason for this was to be found in the fact that the Government had levied yet another ingenious tax, this time upon the powder used to dress wigs and for some ladies, their own hair. It would not be many years before the wig too would pass out of fashion. Fanny had joined those who no longer powdered: 'You can't think how very much Lady Martin admires my black locks, but they won't allow that they are black, but a fine dark brown!' Black hair was not considered to be genteel, it suggested that one came from dubious stock.

Fanny was bubbling with excitement as she wrote; so much to tell but so little time. If she went into detail about all the handsome things Capt. Trigg had said about Nelson, she might find that the messenger who was to carry her letter had tired of waiting and was gone. This was one of Fanny's mistakes. She was too considerate of others and so while she hugged all the praise of Nelson to her bosom, she missed an opportunity to ape Lady Hamilton who it was said 'puffed up the incense', heaping up praises to his face. So, instead of repeating even a sample of the compliments, she hurriedly included the slightly more important news that her cousin Martha was ill, so bad indeed that when Fanny called she had not been admitted to the house. She understood that her headstrong cousin had sought medical advice and then refused to take it. Fanny was cross with her, but of the husband for whom she had held so little regard in the past she said: 'I never beheld a creature with so much patience as Mr Hamilton. He will get all her money which I think he deserves.' There had been a time when Fanny expected to inherit her cousin's wealth but she had long known that under her uncle's will she would receive only £3,000 on Martha's death. Fanny closed this letter in a slightly different form. She often wrote 'God bless you' and sometimes 'your affectionate wife' but on this occasion it was: 'God bless you and believe me my dear husband to be your faithful and affectionate wife.' What had been said to make her feel the need to emphasise her faithfulness?

Christmas came but no Nelson with it. However, Fanny and the rest of the family were delighted to entertain the bluff bachelor Capt. Hardy who brought them first-hand news of his commander. Hardy had made it abundantly clear to Nelson that he did not approve of his intimate friendship with the Hamiltons. However, he was careful to shield Fanny from any hurt, therefore when she mentioned that it seemed to her that when Nelson wrote to her he appeared low and depressed, the faithful Hardy reassured her that that was probably the result of having to deal with tiresome people. He did not elaborate on whom he meant. During their conversation in the drawing room, Fanny, keen to get as much information as she could on all sorts of subjects relating to the fleet, asked after Nelson's nephew, George Bolton, who was supposed to have joined Hardy's ship. The captain seemed at a loss and as his sister Susanna was present, Fanny wisely did not pursue the matter. The following morning when she and Maurice Nelson were alone, he told her that George had died while on passage from Gibraltar to Minorca. Compassionate Fanny feared that the little boy, as she called him, had fallen overboard and drowned but Maurice assured her that was not the case. Her next thoughts were for George's parents. Had they yet received the awful news? Probably not, as Mrs Bolton was at Hollesley and Mr Bolton was with friends in Norwich.

Hardy had brought with him a list of items that Nelson required and Fanny made sure that they went in the next frigate to sail in his direction. Among them had been the request that she select a gift for Lady Hamilton. Fanny complied with this sending; '… a cap (the whim of the moment) and kerchief such as are worn this cold weather.' It is possible that these rather mundane articles were not quite what he had in mind for his dear friend while Fanny may have been trying to emphasise the differences not only in their life-style and fashion but in temperature too. As far as fashion was concerned, Fanny had always dressed the best she could but she had never felt she could spend freely on the latest styles. But now, with her new position, where she was expected to be seen in the right places, in particular the select public functions at Court, she had to have smart new clothes. She wrote that she had ordered an outfit for the Drawing Room to celebrate the Queen's Birthday. A week or so earlier she had described how Lady Parker had taken her to see a famous, and no doubt expensive, French milliner. Fanny possessed the ability to laugh at herself and the headgear she normally wore which, so Lady Parker had said, was so bad that if they put her in a sack and sent her off to Bonaparte, it would scare him off. However at the time of writing, it was so cold Fanny was certainly not clad in her finery. Whatever she was wearing on top, underneath she had been forced to put on not one but two sets of flannel underwear. Only a close intimacy between husband and wife would have let her tell him this and under other circumstances this might well have excited Nelson.

Immediately after the confession that she has been spending on herself, Fanny revealed that she was almost frightened to tell Nelson how much the new chariot had cost. It was not as if the makers had produced anything extraordinary for the money; for £352, including harness for one pair of horses, they had got: 'nothing fine about it, only fashionable.' The carriage had cost almost as much as a year's rent on the London house. To gloss over the tiresome subject of expenses, Fanny related chit-chat about people with whom Nelson was familiar. Capt. Hardy, hoping to hear the news that Nelson was at last on his way home, was a regular and welcome guest. Admiral Pringle called and cleared up the mystery of his ill-fitting wig – he had been seriously ill with what Fanny termed 'a complaint in his head'. Serious too, might have been the accident that had befallen Fanny's good friend Sir Peter Parker. Climbing the stairs to bed and carrying his candlestick, Sir Peter had caught his foot, causing him to fall backwards down the stairs. Fortunately he escaped with only heavy bruising and a cut to one of his legs but the shock to his nearly 80-year-old system was such that he was confined to bed for almost two weeks. Quite apart from the fact that this fall could have led to broken hips or even spinal fracture was the more dreadful prospect that he and the house could have been set on fire.

Fanny started the new decade full of hope. Lieutenant Leahy called to tell her that he had seen Nelson recently and that he was well. She hoped this was true, doubting that men could necessarily recognise the signs of ill health in others. Her own health, she felt was much improved. She still had rheumatism but she brushed that aside saying that the visits from Hardy and Leahy had made her much brighter in her mental outlook. It was difficult to always 'be in spirits' as she expressed it, especially as she was surrounded by those who were in poor health. Nelson's old friend and mentor, Capt.Locker, a frequent visitor, was showing progressive signs of ageing. Since he complained that his hands had become so stiff that he could no longer hold a pen it is likely he had acute arthritis but worse, his short-term memory was failing and he was given to repeating himself. Strangely, while Fanny tolerated this failing, it greatly irritated Edmund, who although himself physically weak was still in possession of a sharp intellect. Thus Fanny found herself torn between the pair of them.

Her love for Edmund must on occasions have been severely tested especially when his physical problems grew worse. At first she only hinted at Edmund's: '...[the] weakness he has had some years rather increases.' However, never one to avoid the truth and in keeping with the vogue of the period to discuss openly all health problems, she told Nelson in early February exactly what that weakness was. First though she paints a depressing picture that must have been familiar throughout London at the time. 'We have a sick house, every servant, one after the other. Susanna [Bolton] very ill with a bilious complaint in her bowels and fever. This day is the sixth she has had a physician.' Far from bemoaning her fate that she should have to bear with all this sickness around her or looking on the black side, she assured Nelson that Susanna was better and would be completely well within a few days. Edmund's state of health however, was a very different matter, he was:

> very ill yesterday, the weakness in his body was so much increased that he could not assist himself, therefore he sent for Mr Younge who took a surgeon (Mr Hawkins) into his room, who replaced his body up; immediately he had relief and is much better this morning.

Her description seems to fit an acute hernia. The problem worsened over the next few days.

> Surgical assistance has been very necessary, from extreme weakness his body comes down too frequently, even turning in his bed quickly. Mr Hawkins has taught our father's servant (who is a good man) to put it up, which he has done these last 48 hours. The least difficulty arising Mr Hawkins is sent for, day or night. A suppression of urine alarmed us all and he has been obliged once to have it drawn off. Mr Hawkins said he never relieved any person with so little difficulty. But he was on the day following sent for for the same purpose, but nature relieved him and he has had no difficulty since. I was not satisfied with the advice of one physician, therefore I desired Dr Baillie to attend which he did. He approved of everything which had been done or given, rich cordials with some few drops of bitters are the only thing taken as medicine. The laudanum is given in ejections [sic].

In giving Nelson this very detailed description of Edmund's condition, Fanny was also conveying to her husband that his father was receiving the very best medical treatment available. No expense had been spared; in calling upon Dr Baillie for a second opinion, she had sought the advice of the most eminent of London physicians.

Illness was rife that winter. Nelson's brother-in-law, George Matcham, gave them serious cause for concern when what appeared to be a cold developed into the same 'bilious fever' for a time leaving him with a paralysis of all his limbs. Kitty Matcham, in a letter to her father giving the news that her husband was recovering, mentioned that they had had an offer of £5,000 for their house, but they would not accept it if there was a likelihood that her brother wished to buy it. Edmund shelved the reply to this on to Fanny, who with all honesty said that it was impossible for her to make such a decision, but she had gathered from what Nelson had said in correspondence that he did not intend to buy anywhere else. Edmund told her to add that if it was possible for them to get such a good sale, they should seize the chance. Matcham had decided that when peace was declared, he would move his family to France. Fanny's comment to Nelson was not one of surprise, quite the opposite. She believed that: 'if there is anything like an established government [there] numbers will do the same.'

Although Fanny had told the Rector quite firmly to stop agitating his father, it did not stop his wife, Sarah, from being almost as obsequious as her husband when she wrote to assure Fanny that there was no one else she would rather look after her daughter Charlotte in London. Totally ignoring the fact that she had a sick and ageing man to look after, 'Mrs Rector' asked Fanny to have the girl to stay until such time as term began and then she could take her to school. Telling her that the Rector and his son and daughter would be in Town within a day or two, she gave Fanny no opportunity to refuse, taking it for granted that Fanny would be only too pleased to take the girl. Charlotte duly arrived and Fanny put herself out for her, taking her to places of interest and into society as well as passing on to the girl some of her own expertise particularly on the piano. In a letter home Charlotte told her mother:

> I hope you will find me very much improved in my music when I come home...we went to Whitelands [the school in Chelsea]. My aunt went in some of the rooms and thinks it a very nice house and gardens. I go on Monday...You will be surprised to hear I and my aunt Papa and Capt. Hardy went to a grand ball and supper on Tuesday. Capt. Hardy danced with me several dances...My aunt was so kind as to lend me a pair of pearl ear-rings and a wreath of flowers to wear on my head and a pair of white kid gloves. So I did very well...My aunt is so good as to order me a cake to take to school. Susanna still continues poorly.

This very affectionate portrait of Fanny revealed yet again her sympathy and understanding of young people. It does not require much imagination to see aunt and niece in Fanny's bedroom going through her jewellery box to find earrings for Charlotte to wear and then lending her gloves; the final touch came in her taking the trouble to make up the circlet of flowers to wear in her hair. All this a fond and indulgent mother would have done; the pity was that she did not have daughters of her own to whom; she would have been a good mother. Certainly she would have taught them to be wary of those who sought their acquaintance for what they could gain from it. At the time Fanny was being courted assiduously by Sir William Calder and his wife:

> [They] have made me two visits before I took it into my head to call upon them once. It certainly shows her extreme anxiety for the honour of my acquaintance. Whether I am flattered to be so noticed is another thing. Some I hear think she can be very ill natured if she pleases, and a little envy sometimes will intrude on her ladyship's mind.

How politely Fanny expressed this but then envy was a trait entirely unknown to her.

As it was, she was too busy to let the pettiness of those engaged in the social scene worry her for Edmund was still ill. Fanny realised that this coloured the tone of her latest letters to Nelson and she apologised for seeming so low spirited.

> Our dear Father was extremely ill, I never thought of seeing him again sitting by the fireside. That pleasure I have really had. He is very, very weak. He tells me thinks he may go on for some time. The fabric has had such a shake that it can never recover its former strength. I rejoice to see him free from pain and I hope he remains so.

Fanny's love for the old man had grown deeper over the years. What had, no doubt, started as a dutiful affection expected from a daughter-in-law had developed into genuine feeling each for the other. Underlying the relationship in the beginning had been the desire of each to please Nelson.

> His affection for me is great his opinion of me will gratify you. I cannot tell you what he says of me. The two physicians and the surgeon and Mr Young will remember it. This best of men often talks of you. He told me when he thought and talked of you he shed tears but now he could not relieve himself in that way.

Fanny followed with a remark that showed Edmund's faith in the strength of his son's relationship with his wife. Did Fanny repeat it in order to jog Nelson's conscience? 'When every one was loud about your coming home, he did not expect you because you had not written to me on that subject.'

She did not dwell on this but turned to more news of sickness, namely the widespread outbreak of yellow fever in the West Indies. Among those afflicted was her young friend Pierson who had been sent home to recover. Just before his leave expired he suffered a relapse and was now dangerously ill. Wherever she turned, it seemed, Fanny encountered sickness and bad news although at last, Susanna had recovered. As a companion for Fanny she had been useless for some weeks but Fanny's concern now was that the girl should thoroughly recoup her strength and this, she felt could only be done through exercise on a scale that was impossible in London, therefore it was planned to send Susanna home.

During this time, which was the height of the London season, Fanny had turned down several invitations. One of them was expected to be a grand affair, her hostess, Lady Walpole promised that the guests would include 'The Prince of Wales, two of his brothers and the Stadtholder, the Duke of Gloucester if he could and a great many fine people.' Telling Nelson she had declined this invitation Fanny suggested, perhaps half in fun, that society hostesses would give up on her for 'being too humdrum'. She also turned down tickets for the opera. She later revealed that it was fear of leaving Edmund that accounted for her supposed lack of sociability. Only once had she left him for an evening because he had insisted she should go to dine with the Davisons, Mr Davison being a particular favourite of his.

Edmund was making some progress; he was getting up most days by 9 o'clock, eating dinner in his own room at 4 pm and then sitting up with Fanny until about 7 pm. Believing he needed to get some air, he had twice gone out in the carriage but the experience had been painful and had irritated his bowels. For someone suffering from a serious hernia, the bumping of a carriage over the cobblestones must have been uncomfortable to say the least. Determined that he should get out for a change of air, Fanny decided she would try to talk him into using the sedan chair instead which would have given a smoother ride. Now that he was somewhat better, Fanny began to think of returning to Round Wood but Edmund had declared that he did not wish to leave London where he could be assured of good surgical attention if it were needed. Fanny herself was obviously run down and the cough that had troubled her for so long showed no signs of abating. Again her doctor had recommended hot sea-bathing as soon as was feasible. Edmund, who whilst at his worst had refused to see any of his family, now thought he might like to see the Matchams who were indeed anxious to see him. Having managed to sell their house, a spell staying with him would solve a problem and at the same time release Fanny to go and recuperate.

Towards the end of February, Fanny returned to the subject of her going out to join Nelson:

> Sir Andrew Hamond called this morning...to offer me every accommodation the *Champion* could afford if I had a wish to go out to you. I told Sir Andrew I had the desire, but without your leave I could not think of undertaking the voyage. You may be assured I felt much obliged to them for thinking of me.

She knew that she would never take the journey and had to content herself that the nearest she would ever get to Italy was through the flowers that would grow from the seeds that Nelson had sent her. These she had sent to the gardener at Round Wood to raise for her.

The Rector, who could so easily have served Jane Austen as the model for Mr Collins in *Pride and Prejudice*, continued to torment Fanny and Edmund in his relentless pursuit of clerical preferment. Now that his brother was a lord, he had every hope of joining him in the House of Lords and he saw just the opening for him. The Bishop of Bangor having recently died, the Rector had his eyes set on becoming the next incumbent. Bishops being political appointees, he was still agitating for Fanny or his father to speak for him in the right quarters. His persistence was almost beyond belief. He referred back to letters that Nelson had written to him years before expressing the hope that he would one day be able to help him to some good office within the church. He even quoted extracts from letters Fanny had written to him in 1797 that mentioned Nelson's desire to help. With such harassment it must have been a relief to look forward to a visit from her friend Lady Berry who was staying in Kensington. 'They tell me she is six months gone with child. She is not in [the] least increased in size. She is to spend a few days with me.' Then pointing to the fact that her house was not large and highlighting a common occurrence of the period: ' [she will] take half of Susanna's bed.' The visit went unrecorded in Fanny's letters to Nelson except for a reference after the event when she told him that it had been a vicious rumour that Lady Berry was pregnant. Vicious, because at the time of the supposed conception, Edward Berry was at sea. Gossip abounded at that period, the more malicious the better as Sheridan's *School for Scandal* epitomised. The very small, close circles within society passed on and embellished the latest bits of tittle-tattle, little caring whose reputation was damaged en route. The newspapers aided and abetted in this, careful never to give names of those involved but sufficient information to make it perfectly clear to readers to whom they were referring. Nelson had access to English newspapers so he was well aware of some of the gossip of the day that Fanny passed on to him but she rarely relished the misfortunes of others. Rather she tended to take a moral stand.

March was halfway through and still there was no sign of Nelson's return nor were his letters arriving. In February she had had to rely on a letter he wrote to Davison to tell her how he was. With nothing to reply to, Fanny did her best to keep her letters light hearted. In the middle of the month she was able to report that Edmund's recovery continued, so much so that he was now talking of returning to Round Wood. But the central item of this letter was of her attendance at St James's Palace where she had been received by both their Majesties. As always, Fanny made light of her appearances at Court, apparently perfectly at ease. However, while describing the occasion to her husband underlying her banter there is more than a hint of reproach:

I shall make you smile at my economy. My birthday suit [the outfit she had made for the Queen's Birthday in January] could not be worn after Easter therefore I took the first tolerable Thursday to pay my respects...Our gracious King thought it was a long time since I heard from you, and told me the wind was changed therefore he hoped I should hear from you very soon. The Queen always speaks to me, with so much condescension [affability] that I like her very much.

Fanny might be forgiven for pointing out to Nelson who was hobnobbing with the King and Queen of Naples that he was not the only one to be well received by royalty. She was still putting pressure on him that apart from the seafarers who had offered to take her out to join him, others thought she should go. 'Lady Harrington endeavoured to persuade me to make you a visit. Spoke of the climate how necessary it was to me who had so bad a cough.' Fanny followed this with the enigmatic sentence: 'She little knew how much virtue I had in not going out.' Was she referring to her selfless dedication to Edmund or hinting that she knew a visit from her would spoil things for Nelson?

But there was little time for her to consider what might be; she was again embroiled in Nelson family affairs. Just as Edmund's physical state was improving, his emotions were severely disturbed by the death of his sister Mary. Aunt Mary had been a special favourite of Nelson's and he often asked Fanny to make sure she wanted for nothing. As might be expected, the Rector, who lived close to Aunt Mary, had a great deal to say about the carrying out of her last wishes. Edmund had her will in his possession and was her main beneficiary. With his accustomed blatancy the Rector informed his father that since he knew Edmund was to inherit everything: 'Mrs Nelson or myself never made use of undue influence with my aunt in her last illness.' However, in sorting through his aunt's belongings he had found various bequests she wished made such as £20 to his daughter Charlotte, £150 to her friend Mrs Goulty and £20 or so for repairs to her house which she had left to her sister Mrs Rolfe. The Rector hoped to buy the house from Mrs Rolfe who did not wish to keep it. However, he had insufficient funds but was quite sure that his father would be only too pleased to assist him in the purchase. Weak in health Edmund might have been yet he had enough strength of mind to throw this letter into the parlour fire. His annoyance with the Rector was so great that he wrote to tell him that he thought children should spend their school holidays with their parents rather than be foisted onto relations. So, with the approach of Easter, Fanny was expecting her in-laws to take lodgings in London. Again emphasising the lack of guest bedrooms in St James's Street, she said she could accommodate Charlotte – no doubt she would also be taking a place in Susanna's bed – but she had no idea where she would put Horace when he came down from Eton.

The problems of family finances were not confined to the Nelson family. The question of the payment of legacies under John Herbert's will had still not been settled and came under discussion when her cousin Sally's husband, Captain Kelly, called on her. The Kellys like Fanny could make good use of the money and were trying to ingratiate themselves with cousin Martha in the hopes that she might expedite the payments. Fanny herself had raised the topic months before, mentioning that the settlement date was now almost a year overdue. 'I have seen such terrible quarrels in my own family about money that I dread to say a word.'

Towards the end of March three letters arrived from Nelson; the first, dated 7 February, was followed five days later by those of 20 and 25 January. Great was the delight when the first arrived: 'I had last night the pleasure of reading your letter to our Father. It made him cheerful and I believe made him sit up one hour later.' There was news too of Josiah and Fanny expressed the hope that he would not come home before Nelson.

In the other letters Nelson showed plainly his dislike of his new commander-in-chief, Lord Keith. As of old he poured out his disgruntled feelings and burdened Fanny with them, railing against his lack of recognition by the authorities.

> I never yet have received any particular mark of favour and have been kept here with all the expenses of a commander-in-chief and not one farthing of profit. From the day I left England I have never received one farthing of prize money, except £500 in dollars for what was taken when I was last in this country and I am forced to an expense of many thousands a year.

Nelson, anchored off Leghorn waiting for Keith to arrive, wrote bitterly: 'I am come to pay homage to him. Now I have only to obey and God only knows on what service he will order me. Josiah is with me and is much improved. I yet hope he will be a comfort to you.' The letter ended with the pathetic lament: 'It has been very hard how I have been kept here since May 1798.' He also, at long last, replied to Fanny's request that she should go to wait for him in Lisbon. The lurid picture he painted would, he thought, be guaranteed to put an end to such a notion.

> Whatever any physicians may say about Lisbon I can have no idea that the most dirty place in Europe covered with fog can be wholesome; to the old debauches who must lead a more regular life from the want of any decent society, it may be of benefit on that account, but I will answer for no other. My abhorrence of it is such from two days' acquaintance that I would rather take a house in the worst part of Portsmouth, and what a sea voyage.

The last referred to the passage through the Bay of Biscay. Then, as he so often did, he passed the responsibility back to her. 'Having said this it is for you to judge.' And just to make sure that his message had been well and truly rammed home: 'I shall never go to Lisbon for if I can get that far, Portsmouth will be the place for me.'

Fanny replied that in the circumstances she was pleased she had ignored the advice of her doctor – and Edmund – to seek the change of climate. Instead she hoped that a warm summer and hot sea-bathing would improve her health. From the generality she suddenly moved to an intensely personal and emotional subject which suggested that she had again heard unsettling rumours. 'I can with safety put my hand on my heart and say it has been my study to please and make you happy, and I still flatter myself we shall meet before very long.' In almost supplicant mood she added: 'I feel most sensibly all your kindness to my dear son, and I hope he will add much to our comfort.' She, who read every word of his letters over and over, had noticed that when he referred to Josiah he had expressed the desire that the young man might one day bring _her_ comfort.

When he did write, Nelson continued to pour out his problems and grievances, so much so that in mid April when replying to his letter of 27 February she remarked on how low-spirited he seemed. With her knowledge of his moods she knew that this was a sure sign that his general health was suffering. Anxious not to upset him further, she gently suggested that once Malta had surrendered and he had restored the Royal family to Naples, he might then consider his own health and affairs: 'and to show yourself in England.' Playing on his need for reassurance – and confounding her later detractors who said she never offered him praise – she added: 'John Bull's eyes sparkle at the sound of the battle of the Nile.' Then, just in case she should have overstepped the mark: 'However your own wishes and experience must be a better guide than anything I can possibly have to offer.'

Perhaps that was Fanny's great failing, she was too amenable; had she been more demanding things might have turned out differently. This trait of wishing to keep the peace and bowing to the wishes of others rather than her own must have been greatly increased by living with an elderly man whose health continued to give intermittent cause for alarm and whose mind was often set on action that Fanny thought unwise. Having previously declared that nothing would make him leave London and his doctors, he then decided he would like to return to Round Wood. He was so enthused with the idea that he had made plans to go alone, except for his manservant. Accommodating as ever, Fanny gave up her own plan of going to Brighton. Instead she would go with him to Ipswich and only when he was comfortably settled, would she go for treatment at the hot baths at nearby Great Yarmouth. Edmund himself, while taking for granted all that Fanny did for him, was concerned for her health and general well being. He knew better than anyone that the constant state of uncertainty over Nelson's return probably caused the nervous allergy which manifested itself as a rash that came out just before they left London. The irritation it caused was severe enough to prevent her going to social functions in hot and crowded rooms.

Unable to go out much, she was forced to rely on visitors to bring her diversion. The most welcome of these was Capt. Hardy, currently at home on sick leave. For Fanny the blunt Dorset man who had sailed and fought alongside her husband brought her even closer to Nelson than his letters. She would listen enrapt as he related anecdotes about life on board, giving her the minutiae that she craved. He also treated Edmund with respect and endeared himself to the old man. Hardy felt at ease with both of them, so much so that when he visited, he felt he could leave: 'his crutch at the drawing room door' and hop in with 'one leg still wrapped up in flannel'. Still single, Hardy, despite having sisters, was not entirely comfortable in the presence of women. His subsequent marriage showed that neither was he a particularly good judge of the female character but where Fanny was concerned, he had a strong affection for her based on admiration and respect. In Hardy's eyes Fanny's behaviour as a wife had always been admirable; she did not deserve to suffer; he wanted to shield and protect her from inevitable hurt.

The last known letter from Fanny to Nelson for 1800 was dated 15 April. In it she referred again to financial matters, in this case a bounty claim that Davison was pursuing with lawyers on Nelson's behalf. Having told him that he could have no idea how much it took to maintain a household in the style of a gentleman, she hoped that Davison was correct in his assertion that: '…he shan't lose one farthing that I can get.' She signed this letter in the unusual form of 'Your affectionate wife my dear husband'. A postscript revealed that Edmund's hint to the Rector about looking after his children had obviously fallen on deaf ears as Charlotte wrote to her uncle: 'Here I am very happy and very well and expect to see you home very soon. I am afraid my aunt is going out of town very soon or I should be much happier.'

The 10 May was letter-writing day at Round Wood. Fanny's letter caught up with Nelson on 20 June while Edmund's to his daughter Kitty was much speedier in its delivery. Her father noted that it appeared probable, though not certain, that Nelson was to be granted leave to come home. More definite news came from Davison to Fanny in early June that indicated that Nelson was on his way to England. This was corroborated by Maurice from the Admiralty Office who sent word to his brother, the Rector, that Nelson could be in London in under a fortnight. The Rector, who was on his way to London, had invited himself to stay with Fanny and his father at Round Wood for a few days. When he received Maurice's letter, the Rector made a somewhat cryptic remark that Fanny duly reported in her reply to Davison. He had asked if she had any objection to his seeing her husband before she did. Whatever implication lay behind this question caused Fanny when relating the conversation to cross out words and render others indistinct but the gist was that she had asked what objection could she have? In view of the Rector's later behaviour it may well be that he was already trying to stir up trouble between husband and wife.

'Your letter was truly acceptable. God grant My Dear Husband safe in England – and soon' wrote Fanny to Davison on 14 June. 'Your friendship for him, and your kind attention to me, deserves my best thanks.' Davison must have raised Nelson's request from the previous year of renting a suitably furnished house in London for the duration of his leave. Fanny, ever conscious that her husband continually reminded her that money was not unlimited, sensibly thought that this would prove a costly operation and asked Davison to suggest to Nelson that a hotel would prove more convenient and

> I am certain cheaper than taking a ready furnished house, [her underlining] where you are obliged to send table linen, knives and forks with many etc. which will amount to more than any extras from an Hotel – and the removing of servants is a great expense.

Having made her point forcibly she added 'all this, I leave to you'. Did she believe that as his financial adviser, Davison might put the economic aspect more strongly than she could or had she another reason for not wishing to have a house? While the main body of this letter was taken up with practicalities and cryptic remarks, Fanny revealed that she had had: 'spasms which has again shook me very much.' This may refer to panic attacks brought on by the excitement and apprehension of Nelson's imminent return, but more likely it was a recurrence of the bronchial cough from which she had suffered the previous winter.

Nelson had reported in March that he was very unwell but by 20 June he claimed:

> My health at times is better but a quiet mind and to give content is necessary for me. A very difficult thing for me to enjoy: I could say much but it would only distress me and be useless. I trust I shall find my dear Father in as perfect health as his age will allow. I shall come to London or where ever he may be the moment I get out of quarantine therefore I would not have you come to Portsmouth on any account.

Fanny must have read and re-read this letter trying to understand its full import. Nowhere did he say how much he was longing to see her yet he did suggest that he would waste no time in coming ashore. But that was to make his way to wherever Edmund was. Of course he knew that Fanny would be with his father but by forbidding her to go to Portsmouth to meet him he was denying her the accepted pleasure of all naval wives.

As far as Edmund was concerned he was in fine form telling Kitty: '…though there may be some few instances of stronger men at 77, yet they are rare.' He was looking forward to Nelson's return and seemed confident that his son would be given a posting that would enable him: '…to settle at home'. When that happened: '…some new domestic arrangements most likely will take place, but whatever they are, I have no doubt of my ease and comfort being considered.' But Nelson did not return swiftly by sea as they expected. When the Admiralty refused permission for his ship to leave the Mediterranean, Nelson, thwarted in his hope of bringing the Hamiltons back with him at the end of Sir William's tour of duty, decided to join his friends and make the long journey overland.

So the days of waiting for her husband's return dragged on. While she waited patiently, Nelson and his party, that included the Hamiltons, Emma's mother, Mrs Cadogan and the young writer, Miss Ellis Cornelia Knight, were enjoying the hospitality of the British Minister in Dresden. Also present at a number of parties was Mrs St George whose detailed diary entries recorded her impressions of her fellow guests. Like Mary Nisbet she was well aware of the gossip about Nelson and Lady Hamilton.

> Oct. 3. Dined at Mr Elliot's with only the Nelson party. It is plain that Lord Nelson thinks of nothing but Lady Hamilton who is totally occupied by the same object. She is bold, forward, coarse, assuming and vain. Her figure is colossal, but excepting her feet which are hideous, well shaped. Her bones are large and she is exceedingly embonpoint. She resembles the bust of Ariadne; the shape of all her features is fine, as is the form of her head, and particularly her ears; her teeth are a little irregular, but tolerably white; her eyes light blue with a brown spot in one which, though a defect, takes nothing away from her beauty or expression. Her eyebrows and hair are dark and her complexion coarse.

Having given grudging tribute to Emma Hamilton's assets she was far less flattering of Nelson.

> Lord Nelson is a little man, without any dignity...Lady H takes possession of him and he is a willing captive, the most submissive and devoted I have seen. Sir William is old, infirm, all admiration of his wife, and never spoke today but to applaud her...After dinner we had several songs in honour of Lord Nelson written by Miss Knight and sung by Lady Hamilton. She puffs the incense full in his face; but he receives it with pleasure and snuffs it up very cordially.

Mrs St George's opinion of Nelson did not improve on further acquaintance.

> Oct.5. Went by invitation to see LN dressed for Court. On his hat he wore the large diamond feather, or ensign of sovereignty, given him by the Grand Signior; on his breast the Order of the Bath, the Order he received as Duke of Bronte, the diamond star, including the sun or crescent given him by the Grand Signior, three gold medals obtained by three different victories and a beautiful present from the King of Naples. On one side is His Majesty's picture, richly set and surrounded with laurels, which spring from two united anchors at bottom and support the Neapolitan crown at top; on the other is the Queen's cipher, which turns so as to appear within the same laurels and is formed of diamonds on green enamel. In short, Lord Nelson was a perfect constellation of stars and Orders.

Nor was she taken in by Lady Hamilton's protestations of friendship even after she had been treated to a private showing of Emma's 'dramatic attitudes' in which she adopted the poses of statues and paintings. Although admitting that these were well done:

> ...her usual dress is tasteless, vulgar, loaded and unbecoming. She has borrowed several of my gowns and much admires my dress; which cannot flatter, as her own is so frightful...She does not gain upon me. I think her bold, daring, vain even to folly and stamped with the manners of her first situation much more strongly than one would suppose, after having represented Majesty and lived in good company fifteen years. Her ruling passions seem to me vanity, avarice and love for the pleasures of the table...Lady Hamilton expressed great anxiety to go to Court and Mrs Elliot assured her it would not amuse her and that the Elector [of Hanover] never gave dinners or suppers –'What?' cried she, 'no guttling!'

Emma not only ate well she also drank copiously. Following a Breakfast given by the Elliots on 9 October, the Nelson party stayed on to dinner as well, after which:

> Lady Hamilton, who declared she was passionately fond of champagne, took such a portion of it as astonished me. Lord Nelson was not behindhand, called more vociferously than usual for songs in his own praise... Poor Mr Elliot...endeavoured to stop the effusion of champagne, and effected it with some difficulty; but not till the Lord and Lady, or as he calls them, Antony and Moll Cleopatra, were pretty far gone.

Mrs St George who had entrée to the best houses had it on good authority that the Electress would not receive Lady Hamilton on account of her former dissolute life and to achieve this no Court functions were held during her stay.

No wonder then that Nelson had no time to write to Fanny beyond the one letter dated 20 September from Vienna that was enclosed with others to Davison:

> Since I wrote you from Trieste we have been so continually prepared to set out that I have not wrote a line till this day. Sir William being recovered we set out tomorrow and shall be in England the second week in October. I have wrote to Davison to take a house or good lodgings for the very short time I shall be in London, to which I shall instantly proceed and hope to meet you in the house. You must expect to find me a worn out old man. Make my kindest love to my Father who I shall see the moment I have been with the King.

The arrival of this letter, which took a month to reach her, threw Fanny into a turmoil of mixed feelings as she told Davison in her reply to him on 20

October: 'How rejoiced you made us yesterday by sending My Dear Lord's letter – I was truly thankful to see his handwriting.' She then copied out the short letter she had received from Nelson giving Davison the injunction to read the letter carefully. If, as Nelson had suggested, he was to be in England in the second week in October, then he must be due at any moment, if indeed, he had not already arrived. Thrown into confusion because of the shortness of time at her disposal, Fanny was of the opinion:

> I think you will see it is best for us to go to an Hotel – it is impossible for me to send linen etc to London – our stock being too scanty to divide – and the expense of the servants travelling amounts to a large sum. My husband says he shall only be a short time in London whether he will return to his Cottage for a long or short time or go to Bath.

Anxiety that she was doing the right thing crept into the letter and so she repeated herself:

> Dodds [an agent] may look out for a house but not engage it – we are at a certain expence [sic] at a Hotel – and the ordering every article for a short time into a house for a family is a great deal of trouble and expence.

The rest of the letter continued in an almost breathless fashion, the next sentence bearing a blot on the opening word: 'Now I have given you my opinion – you must say what you think I had best do – and I will do it.' The lapse in time between Nelson writing his letter and her receiving it weighed heavily upon her. Knowing that Nelson's party would cross to England to one of the East Anglian ports, she told Davison that she had immediately sent letters to await her husband's arrival at either Yarmouth or Harwich. Even in a state of nervousness she was still able to think straight enough to take practical steps to contact her husband wherever he arrived. But to cover herself – she seemed to be anticipating Nelson's criticism – she felt it had been necessary to explain to her husband that as Davison had been out of London with his family in Northumberland he had not been able to forward the letter sooner. She added that she had told him that as a result:

> …it was impossible for me to be in town, no house could be taken and got ready in a few days. I likewise mentioned the convenience of a Hotel and begged My Dear Lord just to stop at his own door for a few minutes and I would have everything ready to sett [sic] off with him – he will then have seen his father who is grown older than anything I can describe – he has been very ill since you last saw him – but is better.

Then having made all her arrangements to stay at home to greet Nelson, she suffered qualms of indecision. Was she doing the right thing? She put it to

Davison: 'Say whether you think I had best leave Round Wood – although I have written these letters to Yarmouth and Harwich.' Still in a highly agitated state she asked Davison to send her letter on to Maurice Nelson to save her having to repeat her plans to him especially as she wanted to write to Josiah who was at Plymouth to tell him the great news. Her Dear Lord would soon be home.

CHAPTER XI

Nelson's Return

I hope it will not be long before Lord Nelson arrives in this part of the world. His further stay in the Mediterranean cannot I am sure contribute either to the public advantage or his own...
The Admiralty, 18 August 1800, marked Private

In her letter of 20 October, Fanny asked Davison's advice as to the best course of action over Nelson's arrival; should she stay at Round Wood or should she do as Nelson had at some time suggested meet him in London? Her natural inclination was to the former as she was longing to show off the home she had created for them. She also knew, no matter what she tried to tell herself and Edmund refused to acknowledge, that things had changed. She had been apprehensive the last time Nelson came home after nearly five years away, but in spite of his severe wound, they had been able happily to pick up the threads of their life together. That their regular letters had been full of each other's daily routine had helped to fill the gap of those years apart. Once they were together they were able to refer to past events, each knowing that the other was able to share in whatever it was. The memory of that happy and loving few months had carried Fanny through Nelson's return to sea and her anxiety for his safety in the months that followed.

This time things were very different. She was acutely aware that the hero of the Nile was going to be a very different man to the wounded hero of Santa Cruz who had returned to her in 1797. While she never failed to give thanks for his survival and was pleased and proud of his success, she would have been completely naïve or obtuse not to realise that she was no longer the centre of his life. Although she had tried to persuade herself that the lack of letters from him was the result of their going astray or taking an extra long time to arrive, when they did come she had to find another excuse for their brevity and lack of intimacy. She was no fool; she knew that Lady Hamilton was exerting undue influence on her husband. While they were far away there was nothing she could do except to continue to send her husband loving letters. But how was she to cope when she inevitably came face to face with one of the most notorious women of the day, a woman who provoked outrageous gossip, a woman possessed of the power to charm most men and some women too; the woman who had apparently turned her husband into someone unrecognisable to those who knew him?

Fanny's intuition told her to adopt the tactic used by many women both before and after her who have found themselves in a similar position. She invited the Hamiltons to dinner and to stay the night at Round Wood on their journey between Great Yarmouth, Nelson's expected port of arrival, and London. Here she would be on her home ground; she would be the hostess welcoming them as guests into the home that was hers and Nelson's. In other words, she would have command of the situation from the outset.

Unfortunately, Fanny did not on this occasion follow her intuition but chose to act on Davison's advice. He had replied by return of post to her letter and on 22 October she wrote:

> I asked your advice with an intention to follow it – therefore tomorrow morning I sett [sic] off from Round Wood and expect to be at your door before six o'clock – if you are gone to Northumberland – I will accept your very friendly offer of your house – if you are still in London I go immediately to the Lothian Hotel. All this I have written to My Dear Lord – both to Yarmouth and Harwich. I would prefer a bedroom upstairs and my Woman servant very near. Samuel the coachman can sleep out.

With uncertainty over how long they might have to wait before Nelson arrived, she had left Edmund at Round Wood with Lady Berry who was staying for a few days to keep him company.

In the absence of any correspondence between 22 October and 6 November we can only speculate about Fanny's movements. It is likely that she had several meetings with Davison in which he must have stressed that although he sympathised with her inclination to stay at an hotel for the duration of his London stay, Nelson had asked him to rent a house and therefore he was under an obligation to do so. It is not known how much Fanny was involved in the choice of 17 Dover Street, centrally situated off Berkeley Square, Bond Street and Piccadilly, which was leased from the beginning of December. Certainly, Edmund was later to find it too big and with far too many servants. Nor is it recorded at what point Edmund joined Fanny. It is most likely that after spending a week sorting out accommodation, she again took Davison's advice that the best place for her and his father to await Nelson's arrival was in London.

So Fanny returned to Round Wood and finding no letters from Nelson awaiting her there, she closed up the house. By the end of the first week in November she and Edmund were settled in the fashionable Nerot's Hotel in King Street, St James's, situated quite close to the house to which they would later move. Fanny was not alone in waiting to hear of Nelson's movements.

Captain Hardy's annoyance that his Admiral should behave with such non-chalance towards those who cared about him showed when he wrote:

> Notwithstanding all the newspapers, his Lordship is not arrived in Town and when he will God only knows. His father has lost all patience and her Ladyship bears up very well as yet but I fear she also will soon despond. He certainly arrived at Yarmouth on Thursday last but there has been no letter received by anybody.

Many of Nelson's later biographers have blamed Fanny for the confusion that occurred over their reunion. On 6 November he and his party landed at Great Yarmouth. *The Ipswich Journal* reported:

> Thursday a.m. arrived at Yarmouth, in the King George packet, *Capt. Deane*, the gallant Admiral Lord Nelson, accompanied by Sir William and Lady Hamilton. His Lordship landed about 12 o'clock and was drawn from the Bridge to the Wrestlers Inn by the populace, where he alighted amidst the loudest acclamations of gratitude.

Such were the demands on his time that Nelson had only time to write a brief note to Fanny, addressed to Round Wood where he expected her to be:

> We are this moment arrived and the post only allows me to say that we shall set off tomorrow noon and be with you on Saturday to dinner. I have only had time to open one of your letters, my visits are so numerous. May God bless you and my dear Father and believe me ever your affectionate Bronte.

The last time he had signed himself 'your affectionate husband' had been on 15 December 1799. The letter from Fanny was the one which contained her invitation to the Hamiltons, hence his comment: 'Sir and Lady Hamilton beg their best regards and will accept your offer of a bed. Mrs Cadogan [Lady Hamilton's mother] and Miss Knight with all the servants will proceed to Colchester.'

Had Nelson bothered to read the rest of the letters Fanny had sent to Yarmouth, then he might have been saved the annoyance of arriving at Round Wood and finding that not only were his wife and father not there but no preparations had been made for him or his guests' entertainment. Any warm emotion Nelson might have felt at the prospect of meeting his wife and seeing their home was promptly turned into irritation and anger. The man who had come to tolerate anything Emma Hamilton did had not expected that his wife would not be there to greet them and provide them with the promised meal and accommodation. He had, had he not, written that they would be there at that time on that day? So within half an hour of his arrival, after a cursory examination of the house he had never lived in and never would, the party was driven into Ipswich to find rooms for the night at Bamford's Hotel. No doubt his temper was calmed when the word having been spread around the town that he was there, the crowds turned out to cheer and several civic dignitaries called upon him. The following day having stepped into his carriage en route for Colchester, some members of the enthusiastic crowd which had gathered to gawp as well as cheer, uncoupled the horses from the carriage and carried it through the town to the point where it met the main London road. It is not recorded how the Hamiltons felt about this unusual mode of transport, but it was one to which they would have to become accustomed.

As she waited, certain in her mind that she had done all that her Dear Lord had required of her, Fanny was suddenly wrong footed by the arrival of Nelson's letter of 6 November that had been immediately forwarded to the hotel from Round Wood. Her anguish that she had not been at home to lovingly greet her husband was compounded by the fact that she knew that she had been found wanting as a hostess. This was what had come of listening to Davison. Had she followed her instincts, she would by now have welcomed her beloved husband, been able to greet her rival on her own territory and display the comfortable home she had waiting for her Lord. Instead, she had been made to feel in the wrong; she had been put in the position where the first thing she would have to do when they did meet was to apologise.

Thus it may be that Fanny was relieved that the meeting, when it finally took place on Sunday 9 November, was both formal and in the full gaze of the public. Somehow word had gone ahead that Nelson would be arriving that afternoon and by the time his coach pulled up outside Nerot's at three o'clock, a large crowd had gathered to welcome him despite the pouring rain. Among them were representatives of the London press eager to capture every detail of the event for their readers. So nothing was omitted – from the fact that the coach was a German travelling carriage to a description of Lady Hamilton's black Egyptian serving-woman who accompanied her mistress, Sir William Hamilton and Nelson in the vehicle. Nelson stepped down from the carriage dressed in full naval uniform displaying on his chest three stars and two gold medals. The rapturous cheers of the crowd showed no signs of abating. Having become accustomed to this sort of reception from the populace over the last three days, the 'illustrious tar' acknowledged the acclamations with a low sweeping bow. The newspapermen noted that while Nelson looked extremely well he was very thin. But so for that matter was Sir William. However, never missing an opportunity to fuel the gossip that had already come from abroad, they also reported that Lady Hamilton looked extremely well.

Waiting in the vestibule of the hotel were Fanny and Edmund. It would have been surprising if Fanny had not suffered palpitations as she waited; a small, slight figure, desperately trying to show outward calm and support for Edmund who, overcome with emotion, stood at her side. Perhaps it was just as well she had him to think about, either by clasping his hand to give him comfort or holding his arm, which in turn gave her the support she so needed to face – what she was not quite sure. Nelson himself had warned her he was a physically changed man. But it was the change in attitude not just to her; the wavering between imperious manner and the conviction that he was not receiving the recognition that was his due that was most worrying. She had perhaps tried to fool herself that everything would be well once he was home with her. She had tried to dismiss as merely malicious the rumours and gossip of the ever-growing intimacy between her husband and Lady Hamilton such as the item which had appeared in *The Morning Post* in September:

> The German State painter, we are assured, is drawing Lady Hamilton and Lord Nelson at full length. An Irish correspondent hopes the artist will have delicacy enough to put Sir William between them.

As she and Edmund stood waiting in that hotel lobby for him to come in she must have had serious doubts about what the future would hold.

Yet as so often happens in moments of great tension the actual entry of Nelson and his party was almost farcical in that Nelson had stood so long outside acknowledging the adulation of his public that he was very wet. That at least must have made the introductions easier. Nelson no doubt embraced his aged father warmly and Edmund was finally unable to hold back the tears of joy for the return of his favourite son. But there is no record of how Nelson and Fanny greeted each other. Her innate sense of decorum would probably have prevented her from throwing her arms around him as she might had she been alone with him and with so many onlookers it was inevitable she should be restrained. But what about Nelson? What move did he make to show how deeply he had missed her and how much he loved her? How does a man react when meeting his wife in the presence of his mistress? Perhaps no more than her hand raised to his lips or a perfunctory kiss on the cheek passed between them. Whatever the case, it was enough for Fanny later to be branded as 'cold'. Fortunately perhaps, there was hardly time for anyone to consider the situation for within ten minutes of his arrival, His Grace the Duke of Queensberry arrived for a visit to Nelson that lasted for an hour or so.

Dinner had been ordered for five o'clock so there was barely time for Nelson to change his clothes before he and Fanny sat down to eat with the Hamiltons. Certainly, there would have been no space for intimate conversation and as the meal progressed it must have been almost inevitable, if not intentional, that Fanny would have felt excluded from the conversation of three people who had spent so long together and had so much shared experience. Of what could Fanny talk? The Hamiltons had been away so long that the social chat of the time would have meant little to them. On the other hand, Fanny was well aware that it would have been impolite for her to talk to Nelson of his friends and family who were not known to the Hamiltons. If she had been able to control her feelings sufficiently then it is most likely that she would have engaged Sir William in conversation. He was a cultured man with a great love of antiquities and under other circumstances Fanny would have found him a pleasant dining companion. It would have been only natural for both the women to take surreptitious glances at each other while maintaining polite conversation. Fanny no doubt felt herself to be under the scrutiny of not only Lady Hamilton but also her husband. If he was mentally comparing them, then Lady Emma's effusiveness served to emphasise Fanny's genteel politeness. Fortunately, Fanny was spared having to spend too long in the Hamiltons' company as at half past seven Nelson was carried away to report to the First Lord of the Admiralty, Lord Spencer. Here at least Fanny scored one little triumph; she received an invitation to spend the evening informally with Lady Spencer. The Hamiltons were not included in the invitation – the first of the many slights that Lady Hamilton, in particular, was to receive.

The Hamiltons then retired to 22 Grosvenor Square, a house loaned them by their friend William Beckford until such time as they were able move into their own home at 23 Piccadilly. Any hopes that Fanny had that this would be the last she would see of them were soon to be dashed. As a result of Nelson having spent much of his leave travelling through Europe with the Hamiltons, he would have only a few weeks ashore before he was recalled to sea; in fact he had placed himself on the active list as soon as he had arrived in Great Yarmouth. Fanny would indeed see very little of her husband as he was so taken up with meetings and celebratory dinners. To make matters worse for her what time he did have free of such engagements was filled with social events that seemed always to include the Hamiltons.

The day after his arrival in London coincided with the annual Lord Mayor's procession. Nelson, as victor of the Nile, was invited to ride in the cavalcade. Again the general public showed their great affection and regard for him, shouting and cheering him as he passed. As had happened at both Yarmouth and Ipswich, some of the crowd paid him the greatest compliment by uncoupling his carriage and carrying it for some length upon their shoulders. Princess Castelcicala, wife of the Neapolitan Ambassador to the Court of St James, took Fanny and Edmund with her to watch from various vantage points the parade which started on decorated barges on the Thames before continuing to the Mansion House by road. It is possible that the Hamiltons were also in the party.

Fanny's enjoyment of the brilliant pageant was marred by two considerations; her anxiety that Edmund should not become over-excited and his health suffer and the fact that she was sharing Nelson's triumph, not just with his father and other members of his family which she was happy to do but also with her husband's 'best friends'. It is not recorded how Fanny spent the rest of her day but she may have been among: '…the four to five thousand ladies and gentlemen who sat down to dinner' at the ensuing

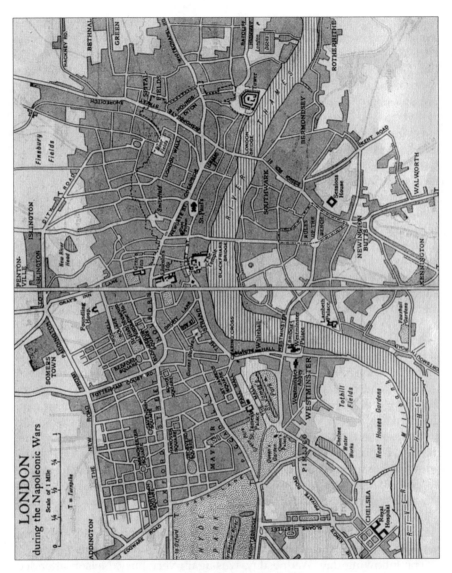

London during the Napoleonic Wars

banquet where Nelson was among the guests of honour. Many were the expressions of gratitude to Nelson for his daring and leadership and toast after toast was raised in his name. This was the first of many such banquets. The Directors of the East India Company gave him a dinner that began at 6pm and ended at midnight and that was followed by dinners and the presentation of valuable pieces of silver in the form of either large cups or plate from the merchants of the Turkey and Levant Companies. When his old friend Lord St Vincent read the newspaper accounts of Nelson's social life, he wrote to give him sensible advice against too much city feasting: '...for there is much risk of illness in going out of smoking hot rooms into the damp putrid air of London streets.'

The following day, Fanny and Edmund were told that they were to accompany Nelson and the Hamiltons to the theatre at Covent Garden. When the party entered the box the whole audience, it seemed, rose to hail the hero. As Nelson acknowledged the applause, it all became too much for Edmund who broke down, weeping tears of joy. The programme that evening included a play called *Comedy Life* and most apt, a musical entertainment dedicated to Nelson, entitled *The Mouth of the Nile*. It is doubtful that many of the audience gave their full attention to the stage. Much more interesting for those who relished intrigue and gossip was the interplay of the characters in Nelson's box. The attire of the two ladies was examined in detail and for those who were not able to be present, the scene was described in the press the following day. Fanny's figure was described as pleasing, her features handsome and exceedingly interesting, with a general appearance that is: 'at once prepossessing and elegant.' How long had it taken Fanny to decide what to wear for this very public occasion? She knew that she would be under severe scrutiny and possible comparison and she had been unerring in her choice of white for her gown, set off by a violet satin head-dress with a single small white feather. Against this understated dress, suggestive of purity, Lady Hamilton appeared overblown in a rich blue satin gown with a matching head-dress topped off by a whole plume of feathers. Those close enough to see her clearly remarked on the difference in size between the two ladies: 'Lady Hamilton is rather embonpoint' adding rather grudgingly, 'but her person is nevertheless highly graceful and her face extremely pretty.'

The following day, Wednesday, was again very busy. Nelson attended a royal Levee at St James's Palace. This was an all-male affair and was an opportunity for the sovereign to meet and talk to prominent people of the day. For Nelson this was his first appearance at Court since he had been ennobled and he went full of good humour expecting the monarch to greet him warmly and no doubt congratulate him on his great victory over the French. Someone should have warned him or perhaps he did not heed the advice if it were given, for he made a terrible blunder in etiquette. Proud as he was of all the foreign decorations and insignia he had been given abroad, he wore them all for his appearance at St James's. This was a faux pas not lightly forgiven; before he could wear these foreign honours alongside his

British ones he needed formal permission from the King. Thus when it was his turn to be presented, the King merely expressed the hope that he had recovered his health and before Nelson had time to reply, His Majesty had turned to a General standing close by whom he proceeded to engage in good humoured conversation for nearly half an hour. Nelson felt gravely slighted by this very tepid reception. It was not what he had expected. In his mind this off-hand treatment confirmed his previously held view that his own country did not appreciate his greatness.

Brooding over what had occurred, he was not in the best of moods for the dinner to which he and Fanny had been invited at the home of the Spencers. The last time the pair had dined there was the occasion when Lady Spencer, who rarely invited many women to her dinners, had given in to his plea to include his beloved Fanny because he held every minute with her as precious. Lady Spencer was well aware of the current gossip and was horrified to see how changed Nelson had become. As a dinner guest he behaved extremely badly, hunched over his plate, speaking to no one and glowering at any attempt at conversation. The main meal over, the guests lingered at table before the ladies left for the drawing room. An incident then took place which has been retold many times since Lady Spencer first related it to Lady Shelley. As the nuts and wine circled the table, Fanny, who was seated opposite her husband, carefully cracked some walnuts, put them into a glass and gently handed it across the table to Nelson. It was a thoughtful and caring wifely gesture on her part since although he had managed to master eating with one hand, there was no way he could have managed to crack a nut. It was related that Nelson churlishly pushed away the proffered glass so roughly that it smashed against one of the dishes on the table. There was one of those pregnant pauses that follow such accidents before Fanny broke the tension by bursting into tears. To those who witnessed the scene it was taken as proof of Nelson's rejection of his wife. Most of those present would have heard the reports from abroad that while on the journey across Europe, Lady Hamilton always sat beside Nelson and cut up his food for him. The story also became current that Nelson had behaved so badly because Lady Spencer had refused to invite the Hamiltons to the dinner. It all added up to a good story. To be fair to Nelson it could be that with his black mood and his partial sight, he did not see the glass properly. Whatever the truth, Fanny had been publicly humiliated. Lady Spencer rapidly took charge of the situation and shepherded the ladies into the drawing room where she attempted to comfort Fanny.

It was not in Fanny's nature to unburden herself to others. Hers had always been the role of comforter and sympathetic listener, but on this occasion she responded to the warmth of Lady Spencer's concern and told her a little of what life had been like for her since her husband's return. Little in the way of concrete facts has come down the ages but just from the public diary of events it was obvious that Nelson and Fanny spent very little time together. Since they were living at an hotel we may assume that they shared a bedroom but it is doubtful that they had marital relations however much Fanny might have desired it initially. In the brief periods during the day when he was not out they would seldom have been alone; Edmund was always there too, while members of the family such as Maurice and the Rector and his wife as well as Nelson's old friends and colleagues who were anxious to see him came and went. The constant flow of visitors must have made Nelson even more annoyed that the house he desired – and had commanded should be ready – had not been immediately available. Conscious of his new status, it was impossible for him to entertain at an hotel as he would have done in his own establishment. It was all Fanny's fault.

Continuing the hectic social round, Thursday found Fanny and Nelson at the Queen's Drawing Room where Fanny was presented to Her Majesty. Being at Court was no longer a novelty for her; she had attended various functions by this time and certainly was able to hold her own. If anything, it is likely that the Queen showed her more attention than was usual for the royal consort had made it very plain that she would not receive Lady Hamilton at Court even though as a returning diplomat, Sir William was expected to pay homage to His Majesty – but not his wife. What sort of reception Nelson received from the Queen is not recorded but he would at least have felt at home amongst the men present for many of the captains who had fought with him at the Nile, including Hardy, had also received invitations. Many of these must have looked closely for indications as to how Nelson was behaving. It was now an open secret among them and others that Nelson wanted Lady Hamilton to be received at Court. On the day he had landed in England, the prescient Lord St Vincent had written to Nepean, the Secretary to the Navy: 'I have no doubt he [Nelson] is pledged to getting Lady Hamilton received at St James's and everywhere, and he will get into much brouillerie about it.'

The Nelsons and the Hamiltons made two more visits to the theatre together. When they revisited Covent Garden, they were given the second box from the stage next to that frequently occupied by the Prince of Wales. The press were quick to report that Nelson sat at the front of the box with Lady Hamilton seated on his right and Fanny on his left. The elderly Edmund and Sir William Hamilton who were much of an age, were relegated to the back. There was much more to fill the columns of the papers and titillate the gossips over the tea-tables when the quintet attended a performance of *Pizarro* at the Drury Lane theatre during the third week in November. The theatre was leased by the dramatist Richard Brinsley Sheridan and most of his own popular plays were performed there. However, he occasionally adapted the work of other playwrights, as was the case with the drama *Pizarro*. The play was in full swing when Fanny fainted and had to be helped from the box. Not willing to concede that she might simply have been overcome by the heat in the theatre, the rumour-mongers related that she had lost consciousness just after the actress on stage had declaimed: 'How a woman can love, Pizarro, thou hast known…how she can hate thou hast yet to learn...wave thy glittering sword, meet and survive an injured woman's fury.' If the bystanders to the Nelsons' domestic drama believed this was the attitude Fanny would adopt, they clearly had no knowledge of the woman she was.

The house in Dover Street became available earlier than expected; Edmund, writing to Kitty Matcham on 15 November, gave it as his address. He remarked that the house was quite large and seemed to him to be over-filled with servants. He did not mention that these included a French butler. Three days later in another letter he gave an insight into the hectic life Nelson was leading. 'He looks well, is active and cannot rest long in a place there-fore I myself can only see him for a minute. Your brother is so constantly upon the wing that I can get a short glimpse myself.' Edmund had waited so very long for the opportunity to sit down and enjoy long talks with his son. Certainly, he would have been the first to admit that where possible he was included in his son's crowded social life but that was not what he had dreamed of. Like Fanny, he was hoping for quiet, intimate sessions but he could not see that these would ever come. In that same letter Edmund gave Kitty the news that the Rector and his wife had taken lodgings close by and were intending to stay for some time. So even if, by chance, there were no other visitors calling, it looked as if the Rector would be much in evidence.

But there always were visitors and most often they were the Hamiltons. It was one of the occasions when they were dining with the Nelsons that gave rise to yet another of those anecdotal stories that has passed down through the ages, reported presumably by someone who was present. During the course of the meal Fanny is supposed to have said something which caused Lady Hamilton to take offence. This may have had to do with an event that had taken place earlier in the day. The Nelsons and Hamiltons had been present at an entertainment which had been graced with the presence of a Duchess. The noble lady had been graciously polite to the Nelsons, engag-ing them both in conversation but had studiously ignored Lady Hamilton even when Nelson had tried to introduce her. Once the Duchess had left the room, several bystanders had remarked on her off-hand manner. Fanny had remained silent – she was not given to making remarks about others in public – but Nelson had joined Lady Hamilton in making contemptuous remarks about the lady. Rather than letting the episode go, Lady Hamilton, who had a reputation for enjoying her food hugely, complained she was feeling nauseous and left the room, accompanied by a servant.

Fanny, as hostess, retained her place at table but Nelson turned upon her, accused her of trying to poison Lady Hamilton and demanded that she go and attend to her. Justifiably, Fanny was reported to have replied that her ministrations were not needed as there were plenty of servants to make sure the lady was well looked after. Nelson was then said to have ordered Fanny to do his bidding. Obediently, she went in search of her guest. The final touch to the story was that Fanny was later to be found holding the basin while Lady Hamilton vomited. This tale, if true, must have confirmed Fanny's suspicions that Emma, as had been whispered abroad, was pregnant. It is possible that this event took place a day or two before the visit to Drury Lane and provided onlookers with another reason for those words from Pizarro to have significance. Who could not feel sympathy for a woman who was constantly being publicly humiliated by her husband? Sir William Hotham who had known Nelson for years summed up the feelings of many at that time.

> His [Nelson's] conduct to Lady Nelson was the very extreme of unjustifiable weakness, for he should have at least attempted to conceal his infirmities without publicly wounding the feelings of a woman whose conduct he knew well was irreproachable.

The mores of the period accepted that within a marriage one or other might take a lover or mistress but it was expected that the affair would be conducted with discretion. Fanny, suffering emotional anguish at her own treatment, at times must have marvelled at the blind acquiescence of Sir William Hamilton.

In a matter of sixteen days, all Fanny's hopes for a happy reunion with her husband had been crushed. It has been said that because she was shy and retiring, she was unable to cope with the demands of the high society in which she found herself. That picture does not fit the Fanny who, as her uncle's hostess, had entertained people of different nationalities and from all ranks of society. Although during the years of her marriage she had by necessity of circumstances and income led a fairly retired life, when given the opportunity she quite happily socialised with those of high standing. So it was not the social life that Fanny could not cope with, it was the negligent attitude of her husband. We can only surmise her feelings when Nelson informed her that he had received an invitation to accompany the Hamiltons to spend Christmas with Sir William's relation the eccentric author, William Beckford, at his country house, Fonthill, in Wiltshire. Lady Hamilton had received the invitation on 24 November – the same day they attended that performance of *Pizarro*. Perhaps she conveyed it to him as they sat in the theatre and Nelson casually informed his wife he would not be spending Christmas with her. That may well have been the reason for the fainting fit.

It would hardly have been surprising if Fanny had taken to her bed after this but the evidence is that she continued to appear with Nelson at any function to which she was asked, as, for example, to the house of the Marquis of Abercorn at the beginning of December. However, she was not with him and the Hamiltons on 16 December when Nelson's distant relative, George Walpole, an MP and younger brother of Lord Walpole, entertained them. Another long established story relating to this time tells that following a blazing row late one evening, Nelson left the house and walked the streets of London, before turning up at the Hamiltons' house in the early hours. Quite who heard the 'row' and who knew that he had roamed the streets has never been revealed but if it did happen then it suggests servants' gossip. Nor is it clear whether this was supposed to have occurred before or after Christmas. What is certain is that Nelson joined the Hamiltons on 20 December for the Christmas festivities at Fonthill. These were lavish and 'artistic'. Lady Hamilton, as always, excelled herself, entertaining the company with her singing and her various statue poses. Here the subtle use of draperies managed to conceal her swelling body now in the last stage of pregnancy. The grand festivities lasted six days bringing Nelson back to Dover Street on Boxing Day.

Fanny and Edmund spent Christmas together as they had done in preceding years. Only this time they were in a large house with a small army of servants to provide them with whatever they liked to order. It is likely that their needs were simple; Edmund had to watch his digestion and Fanny was not a great eater so any large meals would have been for the benefit of others. There is some evidence that Josiah managed to join his mother for the first time in years, so that was some compensation to her for Nelson's absence. It is almost certain that the Rector and his family, and possibly other family members gathered for the Christmas meal. And there is no doubt that Fanny and Edmund would have attended church on Christmas Day but it is very doubtful if Nelson, to whom his faith had once meant so much, found time to go to a service while at Fonthill. But how did the family explain Nelson's absence to themselves? Did they openly face the fact that their beloved husband, son, brother had deserted them for the woman who had captivated him or did they all pretend that Mr Beckford's invitation was one he could not politely refuse; that his ennoblement had placed certain constraints upon him that must be obeyed?

Nelson had taken his seat in the House of Lords in mid November and on New Year's Eve, he and Lord Hood had the privilege of playing a part in the time honoured ritual of escorting the King from the Presence Chamber to the throne in the House of Lords. If this was not honour enough for Nelson, then more was to follow the next day when he was finally promoted to be a Vice-Admiral of the Blue.

But time was now running out fast. Nelson's leave would shortly be at an end and, although Fanny had not yet faced it, so would her marriage. No letters exist from either of them to show that this was to happen as rapidly as it did. There are however, two accounts of what occurred during those final days that have been repeated over and over. Again the question has to be asked, who observed the scene and under what circumstances was it later reported? The most likely candidate for the first event would have been Fanny's personal maid who may have talked to those sympathetic to her mistress. It is said that on his return to Dover Street, possibly after the Fonthill visit, Nelson found Fanny in bed. It is not recorded if this was because it was late at night or if she was ill. He is said to have taken her hand, presumably in a loving gesture and she, anxious to explain his treatment of her as her fault, asked him if she had ever given him cause for complaint or suspicion. He answered honestly that she had not.

The second story appeared many years after the event and is ascribed to Nelson's solicitor William Haslewood who called, so it was said, on Nelson as he and Fanny were having breakfast. In the course of conversation, Nelson mentioned Lady Hamilton at which, so the story goes, Fanny stood up and issued an ultimatum: 'I am sick of hearing of dear Lady Hamilton and am resolved that you shall give up either her or me.' To this Nelson is supposed to have retorted: 'Take care, Fanny, what you say. I love you sincerely but I cannot forget my obligations to Lady Hamilton and speak of her otherwise than with affection and admiration.' The story concludes with Fanny sweeping out of the room declaring that her mind was made up and Nelson left the house – and her – forever. The problem with this dramatic denouement is that it seems out of keeping for Fanny to behave with such determination. One can believe that she might well have said she was heartily sick of hearing about Emma, even employing the sarcasm of 'dear Lady Hamilton', but it is unlikely that she would have tried to force Nelson into choosing between them. She would have been only too aware that at that moment she would have lost whereas, if she played her cards carefully and waited, there was a possibility that the affair might peter out and they could resume their life together. It should be noted that Haslewood was later to act as solicitor for the Rector when he became the successor to Nelson's titles. After Nelson's death, the family was anxious that the hero's name should be untarnished and while trying to insist that in the beginning the affair between Nelson and Lady Hamilton was purely platonic, they set about casting Fanny into the role of the cold, unresponsive wife who had pushed her husband into the arms of another woman. Haslewood's story was ideal as corroborative evidence but it overlooked the fact that Nelson remained with Fanny in the house until it was time for him to rejoin his ship.

The order came to hoist his flag at Plymouth on 9 January 1801 but before he left London, he had the sad duty to attend the funeral of his old friend, Capt. Locker. Then, two days before his departure, there was another Royal Levee at which Nelson and many of his fellow appointees for promotion were presented to the King. Sir William Hamilton was also among the guests but neither he nor Nelson had been able to gratify Lady Hamilton's deepest desire to be presented to the Queen, as the press were keen to point out to their readers, reporting in late December: 'Lady Hamilton had not yet been at Court, not having received any answer from her Majesty to a letter of recommendation of which her Ladyship was the bearer from the Queen of Naples.' Then on 10 January, having reported that Nelson had been expected to leave Town on the previous day, came the paragraph:

> Lady Hamilton has received no answer whatsoever to the recommendatory letter from the Queen of Naples although a great personage received it at the Levee from Sir William Hamilton and was himself the bearer of this courtly epistle to his Royal Consort.

The Queen's determination to refuse to recognise her was so strong that not even the King's recommendation could overcome her decision. This very public slight must have rankled with Lady Hamilton and was perhaps the cause of Nelson's remark that Emma knew how to raise the hell of a dust when she couldn't have her own way.

Just before he left, Fanny received an undated letter from Lady Hamilton which showed that that lady either had supreme confidence in her position or that she totally lacked sensitivity:

> I would have done myself the honour of calling on you and Lord Nelson this day, but I am not well nor in spirits. Sir William and self feel the loss of our good friend, the good Lord Nelson. Permit me in the morning to have the pleasure of seeing you and hoping, my dear Lady Nelson, the con-tinuance of your friendship, which will be in Sir William and myself for everlasting to you and your family. Sir William begs to say, as an old and true friend of Lord Nelson, if he can be of any use to you in his Lordship's absence, he shall be very happy and will call to pay his respects to you and Mr Nelson, to whom I beg my compliments and to Capt. Nesbit.

Can she really have been so naïve as to believe that Fanny would wish to continue an acquaintance with her? And although Sir William may have offered his services to her out of sheer good manners, it was an offer that Fanny could do without. She had sufficient gentlemen among her circle of friends on whom she could call for help or advice. Perhaps Lady Hamilton was suggesting, as has been speculated upon over the years, that they should form a ménage à trois – or rather a ménage à quatre – with Fanny accepting the situation with the same complaisance as Sir William.

The short letter from Southampton on 13 January hardly suggests that Nelson had decided to sever all connection with his wife: 'My Dear Fanny, We are arrived and heartily tired, so tell Mrs Nelson [the Rector's wife] and with kindest regards to my Father and all the family. Believe me, your affec-tionate Nelson.' Perhaps it had become ingrained upon him that he should address her as 'My Dear Fanny' and end 'your affectionate Nelson' but this letter is no more terse than many he had written during the previous year. What is interesting is that he has reverted to the signature 'Nelson' when from 7 November 1799 he had signed himself 'Bronte Nelson'. If relations between them had reached the pitch that they were neither living under the same roof nor communicating, this letter does not seem to bear that out. Had he really decided to separate from Fanny or was it possible that he believed he could have both of them?

From Southampton, Nelson set out for Plymouth calling on the way at Torr Abbey, the home of his old friend Lord St Vincent. When he left, his host wrote to the Secretary of the Admiralty: 'Poor man! He is devoured with vanity, weakness and folly: was strung with ribbons, medals etc and yet pretended that he wished to avoid the honour and ceremonies he everywhere met with upon the road.' St Vincent saw, as others had done, the vanity of the man but in mentioning folly was he referring to Nelson's behaviour generally or with Emma Hamilton in particular? Was he aware that Nelson himself did not seem to know what he wanted at that stage?

Two of the next three letters, written from Plymouth on 16, 19 and 21 January, must have reminded Fanny of the husband who some years before had taken her to task for what he considered to be her incompetent packing. Did he feel that Emma Hamilton would have managed things better? Or was it that he had become so accustomed to off-loading his frustration upon Fanny that he quite forgot their present situation? Whatever his motives, he obviously thought that it was her fault that:

...all my things are now breaking open for only one key can be found. My steward says I have no one thing for comfort come but a load of useless articles from Burgess's & a large chest of green tea. I have been buying a few things just to make me comfortable for in fact I have nothing but two chairs. £100 I have paid for carriage, £20 would have bought me more than I could want from Mr Burgess. [John Burgess & Sons whose premises were at 107, in the Corner of the Savoy Steps in The Strand were well known purveyors of high class meat, fish and other delicacies, particularly from Italy. Whatever opinion Nelson held at that time, Burgess was chosen to victual the Victory in 1805.] I know not where I shall be in a week, with my kindest regards to my father and Mrs N.

His annoyance did not abate and a further list of complaints was sent:

...half my wardrobe is left behind & that butler, a French rascal, ought to be hanged and I hope you will never lay out a farthing with Mr Burgess. Had the waste of money been laid out in Wedgewood's ware, forks for servants or cooking utensils it would have been well, but I am forced to buy everything, even a little tea for who would open a large chest? In short I find myself without anything comfortable or convenient. In glasses of some kind the steward tells me he finds a useless quantity of decanters, as yet no one can be found, and if he cannot find them today I must buy. In short I only regret that I desired any person to order things for me. I could have done all in ten minutes and for a tenth part of the expense, but never mind I can eat off a yellow ware plate. It is now too late to send my half wardrobe, as I know not what is to become of me, nor do I care.

Fanny would never have retaliated to this with the comment that perhaps he should have done it himself or at least supervised the ordering himself, rather she took the tirade as proof that he still needed her. Little did she know that while she bore the brunt of his anger, Lady Hamilton was receiving almost daily declarations of his love for her.

CHAPTER XII
Marriage Breakdown

When Miss Knight had observed that victory in Abu Qir bay must have been the happiest day of his life, he had replied, 'No, the happiest was that on which I married Lady Nelson.'
The Ipswich Journal, April 1801

Once Nelson had left Town, there was little reason for Fanny to remain there even though the Dover Street house had been taken for a year. Neither she nor Edmund felt comfortable in it; it was far too big for them and it held too many painful reminders of the hectic social round and upheavals of the previous eight weeks. Both were anxious to have time to rest and recoup themselves. The winter was never the best of time for Fanny's health but all the emotional strain of the months leading up to Nelson's return and the problems that had followed must have taken their toll. So it was with some relief that she looked forward to going not to Bath but to Brighton for a change of air and a course of treatment at the hot sea-baths.

Plans to take a house there must have been made when Nelson first arrived home. It may be that being uncertain as to when he would be recalled to sea, he had anticipated joining Fanny there so that he too could enjoy the change of air and take part in the therapeutic treatments that the seaside resort had to offer. Brighton was not only closer to London should he need to go quickly to the Admiralty, but with its associations with the Prince of Wales it attracted a different class of society than Bath. Once Nelson had returned to sea, there seemed no reason why she should not continue with the original plan which was to take the Brighton house from the last week in January. Once it became clear that Nelson was not able to join her, she had invited the Rector's wife Sarah to join her for part, if not all, of her stay. Sarah, however, suddenly withdrew from the arrangement, no doubt at the instigation of her husband. The Rector had accompanied his brother to Southampton and although Nelson had often professed to dislike much of what his brother did, it seems, he now became his close confidant.

Having lived away from his family since his early adolescence, Nelson had an almost childlike, idealistic belief in the close relationships within a family. It was almost as if he needed to have the total and unreserved approval of his father and siblings for his actions. He also needed someone who would listen to his problems but more important, he needed someone who would give him the answers he wanted. If on the long journey to Plymouth and during their overnight stays, Nelson had discussed his feelings for Emma, and his responsibilities especially as the birth of their child was getting closer, it was possible he had sought the advice of his brother. If he had expected a homily on his duty and the sanctity of marriage, then he had chosen the wrong person.

The Rector exemplified the stereotypical picture of the eighteenth-century cleric who had entered the church for all the wrong reasons. Jane Austen's Mr Collins and Mr Elton would have recognised William Nelson as a kindred spirit. Not wishing to jeopardise whatever benefits might come his way by remaining close to Nelson, the Rector was only too eager to say what his brother wanted to hear and do whatever his brother wanted of him. And if that meant withdrawing his wife from the company of Fanny, so be it. Of course, Fanny had been exceedingly useful to him and Sarah in providing a home for their children in the holidays and in looking after Edmund but against that Fanny had not always done what he asked her to do, witness her refusal to make approaches to those in high places who might grant him clerical preferment. So the Rector and Sarah detached themselves from Fanny and perhaps at Nelson's request, set about cultivating the friendship of Lady Hamilton.

Fanny had no doubt invited Sarah to join her because it seemed the familial thing to do but she may have already sensed a cooling off towards her by the Rector and his wife: 'I am sure I need not repeat my constant desire to do anything in my power to serve or accommodate my Dear Lord's family.' But the women had little in common so when Sarah declined the invitation, Fanny asked Elizabeth Locker to join her. Again Fanny put the considerations of others before her own as this lady was hardly likely to be the brightest of companions, having so recently been bereaved of the father with whom she had lived. Neither had she much money but Fanny was quite happy to take care of the expenses for both of them. However, her motive in inviting Miss Locker was not entirely altruistic nor was it the action of a woman who had become embittered with her husband. Had her love for Nelson diminished to the extent that she could hardly bear to hear his name mentioned, she would certainly not have invited someone who had known Nelson for many years to join her. Because Fanny's love was constant, she needed someone with her to whom she could talk about him as he had been and could add her own contribution of recollections of the man she had always admired.

A matter that must have been discussed before Nelson left was what was to happen to Round Wood. Despite *The Ipswich Journal*'s report that his

Lordship was very pleased with all the improvements that had been made, it was clear from his earlier letters that Nelson was really not interested in a property that was too far from Town and did not possess the features of a substantial landed estate. In earlier letters to both Davison and Fanny, Nelson had made it clear that the idea of a country cottage had faded in favour of a house in London. If this was his desire then Round Wood had to go. Plans to dispose of the property were put into action very swiftly and fortunately, Fuller, the farm tenant, was anxious to acquire it. The transaction was completed reasonably quickly; by the time the land tax on it was due in April, the property was marked as belonging to 'formerly Nelson' and by the next quarter Fuller was named as the owner. No doubt the solicitor William Haslewood conducted the legal negotiations for the sale, which could account for his breakfast meeting in early January with Nelson.

There is no record of Fanny returning to Ipswich in the period before she left for Brighton but it would have been out of character for her to leave others to pack up the house and arrange for the furniture either to be disposed of or go into store. She had after all undertaken the arrangements for the move from Bath to Ipswich. Fanny's detractors believed that she was not a homemaker, that she was much happier living in rented houses with other people's belongings. This was patently not true; she had delighted in Round Wood as she would in later homes. The house she was leaving had been filled with additional furniture and fittings she had purchased in London as well as decorative items bought locally. The fate of all these had to be considered as well as what was to be done about the staff she had left there in her absence. Not only that, she had the good friends she had made, like Admiral Reeve, of whom she would wish to take her leave.

So sometime during the ten days between Nelson's leaving and her going to Brighton she went to Ipswich. Next she had to make arrangements for Edmund. He chose to return to Bath where he had always intended spending the winter. His health and his spirits had been considerably undermined by the previous weeks' events and he longed now for a return to the security and serenity of his old life. He knew the waters of Bath would do him good and he must have hoped that being amongst those he knew well would lessen the pain of the gossip that was rife about his son. As far as he was concerned, once Fanny had taken her treatments at Brighton, then he and she would be together again, and everything would be back to the way it was. So away he went to Bath leaving Fanny and Miss Locker to take up residence in Rock Buildings Parade, Brighton on 24 January 1801.

Whatever had been said between them, Fanny certainly did not believe her marriage was over. She went to Brighton as so many other people did, for the sake of her health, not to hide away from the general gaze and nurse her wounded spirits. As far as she was concerned, she was convinced that once Nelson returned to sea his friendship with the Hamiltons would wane and that she and her husband would forget their differences and resume their 'normal' life. The letters he wrote to her immediately after he left

London, although terse and fault-finding, offered some hope, so she continued to write to him. Unfortunately none of those letters has survived. He did not reply; he was too busy writing to Lady Hamilton, letters that betray a cruel, callous streak whenever it was necessary to refer to Fanny. In response to Emma Hamilton's account of Fanny's movements, he wrote on 25 January: 'Let her go to Brighton or where she pleases, I care not; she is a great fool, and thank God you are not the least like her.'

In that last statement he was correct; the two women could not have been more different both physically and in character. How much of the bitterness in the letter was for Emma's benefit, his feelings of guilt or the result of ill health is debatable. Three days later he explained:

> My eye is very bad. I have had the Physician to the Fleet to examine it. He has directed me not to write…not to eat anything but the most simple food; not to touch wine or porter; to sit in a dark room, to have green shades for my eyes – will you, my dear friend make me one or two – nobody else shall; and to bathe them in cold water every hour. I fear, it is the writing has brought on this complaint. My eye is like blood; and the film so extended that I only see from the corner farthest from my nose.

This was hardly a passionate letter to his love, much more the kind he had often sent Fanny. He complained that although ordered not to, he was compelled to write many official letters but he assured her that she was: 'the only female I write to.' Feeling thoroughly sorry for himself, he was also consumed by insecurity and jealousy. Emma had told him of the Prince of Wales's visits to the Hamiltons' home in Piccadilly and he was convinced that she might succumb to the Prince's attention and become his mistress. While he was so besotted by her that he imagined every other man found her irresistible he also showed a decided lack of trust in her ability to remain faithful to him.

Although he would have Emma believe he had ceased to communicate with Fanny, he had replied to his wife's response to his criticisms of the purchasing and packing arrangements mentioned earlier. The tone of this was intended to be placatory:

> Feb.3.1801, *San Josef*, Torbay…I received yesterday your letter from Brighton. It never was my intention to find [fault] but the fact is I have nothing and everything. If I want a piece of pickle it must be put in a saucer, if a piece of butter on an earthen plate…

As it continued, it became a catalogue of mismanagement: 'large nails drove through the mahogany table and drawers; only three keys and none for the wardrobe and trunk; the trident of Neptune bent double from ill package.' However he had determined: 'I shall direct what things I want in future.' He ended the list of complaints stating that he had six silver bottle stands but no decanters to fit the: '...you told me six of the house ones should be sent for.' This suggests that they had discussed the disposal of items from Round Wood. The letter ends on friendly terms: 'I beg my kindest regards to Josiah and Miss Locker, the Ellises etc.' This letter did not reach her for some time.

At this period it seemed that Nelson was deliberately leading Lady Hamilton to believe that he disliked and intended to have nothing more to do with the wife whose name he could no longer bring himself to mention. On 18 February he wrote:

> I had a letter from that person at Brighton saying she had heard from my brother that I was ill and offered to come and nurse me but I have sent up such an answer that will convince her she would not be received. I am almost afraid you will think I have gone too far, for she must see there is some strong reason but my intentions are in everything to give you satis-faction, therefore do not be angry for the strength of my letter.

Was he so blind to Emma's character that he could honestly believe that she would chide him for being harsh with Fanny? When it came to harshness, Lady Hamilton later led the field in caustic comments about Fanny.

Previous chroniclers of what happened to Fanny after Nelson deserted her have had to rely mainly on references that appeared in the press and in other people's letters. However, her correspondence with Davison now helps us to have a better understanding of her feelings at this time of crisis. Probably one of the longest letters she ever wrote was sent from Brighton on 5 February and gives an insight into her emotional turmoil. She wasted no time in open-ing pleasantries but went straight to what was worrying her. First was the question of why she had had no response to the letters she had sent to Torbay to await Nelson's arrival there, especially as she had read in the previous day's papers that he had arrived there some time earlier. Fearing the letters had gone astray she had sent others enclosed in a packet addressed to the home of Lord St Vincent. Now she was anxious that this too had miscarried, as she had not had a reply from her letter to Lady St Vincent.

Without a pause she went on to report that she had heard that Edmund was safely arrived in Bath, then casually slipped in that she had a few lines from the Rector's wife that was full of the attention being paid to her by: 'her friend in Piccadilly.' And then came the subject that was really upset-ting her – and that she desperately needed to share with someone.

> I will relate to you a thing which seems nothing but coming from Lady Hamilton I am certain some mischief is brewing. After I left London she sent for Bartinelle and offered him her Butler's place, telling him she feared he would find things in confusion but that she hoped they would soon be settled.

Fanny then gives a verbatim account of what Lady Hamilton said to the butler which was:

> I am extremely surprised at Lady Nelson's leaving London at this time of the year, giving up the house and parting with all the servants. I cannot think the reason of it, to my knowledge Lord Nelson allows her £2,000 a year and with that she might make a pretty appearance – it looks very odd.

Fanny continued, explaining that Bartinelle had told all this to one of the servants who had been ordered to follow Fanny from Dover Street to Brighton. Once there the servant had gossiped to the other staff until:

> … my housekeeper made some apologies for telling it to me, but as it was the talk of the kitchen she thought it was right for me to know it. None of us I believe like the servants to know our incomes – I can only say no woman can feel the least attention from a husband more than I do – and I will say I never will withhold from the world anything that will add to his credit.

When Lady Hamilton had tried to poach the butler to work for her, had she known that Nelson had a very poor opinion of him describing him in one of those complaining letters to Fanny as a French ruffian?

At least Nelson had acted honourably in arranging for Fanny to receive a regular income, although that should have been an indication that he was formally separating from her. Since the days when he had first returned to the sea, he had left it to her to apply to his agents for money as and when she needed it. While the allowance was generous, Fanny, understandably, resented others knowing her personal business. The fact that Emma Hamilton could gossip with servants merely confirmed her lack of breeding. The letter to Davison continued on the subject of the allowance and Fanny, in her distress, must have confused him as to exactly who had said what when she suddenly mentioned Mrs Mills, an old friend from Nevis who, during a carriage ride to a social engagement, had revealed a conversation with Nelson she had had some time earlier.

> I was a little surprised by Mrs Mills, who told me what my husband had allowed me, and that the £4,000 my uncle gave My Lord, he had given to me saying I have done a great deal more than that, but she said [I] 'will tell it all to you ' (which I assured Mrs Mills I should not have particularised the sum to any creature living thinking it a breach of confidence) 'you seem surprised but I will surprise you still more.'

According to Mrs Mills, Nelson had told her that he was unhappy that Fanny seemed so lacking in health, was deeply depressed and looked miserable. He really had no idea why this should be so. Mrs Mills, only too well aware of the cause, had refrained from telling him because she: '…did not know how he would like the truth.' However, Nelson had admitted to Mrs Mills that in spite of these present failings, Fanny was an 'exemplary woman.' Mrs Mills had gone out of her way to arrange that she and Fanny should travel together to Mr Coleman's entertainment so that she would have the opportunity to tell her of the conversation.

Having reported this conversation, Fanny needed Davison's assurance that she had done the right thing in repeating it and, as if to excuse herself, she quoted Edmund's advice to '…consult Mr Davison upon all occasions'.

The day after Fanny had written this long letter she wrote one that went to the other extreme. Having announced that Josiah's ship had gone into dock and that she expected him for a visit the following day, she begged Davison to take no notice of what she had previously said to him. On 13 February she enlisted Davison's help with a matter which was unexplained but had to do with a letter she had received from Bath and involved a Mr Ryder. But the real purpose of that particular letter lay in seeking information about Nelson's health. When Josiah had been in London he had met the Rector who had told him of Nelson's eye problems. Fanny was so concerned that she had immediately written to 'my Dear Lord' offering to go to him, assuring him he would find her 'an affectionate nurse'.

Nelson's ill health provided him with the perfect excuse not to reply to the offer but Davison gave her the information she wanted. On 20 February she thanked him for: 'the account you give me of my Lord's health and his speaking of me with affection are truly glad tidings, and I hope in God all you say will prove true.' How is that last remark to be interpreted? Had Davison simply told her that there was no cause for alarm where the eye was concerned or had he held out the hope of reconciliation? Eagerly she had grasped at the news that Nelson had talked of her with affection but was Davison telling her what she wanted to hear? In this letter, Fanny told him: 'My mind has not yet recovered its natural calmness – or do I think it ever will – I am now distrustful and fearful of my own shadow.' This picture of a poor pathetic creature is in part dispelled by Fanny's innate sense of humour in the next sentence.

> In consequence of my not hearing of the arrival of the papers I enclosed to Earl St Vincent I wrote to her Ladyship, really and truly what Miss Locker and I termed a pretty epistle, and what might be read to all the breakfast company.

She then reiterated that Josiah had called on Sarah Nelson only minutes before the Rector arrived back from Torbay with the news about Nelson's inflammation of the eye. On hearing that she said:

...my affection, my anxiety, my fondness for him all rushed forth and I wrote to him on last Wednesday week and offered to nurse him and that he should find me the same I had ever been to him, faithful, affectionate and anxious to do everything I could to please him.

What Fanny did not realise was that when Josiah called on Sarah Nelson, a woman he had known since childhood and no doubt regarded with affection, she would report his conversation and news about his mother back to her new best friend, Lady Hamilton. In their correspondence the two women referred to Josiah as the Cub while Fanny was given the cruel nickname of Tom Tit, thought to be a reference to her manner of walking.

Continuing her letter to Davison she told him that she had written almost no other letters except to a friend and to Nelson's sister Kitty Matcham who had: '...certainly written me one of the most affectionate letters ever written to a sister-in-law.' While pleased with that, she had been upset that Kitty had made no reference at all to Nelson as if he was no longer part of Fanny's life. As she often did, Fanny asked Davison to send her greetings to her brother-in-law Maurice. This request was written across the sheet of paper followed by the inquiry: 'do you think they will give My Lord the North Sea Command – I hope they will do everything he deserves.'

Buoyed up with the hope that Nelson might yet send for her, her heart must have raced when she finally received a letter from him. When she could bring herself to do so, she sent an extract from it to Davison, asking him for his candid opinion on the contents. He would have been totally insensitive if he had not been shocked by the callousness of Nelson's words:

I have received your letter of the 12th I only wish people would never mention My Name to you, for whether I am blind or not, it is nothing to any person. I want neither nursing or attention. And had you come here, I should not have gone on shore nor would you have come afloat. I fixed as I thought a proper allowance to enable you to remain quiet, and not to be posting from one end of the kingdom to the other. Whether I live or die, am sick or well I want from no one, the sensation of pain or pleasure. And I expect no comfort till I am removed from this world.

It took Fanny several days to compose herself sufficiently to write to Davison. When she did, she admitted, perhaps for the first time, that she had not really dared to hold out hope that things would change in her favour. But, she declared, her affection for Nelson was unchanged and she wished to demonstrate that to him. Sensibly, she had not replied to the letter, indeed she intended to take some days to consider how it should be answered. She then referred to an observation Edmund had made, whether in a recent letter or before he left for Bath, that she had seen enough (presumably of Nelson's conduct with Lady Hamilton) not to be surprised at anything. Edmund, she said, was anxious that she should now consider her own comfort and convenience and when choosing a house he would be only too pleased to help financially with its furnishing. Quoting Edmund again, he had said that the Rector had never forgiven her for not choosing to employ the coachbuilder he had recommended.

Understandably, the letter is disjointed; her mind hopped from one subject to another and then reverted to a previous one. In addition to all her other worries, she was concerned for Josiah's future; he had yet to secure command of another ship. With promotion so dependent on patronage would he, under these present circumstances, be able to rely on his stepfather's help? She hoped that he might. As to her future:

> a conscious rectitude will carry me through but what will await me –...I think you had better not mention my name and leave me to my fate – I am resigned and trust to my God who has been a merciful Father in many a difficulty.

But Fanny could not wallow in self-pity for long. There were other matters that needed Davison's attention on her behalf. Mr Fuller who had bought some of the furniture at Round Wood was now laying claim to a canopied bedstead that she had loaned to a friend. Just for a minute there is a fleeting glimpse of her fighting spirit: '...he shall not have it as I positively mentioned it before witnesses it was to be reserved for me.' And she wished to remind Fuller that he still owed her twenty pounds.

On the same day (24 February) that Fanny had written the foregoing lines, Nelson sent her a note to say that he was going to be in London for a day or two on business but that on no account was she to leave Brighton to join him nor was she to think of going to Portsmouth as he never went ashore. The short letter concluded with his hope that the change of ministers at the Admiralty would ensure a ship for Josiah. He signed this letter: 'As ever your affectionate Nelson.' While making it clear he did not wish to see her, this was hardly the cruel dismissal of the week before. If she was nonplussed as to how to react to this, the postscript focussed her attention elsewhere.

> Josiah is to have the *Thalia,* and I want to know from him two good lieutenants, they must be of my approval. I wish L. Champion to be second, would he like Mr Yule to be first if I can induce him to quit the *St George*? He [Josiah] must return an answer by the post direct to me, Lothians Hotel.

One cannot help wondering why Nelson did not communicate this directly to Josiah rather than going through his mother. Could it be that he was reminding Fanny that he alone had the power to secure Josiah's promotion or had he, just for a moment, remembered their shared interest in the young man?

At least that was one worry less for Fanny and on 2 March she wrote to tell Davison that Josiah had just returned from Town where he had been to thank Nelson for the news. Unfortunately it looked as if it would be some time before the repairs to the *Thalia* were complete and in the meantime Josiah was bored by the lack of entertainment and company in Brighton. Fanny had given her son a letter to take to Nelson thanking him: 'for his goodness in getting him a ship.' She had made no allusion to his previous letter but she was resolved that she would never again offer her nursing services. She also asked Davison if he thought that the best way to deal with Nelson's very harsh letter was to make no comment on it. Poor Davison must have found it extremely difficult to answer Fanny at times; she regarded him as her friend and confidant, as did Nelson who in turn used him in his dealings with Lady Hamilton.

Another aspect of the rift with Nelson that caused her concern was something she had mentioned earlier in relation to Kitty Matcham's letter where there had been no reference to Nelson. Now she was finding that other people were keeping silent. 'You will be surprised when I tell you I have never once been gratified by any person's (excepting Mr Ellis, the apothecary) enquiring after my Lord.' She went on to relate how when she had first arrived in Brighton, Lord Tankerville had asked how long she intended to stay. She had answered that her stay was dependent upon however long Nelson stayed in home waters. She had been taken aback that Tankerville had merely bowed at this point but had made no inquiry about her husband. She could not understand why people were behaving like this especially, as she assured Davison: 'I never spoke of my extreme misery at the loss of his affection [next words erased] to any but those who had been eye witnesses and yourself.'

She had always tried to conceal her feelings even though, she now revealed, a number of people had spoken openly to her on the subject: 'even at the Drawing Room and Lord St Vincent's long conversation twelve months before his Lordship's arrival.' As to the current situation: 'no one shall know of those harsh cruel letters –I still feel too much on the occasion.' Even though she had been unable to banish the 'cruel letters' from her mind, she did not let them sour her and with much generosity towards Nelson, she remarked that she was: 'truly thankful he is well and [I] hope happy.' Neither did she allow bitterness to prevent her from getting on with her daily life which included resolving the problem of where she was to make a permanent home. In the conclusion of this letter she asked Davison if he had yet had a chance to speak to Nelson about a house for her.

Whatever Nelson's feelings for Fanny were at this time, she took some comfort that it had now been proved that the rift between them was not to include Josiah. He had come back from his meeting with his stepfather full of joy. Nelson had received him warmly, shown him great affection, and insisted that they should spend as much time together as possible, even to the extent that Nelson promised to get Josiah invitations to dine wherever he was invited. Josiah who, while supporting his mother, had the optimism (and the selfishness) of the young, could not resist telling his mother: 'I told you all would end well, he has the best of hearts.' The elation and hope was short lived for within days came another letter from Nelson which not only showed no affection for Josiah but also accused him of plotting against his stepfather.

> Josiah is to have another ship and to go abroad if the *Thalia* cannot soon be got ready. I have done all for him, and he may again, as he has often done before, wish me to break my neck and be abetted in it by his friends, who are likewise my enemies; but I have done my duty as an honest, generous man and I neither want nor wish for any one to care what becomes of me, whether I return or am left in the Baltic. Living I have done all in my power for you, and dead you will find I have done the same, therefore, my only wish is to be left to myself.

These violent mood swings were surely not reserved entirely for Fanny. They must have caused concern to others who were close to Nelson who perhaps explained them as the result of the drugs he was taking for his eye condition. It is impossible to know now if there was some other physical reason such as pressure on the brain brought about by the injuries he had received. What is certain is that he was under emotional pressure from his relationship with Lady Hamilton and that had brought with it the critical pressure from his naval peers. From this letter it would appear that his earlier belief that he was not fully appreciated by those in authority had developed into full-blown paranoia that he had enemies who wished him ill.

Fanny, however, was not an amateur psychologist; she was simply totally bemused by this attack on Josiah. Nelson's plea to be left to himself she may have taken as a sign that he felt alone and deserted and so she made him an offer using Davison as her intermediary. That this was intended to be taken very seriously was reinforced by the fact that immediately before sitting down to write, she had taken the Sacrament at church. Thus it was in a spirit of unreserved forgiveness that she vowed: '…if at any future time My Husband will make my house his home – I will receive him with joy; and whatever has passed shall never pass my lips.' Expressing the hope that Nelson would return safely and victoriously from the Baltic campaign, she continued in liturgical vein: 'I forgive my cruel enemies…I have injured no one intentionally.' Then, with thoughts racing on to more practical matters, she urged Davison to find her a house in the part of London that would please Nelson. She mentioned one in Grosvenor Square that she knew was available on a yearly lease but she was quite ready to go to Town to view anything he thought suitable; she knew she could stay with the Ellises while she was looking. She was anxious for a more settled life, not just to be able to offer Nelson a home but because she was finding life in Brighton more expensive than she had anticipated. She had already drawn on some of the money she had earmarked for furniture. To make that up, she proposed to make savings on her clothes.

The desire for a house in London may have been given added impetus by a letter from Nelson's sister, Susannah Bolton. Over the years, Fanny and Mrs Bolton had spent long periods together, each getting to know some of the innermost workings of the other's marriage. When her financial situation was strained, Susannah knew she could rely on Fanny for help, not just for a donation but the more long-term assistance that came in the form of Fanny taking one or other of the twin girls to live with her. So, Fanny must have been hurt that she had heard nothing from her sister-in-law since leaving London at the end of January until she finally took the initiative and wrote to her. It was during March that Susannah replied, full of apologies, assuring Fanny that the reason for her silence was not knowing where she was living. In a warm, sisterly fashion she offered some advice:

> Will you excuse what I am going to say? I wish you had continued in Town a little longer, as I have heard my brother regretted he had not a house he could call his own when he returned. Do, whenever you hear he is likely to return, have a house to receive him. If you absent yourself entirely from him, there can never be a reconciliation…I hope in God one day I shall have the pleasure of seeing you together as happy as ever, he certainly as far as I hear is not a happy man.

Fanny must have taken comfort from Susannah's sensible counsel not least that it reassured her that she had not been discarded by most of Nelson's family. She would have been delighted that his sister had acknowledged that Fanny and Nelson had been happy together. As for that final phrase which suggested that there might yet be a chance of Nelson returning to her, she would dearly like to believe that might be true. As she wrote to Edmund: '…things do not appear in bright colours at present still I had hopes all would be well.' Writing to Davison on 17 March she enclosed a copy of Edmund's letter. The contents of that we have to guess but it would seem that Edmund had wanted to know what was the current situation and had perhaps suggested that Fanny was not making sufficient effort to win Nelson back. Fanny's response was an offer to let Edmund see all the letters she had received from her husband in the past two months or so. Fanny also told Davison that she had offered to join Edmund at Bath now she felt better for having had sea air.

In the pursuit of his own happiness, Nelson had not considered the effect his separation from Fanny was likely to have on his father. Edmund and Fanny had shared a home on and off for a dozen years; they had established a close domestic routine and each had come to rely heavily on the other. Edmund needed Fanny. A good housekeeper and domestic servants could have looked after his physical welfare but Fanny gave him both affection and respect. This would have been expected in the blood relationship of father and daughter, though there was no guarantee it would exist. What had started out as a rather cautious respect of one for the other had grown into the deep and strong affection of two very good friends. In many respects Edmund supplied Fanny's need to nurture while Edmund was able to retain his feeling of usefulness in being able to offer advice and counsel. As friends they were able to confide in each other, Edmund, in particular, saying things about his own children that he could not discuss with another member of the family. There were attached yet detached. So, it must have been very difficult for Edmund to go to Bath without Fanny. She had left him occasionally in the past but only for a week or so. On this occasion he had his favourite daughter Kitty Matcham with him but however much he may have enjoyed her company, he would have had to share her with her family and fit into a routine that did not centre on him. It would not have been long before he missed the quiet, calm life he had shared with Fanny. Hence his desire to set up home with her in London and his offer to pay towards the furnishing of a house.

Fanny threw herself into the project with enthusiasm telling Davison: 'I think I shall never have a better opportunity of furnishing a house than now.' Ever practical she made the best of the situation: 'the summer coming on I need no curtains to the windows. I have many articles of furniture such as beds, bedsteads, linen, china, glass, knives and forks and some kitchen furniture.' She added that she had told Edmund that she was to go to London the following week to look for a house, acknowledging that Nelson's generous allowance to her made this possible. When it came to selecting a suitable property, she put Edmund's welfare before her own. Some unfurnished houses in Albemarle Street were rejected on the grounds that they would not be airy enough for him. Having committed herself to a course of action she laid out her plans; she would bring her own carriage up to London so that she did not have to rely on others for transport, she would take a bed at the house of Mrs Ellis and invite herself to dinner with Davison's wife. There was also just a hint that Miss Locker had outstayed her welcome. 'I should like very well for Miss Locker to have the opportunity of returning to some friends.' Then perhaps fearing that this sounded unfeeling, she assured Davison: 'at any other time [I] will be glad to see her.'

There were other matters to distract her at this time. Having kicked his heels ashore for the longest period in his sea-going career, Josiah had finally received his orders to return to sea and was due to leave Brighton just before his mother did. His departure must have brought mixed feelings. On the one hand she had not had him with her for so long since he was a child that it must, at times, have been difficult for both of them, while on the other, he had been there to support her during the most testing time of her life. We shall never know how much the young man told his mother about the events that led to Nelson's infatuation with Lady Hamilton. The only indication that they ever discussed the matter is a note at the bottom of one of Nelson's letters appended by Fanny some years after his death that read: 'My son did not much care for the Hamiltons.' In the weeks leading up to his being given a ship, Lady Hamilton had tried to win him over to her side and so cause a rift between mother and son, a ploy that bemused Nelson who took her to task for one moment saying she would not have him in her house and the next inviting him to dinner. As for Fanny, her concern was that her son should be employed.

Nelson may have led Lady Hamilton to believe that in his eyes she was now his wife but as far as the rest of the world was concerned there was only one Lady Nelson and that was Fanny. Her husband might no longer communicate with her but she was not left in the dark concerning his naval activities. Following the Battle of Copenhagen, Lord Spencer had sent her:

> ...the account...received from the Admiralty of the glorious victory obtained under the Command of Lord Nelson....Every one speaks in the highest terms of his Lordship's conduct on the occasion and in a line he has written to Mr Addington he says that he thinks this action will put an end to all further contest.

Proud though Fanny would have been to receive this account, she perhaps took note of, as no doubt those at the Admiralty had, the confidence of Nelson that he had ended the war in that area. Nonetheless, this also gave Fanny the opportunity to write to Nelson to offer her own congratulations. Just as had happened following the Battle of the Nile, Fanny found herself the recipient of congratulations from many sources, among them a Count de Lille who had sent his sincere compliments to the Matchams with an enquiry for Fanny's address in order that he might convey his respects to her in person.

After her brief visit to London, Fanny had received a sad letter from Edmund. He was worried that having not heard from her for some time she must be ill. He told her his own health was weak and uncertain: 'a frame broken almost to pieces by time.' There was no doubt that he was missing her even though he had his daughter Kitty next door but that was not the same as having Fanny. 'My daughter I see for a short time every day, tho' seven infants require much care and demand great and anxious attention.' He repeated in a number of different ways that Fanny meant much to him. 'Can I contribute anything to the farther increase of your comfort', and 'believe me ...a sincere wish to prove that I am truly yours.' He so hoped that the breach between her and Nelson would soon be healed. As he said to his son when he wrote to congratulate him on his latest victory:

> I have sometimes a hope of receiving you once more surrounded not with public honours alone, but what must add pleasures to every other gratification, a return to domestic joys, the most durable and solid of all others. Be it so O God.

Responding to his very evident need, Fanny went some time in April to join Edmund in Bath where for the next few weeks she rarely ventured out into society except in company with Mrs Matcham. With a touch of humour she described herself: ' as more circumspect and cautious than any young Miss of 16.' What little social life she had was curtailed when on 21 April she received news from Davison that her brother-in-law, Maurice was seriously ill. Fanny who referred to Maurice as her friend, a good and honourable man, begged Davison who was himself ill, to let her have as much detail of Maurice's condition as possible. She had so far kept the information from Edmund, believing he had enough to bear without adding to his 'uneasiness of mind'. Part of this uneasiness must have been caused by the news that Nelson had been engaged in the decisive Battle of Copenhagen. Fanny's comment on that: 'I thank God My Lord Nelson's life has been spared –had anything happened to him I should be wretched.' This letter can barely have reached London before Davison had to break the news of Maurice's death. Fanny's instant reply was spontaneous and from the heart.

I am truly grieved at your letter, I feel sensibly the loss of my dear brother Maurice – I have truly lost a friend. My father will write you tomorrow, he is the best of fathers and much attached to his children. Every attention will I pay Mrs Nelson I am not one of those who forget past kindnesses. My heart is full, so full…We long to hear of your own health.

In the midst of the very real grief Fanny and Edmund were suffering came one of those family upsets that so often emerge following a death. Instead of writing to Fanny as he would have done in the past, the Rector wrote to his brother-in-law, Matcham, asking him to break the news of the death to Edmund. Matcham had replied that he had left it to Fanny as she was in the habit of doing everything for Edmund and that in any case, she had had the most recent information from Davison. He had then said he would be prepared to go to London and go with the Rector to attend Maurice's funeral and interment at Burnham. The idea of the Rector and Matcham attending the funeral together upset Edmund as he remembered that the last time the two had met they had quarrelled violently. Fanny in relating this to the ailing Davison was aware that she ought not to be burdening him with her cares when he too, was suffering from the loss of a friend. But even so, she could not refrain from mentioning Nelson.

My Lord Nelson will be grieved to hear of his brother's death he loved him most sincerely. I have not the happiness of hearing from My Lord it hurts me too much even to mention it to you. Do not mention me in your letters better not…pray do not.

But her own concerns and to some extent her grief were subsumed by anger at the behaviour of the Rector who had complained to Edmund that he had been rather shabbily treated. First, when he had called at Davison's house to find out details of Maurice's death, he had been told that Davison was too ill to see him. This, he obviously felt, was an excuse but then he went to Dodds where he was told that all the funeral arrangements were in hand. He was furious that Edmund had not asked him to take care of things. But, he intended to go to Burnham with his wife and there he would: 'shew every attention to his Dear Brother's memory.' When she had read this, Fanny had exploded inwardly as she then did on paper to Davison:

> My Dear Sir, God forgive if I judge harsh – but are these words true – dear brother – a man to my knowledge he treated with contempt and only is fearful the world will in time know his disposition – and what motives guided him.

She returned to the subject of the Rector's insincerity in her next letter in reply to observations that Davison had made about him, saying that nothing he said would surprise her. All her pent up feelings of animosity against the Rector are now aired.

> I have been acquainted with him thirteen years – during which time his brother Edmund died with us at Burnham of a deep decline. I was his friend and nurse to the last. Suckling who died two years ago he spoke of in such cruel terms at Norwich at the very time he laid dead, that everybody cried out shame although this poor brother died in a fit only forty miles from him, he never rode over to see him.

Then Fanny revealed that she had been the cause of that quarrel between the Rector and Mr Matcham mentioned earlier. The Rector's behaviour towards her on his last visit to Bath had been so – Fanny described it as 'glaring' – that Kitty Matcham had declared to her husband that if, as it appeared, there were those who were aligning themselves against Fanny, she certainly had no intention of deserting Fanny, whatever the consequences might be. Matcham presumably repeated his wife's views to the Rector and during the violent exchange that followed, the Rector had spitefully declared that Nelson had told him the only members of the family he cared for were the Rector and his children. The implication was that they would be the only ones to enjoy any financial gifts from Nelson. This had angered Matcham who was a fiercely independent man but one who had never hesitated to help any of the Nelson family when he could. Battle lines were being drawn within the family.

The Rector and his wife had ingratiated themselves with Lady Hamilton, Sarah Nelson becoming her bosom companion while the Rector was on his travels. On the other side, Fanny still had the support of the Matchams and the Boltons and Edmund, of course. And in describing how these lines were being drawn, Fanny told Davison why Edmund had been so anxious for her to come to him in Bath.

Mrs Jeffreys, Wilkes' sister told him of the report of Lord Nelson's determination not to live with me – he [Edmund] was so shocked ...he then told
his daughter he would try and get me here and that would silence people
– it has some but not all – Mrs Matcham tells me it is the conversation
before them everywhere. The lady of 23 Piccadilly's character she hears
from everybody.

Kitty Matcham had expressed the fear that the Rector, believing Davison
had slighted him, would turn Nelson against his old friend and advisor. If
that should happen, Fanny wisely commented: 'then he will have no one
to tell him the truth.'

The death of Maurice continued to cause friction between members of
the family. Fanny contributed to the disagreements by wanting to go into
mourning for her brother-in-law. This was not just a question of her adopting black clothes for a set length of time; her household staff would be
expected to have mourning livery. She was advised by Edmund to consider
the expense this would involve but for once, she was adamant that this
was a way in which she could pay her own tribute to Maurice and to do
what was right in order to please Nelson. Therefore she proposed to send
an order to the tailor to provide the requisite garments for all the servants,
including the coachman and the footman, leaving Davison to make the
necessary payment on her behalf.

The practicalities involved helped to take her mind off the constant
stream of letters which passed between the Rector and Edmund. Since
Fanny was always given these to read she knew both sides of the argument.
The father had reprimanded his son for his neglect of his parochial duties
in pursuit of ambition but more important he had warned the Rector that
his wife should be fully aware of what it was she was doing. His criticism
of her close friendship with Lady Hamilton, although veiled, was nonetheless forthright. Sarah should remember: '...this was a very seducing and
licentious Age.' If that was not strong enough, Edmund reminded both
the Rector and his wife that they had a duty to consider the safety of their
daughter. Edmund knew his granddaughter Charlotte well as she had been
a frequent visitor at the home he and Fanny had shared in London. He had
been quite happy for Fanny to be her mentor, knowing that the girl would
learn nothing but good habits from her aunt. The fact that he voiced his
concern that the influence she was now under could only morally harm her,
showed that his own encounters with the Hamiltons, as well as the gossip
he had heard, had left him deeply unhappy.

Much of the argument between Edmund and the Rector still centred on
the latter attending the interment of Maurice's body into the family vault at
Burnham Thorpe. As the only son now in the country, Edmund felt it was
the Rector's duty to perform the last offices for his brother, especially as
Edmund was too frail to do so. But the Rector was torn between duty to a
dead brother and what he saw as duty to the living one who was expected

back in England at any moment. The fact that the dead brother had nothing to give him while the living one had a great deal, weighed heavily on his decision-making. Maurice had died on 24 or 25 April and his funeral, for which Davison had made all the arrangements, finally took place in London on 2 May. In offering her personal and very sincere thanks, Fanny paid tribute to the strength of Davison's friendship not just to Maurice but for the whole family. It grieved her that his kindness should be rewarded by the ill natured behaviour of the Rector who by making wild accusations against him was endeavouring to blacken Davison's good name. None of this surprised Fanny. She had reached the point that when either Edmund or Mrs Matcham was about to read aloud one of the Rector's letters she took herself out of the room rather than having to listen to the revelation of yet another aspect of his despicable character. 'I own when I hear his name mentioned I give an involuntary movement.' When she did eventually read them she discovered that the Rector pointedly made no reference to her whatsoever – not even a polite enquiry into her health. Nor did he actually name 'the Lady of 23 Piccadilly'(Lady Hamilton) although he gave so many accounts on that subject that they: 'caused her heart to shudder.'

With all the upset caused by the Rector, little consideration was given to Maurice's widow. Fanny's natural inclination had been to write to her immediately and offer any help she could but Edmund had advised her to wait. Although Fanny had corresponded regularly with Maurice and frequently met him in London, there is no record of her having visited his home at Laleham or ever having met his wife, who was known in the family as 'poor blind Sukey'. Neither is there ever any mention of her being included in the family meetings. That is not to imply that she was ignored by the family; we have had evidence that Mrs Bolton and the twins stayed with Maurice at Laleham and the Rector's son found it convenient to visit his uncle when he was at school at Eton. When the news of Maurice's death had first been broken to him, Edmund had been very anxious to know if Maurice had left a will and he had been greatly reassured when Davison was able to confirm that there was one. But there was still something bothering Edmund: '…his mind is not quite satisfied about our dear friend's marriage, the unfortunate Mrs Nelson – he says must be taken care of but still he harps upon the word marriage.'

Edmund was in a moral dilemma. If his son had not left sufficient funds to support his widow, then the father would feel duty bound to assist his daughter-in-law to the best of his ability. But, and here was the crux of the matter, what was his responsibility if she were not his legal daughter-in-law? For a man of strong religious principle was he duty bound to look after a woman who might not have had her marriage blessed by the church? It would appear that the family feared that the woman who was known as Mrs Maurice Nelson had no legal right to that surname. The will was to provide the answer. Not wishing to waste money on employing an attorney, Maurice had drawn up his own will in July 1795. It was quite straightforward. He left all the interest on what money he had invested together with what ever was owed him at the time of his death:

> …to Mrs Susannah Ford (alias) Nelson with whom I have lived in the habits of the utmost friendship for many years for the term of her natural life which she is to enjoy without molestation from any one.

Had Maurice anyone in particular in mind when he added that phrase 'without molestation'? It is tempting to think, though there is no definite proof, that he might have foreseen the Rector as a potential trial to his Susannah. With the publication of the will the skeleton in the family closet was there for all to see. Maurice had not married; the naming of his partner as Mrs Ford suggests this was because she was already married. Their relationship could explain why Maurice had been passed over as Nelson's heir. Having ensured Susannah's welfare for her lifetime, at her death the principal which was invested at five per cent was to provide £500 to his brother Horatio, at the time of the making of the will, a mere captain, and £500 a piece to his nieces Susanna and Catharine Bolton. If they were under age at the time, it was left to Nelson's discretion whether they should receive their legacies at either 21 or on marriage. Should either one or both of them die before that, the legacy was to go to Nelson. Why out of all the nephews and nieces the twins were singled out is a matter for speculation. It may be that Maurice wished to acknowledge his affection for his sister, their mother; he may have had more contact with them than any of the others or he may have felt, given that their father was often in financial difficulty, that they might have few marriage prospects. The legacy might thus be either a small dowry on marriage or the independence of a small income in spinsterhood.

Perhaps the most significant words in Maurice's will are 'lived in the habits of utmost friendship'. In many of his earlier letters Nelson had referred to Fanny as his friend, a term which may present difficulties to a reader in the twenty-first century but would have been understood by those in the seventeen and eighteen hundreds to denote an intimate and loving relationship between those who lived together, usually in marriage.

In the letter of 3 May Fanny mentioned that she had read newspaper reports that Nelson had asked for sick leave. Her comment: 'God grant him health and happiness is the sincere wish of his affectionate wife' was intended for Davison's eyes only as she begged him not to mention her when he wrote to Nelson. She showed a clear understanding of her husband's character having come to the opinion that so many people had spoken to him about his behaviour towards her that rather than doing her case any good, it had done the reverse and antagonised him further. Fully aware too, that Davison's position with Nelson was such that he would have visited at '23 Piccadilly' she implored him never to mention her there either.

What Fanny did not know was that Nelson had written to Davison:

You will, at a proper time and before my arrival in England, signify to Lady Nelson that I expect to be left to myself without any enquiries from her: for sooner than live the unhappy life I did when I last came to England, I would stay abroad for ever. My mind is as fixed as fate.

The blame for his unhappiness had been shifted entirely on to Fanny. Unaware of this, Fanny was still hanging on to a thin thread of hope. Seated at her desk on 7 May, writing a few lines and then discarding sheet after sheet of precious paper, she tried to sort out the many thoughts milling around in her head. Finally, it all poured out. First, she wanted Davison to know that she had written to Nelson. Making no reference to that cruel letter he had sent in March, she had offered her congratulations on his victory in the Baltic and his ennoblement as a viscount. She had again asked his forgiveness for any unintended offence she had given him and explained she had gone to Bath at Edmund's request. She had tried to make sure that this letter would reach him by enclosing it in one to Nelson's colleague, Troubridge, whose delighted response had been to urge her to write often to Nelson as he thought such action could do no harm and might even do some good. Fanny in recounting this was realistic enough to comment: ' [I] am afraid he is too sanguine.'

A more immediate concern was what she should do about a house. Both she and Edmund had taken a fancy to one in George Street that had excellent accommodation to suit Edmund's needs. But Fanny was having second thoughts. As she had had no communication from Nelson, she thought it might be better if she stayed away from London where they might meet accidentally. If he did want to see her, he knew very well where she was. However, Edmund was pressing her to take the house, dismissing her qualms. So, practicality to the fore again, she detailed the yearly expenses involved. Edmund thought £230 for the rent was reasonable; taxes, repairs and fixtures were another £300 to which he intended to contribute £200 and she estimated that £500 should cover the furniture. Her father-in-law told her that Nelson had said he had never intended to be so restrictive with her allowance that she could not have another two or three hundred pounds if she wanted it. Fanny's hurt broke through in her response to this: 'I told him my spirits were so truly broken I dare not ask.' But, careful not to sound too self-pitying she went on to tell Davison of their more immediate plans.

Edmund was thinking of going to Norfolk while she intended to stay on in Bath for as long as she could even though she felt the air did not suit her. She had an invitation from Lady Walpole to visit Wolterton to which she looked forward and after that she thought she might try spending the summer in Cromer. And then just to prove to Davison that indeed her thoughts were all over the place, she reverted to the subject of money, detailing how she and Edmund arranged their domestic expenses: 'Mr N finds house rent and cook and housemaids wages – the wine bill and all other expenses I pay.' She then lamented the high cost of stabling for the carriage horses; the inflation caused, she thought, by the large number of horse troops quartered in the town.

Two weeks passed before Fanny wrote again to 'her dear friend' Davison who had written to advise her not to take the house in George Street, as he believed that the cost of refurbishment before she and Edmund could think of moving in was too great. Edmund had been building his hopes on this house and was bitterly disappointed that it had been given up but had told Fanny in front of his daughter Kitty that Davison's advice was always sound and it was right that Fanny should follow it. The rest of this letter of 20 May described the strain Fanny was under from Edmund's anxious and disturbed mind. 'So far from giving pleasure to my good Mr N, Lord Nelson's appointment in the Baltic was [word crossed through] his spirits are much depressed.' Fanny made such a good job of the erasure, there is no chance of even guessing what it was Edmund felt. She had over the years become accustomed to the old man doggedly pursuing the subject of his son's movements at sea, speculating when he would return or questioning why letters had not arrived but now Fanny was finding his circular conversation both worrying and wearisome. 'All ways asking some question which leads me to say something on the subject – that the Fleet returns in the autumn – and in short I do not know what to say.' She was genuinely upset to see the old man so torn apart by his son's behaviour towards her that he had declared that there was now nothing in the world that could give him pleasure.

Trying to relieve his great distress took precedence over her own feelings but the strain was taking its toll on her health and a Mr Spry, whom Edmund held in high esteem, had said in front of him that what she needed was sea air and bathing. With that advice she had decided to go fairly soon. She believed Edmund intended to go to Burnham for a few weeks – he had told Kitty one day that he was thinking of returning to live there but the next he had changed his mind. Although Fanny worried greatly about him, she knew that if she did not have a break from him and the air of Bath, her own health would get worse. She felt she could leave him with a clear conscience because, for the first time, one of his own family was on hand to watch over him. Kitty Matcham who was living in the house next door already spent much of the day with him.

However, before Fanny could make her plans to visit the seaside she was faced with a problem of etiquette. Nelson's recent honour had turned Fanny into Viscountess Nelson and presented her with a quandary which she explained to Davison. 'I have written to Lady Spencer to know if it is necessary for me to go to Court on the recent honours confirmed on My Lord Nelson.' Uncertain what her position was, she had not given it much thought until Edmund had asked her if she would be attending the Court celebration of the King's Birthday. He did not know if she should go but had advised her to ask those who would know. She had not much time and there were practicalities to be attended to. No time now to think of ailments, here was something for Fanny to focus on; a consultation over the ordering of a new dress; the consideration of how long the journey would take if she went to Town with her own horses (considerably longer than travelling by coach) and the booking of rooms at Nerot's Hotel for her and Miss Locker who she would ask to join her there.

The letter of 27 May was short and business-like.

> I have been advised to go to St James's on the Birthday, therefore I begin
> my journey tomorrow & shall be in London on Sunday or Monday and
> take up my quarters at Nerot's as it was thought a proper place for me
> last November. I do not intend staying many days after Thursday [the
> Birthday]. I assure you Mr N & I have talked the matter over several times.
> Good Old Man – he says he is afraid I should run my head against any of
> them. He thinks of going into Norfolk.

Fanny's remark about staying at Nerot's Hotel showed her concern not
to do anything that might harm Nelson's reputation; a subject she was to
return to almost three weeks later. After she had told Davison that her recent
silence had been occasioned by a severe and lengthy attack of biliousness
probably picked up in London, she related that both she and Edmund were
satisfied that she had done the right thing in going to Town. She justified her
action by quoting from letters that Nelson had written her from the Nile: 'if
the King confers any honours on me I need not point out the propriety of
your going to St James's' and 'Support my rank and do not let me down.'
She continued: 'I assure you I did my very best and I am fully satisfied that
I have strictly adhered to My Lord's injunctions. No one ever felt so anxious
to please and make him happy as I did.'

It is certain that with the gossip that had surrounded Nelson and Lady
Hamilton, public opinion generally had rallied to Fanny. *The Ipswich Journal*
was no exception. It had at the end of April begun a series of biographies
of notable living East Anglians and in the two issues preceding that of 9
May had dealt with the artists Gainsborough and Constable. In a fulsome
account of Nelson's life to date, Fanny was picked out for her own praise.

> The pious attention paid by Lady Nelson to her venerable father-in-law
> (who resided near Ipswich sometime)…as well as her exemplary conduct
> during the absence of her Lord, will long be the theme of admiration
> amongst the inhabitants of that town, who witnessed her departure for
> Bath (where she now resides) with much regret…The Letter of Lord
> Nelson to his Lady (1798) evinces how much a man is calculated to enjoy
> repose from his public labours in the bosom of domestic felicity.

Nelson must have regretted bitterly that he had allowed a copy of that letter to be published. It was not by chance that the compiler of the biography
made such pointed reference to Fanny's exemplary conduct during Nelson's
absence nor that he deliberately omitted any mention of the Hamiltons.

But then neither did Susannah Bolton when she wrote during May, a letter that was full of warmth and affection for Fanny. Discussing Fanny's visit
to London for the Drawing Room she reveals that she has heard that Fanny
had met the Rector's wife, who, she hinted was becoming tired of London

and was thinking of taking her daughter back to Hilborough for the summer. Was Fanny meant to understand from this that the friendship between Lady Hamilton and the Rector's wife was fading? Susannah's letter was full of the excitement of now being settled at the farm in Cranwich, their first invitation out and their own very first dinner party in their new home. And she longed to welcome Fanny into that home, begging her that if she were going to Wolterton, she would extend her vacation and stay with them as well. She then stoutly defended her own position with regard to Fanny.

> Do not say you will not suffer us to take too much notice of you for fear it should injure us with Lord Nelson. I assure you I have a pride, as well as himself, in doing what is right, and that surely is to be attentive to those who have been so to us and I am sure my brother would despise us if we acted contrary.

Fanny desperately wanted to believe that Nelson's infatuation for Emma Hamilton would pass and that she would regain his favour. They had shared so much in the past; perhaps only she could say: 'I know he possesses the best of hearts.' It was not easy simply to dismiss him from her life and she continued to worry about his health and state of mind just as she always had. She and Edmund must have had interminable discussions about Nelson's health problems for she told Davison that Edmund was determined that when Nelson returned he must be seen by the two leading physicians of the time. Her own health had caused concern; when her fever showed no sign of abating, the apothecary who had treated her initially on her return to Bath had felt her condition to be serious enough to seek a second opinion from a Dr Falconer. He prescribed medication to reduce the fever and control the bilious condition. It was hardly surprising after this long bout of sickness that Dr Falconer declared her as greatly debilitated and indeed the fact that she crammed this information in at the end of the letter in note form leaving it unfinished, suggests that she might suddenly have felt very unwell.

However, by 22 June her physical condition was much improved. She was full of praise for Dr Falconer whose treatment had been: 'chiefly by Ice – a cold bath to my stomach.' But now, as she said, despite the fact that her spirits were still agitated, she needed to exert herself ready for Nelson's homecoming which was expected within the next few days. Both she and Edmund had written to Nelson but Fanny must have feared that he would ignore her letter so she begged Davison to tell her husband on her behalf that she:

> never had any other wish than to please him. I am ready, willing and desirous to live with him and will do everything in my power to oblige him. I think I cannot say more. If I could I would.

Four days later her mind was showing even greater signs of agitation as excited anticipation mixed with recollection and realisation of what might be the outcome of the imminent arrival of 'My Dear Lord'. In this letter to Davison, she dropped all restraint and wrote directly as she felt.

> I love him – I would do anything in the world to convince him of my affection. I was truly sensible of my good fortune in having such a Husband – Surely I have angered him – it was done unconsciously and without the least intention – I can truly say, my wish, my desire was to please him. And if he will have the goodness to send for me I will make it my study to obey him in every wish or desire of his – And with cheerfulness – I still hope – he is affectionate and possess the best of hearts – he will not make me miserable – I hope I have not deserved so severe a punishment from him.

This passionate declaration cannot have failed to move Davison especially when she pleaded with him:

> if you find that you can <u>mention</u> me – I will thank, I will esteem it the greatest favour you can confer on me. I shall feel myself under very, very great obligations – you or no one can tell my feelings – or what I have suffered since My Lord left England.

Davison had written to Fanny before that letter reached him. His must have arrived either on the afternoon of 26 June or the morning of the following day which was when Fanny replied. Judging by her response it appears that Davison must have repeated Nelson's accusation that her reception of him in November had been lacking in warmth:

> Be assured I did not mean the least coolness or indifference to My Dear Lord far from – but my poor mind is so distressed and disturbed that I <u>dare</u> not write and particularly of what makes me <u>wretched</u>. If you do not think I have expressed my feelings my affection and my sincere desire to do everything he wishes me I am willing to say more – if possible. Should he receive me with affection I will do everything he desires and in a gracious manner. He shall have no reason to regret his goodness, to me, I give you my honour.

Fanny was not the only one suffering on an emotional roller coaster. The usually calm and sensible Edmund had surprised all those who knew him by becoming exceedingly irritable and short tempered. Under the strain of the situation he became selfish and demanding, even frightening his young Matcham grandson. The boy was ill yet Edmund expected him and his mother to accompany him on his daily carriage drive. His grandfather's irascible behaviour had so scared the child, he begged his mother not to make him go. Fanny blamed the change in Edmund on his fatherly concern for his son, relating that he had told a very close friend: 'My Horace was always a good boy – but he is gone a little out of the straight road. He will see his error. And be as good as ever.' But in that hope, Edmund was to be disappointed.

CHAPTER XIII

The Faithful Wife

Be assured every wish, every desire of mine is to please the man whose affection constitutes my happiness. God bless my dear husband.
Fanny Nelson, July 1801

At the beginning of July Fanny would have read in the papers that Nelson had arrived in Great Yarmouth for a hospital visit to the wounded from the Battle of Copenhagen. From there he had proceeded to Ipswich where, in spite of arriving late in the evening, he had again received a rapturous welcome from the townspeople. As he was driven along the road, passing Round Wood, did he, even for one minute, think of what might have been or was he concerned only with getting back to London for his reunion with Lady Hamilton and possibly the daughter she had borne him in late January? He spent the next three weeks in Town and then went with the Hamiltons to Box Hill for a few days and then to a fishing party at Staines. Sir William Hamilton was reckoned to be one of the finest anglers in the country and devoted much of his time to the sport thus leaving his wife free to indulge in her own pastimes.

Fanny, too, was at last able to go to Lymington where the change of air and the opportunity for sea-bathing appear to have had a good effect on her state of mind. It may be that the company she was with had something to do with lifting her spirits, since it is more than likely that she joined her old friend Mrs Pinney and her family who included Lymington along with Lyme Regis and Weymouth as favoured seaside holiday destinations. Her Nevis and Bristol friends would have made a welcome change from the almost claustrophobic effect of being in Bath with Edmund. She had not been there long when she received a letter from Davison to tell her that Nelson's health was much better than he had dared to hope. After being extremely ill, he now had a troublesome cough; worrying in itself as both she and Davison were well aware of Nelson's propensity to lung problems. Davison decided that what he needed most was a few days' rest and quiet in the country. Again both she and Davison must have been aware that he was unlikely to get much quiet with Lady Hamilton. In some ways, Davison's next remark was cruel for he must have known that it would give Fanny a vain hope.

> I hardly need to repeat how happy I should have been to have seen him with you, the happiest. His heart is so pure and so extremely good that I flatter myself he never can be divested from his affection. I have the same opinion I ever had of his sincere respect for you.

When she replied on 23 July, she told Davison how distressed she had been to hear that Nelson's health was not good. From the formality of its expression, her: 'I sincerely hope he will find every benefit we can wish him from change of air', can be read as the dispassionate sentiment of someone making a solicitous comment rather than the intense wish that it was. Perhaps resignation to the situation was beginning to creep in and with it the realisation that she could not continue to pour out her emotions to Davison. Or maybe now that she was away from Edmund, she was not forced to spend all her time thinking about Nelson and their current situation. And in that particular letter her mind was very definitely on other things. It was short and businesslike and was, in fact, a covering note for a ring that she enclosed with it. This belonged to her son and he 'wished to part with it', was a polite way of saying that Josiah was in need of money, as he probably was for his expected promotion to a ship had not yet taken place. It would seem that Davison's business activities included a form of pawn-broking or as Fanny expressed it: 'I know you lay out money in pretty things therefore I will thank you to look at it.'

While Fanny was in Lymington, Edmund decided to go to Burnham Thorpe breaking his journey in London where he hoped he might see his son. His letter to Nelson was very short, suggesting he felt there was a coolness between them:

> On Tuesday next I intend (God willing) to leave Bath and tho' not very strong, yet, hope to reach Lothian [hotel] on Thursday, and as I must remain a few days in London, let me not interrupt any of your engagements.... I am my dear Son your most affectionate Edmund Nelson.

If, during his visit, Edmund had tried to talk to his son about a reconciliation he would have found him unresponsive and the old man must have despaired. In turn he felt even more that it was up to him to look after Fanny – or at least that is what he told himself – not that he needed her. He wrote to her in London from Norfolk on 21 August saluting her with the affectionate: 'My Good Friend.' He repeated that whenever she had a house that had room for him in it, he would be ready to join her, wherever it was.

> Whether London is the spot most eligible, supposing all your wishes cannot be accomplished there you must judge, or whether Bath may not be a place more likely to answer every probable purpose of making you as happy as the present appearance of things will permit you to hope for.

In his 'supposing all your wishes cannot be accomplished' he was admitting that it now looked certain that her separation from Nelson was permanent.

Unless there were letters, now missing, it was over a month before Fanny next wrote to Davison. Like many other city dwellers he had taken his family out of London during the summer to spend time at his country home near Alnwick in Northumberland. Davison himself was in need of rest and that beneficial 'change of air', for his health had suffered greatly during the preceding months. Fanny and Edmund had shown great concern for his condition, alluded to but unspecified in his letters, but which Fanny had decided was definitely not gout. Then, some time in June, he had been involved in a traffic accident that resulted in his being thrown out of an open carriage. Although he had not sustained any serious injury the shock had taken its toll. Apart from his physical strains, Davison was under considerable mental pressure from being caught up in the middle of the domestic triangle formed by Fanny, Nelson and Emma Hamilton, all of whom confided in him. Replying to him on 3 September from London where she was staying at 66 Wimpole Street, Fanny hoped:

> the air of Swanland [his home in Northumberland] has been of service to you and that you have found every benefit you hoped for, or that your friends could wish you.

She then gave him the news that since she and Edmund had decided to settle in London she had, without Davison's assistance, been house hunting again, a task she had not found pleasant but she had been successful in securing a house in Somerset Street. She went on to tell him:

> I intend desiring Mr Dods [sic] to send the things I left in his house …which consists of the Table Linen, China, glass etc and no great quantity but of great consequence to me.

With the poignancy that accompanies the dispersal of possessions when any partnership breaks down, she continued: 'I look upon these things as mine although nothing passed on the subject.'

Fanny's comment that there had been no discussion or legal action with regard to the household items may be an allusion to a formal contract that Davison had mentioned in his letter. Certainly it is to be hoped that Fanny had already been informed of events privately otherwise she would have been mortified to read in the paper as the readers of *The Ipswich Journal* did on 5 September: 'Lord Nelson has increased Lady Nelson's settlement to £2000 a year. Her Ladyship divides her residence between London and Norfolk.' The word settlement made it final. In the eyes of the world Nelson had divorced himself from Fanny.

The following week readers in East Anglia were informed: 'Lady Nelson arrived here (Ipswich) on Thursday at the house of Admiral Reeve and [on Friday] proceeded on her way to Burnham Thorpe.' Also staying with Reeve were her friends Sir Edward and Lady Berry and Sir Richard Hughes, so the talk was bound to have been on naval affairs. A month earlier, Berry had brought his ship into Hollesley Bay on coastal protection duties. Lady Berry must have regretted that her friend Fanny was no longer at Round Wood which would have been a perfect location for her to stay to be near to her husband.

Newspapers do not always get their information right and as far as Fanny's destination was concerned, they were wrong. She was on her way to stay at Wolterton. Although Fanny had always felt comfortable there, she had accepted this particular invitation with some trepidation, uncertain if her changed position would make a difference to the Walpoles who were, after all, Nelson's kin. She need not have worried, as she wrote to Edmund: 'The reception of my friends on Saturday was truly gratifying.' That she had been accepted for herself had given a tremendous boost to her self-confidence; enough that she felt she could do almost anything, but what she had in mind was to visit Edmund at Burnham Thorpe. Telling him when she expected to arrive, she begged him not to go to any trouble on her account; she was happy to sleep for a couple of nights at one or other of the neighbouring village inns, leaving her free to spend the day with him at the parsonage. In a letter no longer extant Edmund must have queried whether, under the present circumstances, she was still willing to consider making room for him in her house, particularly now that there was a possibility that Josiah might wish to live with her. Fanny assured him:

I shall have great pleasure in paying you every attention in my power – and at the same time you do not deprive Captain Nisbet of any rooms in my house – he will be *very, very* welcome in Town – and a back parlour is all he would ever wish for.

While Fanny was still enjoying her visit with the Walpoles, Lady Hamilton, who had by then moved into the house Nelson had bought for them at Merton, was conducting her own campaign to displace Fanny entirely from the lives of the Nelson family. She had a willing and ready ally in Sarah Nelson, the Rector's wife. Knowing of the Rector's ambitions, Emma set about hinting that if Fanny had had her way, the Rector, Nelson's 'beloved brother', would have been denied his legal right to be his heir. According to her, Fanny had tried to manipulate matters so:

his own flesh and blood [would be] set aside for who? For Nesbit's, the doctor's son, a villain who many times called the glorious Nelson villain and that he would do for him, yet this boy the --- son would, if this designing woman had had her way, have put you all aside.

Having sown the seed of distrust against Josiah, Lady Hamilton decided to include the rest of the family in the conspiracy against Nelson.

And your father, Nelson's father, protects this woman and gives a mortal blow to his son. The old man could never hear [bear?] her till now and now he conspires *against the saviour of his country* and his darling, who has risen him to such a height of honour, and for whom? *A wicked false malicious* wretch who rendered his days wretched and his nights miserable; *And the father* of Nelson says, 'I will stab my son to the heart,' but indeed, he [Nelson] says, 'my poor father is led now he does not know what he does.' But oh! How cruel, shocking it is and I am afraid the Boltons are not without their share of guilt in this affair. Jealous of you all they have, with the Matchams, pushed this poor dear old gentleman to act this bad and horrible part, to support a false proud bad woman, artful, and with every bad quality to make wretched those she belongs to and yet command over her own cold heart and infamous soul to shew an appearance to the bad part of the world of gentleness and struggling with oppression, but let her own wickedness be her punishment.

It is to be hoped that this vitriolic letter made Sarah Nelson pause for a moment but perhaps in the quest for her husband's aggrandisement she had forgotten all the kindness she had received from Fanny in the past, the free accommodation not only for herself and the Rector but her daughter too. How did she quieten her conscience that she had once considered Fanny to be a role model for her daughter? Equally, it has to be asked why Lady Hamilton felt the need to write such a letter. Had she been the 'wronged' wife, there might have been some excuse for her bitterness towards the 'other woman'. As it was, she appeared to have everything; she had managed to separate Fanny from Nelson, she had given him a child and now had a free hand to spend lavishly on making a home for them in an expensive country house.

She was, apparently, everything that Nelson had dreamed of so she ought to have felt secure. So why was she so angry that Edmund wished to go on living with Fanny as he had done for so long? Commonsense ought to have told her that the chances were that he would not live much longer and would it not be better if he was quietly left alone with her, tucked away in Bath? The answer to that was that Fanny had no intention of burying herself away from society and that if Edmund remained with her, it would be a constant reminder – and cause of gossip – to those whom they met, that Nelson's father lived with his estranged wife. Nelson and Lady Hamilton would have preferred it if they never had to think about Fanny – her death was the best they could hope for. It may be an injustice to Lady Hamilton to suggest that not having had strong family relationships herself, she resented Nelson's attachment to his family. Though just how strong that was may well have become part of the legend that came to surround him assisted by the fact that in the next four years Merton would be filled with assorted Nelson family members, usually assembled at Lady Hamilton's request. Where the family was concerned she held the whip hand and understood well the concept of 'divide and rule'.

It is possible that at that stage Fanny had little idea of Lady Hamilton's malicious campaign against her. Thus it came as a shock when she broke her visit to the Walpoles to go and see Edmund at Burnham at the end of September to find him in a distressed state. Naturally the question of their living together had been discussed and then Edmund had revealed that his son was very much against the idea. He had, it would seem, told Edmund that he must choose between him and Fanny. If he chose to live with Fanny, then as far as Nelson was concerned, he would no longer have any contact with him and further, it was implied that the rest of the family would ostracise him too. The latter threat may well have been the work of the Rector. What actually passed between Fanny and Edmund on that occasion must have been highly emotionally charged and much may have been left unsaid, leaving it to Fanny to write to him when she had had time to think.

> The impression your situation has left on my mind is so strong that I cannot delay any longer offering my opinion on the subject of your living with me, which from your conversation makes it impracticable; the deprivation of seeing your children is so cruel, even in thought, it is impossible you can any longer desire…

This was a draft of the letter sent to Edmund and what had completed that sentence was cut out, probably by Fanny at some later stage. She continued: 'I am not surprised for I knew Lord Nelson's friends could not like it.' Understanding the workings of Nelson's mind she had, while still in Bath, told Kitty Matcham that she did not think Nelson would allow Edmund to continue with her. Kitty had relied: 'Oh my dear Lady Nelson. My brother will thank you in his heart for he knows no one can attend to my father as you do.' Fanny's comment on that was that she had seen the unbelievable change that had taken place in Nelson and his sister had not. During their meeting Edmund had fussed about how much rent Fanny would have to pay if he were not with her and in the conclusion to her letter she reiterated the point, finishing with the formal yet genuinely affectionate: 'Be assured if at any time I can be of the least use to you, command my services and you shall always find me the same.' Fanny returned to Wolterton having faced up to her second separation.

However, she had underestimated Edmund. Infirm he might be, no longer able to take services or even walk very far but he was not to be threatened. He wrote to his son to tell him how much he would like to see him:

'...here is still room enough to give you a warm a joyful and affectionate reception.' He was also willing to visit Nelson at his 'general place of residence'. Quite calmly Edmund had revealed that he had received an anonymous letter that berated him for his conduct to his son, '...which is such, it seems, as will totally separate us.' If Nelson was aware of this unsigned letter which surely must have come from Lady Hamilton's prolific pen, then he must have been even more annoyed when Edmund wrote: 'Most likely this winter may be too cold for me to continue here, and I mean to spend it between Bath and London. If Lady Nelson is in a hired house and by herself, gratitude requires that I should sometimes be with her, if it is likely to be of any comfort to her.' Lady Hamilton might protest all she liked that Nelson believed his father: '...was led now he does not know what he does', and 'the poor old man could never bear her till now', but Edmund knew exactly what he was doing. He loved Fanny like a daughter, she had put up with him, nursed him and been a constant friend to him for many years and now it was only right that he should show his gratitude and comfort her. His son did not wish to be reminded where his duty lay.

A week later Edmund informed Fanny that he had made his decision to join her in the London house they had chosen.

> In respect to this business, the opinion of others must rest with themselves, and not make any alteration with us. I have not offended any man and do rely upon my children's affection that notwithstanding all that have been said, they will not in my old age forsake me.

He planned to leave Burnham at the beginning of November ready to join her. Only if there were good reasons to alter their plans would he go instead to Bath for the winter. So in early November Fanny came up to London to purchase anything they needed to make themselves comfortable at 16 Somerset Street. She was then ready to receive the linen, china and glass which had been brought from Ipswich and kept in store at Dodds' Depository. Making arrangements for its delivery she asked Dodds to call at Davison's house to pick up the wine that Nelson had given her from the wine cellar at Round Wood.

The only thing left to do was to make sure that the servants had the house thoroughly warmed ready for Edmund's arrival. But he did not come. After all he had said, he had been unable to withstand his son's emotional blackmail. On the very day, 17 October, that he had written to Fanny telling her of his decision to join her, Lady Hamilton had sent her 'Dearest Friend' Sarah Nelson, a copy of the letter that Nelson had sent to his father in reply to his of 8 October. Nelson had enclosed the letter in one to Lady Hamilton, asking her to post it for him and had, according to her, left it open for her to read. It is not known if he intended she should send copies of it to the rest of the family. The letter is such a mixture of accusations and excuses that to paraphrase it would do injustice to his style:

My Dear Father – I have received your letter and of which you must be sensible I cannot like for as you seem by your conduct to put me in the wrong it is no wonder that they who do not know me and my disposition should. But Nelson soars above them all and time will do that justice to my private character which she has to my public one. I that have given her, with her falsity and his £2000 a year and £4000 in money and which she calls a poor pittance, and with all that to abandon her son bad as he is and going about defaming me. May God's vengeance strike me dead if I would abandon my children. If he wants reformation, who should reclaim him but the mother? I could say much more but will not out of respect to you, my dear Father, but you know her, therefore I finish. On the 23rd I shall be at Merton with Sir William and Lady Hamilton and them with myself shall be happy, most happy to see you, my beloved father, that is your home. My brother and sister, the dear children will soon be with us and happy shall we all be, but more so if you will come.

Lady Hamilton, after revealing that she had now taken over the provision and supervision of young Charlotte Nelson's extra-curricular activities, begged her dearest friend to burn the copy after the Rector had seen it.

This letter is important for a number of reasons, the most important being that it bore all the hallmarks of someone no longer able to make cool and rational judgements within his personal life. Like a spoilt child Nelson accused his father of wronging him, arguing that if his own parent thought ill of him, was it any wonder that others did too? It becomes painfully obvious that Nelson had become so aware of the general criticism of his behaviour that he needed to lash out and blame anyone but himself. And Fanny bore the brunt of it. Except in his diatribe he lumps Fanny and Josiah together until it is almost impossible to decide who has done what to him. Perhaps it was because he could ill afford the excessive amount of money that Lady Hamilton was spending that he referred to his allowance to Fanny. Who had reported to him that Fanny regarded the £2,000 a year as 'a poor pittance' when she herself had written to him in July:

My Dearest Husband – Your generosity and tenderness was never more strongly shewn than your ...very handsome quarterly allowance, which far exceeded my expectation, knowing your income and had you left it to me, I could not in conscience have said so much. Accept my warmest, my most affectionate and grateful thanks.

That surely, had not shown her to be grasping. But maybe that was part of what he called her falsity. As for the £4,000 lump sum, it should be remembered that it was her money anyway, having been left to her by her uncle. But what of the references to Josiah? Was there any truth in the accusation that Josiah had been plotting with others against Nelson, if so who were they and why did they want to do him harm or was that all part of Nelson's mental instability? He had made a similar allegation when he had informed Fanny on 4 March that Josiah was to have a new command.

More confusing is the accusation that Josiah had done something that had caused Fanny to turn against her son, something Lady Hamilton had hinted at several months before. No details have ever emerged as to what his 'crime' was. Certainly Fanny had mentioned Josiah in her letters with no hint of a breach but a possible explanation is that he had got into severe financial difficulties but even so, as we know from her letter to Davison, she had tried to help by pawning his gold ring for him. Nelson's vehement declaration that Fanny should not have abandoned her son however bad he was needs to be read with: 'May God's vengeance strike me dead if I should abandon my children...I could say much more but will not out of respect to you, my dear Father.' Edmund was meant to understand that Nelson believed his father should stand by him.

Edmund accepted the invitation to visit Merton in November, possibly thinking he could do so before he moved in with Fanny. Nelson, having got his father under his roof, appeared to Edmund to be in better health and spirits than he had been for some time. Somehow, during the time he spent there, Edmund was persuaded that it would be better that he should return to Bath for the winter. It is not recorded when he made Fanny aware of his decision or what he said to her, though it is likely that in their now missing correspondence, Edmund may have urged Fanny not to give up hope of Nelson returning to her. Therefore just before Christmas, on 18 December, she sent a letter to him, care of Davison:

> My Dear Husband – It is some time since I have written to you. The silence you have imposed is more than my affections will allow me and in this instance I hope you will forgive me in not obeying you. One thing I omitted in my letter of July which I now have to offer for your accommodation, a comfortable warm house. Do, my dear husband, let us live together. I can never be happy till such an event takes place. I assure you again I have but one wish in the world, to please you. Let everything be buried in oblivion, it will pass away like a dream. I can now only intreat you to believe I am most sincerely and affectionately your wife, Frances H.Nelson.

That was not the letter of a cold and heartless woman, rather one who was doing everything in her power to show her love in a tangible form. What was cold and heartless was the note that accompanied the return of this letter. Davison had written, presumably at Nelson's dictation: 'Opened by mistake by Lord Nelson, but not read.'

Although she was not one to bear grudges, Fanny's relationship with Davison must have changed after that. When, in November, she had made her plans to have her wine collected from his house, she had not realised that he would be away at the time, so the wine had remained where it was.

As things turned out, this was fortuitous, as once she had moved into the house she was confronted with a shortage of space. So, on 27 December she asked him to: 'have the goodness to give my Lord Nelson's wine house room for truly we know not where to put it.' On this occasion she refers to a message that Davison had passed to her from Nelson concerning the sale of Round Wood. She wrote: 'I am glad my Lord has positively said Mr Fuller must pay that money down for Round Wood and then we shall have a good house in Town.' There had been a number of hints during the course of the year that Fuller was being very slow in settling what he owed for the house. But the second half of the sentence: ' then we shall have a good house in Town' is puzzling. Surely, with her rejection of the week before, Fanny was not still clinging to the belief that she and Nelson could have a home together in London or anywhere else?

After what must have been the most gruesome year in Fanny's life in which she had managed to keep up a dignified appearance, she continued much as she had done in past years; taking her place in London society, exchanging visits with her friends and relations, all of whom had rallied to her support. It must have been strange for her, after all the years she had spent looking after Edmund, not to have to consider him. Although no letters survive, it is very likely that they remained in touch. Edmund's health had deteriorated, no doubt assisted by the emotional repercussions of the Nelsons' separation, but he hoped that when the warmer weather came, he would be able to face leaving Bath to make the journey to London. There was no doubt that he missed the solicitous and undivided care of Fanny. True, he had his beloved Kitty living very near him but he had to share her with her husband and seven, soon to be eight, children. She tried to visit and dine with him each day but even that small pleasure would be denied him when she came to her lying-in period. On 20 April 1802 Edmund wrote his last letter to Fanny telling her that Kitty had had a daughter and that mother and child were both doing well. He also told her that a mutual acquaintance, a Mr Tarleton, recently arrived in Bath had given him good reports of her health and her plans for the summer. His closing words to her were: 'Of this rest assured that in all places I wish for your happiness…'

Six days later he was dead. It is not recorded, though it was most likely George Matcham, who sent to tell Fanny that Edmund was dying. She went to Bath immediately. It has always been believed that she arrived in time to be at his side when he died. However, among the recently discovered Davison letters there is an undated very short one that reads:

> … I am just returned from a sad journey. I was too late to see my dear friend God Bless him. His attachment to me…most sincere – had the letters been sent by Saturday's coach I should have seen him.

Matcham had written first to Nelson, who was ashore at the time, to tell him what the situation was. The reply came back:

Had my father expressed a wish to see me, unwell as I am, I should have flown to Bath, but I believe it would be too late, however should it be otherwise and he wishes to see me no consideration shall detain me for a moment.

But he did not make a deathbed visit to his father in Bath, nor did he attend the funeral that was held at Burnham Thorpe two weeks later. It was said that he was too ill to make the journeys. It does seem strange that the man who made every effort to attend the funerals of his naval friends and often wept copiously throughout the services, could not summon up the strength to go to his father's funeral. Edmund's coffin was carried by six local clergymen into the large church at Burnham Thorpe which was packed and, according to Mrs Bolton: 'the farmers in three parishes followed [the coffin].' What was so sad was the fact that there were only three family mourners present; of these one was a son-in-law, Thomas Bolton, the second, a nephew, the Revd Robert Rolfe; only the Rector, now Dr William Nelson, could claim to be directly related to the deceased.

Nelson's reason for not attending must be questioned. It may be that the simplest explanation was, as he had said, that he was too ill to attend. It is also possible that he felt that as a public figure, his going to Burnham might deflect proper attention and respect from his father's memory. The same argument could be used against his going to Bath to Edmund's bedside, though it ought to have been possible for him to 'slip into the house' without provoking too much attention. But there was another more compelling reason for not going to Bath. He knew that it was likely he would come face to face with Fanny. Whatever he might say about her, deep down he had to recognise that she had been a faithful friend to Edmund and would have gone to be with him in his final hours. Had his conscience persuaded him he ought to go, then it would appear he was unable to withstand Lady Hamilton's pleas not to put himself into the position of having to meet Fanny. As for the funeral, he may have been so overcome by his father's death, perhaps even realising that he might have played a part in it, that he could not face witnessing the interment.

It was her sister-in-law Bolton who sent Fanny the details of the funeral in a letter dated 15 May 1802. She began by paying tribute to Fanny: 'Your going to Bath my dear Lady Nelson was a piece with all your conduct to my beloved father.' Mrs Bolton at least was prepared to acknowledge, what all the rest of the family knew, that Fanny had devoted a major part of the previous thirteen years to the devoted care of their father thus relieving them of the responsibility. Susannah, the down-to-earth member of the family, wrote as she felt. She did not prevaricate when she told Fanny that she expected to go to Merton on a visit but that much as she wanted to she was unlikely to be able to include a call on Fanny:

...but my dear Lady N. we cannot meet as I wished for everybody is known who visits you. Indeed I do not think I shall be permitted even to go to town. But be assured I always have [been] and shall always be your sincere friend.

Fanny must have appreciated Susannah's loyalty but at the same time she was well aware that her sister-in-law was unable to stand out against Nelson's wishes for the truth was that he held the purse strings. He already paid out £150 a year towards the education of his Bolton nephews and on 11 June he gave her another £100 and promised to pay her that annually for the following three years for the same purpose. The first part of that letter could suggest that Nelson paid his family in an effort to retain their support but the second part implied that Susannah herself had broached the question of a further donation: 'All I desire is that you would not say or write me a syllable on the subject for I am sorry I cannot do more.' Fanny, of course, would have had no knowledge of that letter but referring back to Susannah's she must have been concerned by the phrase 'everybody is known who visits you'. If this was to be taken literally, then someone within Fanny's household was passing the information to Merton. It was an uncomfortable feeling to think that one of her employees was untrustworthy and that she was being spied upon – but for what reason? Why should it be so important for Lady Hamilton or Nelson to know who Fanny's friends were? Was this all part of a plan to steadily woo them from her and thus isolate her? Susannah made the tightening of the net around those who stayed at Merton seem almost sinister with her comment: 'I do not think I shall be permitted even to go to town.' However, she may have meant quite simply that there was so much entertainment provided at Merton that she would have neither time nor need to go to London.

After Edmund's death and with Nelson's brother and sisters pledging their allegiance to Lady Hamilton, there was no longer any exchange of letters between them and Fanny, so it becomes difficult to follow her in any detail over the next years. Occasional references to her appeared in the newspapers but on the whole we have to conclude that her life continued quietly, following a regular pattern of visits to friends throughout the country. George Matcham writing to Nelson on money matters on 9 January 1803 told him that he had heard that Fanny had taken a house at Clifton, instead of Bath, for the winter. He described how Fanny had arrived at the Matchams' house in Lord Hood's carriage, but instead of calling upon them had merely sent a servant to present her visiting card and then had driven off. Matcham, although under a financial obligation to Nelson, told him that had Fanny called she would have been welcomed: 'it is our maxim if possible to be at peace with all the world'.

It was clear that the Matchams had regarded Fanny's calling card as a snub but it is likely that they misinterpreted its meaning. Fanny was aware that Nelson wished to separate her from his sisters yet they had, in the past, been good friends and this Fanny wished to acknowledge by letting them know that she was in the area and was thinking of them. Matcham's description of how she: 'rolled off as she came in Lord Hood's carriage and four', implied that Fanny was giving herself airs. Yet riding with the Hoods was nothing new for her, they were very old friends, as the Matchams knew very well. By

March Fanny was at 54 Welbeck Street in London where she received a letter from John Pinney in Bristol. The gist of his letter of thanks to her showed
that in spite of everything that had happened to her, Fanny was still showing
concern for others' welfare. In this instance she had taken the trouble to go
and visit Mary Pinney who was at that time under the care of a Mrs Jackson
who most likely ran a school for young ladies. Fanny had not only made the
visit, she had written to let Mrs Pinney know that the girl was well.

At the beginning of April, the newspapers and the local gossips would
have informed her of the death of Sir William Hamilton, at his house in
Piccadilly where he had removed himself to find the peace and quiet that
was in short supply at Merton. Now that Lady Hamilton was a widow, it
would be more difficult to keep up the pretence that Nelson was simply
the dear friend of the couple. Fanny may have felt some sympathy for Sir
William yet it is unlikely that she could admire a man who could so will-
ingly collude with his wife and her lover. It would be interesting to know if
Fanny found it within her to conform to etiquette and send her condolences
to Lady Hamilton – or maybe to Nelson.

May brought the news of another death, that of her old Ipswich friend,
Admiral Reeve. The 71-year-old had been involved in a traffic accident following a late morning visit to Sir Robert Harland (he of the interesting statues but now a married man) at Wherstead. Reeve, accompanied by his servant, had driven the one-horse chaise himself. *The Ipswich Journal* reported:

> On his return, the horse became unmanageable, ran the chaise against a
> bank in the road and both were thrown out. The Admiral dislocated his
> neck and instantly expired, the servant was uninjured.

Brighter news that would have particularly interested Fanny was the marriage of Catherine Bolton to her cousin Captain Bolton. It would be pleasant
to think that Susannah Bolton had not been so warped by Lady Hamilton
that she had let Fanny know of this event. Fanny had had much to do with
shaping the tastes and manners of Kitty and her sister, both girls had much
to thank her for although they never did.

June saw Fanny widening her experience of watering places with a visit
to Tunbridge Wells from where she wrote to Davison saying she was there
on medical advice. The purpose of that letter was to remind Davison that
he had not carried out his part in a Trust Deed. Following the death of
Fanny's former brother-in-law, Walter Nisbet, Josiah had received a legacy
of £1,000, payable on his coming of age. The money was paid into a Trust
Fund for him on the understanding that he would receive the interest of
£300 a year until he could claim the principal. The two people Fanny trusted
most, Maurice Nelson and Alexander Davison, were made Trustees. When
Maurice died his name should have been removed from the Deed and
another Trustee appointed. This had not been done. And since the Deed
could not be legally executed without the necessary signatures, the whole

question of Josiah's Trust Fund had reached stalemate and Josiah was unable to claim his annual dividend.

From Tunbridge Wells, Fanny returned to Town before setting off to spend the summer in Exmouth but her departure for Devon had been delayed because she was house hunting. She had decided to give up her house in London and was looking for a suitable small property in the country. She had had to wait in Town to receive the promising-sounding details of a house near Newbury. However, when the plans arrived, although there was thirteen acres of land and the price was only £3,000, she discovered that the largest room in the house was only 16 feet by 13½ feet. So, she had rejected that but she was continuing with her search for what, as it became clear in the letter to Davison, was to be a permanent home for her and Josiah, for in spite of the insinuations of Nelson and Lady Hamilton, he spent most of his time with his mother.

That Fanny continued to be a source of malicious interest to members of the Nelson family is shown in the few extant letters exchanged between them and Lady Hamilton. On 1 December 1804 Kitty Matcham wrote what can only be described as a fawning letter to Lady Hamilton who had, it appeared, written to her to find out why she had not heard from her. Kitty, anxious not to antagonise the lady, excused her omission by reminding her that she did have a large household to consider and that they had also recently moved house. It is difficult when reading this letter not to form the impression that Kitty deliberately fed Lady Hamilton with information which she knew would please her, namely the activities of Fanny while at the same time reassuring the lady that she, Kitty, was in no danger of renewing her relationship with her sister-in-law.

> The Lady is I believe in Bath, but too great a distance for us ever to see her. We have been at a ball, a concert and a play this week but she was not at either. My only desire is that we shall not be in the same room and circumstances are now so well understood by our friends that I don't think it likely we shall ever meet her…

The phrase 'too great a distance' was meant to imply that Fanny was mixing in the higher echelons of society and considered herself 'above' her in-laws. This was the same complaint that George Matcham had expressed earlier and it obviously worried the Matchams greatly. As to their friends 'understanding the circumstances' this suggests more malicious gossiping among their own circle to ensure that they did not meet Fanny at a social function.

That was not always possible as Kitty discovered about six weeks after her earlier letter to Lady Hamilton when she found herself in the same room as Fanny. Kitty was quick to paint the picture that Lady Hamilton wanted of the cold woman who was constantly stirring up antagonism towards Nelson.

She had then an opportunity of showing her insolence as far as looks could express, so I was told by some friends of mine who said she looked as I passed her in that scornful way, which could not but be noticed by all that saw her.

Kitty in accusing Fanny of looking at her scornfully, omitted to mention that she must have totally ignored Fanny when she passed her. The scornful look described by Kitty's friends might well have been one of hurt or even puzzlement on Fanny's part that Kitty could not even bring herself to acknowledge her with a look or smile or a simple inclination of the head. Kitty went on to relate – and thereby stirring even further Lady Hamilton's indignation – that there were many in Bath who were opposed to Nelson: 'whom we know to be all goodness and liberality. Different tales are told in different parties, but I think a time must come when everything will appear in a true light.'

Fanny had been in Bath since August of the previous year (1804) in order to drink the waters and take the hot baths. Both she had found beneficial but some time during the late autumn she had twisted the tendon in her right foot and that had severely restricted her going out and then when she had recovered she had caught a severe cold that again confined her to the house. But as she told Davison on 30 January she was now almost well again. However, she had not written to talk about her health but rather to find out what he had done about the Deed of Trust to which she had drawn his attention when she had been at Tunbridge Wells the previous spring. His reply at that time had led her to believe that everything was in hand but when in June she had visited her bankers she found that the dividend that was due had not been paid in. She had asked Mr Marsh, one of Nelson's agents, to collect the money for her but he had been unable to do so because the Trust was still in the name of Davison and the deceased Maurice Nelson. Until such time as Maurice's name was removed and another Trustee appointed, she was unable legally to receive the money. Although she had been ill at the time this had come up she had taken legal advice and had asked that Mr Ryder should call on Davison to sort things out. There was almost an air of weary desperation in her: 'God knows which of us are to go first, and your executing your part of the Deed would very much oblige me and relieve me from great uneasiness.'

At the beginning of July Miss Susanna Bolton who was staying in Bath with her aunt Matcham sent a gossipy letter to Lady Hamilton. None of the Matcham or Bolton women emerged unscathed by the influence of Lady Hamilton; she seemed to have the capacity to draw out the very worst of their natures. Years before Edmund and Fanny had despaired of the twins' fiery tempers and lack of sensitivity but if what Susanna said were true then Kitty Matcham was the worst of them all:

We hear that Tom Tit has been very ill and attended by two physicians. She is now however got quite well. She looks shockingly really and very old. Mrs Matcham often wishes she was in heaven, we join and make no doubt we have your good wishes on the occasion.

If Susanna's information that Fanny, having been ill, had by 7 July recovered, then she must have had a relapse almost immediately afterwards. It was on 28 July that she wrote yet again to Davison on that vexed subject of the Deed. It was six months since she had asked him to meet Ryder to fill out the required forms and she still had heard nothing. This, she told him was: 'The only earthly business I have to do.' Aware that this was a somewhat dramatic expression she explained that she had been seriously ill with a bronchial complaint, so ill that her doctor had thought her in danger of dying. Fearing that he might be correct she had even considered asking the doctor to write to Davison to expedite matters. Now, she hoped, at last matters would be settled as soon as possible for within the week she was to go to Clifton to try the water from the hot well there. That was her intention but her arrangements were dependent on her carriage being ready. She wrote: '...if I can get my carriage from the coach maker' without making it clear if she had ordered a new carriage or if her old one was undergoing repair.

That Trust Deed was still bothering her but at least by the time she wrote to Davison from Clifton on 18 August, she had heard that he had arranged for three dividends to be paid. Davison had excused himself from dealing with matters with the explanation that Mrs Davison and the children had all been ill. Fanny sympathetically replied that she hoped they were now fully recovered and:

> that you will spare a short time from them to oblige me by executing the Deed – it has given me great pain in soliciting this trifling boon so frequently as I have done in the course of four years and four months; all you have to do is to prove my friend's Maurice's death – if you will do it immediately you will have no further trouble.

That last was not a threat, she was simply telling him that if he did what was required then she would have no need to bother him further. The need to get her affairs in order was necessary as not only had she been ill since arriving in Clifton, she had now been told that her liver was affected.

Following her stay in Clifton she returned to Bath where on 16 October she had been spied briefly by Mrs Bolton who could not wait to write to Lady Hamilton:

> I saw Tom Tit yesterday in her carriage at the next door come to take Lady Charlotte Drummond out with her. She looked then much as usual had I seen only her hands spreading out I should have known her.

Susannah could have saved that piece of news for within days she was expected to join Lady Hamilton at Merton. When she chivvied that lady for being in low spirits: 'What in the world will my Lord think if he comes back and finds you grown thin and looking ill?' No one in England was aware that four days after she wrote her letter, her brother, Lady Hamilton's lover and Fanny's husband, would be dead. And it was to Fanny, not Lady Hamilton, that the death of Nelson was officially conveyed on 6 November when the dispatches containing details of the Battle of Trafalgar reached the Admiralty. Lord Barham, the new First Lord of the Admiralty wrote: 'It is with utmost concern that in the midst of victory I have to inform your lady-ship of the death of your illustrious partner Lord Viscount Nelson...'

It is impossible to know what Fanny's reaction was to this news. The man she loved and adored would now never return to her – but neither would he to her rival. It was almost inevitable that in the aftermath that surrounded Nelson's death, she would idealise the man and see herself as an inconsolable widow. In this she would have been aided by the many letters of condolence she received. Her closest friends who knew how perilous her health had been in the past year must have worried that the shock would be too much for her. Their loving concern for her was epitomised in a letter from Katherine Walpole written, not to Fanny herself, but to Josiah the day after the news had been received:

> No words my dear Sir can express our feelings at this present moment, you must forgive our anxiety for Lady Nelson, if I trespass upon you. I beg of you to tell me how she supports herself under the shock of Lord Nelson's death. I well know how sincerely she will feel, notwithstanding all that has passed, as I know how well she loved him. ... When she can bear it, may I beg of you to assure her how anxious we are for her.

Miss Walpole was of course, distantly related to Nelson but there was no doubt that her loyalty was to Fanny and she wanted her to know it at this difficult time. She probably echoed the thoughts of all Fanny's friends who admired her for never wavering in her love of Nelson in spite of what he had done to her. On a more practical level, Lady Berry who was staying at Wolterton sent a message in Miss Walpole's letter that she would go at once to Fanny if she would like it.

Among the huge correspondence that must have arrived daily at her home was a communication from the Rector just three days after the news of his brother's death and on the very day that he was created Earl Nelson, a title allowing him to sign his letters, as he did this one to Fanny, with the simple 'Nelson'. Only this oleaginous man could have written at such a time:

> I have just gone through the painful task of perusing that last will of that great man whose name I have now the honour to bear. Being appointed (jointly with Mr Haslewood) executor it becomes my duty to acquaint your Ladyship with so much of the will [as] more immediately concerns your [ladyship].

He then promised that he would give instructions for her to receive a complete copy of the will as soon as possible. No doubt, although the last thing on Fanny's mind at the time would have been the contents of the will, she would have been prepared for that as being a necessary part of the rituals surrounding a death. But having been made only too aware of the Rector's feelings towards her in the past five years she must have been completely taken aback by the rest of his remarks.

> ...if I could feel pleasure amidst so many mournful reflections as press upon my mind it would be in the opportunity afforded me of renewing with your Ladyship that intercourse of kind offices which I once hoped would have always marked our lives – which untoward circumstances have occasioned some interruption of, but which I trust will never again be suspended. Believe me to remain with truest regard dear Madam, your most affectionate brother, Nelson.

Had Fanny been feeling sad and dispirited when she read that it would not have been out of character if she had laughed aloud at the sheer effrontery of the man. He, who had been among the first to ingratiate himself with Lady Hamilton, who had encouraged his wife to do the same and spurn Fanny, how could he now refer to all that had passed as 'untoward circumstances' and call himself her affectionate brother? It is a great pity that Fanny's reply, if there was one has not been preserved.

Nelson had made his final will in May 1803 thus revoking the earlier one in which, apart from a couple of small bequests, everything had gone to Fanny and on her death to Josiah. This one was much more complicated. His presentation pieces from various sources he bequeathed to Lady Hamilton, his brother and sisters and Davison. Capt. Hardy was to have his telescopes and sea glasses and one hundred pounds though there was no mention of the plot of land he was supposed to inherit in Bronte. Everything else, except the contents of the house at Merton, was left to the executors, the Rector and Haslewood, to set up a trust fund to produce £1,000 a year for the natural life of Fanny, payable in addition to the £4,000 he had already allowed her. He expected that she would take that:

> ...in lieu and full satisfaction of all dower right and title of dower and free bench of her the said Viscountess Nelson my wife of and in all of any of the freehold and copyhold lands etc. of which I am now possessed.

In other words, she was not to expect anything else but he did allow that in the event that there were insufficient funds to meet her £1,000, then it should be supplemented from the rents of his lands in Sicily.

Although the news of Nelson's death was confirmed in early November it would be some weeks before his body would arrive in England for the splendid state funeral that was being planned to take place in St Paul's

Cathedral. Fanny stayed on in Bath for a while before going to London. The press had not yet been supplied with sufficient details of what had happened on board Nelson's flagship, the *Victory*, to foster the many legends that would abound in the future. Fanny, in her desire to know exactly how Nelson had died, consulted her old friend Lord Hood, but even he, she told Davison on 4 December, had heard no official accounts. Using paper edged with the traditional black for mourning she had written a very short note thanking Davison for: '…your kind information and the Patriotic Funds for these marks of consideration and respects for my lamented Lord's memory.' When the news of Trafalgar had reached England, a Day of Thanksgiving had been declared and at church services throughout the country collections amounting to £64,000 had been deposited with Lloyds to become the Patriotic Fund. Donations continued to flow in and by the time Nelson's funeral was held they had reached £104,000 and were still rising.

Sometime before 14 December when she again wrote to Davison, Fanny and Josiah went up to London to attend to various matters. That Fanny was distraught by events is evinced in her somewhat chiding manner to Davison about the call he had made on her the previous day. He had placed her in a difficult position by bringing his sons with him. He, knowing how fond Fanny had always been of his children, may have thought the young men would help lift her spirits but Fanny had not appreciated what amounted to a breach of etiquette.

> I was very much surprised to see your sons with you yesterday, recollect I have refused to see some of my Lord's old acquaintance and even my female friends, therefore never bring any person with you, without previously acquainting me, and I will then say what I think right.

Grief-stricken though she might be, Fanny remained, as she had always had to be, practical where her own future was concerned so she told Davison that she would wait in London for a few more days in the hope that she might hear the full contents of Nelson's will and the codicil it was said to contain. One could charge her here with sounding mercenary when she should have been immersed only in her sorrow, but can there have been any widow who has not, amidst her tears, paused to consider how she will manage financially?

Like the majority of English men and women outside London, Fanny had to rely on the reports of the newspapers and the first-hand accounts of her friends for the details of her husband's final great triumph, his state funeral. For the man who had longed to be recognised by his country as a hero and patriot, he could not have received a greater testimony of its appreciation. Everything that could be done to honour him in death was carried out with precision and respect. His coffin was taken from Greenwich by river on Wednesday 8 January. A long procession of barges carrying naval dignitaries and others moved silently upstream between the crowded banks of noiseless spectators. No other vessel was allowed to move and so disturb the procession. By quarter to three in the afternoon the procession had reached the Palace of Westminster where it was greeted by bands playing the 'Dead March in Saul' and other mournful strains. At exactly three o'clock as the funeral barge was about to disembark its precious charge, the sky darkened as heavy clouds lowered and, without warning, hailstones bombarded the earth, ceasing only when the body was safely landed. After lying overnight at the Admiralty, the all-male funeral procession led by the Duke of York and hundreds of other dignitaries including the Prince of Wales, the Duke of Kent and Nelson's old friend, the former Prince William, now the Duke of Clarence, set off at 10 am for the service in St Paul's Cathedral. The chief mourners were Capt. Hardy and the Revd Earl Nelson, dressed in the deepest sables, and his son, now Lord Merton. Sixty-three mourning coaches attended and these were followed by one hundred and twenty three private coaches, sent by their owners to show their respects. Fanny's was among them. A tiny note in *The Ipswich Journal*'s account revealed that on the Saturday evening preceding the funeral as Nelson's coffin lay-in-state at Greenwich: 'A few personages of high respectability' were admitted for a private leave taking. The newspaper mentioned by name only the Princess of Wales and her suite. It would have been surprising if Fanny had not been taken by one of the Lords of the Admiralty or perhaps Capt. Hardy to make her own farewell.

As still happens after the death of a family member, the wrangles over the will and who shall have what cause tension and often bitterness. During the early months of 1806, Fanny was in almost constant correspondence with either Nelson's former agent William Marsh and his colleagues Sibbald, Stacey & Fauntleroy in the business at Berners Street in London or her solicitor James Western in Grays Inn Square. Fanny had been told by the Rector earlier that under Nelson's will, she was to receive an annuity of £1,000. However, when the whole document was read, it was discovered that Nelson had stipulated that if Parliament should grant her a pension amounting to £1,000, then his provision should be null and void. Fanny had instructed James Western to call on the Rector, now Earl Nelson, one of the executors to find out how matters stood. Western reported to her on 4 February that the Earl had referred him to his solicitor, Haslewood from whom he discovered:

> ... the only funded property of which Lord Nelson died possessed was the
> sum of £15,600 in three per cents, and that his Lordship was indebted to
> Mr Davison in the sum of £3,000 and the executors have since borrowed
> £2,000 more from him. From the prize money which is expected to be
> received and the produce of the estate at Merton which is to be sold in the
> spring, there will be more than sufficient for the payment of all the debts,
> legacies and other charges and...it was the intention of the executors to
> provide for the payment of your annuity out of the first monies that might

be received which they expect will be in the course of three month and
that they consider your Ladyship as entitled to half a year's annuity due
at Christmas last.

Western further told her that she could not expect to call on the executors
for the annuity until a year after Nelson's death.

Under circumstances such as these, it was just as well that trades people
were often prepared to wait for their bills to be settled. In January Fanny
had ordered a black silk mourning dress to be made for her by E Franks,
Milliner and Dressmaker of St James's Street, London at a cost of seven and
a half guineas. Etiquette required that she remain in mourning so that later,
in May, it had become necessary to order a complete summer outfit in black,
resulting in a bill amounting to £48.17.0.

But before that there were more pressing matters to be settled. A long
letter from William Marsh on 19 February found Fanny and Josiah in
Exmouth, a place according to Marsh: 'which I think a better place for
people in health, than invalids. I must sincerely hope your Ladyship will
very soon be completely upon the first list.' Tired of waiting for Davison to
sort out Josiah's Trust Deed Fanny had asked Marsh to see what he could
do. She had sent him the certificate of her marriage to Dr Josiah Nisbet
which was needed to establish Josiah's claim on the Nisbet estate. Part
of the problem with the Deed was that it had been drawn up by Nisbet's
brother-in-law, Lockhart, under Scottish law but Marsh thought they would
be able to work round that. Fanny had also sent other documents, some of
which related to the pension of £2,000 that Parliament had voted her. The
letter was very detailed, containing facts and figures as well as references
to financial dealings that Davison had undertaken on her behalf some of
which were, to say the least, suspect. Marsh knew when he wrote this letter
that Fanny would have understood him; he was writing to an intelligent
woman with a fine grasp of affairs. His letter crossed with one from her to
which he straightaway replied, telling her that that very morning he had
received the sum of £912.10.0. payable to her from a Bounty Bill, that is a
share of Nelson's prize money. He also thought that it was most likely that
her pension would be backdated to the day of the action that had caused
Nelson's death.

As with Fanny's relationship with Davison, so that with Marsh was a
mixture of business and sincere friendship. Although we do not have her
side of the correspondence, we can judge by the tone of his replies that he
knew her well enough to make small jokes and make references to his own
affairs.

I am going on Tuesday next to take my little Fanny (who has been so
long at the sea) to Malvern Wells, & as I shall then go on to [? Park] near
Leominster, to see an old friend, it will be a fortnight at least before I
get back.

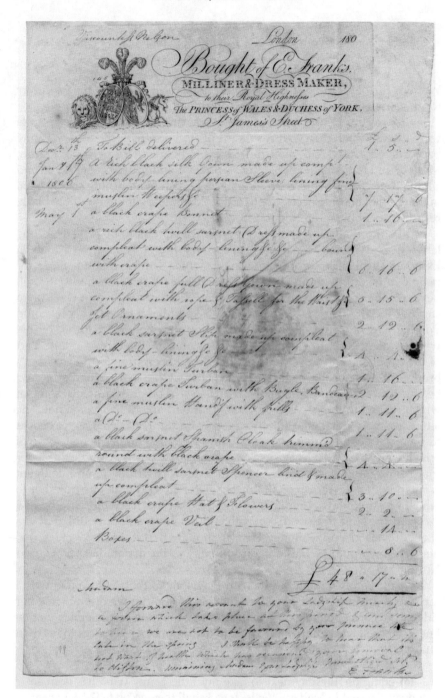

Fanny's Dressmaker's Bill.
© *The Nelson Museum and Local History Centre, Monmouth.*

Marsh wanted her to know however, that though he was away from the business, if she had any commands for him, a letter to the office would be forwarded to him immediately.

March brought news from Western, the solicitor. When he had again asked Haslewood when she would receive the previous half year's money due to her, he was told that the executors still had not sufficient actual cash to pay it and again suggested they would have to borrow it from Davison. Haslewood had then written to Western saying that there was an aspect of the Will on which he needed to take Counsel's opinion. Then Haslewood had sent a letter on another subject altogether. This had emanated from the Earl and speaks for itself.

> By the will of the late Lord Nelson, a gold box presented to his lordship by the City of London is bequeathed to his brother, the present Earl. This box is understood to be in the Viscountess Nelson's possession. And I shall be obliged by your communicating to her Ladyship the joint request of Earl Nelson and myself, that, if the above information be correct, she will have the goodness to direct the box to be left at the Earl's house No.10 Charles Street Square.

Unfortunately, Fanny's reply to this letter has not survived.

Counsel gave his opinion on 25 March but it was 23 April before Western learned of it: '…the copy having been mislaid in Mr Haslewood's office.' The opinion was that all the legacies were to be paid before a fund was set up to provide Fanny's annuity but that she was entitled to the arrears as soon as there was money to pay them. Haslewood had pointed out that as things stood once the debts had been paid there would be about £3,000 independent of any prize money. The estate at Merton, which was to be sold immediately, was expected to raise between twenty and thirty thousand pounds and that should ensure enough to pay her annuity.

If Fanny thought that was the end of the matter, then she would find out in the following month that the Earl, through Mr Haslewood, had conveyed to Western that he was not going to pay her arrears until all the legacies were settled. In the meantime Western had been talking to another learned Counsel who had recommended taking the advice of Sir Samuel Romilly, the Solicitor General. Fanny, the daughter of a lawyer, knew enough to know that all this was going to cost her a great deal if and when she finally did get her annuity. This long letter revealed that one of the legacies that had to be met was the £4,000 Nelson had left for his 'adopted daughter' Miss Thompson. It also answered a query from Fanny, possibly fed to her from other sources, that as his widow was she entitled to a third of Nelson's personal estate? At great length the answer was no. Tucked right at the end of this letter was a note – without any apology – to say that the missing gold box had been located. It had been found at Merton – presumably in Lady Hamilton's safe keeping.

While Western was pursuing Fanny's annuity for her, William Marsh was doing his best to sort out Josiah's inheritance. Apparently when Mr Lockhart, his uncle by marriage, had drawn up the trust Bond he made 'an informality in the date written into the Bond' – strangely, Fanny was to do the same many years later in her own will. However, the Bond was legal in Scotland but if Josiah wanted to make a claim on his uncle's property in Nevis, then it would have to be redrawn in an English form. Having told Fanny how her account stood at the time, Marsh then turned to a very personal matter. He knew that she had recently sent Mr Fauntleroy, one of his partners, a very precious present and Marsh hoped he might be honoured with a similar gift:

> I mean a lock of dear Lord Nelson's hair – if you have enough to spare me one I shall feel particularly obliged to your Ladyship at leisure to send it me accompanied by such a note of Ladyship (unblended with other matter) as may forever authenticate the [? - unreadable].

This truly personal gift revealed the sentimental side of Fanny's nature. When, we may wonder, did she gently cut a few locks of Nelson's hair to keep by her while he was away; perhaps in those happy days spent in Exmouth in the first year of their marriage or when he went to sea in 1793 or even after that very special time they had spent together in 1797/8?

By June Fanny had moved on to Clifton for the summer and it was there she received the news that Marsh had finally secured from the Government her pension for the previous half year up to 5 April amounting to £936.15.6. The correct amount had been £936.15.7 ½ d but according to Marsh: 'the odd halfpence they never pay.' Rounding off figures was always up for the Exchequer and down for the public. Marsh confided that he had encountered many delays before securing the warrant from the Treasury who even then would not release it until he had paid the stamp duty of £20.2.6. He wanted to make an appeal against that but was advised it would be better not to contend that issue, especially as he was about to do battle against the demands for the Property Tax and other taxes that Fanny had already received and had passed to him to deal with.

If the lack of extant letters is anything to go by, then the summer seems to have passed quietly and it was October before Western contacted Fanny to inform her that finally Nelson's executors had purchased £33,333.6.8. in 3% Consols to cover the payments of her annuity and were willing to execute a power of attorney to enable her bankers to receive the dividends as they became due. He enclosed a receipt for the year's annuity payable up to Midsummer minus the inevitable Property Tax. He also congratulated her that her case against the executors in the Chancery had gone through so quickly. Fanny wrote to Marsh enclosing Western's letter. 'I am glad the business is all settled.' She then asked that Marsh purchase a thousand pounds' worth of stock in the same Consols. She thought that would leave enough in her account for her living expenses until the New Year. As she did not intend to go to London until the spring, she had asked Western to send his bill to Marsh for him to settle for her. 'As to the amount, I can form no idea, but I beg you will do what is proper and customary on these occasions.'

Marsh's reply the following day, 21 October, brought a poignant reminder that it was exactly one year since Nelson had died: 'I assure you your Ladyship – many past occurrences rushed into my mind this morning before I had the honour of reading your Ladyship's letter.' On the following day he had to write to tell her that the executors were now objecting to the provision of her power of attorney.

Western had been precipitate in his congratulations on her winning her case. A week later he had to tell her that when he had received £918.15.0. from Nelson's executors, he had informed Haslewood that the executors would be expected to pay the legal costs incurred in filing the case in the Chancery Court. Haslewood, while admitting the executors' legal liability, thought it rather harsh and hoped that her Ladyship would not insist upon it. Western advised Fanny that she had no reason to allow Haslewood's request especially as it was the executors who had made it necessary to go to court. The amount of costs involved would, he thought, be around twenty-three or twenty-four pounds. Fanny obviously decided not to be swayed by Haslewood's pleas but the matter still had not been resolved by December despite promises they soon would be. Until that matter was cleared up, Western could not submit his own bill to Marsh for payment. Haslewood was making other difficulties. He was not happy with the power of attorney that had been granted to Fanny's bankers to receive the annuity, because it would mean that they would be able to receive the dividend on all the stock in Consols that might have been invested in the names of the executors. Therefore Haslewood proposed instead of the power of attorney, an order should be given to Davison to pay the annuity regularly to Marsh as soon as the dividend was received.

Unfortunately there remains no further correspondence on this subject but Fanny may have felt uneasy to hear that her future payments depended on Davison – and she would have been right to do so; in 1808 Davison stood trial for fraud over Government stock.

CHAPTER XIV
The Widow

Little has been published regarding the lady Nelson married, Mrs Nisbet…a lady of that calm and equable temperament, governed chiefly by common sense, which has no sympathy with, and is nearly incapable of understanding the waywardness of genius.

T Knox Laughton, *British Sailor Heroes*

Just when Fanny might have felt that she could begin to lead a life untroubled by financial matters and court cases and the initial grief over her husband's death had passed, there came an event that not only stirred up memories but was also guaranteed to create even more rifts. It had been inevitable that there would be a public demand for a biography of Nelson and the Revd J S Clarke, a former naval chaplain and Dr J McArthur, a naval man who had been secretary to Lord Hood, were considered eminently suitable to produce a thoroughly sound record of Nelson's achievements. They had begun their painstaking research, carefully collecting information from many sources including Fanny who was willing to co-operate and lend them such letters from Nelson that would be useful.

However, they were beaten to it in the latter part of 1806, when James Harrison published a hastily put together *Life of Nelson*. Harrison had relied heavily for much of its content on Lady Hamilton, who may actually have suggested the work as part of her continuing campaign to remove all public sympathy from Fanny. Being based mainly on hearsay and gossip, it was both inaccurate and sensationalist. When Fanny read it, she was appalled. Writing to McArthur on 28 February 1807 she left him in no doubt of her feelings on the subject.

I think without exception Mr Harris's *Life of Nelson* is the basest production that ever was offered to the public. It is replete with untruths – in regards to my dear son and self – when my son was told what Mr H said in regard to his saving Lord Nelson's life at Teneriffe, [sic] all the answer he made was 'God knows I saved Lord N's life at T. That's a pleasure no one can take from me'. Lord Nelson often said to me, 'it was not so much Josiah's tying up my arm' (Nisbet says a man in the boat, Lovel, assisted him) 'the grasp he gave it stopped the blood immediately, but his judgement in getting me to the ship.' By all account he rowed very very hard that night and steered well too under the batteries.

This was a reference to the unsuccessful attack on Santa Cruz during which Nelson received the severe wound to his right arm. When Nelson had written to Fanny nearly two weeks after the battle, using his left hand for the first time he had told her briefly: 'I know it will add much to your pleasure in finding that Josiah under God's providence was principally instrumental in saving my life.' The full account of what took place was given to Fanny later but as recognition of Josiah's part in the action: 'Good Earl St Vincent has made Josiah master and commander.' He was given command of the hospital ship, the *Dolphin*. Fanny had been so incensed by Harrison's distortion of the account that she had acquired copies of letters from Lord St Vincent that would negate the libel that had been made on Josiah's character as well as his seamanship. St Vincent wrote:

> Lord Nelson assured me, that he owed his life to the resolution and admirable conduct of his son-in-law [i.e. stepson] when wounded at Teneriffe, and that he had witnessed many instances of his courage and enterprise.

For the next few years Fanny's life was to follow a pattern similar to that of many of her social equals: winter in either Bath or Exmouth, the occasional visit to London and one or other of the other fashionable watering places such as Weymouth, very popular with the royal family, where she stayed with the Pinneys. Among the papers in the Monmouth collection, a series of tradesmen's bills give a fleeting insight into Fanny's domestic habits while she was staying at Great Malvern. In nearby Worcester, at F Dipper & Co's shop, she bought a black straw riding hat that cost her 16/-. Riding in that context referred to the practice of sitting in an open carriage drawn, in Fanny's case, by a pair of chariot horses that she hired at £30 for three months. With a quarter's rent amounting to £53.5.0, repairs to her coach at 10/- and half a dozen bottles of Bristol Water at 3/9d, not to mention fine lump sugar at 8/-, it is not difficult to see that the cost of living was high.

One way many of the upper classes took to cut down on their expenses was to make long visits to other households. Lady Nugent, the wife of a diplomat, described a house party of the period:

22 September 1809 – Ramsgate & Deal – This morning very busy & we all dined again at Sir Henry Dashwood's. The Duchess of Manchester

etc. Very amusing arrangement of carriage for the party to go to the ball at Broadstairs. At last the Duchess and General Nugent went in a hack chaise, with the singing Mr Mercer, as a bodkin [squeezed between them]. The events of the ball equally amusing. Old Lady Nelson shocked at Lady John Campbell & the Duchess of Manchester asking their own partners etc. She assured me that Lady J Campbell must be mad, or worse; for she wore half boots & had a dog called Devil...

This reference presents a problem. It would be easy to assume that Lady Nugent is referring to Fanny who, at almost 50, might be allowed the appellation of old and she certainly knew Henry Dashwood. But at that time Fanny was usually referred to as Viscountess Nelson and Bronte. There was, however, another 'Lady Nelson', the wife of the Rector, but since he was now an Earl, she was officially the Countess. The editor of Lady Nugent's journal believed the reference was to the latter lady but it is open to question and underlines the point that casual mention in the press or other documents cannot always be relied upon. However, Lady Nugent did include another small piece of information in her journal that indirectly threw light on to both Fanny and Lady Hamilton. When Nelson's 'dear friend' arrived in London in 1800, much comment was made both in the press and by those who met her as to her voluptuous figure that was not just the result of her pregnancy. In comparison, Fanny was described as a slight figure and her supposedly excessive thinness has often been quoted as another reason for Nelson rejecting her in favour of the more generous proportions of the other. Lady Nugent made it clear that slender figures were not unusual when she reported from Bath:

> After we had taken our glass of water, went with little ones to Rosenberg's & had them weighed. George 2 st. 9, Louisa 2st. I was 6st. 8.

One of the last extant letters Fanny sent to William Marsh personally was on 29 January 1810. From Bath she wrote to tell him that she had heard that the memorial vase commissioned for her by the Patriotic Fund was now ready. She asked Marsh to make arrangements for it to be sent to her at her house in Russell Street, begging him to make sure that if it was necessary it was adequately insured. She had also received another presentation, an advance copy of the official biography. She was obviously pleased with it, and said she hoped it would give pleasure and satisfaction to its readers. Then she related a story of reconciliation. The former Rector, now the Earl, had brought his wife and daughter Charlotte, now a young woman in her early 20s, to Bath three weeks earlier. Fanny had been very moved when:

> their good child not only sought me, but brought her father and mother to my house: I received them, they were much affected and I think they have received some satisfaction from a shake of my hand.

This must have been a difficult moment for all of them. The Rector and his wife had been quick to turn their backs on Fanny when they thought they had more to gain by befriending Lady Hamilton. Sarah, in particular, had joined in the vicious attacks on Fanny's reputation and both of them may have assisted Harrison in the preparation of his book. In addition, the Earl, as executor to Nelson's will, had made it as difficult as possible for Fanny to get her annuity. As for Charlotte, in her early years she had been very fond of Fanny and it is to be hoped that it was the good taste and manners that she learned from her that withstood the later influences of Lady Hamilton. That lady was no longer any use to the Nelson family; she had neither money nor influence; she had not received the pension that Nelson had hoped the country would give her, and her extravagant ways had led her into penury. She was certainly in no position to do anything to further the Rector's ambitions – his brother's death had done that. In the circumstances, Fanny could have been forgiven for not being in any hurry to stretch out the hand of forgiveness to her brother-in-law and his family but as she herself had said long ago, she was not one to hold grudges and her heart had melted when she saw Charlotte, as her words 'good child' show only too clearly. The healing of the breach with Charlotte in particular brought Fanny great joy and when the young woman married the grandson of her great friend, Lord Hood, this brought them even closer.

As has already been said, information about this final section of Fanny's life is intermittent as well as sparse. What is known, however, is that Lady Hamilton made one final attempt to banish Fanny from being remembered as having played a part in Nelson's life. It may have been a desire to take her revenge on the woman who continued to live and bear the title of Viscountess Nelson and Bronte, thereby indelibly identifying herself as Nelson's wife or the very necessary need to make money, that led Lady Hamilton to publish Nelson's letters to her. The two volumes entitled *The Letters of Lord Nelson to Lady Hamilton; with a Supplement of interesting Letters by distinguished Characters* were published in London in 1814. While many rushed to read the passionate outpourings of their hero to his mistress: 'Blazoned in every newspaper, and in every shop window in the kingdom', others found the work thoroughly distasteful. *The Edinburgh Review* for September 1814 devoted thirteen pages to it beginning:

> We scarcely remember to have seen a more reprehensible publication; or one in which the frailties of the Mighty Dead have been more wantonly and barbarously unveiled – without the possibility or indeed the pretext of any other motive than that of the sordid and miserable profit that may be made of the exhibition...who but the receiver of these letters could have the means of giving them to the public? Who but the object of this guilty, but ardent and devoted love, could have betrayed its follies and its phrenzy [sic] to our gaze?

The article went on to point out that although Lady Hamilton had put notices in the papers disclaiming any part in it, it was very difficult to believe since she had made no effort to stop its publication. The reviewer could only assume that as the letters had not been reported missing, then Lady Hamilton had sold:

> ...the indefensible and imprudent, but most confidential letters – addressed to her by Lord Nelson, to a bookseller for money!...had, for the sake of a few pounds, exposed them to the eyes of the world!

The astute reviewer was conscious that in mentioning the book at all, he was contributing to its publicity but he wished to draw attention to a promise within its pages, that was probably intended as a threat, that there were a great many more letters being prepared for publication which would: 'throw light on political transactions at present *very imperfectly understood.*' Beginning his next paragraph with the benign words that the published letters showed Nelson to have 'a warm, affectionate and generous nature', he quickly moved in to an attack that would have sickened Lady Hamilton.

> There is a culpable disregard of domestic ties, and a neglect, approaching to cruelty, of one he was bound by honour, as well as religion, morality and law, to cherish. This neglect, the consequence of an improper passion, seems (as frequently happens in minds otherwise virtuous) to have rankled to a degree of hatred, from the workings of self-reproach. Nor can a more melancholy instance be found of the maxim, that we are apt to dislike those whom we have wronged, and thus preposterously to visit on them the sins of our own injustice.

He then wrote glowingly of Fanny, calling her an amiable woman while emphasising Nelson's growing hatred towards her once he had fallen in love with Lady Hamilton. In supporting Fanny, he was making a moral point that by condoning Nelson's behaviour, the general public had the excuse to do the same because 'Nelson did it.' He also noted that these letters showed that Nelson had alienated himself from others:

> The effusions of his passion, with such trifles as lovers write about, and a petty indiscriminate abuse of every man, woman, and child, whom he has occasion to mention, except Sir William and Lady Hamilton, and one or two of their common friends, not amounting to quite six privileged persons, make up the bulk, if not the whole, of his letters.

Pursuing the theme, the reviewer pointed out how abusive Nelson had been about almost all his friends, particularly his naval colleagues, most of whom had always spoken highly of him. He also called into question Nelson's often self-opinionated action during battles: 'If every commanding officer had acted so…nay if only a very few officers had acted so, the speedy ruin of our affairs must have ensued.'

Not to be entirely negative in his approach the reviewer drew attention to the compassionate side of Nelson's nature citing his attitude to his friend Capt. Parker who had died from his wounds. More interesting was his mention of 'a Mrs Thomson and her child [who] appear, after Lady Hamilton, principally to occupy his thoughts'. Perhaps the reviewer was unaware that the references to Mrs Thomson were all part of the elaborate code devised by Nelson. The state of Mrs Thomson's health alluded to Lady Hamilton's final weeks of pregnancy and the birth of the child named Horatia, whom Nelson was to claim as his adopted daughter. It is difficult to know how many of the general public were aware of the true nature of the relationship to the child.

There is no extant evidence that Fanny read these volumes; it would have been against her natural instincts to pry into others' correspondence even when it was offered to public view. But she might have found it difficult to escape from extracts that appeared in the press and people around her may have read the work, not because they wanted to but because they thought they ought. One imagines that Josiah, who had watched his stepfather in the early stages of his love affair, would have wanted to know exactly what had been said about him. If the other letters, as was hinted at in *The Edinburgh Review's* article, included many of those from the Nelson family, then Fanny would have learned the true extent of their treachery against her. There was even one from Edmund which praised Lady Hamilton in terms that the old gentleman had known would please his son. Suddenly, it seemed that all the bitterness and hurt was to be brought to the surface and raked through again. It would also have affected Fanny's attitude to those who had attempted to regain her friendship.

It must have come as a relief to Fanny when she heard of Lady Hamilton's death. She would have appreciated the irony that she should outlive the woman who had so often wished her dead. Perhaps now, Fanny would be free to enjoy the rest of her life without the shadow of 'the lady from 23 Piccadilly' forever at her elbow. So, in 1815, Fanny finally put down roots and took an elegant but not overlarge house in Exmouth, on the cliff top known as The Beacon from which she could enjoy a panoramic view of the ocean. Once there, she invited one of her many goddaughters to come and make her home with her. Like most of the others, this one also had her godmother's name of Frances and since she was distantly related, they also shared in common the second name of Herbert. This Frances was the fourth daughter of Henry Evans, a solicitor who lived in Glamorgan in a property known as Eagles Bush. Almost nothing is known about this gentleman, except that he had at least four daughters to marry off, an expensive business as has been seen. It is not known how Fanny came to make the acquaintance of this remote cousin, he was never mentioned in any of her letters but it is likely that he was connected with her Bristol friends and rela-

tions and may also have had links with Nevis. It is possible that the actual
family relationship came through his wife. The fact that Fanny had stood
godmother to Frances, who was born around 1792, shows that the relationship, whatever it was, was of long standing. In the past, Fanny had taken
girls like Nelson's nieces, the Bolton twins and Charlotte Nelson under her
wing and had helped educate them and prepare them for entry into society.
But this was different. Frances Evans was in her early 20s and at the age
when she ought to have been married. It is possible that in having her live
with her, Fanny hoped that Exmouth might widen her chances of finding
a husband – she may even have had her son in mind. Alternatively, Fanny
may have wanted her solely to provide her with female companionship and
take the place of the daughter she had never had.

In the following year, Frances accompanied her godmother and Josiah to
spend the summer at Teignmouth and Torquay. Josiah, who was still on half
pay from the Navy but otherwise unemployed, like so many young men of
his social class was left to fill his days as best he could. With a certain amount
of financial independence from his Nisbet inheritance he was able to indulge
his love of the sea by sailing. He started with a small yacht and eventually,
with Fanny's assistance, he was able to afford a boat capable of crossing the
channel. Frances shared his love of sailing and in the spring of 1819 they married. There is an amusing anecdote that has been passed down through the
ages relating to this marriage. It was said that the mysterious strife, referred
to so long before by Nelson between Josiah and his mother, had continued
until 1819. Whenever they met, Fanny is supposed to have nagged Josiah
to find himself a wife. On one occasion as she is reputed to have done so
yet again, Josiah shocked her into silence by telling her that he was already
married. He then turned to Frances who was sitting on a sofa beside Fanny,
saying: 'Lady Nelson, there is Mrs Nisbet. Fanny, my love, kiss your mother.'
A highly romantic idea that may well have appealed to the grandchildren
of the Matcham family, whence this story emanated but it will not stand up
to scrutiny. There is ample proof that Fanny and her son had lived happily
together for many years and as for Josiah creeping off to marry his Frances
secretly, how would they explain the fact that the Viscountess Nelson and
Bronte signed their marriage certificate at Littleham church?

For Fanny, life changed dramatically with the marriage of her son. One
might assume that having now reached 60 she was prepared to settle into
the sedate, somewhat restricted life suited to a dowager of mature years.
Far from it! If anything, life for Fanny for the next ten years was to be more
full and more active than ever before. Certainly she widened her horizons,
no longer was her time spent between the watering places of the south
west of England. Europe beckoned. Following the defeat of Napoleon at
Waterloo, the English nobility had speedily renewed its love affair with
France, quickly establishing little British enclaves in Paris and the coastal
resorts. It is said that Josiah and Frances spent their honeymoon sailing
along the French coast and it would appear that Fanny was with them,

at least for part of the journey, before spending the summer at an hotel in Dieppe where she was joined by many other fashionable people, among them, the Duchess of Wellington. The two ladies had at least two things in common; their husbands had become national heroes for their part in the war against Napoleon and they had both been cast aside for a mistress.

The following year, 1820, the family was back in Exmouth for the birth in February of Fanny's first grandchild, a boy named Horatio, in honour of her husband, and Woolward to commemorate her family name. It is said that it was this year too, that Fanny indulged her son and daughter-in-law by buying them their own carriage. Most of her adult life Fanny had had to be very money conscious. She did not have what she could not pay for and she did not waste money either. How pleasurable then, it must have been for her to suddenly find that she had more than she needed. So, she was able to indulge her son – something she had been unable to do when he was young, but more important, she was able to indulge in the pleasure of helping others in need.

Instructions to Marsh & Co at intervals over the next few years reveal that she subscribed annually to the charity set up to help those injured at the Battle of Trafalgar. Sometimes these were simply donations to the general fund, at others, a large donation to help a specific officer wounded in the battle. But she also helped her friends. Her sister-in-law Miss Anne Nisbet had obviously fallen on hard times for Fanny gave orders to her bankers on several occasions to send her quite large gifts. Similarly, she helped make the life of Miss Elizabeth Locker, the daughter of Nelson's old friend, a little more comfortable with regular monetary gifts. And it is reported that on 31 January 1821, Fanny and Josiah threw a lavish dinner and ball in Exmouth. It may be that this was to mark Josiah's and Frances' departure from the town because Josiah, now with the responsibility of a wife and a family, had decided to go into business. He was entering the world of finance in Paris.

During the French Revolution, much of old Paris had been destroyed. Redevelopment was now in progress so Capt. (as he was still termed, although he never went back to sea) and Mrs Nisbet set up home in one of the newly built houses at the top of the Champs Elysées. Here Fanny would join them for months on end and certainly for the birth of their second son on the last day of 1821. He was named Josiah for his father and grandfather and Herbert to commemorate the family heritage. A weak baby, he survived for just over two weeks.

Fanny spent much of 1822 travelling in other parts of France and Switzerland. Lady Hardy, the wife of Fanny's devoted admirer and Nelson's flag captain, who did not really like Fanny, perhaps because her husband sang her praises too often, wrote in her *Memoirs*:

In July the Viscountess Nelson, widow of Lord Nelson came to Lausanne for a few weeks with her daughter-in-law and her three granddaughters and I gave her a soiree on 6 July.

Lady Hardy's *Memoirs*, written towards the end of her life, are based on diary notes she kept at the time so although she may be accurate as far as the date was concerned when she gave the evening entertainment in honour of the Viscountess, one detail was incorrect and based on much later knowledge. In July 1822 Fanny had but one grandchild, the 2-year-old Horatio. It was during this visit that Fanny and the Nisbets are reputed to have met Lord Byron. The story goes that Byron took them all out on the lake in his rowing boat and that <u>one</u> of the Nisbet children fell overboard but was rescued by the gallant poet. It was feasible that with Josiah's love of sailing, he and Byron had something in common and that had they met, they might have all gone out in Byron's boat but again there was only one child and it would seem very unlikely that one so young would have been in a position to fall overboard. Quite how this story arose is unknown but it has persisted even though the present Byron Society is unable to offer any proof of its likely veracity. From Lausanne, they crossed back into France to Strasbourg and in early September they were in Colmar, a town close to the Rhine border between Strasbourg and Basel en route to Zurich. Here it was necessary for Fanny to catch up on her correspondence and attend to her business affairs. On 5 September she wrote to Marsh & Co:

> Gentlemen – On the 30th of August I drew on your House for three hundred pounds Sterling in favour of Mr J P Franks of Strasbourg. I wish you to send a Bank Post Bill of fifty pounds to Mr Black Surgeon Exmouth.

October found her at the Hôtel Roi d'Angleterre in Dieppe from where she again had business to attend to, in this case with the Post Office in Zurich. In a clear, flowing hand she wrote:

> Sir – I have received a letter from the Post Office Exmouth Devonshire informing me that a letter directed to the Viscountess Nelson has been forwarded Sept. 7th to the Post office Zurich Switzerland, which letter I request may be forwarded to me at Dieppe. I am – your Humble Servant – Frances H Nelson & Bronte.

Fanny was still in Dieppe at the beginning of December when she found it necessary to write a very strong letter to the bankers reminding them that she had written to them four times and had not received an answer to any of her letters. On this occasion she directed that £30 was to be sent to the Exmouth surgeon and £20 to a Mrs Dare of Bridgend. In this same letter she revealed that Josiah was also paying two annual subscriptions to support named officers injured at Trafalgar.

The winter of 1823 found Fanny back in Paris for the arrival of her first granddaughter who on 16 February was baptised in honour of her grandmother, Frances Herbert Nisbet. June of that year found her in the Hôtel Maurice, probably in Dieppe, she staying on land while the Nisbets sailed their yacht. It was from the Hôtel Maurice that Fanny wrote about one of her gifts, that twenty pounds to Mrs Dare of Bridgend in Glamorganshire. This may have been a second donation but the tone of Fanny's letter to Marsh & Co. suggests that they had failed to carry out her original request, hence Fanny's comment that she had told Mrs Dare to write to her immediately she received the Bank Post Bill. There was no indication as to who this lady was or why she should merit the gift but the note of urgency in Fanny's letter suggests that Mrs Dare was in need of the money.

The following year brought another granddaughter, Sarah born at the end of August. She, like her brothers Horatio and Josiah, was to die young. By now Fanny was spending more and more time in Paris and was becoming part of the English society there. It was in Paris that she was to repair the last of the Nelson family fences when she encountered some of the Matcham girls at an evening entertainment. The renewed relationship became strong enough that Kitty Matcham would later enlist Fanny's aid to write to Prince William to plead the cause for employment for one of her sons-in-law. Old habits die hard and Fanny was still willing to be used by her in-laws in spite of their disloyalty.

But Paris also gave her the chance to catch up with other old friends, in particular Sir Edward and Lady Berry and the Hardys who often stayed at the Embassy in Paris. The Ambassador's wife, Harriet Countess Granville, kept up an unflagging correspondence with her sister, Lady Morpeth and her brother, the Duke of Devonshire. Unreserved in her comments, she painted a lively picture of her everyday life in Paris from 1824. From her we learn about the theatres and opera as well as all the dinners, balls and soirees which provided entertainment for the English, among them:

> Ladies Jersey, Gwydr, Tankerville, Mrs Hope etc – their conversation is all upon dress, the Opera, Talma. There is not as much mind as would fill a pea-shell.

An idea of just how many of the nobility were in Paris at one time is revealed when the countess had to select some ladies to accompany her to her presentation at the French Court. From the peeresses alone she had the choice of Ladies Abercorn, Newburgh, Caroline Lamb, Northland, Belfast, Granard, Thomond, Waterford, Ailesbury, Worcester, Aldborough, Glenlyon and Strathall.

Although Fanny does not feature in the countess's letters, that is not to say that she did not visit the Embassy. Certainly, in the early days before St George's Anglican church was built, she would have attended the Sunday services held in the Embassy dining room where several of her grandchildren would have been baptised by the very evangelical minister, Lewis Wray, who was known not just for his impressive sermons but also for his imperious manner, pausing, should anyone dare to whisper while he was speaking and saying, 'when So & So has done talking, I will proceed.' From the countess we get glimpses of everyday life, from her garden: 'looking out upon the Champs Elysées all alive with cabriolets, horse and foot passengers ' and taking her children to the Ecole de Natation to learn to swim or to the Bois de Boulogne to ride their ponies, activities that would have been available to Fanny's grandchildren.

In September 1826 and December 1829, two more granddaughters were born, Mary and Georgina, making the three little Nisbet girls. The eldest son, Horatio, had joined his brother Josiah and sister Sarah in the Paris graveyard. Fanny was spending so little time in England that she gave up the house in Exmouth, deciding instead to take a house in London's Harley Street which would provide a base for the Nisbets should they ever leave Paris. Her companion when she was in London was Mrs Francklyn, formerly Frances Webbe, a cousin of her first husband, who lived in nearby Baker Street. Younger than Fanny, she too had an only son. She may also have been a widow but there may have been some scandal or mystery about her husband as her son in later life dropped his father's surname in favour of his mother's maiden name.

It is not known if Josiah had been in indifferent health for some time. It is likely that whatever caused his death, said by some to be dropsy, he had time to draw up his will on 13 May 1830, two months before he died. This close written document ran to six pages and was full of instructions. Many of the comments he made show that he had learnt lessons from his past. He started by confirming the sum of money he had settled upon his wife upon their marriage thus making sure his wife would not suffer from lack of funds as his mother had done. It is not clear why he also stipulated that his children should during their childhood live in Great Britain, unless their health required otherwise, and that they should be brought up according to the teachings of the Church of England. Possibly he was disillusioned by life in Paris or perhaps the growing signs of trouble within the country worried him. Significantly, he left the children under the care and management of their mother for her life:

> ...or until my said wife shall contract a second marriage in which case... the child or children shall be immediately removed by the trustees from... their said mother and no longer permitted to reside with her...

It is difficult not to draw the conclusion from this harsh injunction that Josiah was reacting strongly to his own experience with a stepparent. He made Fanny one of his trustees, the others being George, Lord Vernon and Christopher Mansell Talbot. Apart from the £100 he left to his friend, Admiral the Hon. Thomas Bladen Capel, the rest of his estate was put in trust for his children until they reached 21 or in the case of girls, when they married if that came earlier. In the event of his children dying before they came of age or failing to have issue then his estate passed to others. Of these he mentioned his Nisbet cousins and one whose Christian name he had either forgotten or did not know: 'In trust for [blank] Woolward a distant relation now in the West Indies.' Fortunately the trustees did not have to trace the unknown cousin as all three of Josiah's remaining daughters not only survived to 21 but they also married and lived to an old age. Fanny might not hold grudges, but it seems that Josiah did and toward the end of his will he added another strong injunction:

I do hereby expressly prohibit my said trustees or any or either of them from employing or consulting professionally or otherwise Herbert Mansell Evans of Eagles Bush…concerning the execution of this trusts of my will or in or about the management of my estate or effects or in any manner relating thereto…

Josiah's father-in-law must have upset him badly to merit such strong words.

Josiah died on 14 July. To have one's children predecease them is difficult for any parent. At a time of high infant mortality, it was something to be borne with resignation, as they had with the untimely deaths of three of the Nisbet children. But for Fanny, to see one's child go first when he had reached 50 was exceptionally hard to bear. But she could not give in to her grief, she had to be strong as she had so often in the past, for now she had the responsibility of Frances and her three little girls aged 7, almost 4 and six months. One thing was certain. Josiah should not be buried in foreign soil. Fanny wanted to take him home – home being Exmouth, the place where Josiah had found happiness and where she had determined she should be buried.

So Fanny took charge of the situation. But before she arranged to have his body transported home, there were other arrangements to be made. If they were to leave Paris for good, Frances was reluctant to leave her three dead children behind. This was not so much the sentimentality of an over-wrought, bereaved woman as a genuine fear that harm might be done to the children's graves. Trouble was brewing in Paris. For some time there had been rumblings of discontent amongst the French middle class and in the press against the inept government of the king, Charles X. When he directed his favourite, the reactionary Polignac, to form a new ministry, the Chamber of Deputies objected strongly, resulting in the king dismissing it and calling an election. When that produced a Chamber even more strongly opposed to Polignac, the king dismissed that too. Realising that the press had much to do with stirring up the educated middle classes, he and Polignac attempted to impose strong control over the newspapers and at the same time altered the criteria which proved eligibility to vote, thus substantially reducing the electorate. Those living in Paris realised they were sitting on a powder keg and that it would take little to set it alight. Although the middle classes were hardly thought to do more than simply protest, past experience had shown what could happen once the masses were aroused. Last time had seen looting and desecration of places that had nothing to do with those in power and graveyards had not escaped the attacks. So there was nothing for it, the bodies of the children would have to be exhumed and taken back to England.

This would not have been a simple matter; there would have been legalities and all the pettifogging bureaucracy that went with them. Fanny must have been thankful that her French was fluent enough for her to deal with the officials as well as the undertakers who were required to perform the operation. Finally the bodies were retrieved and with that of Josiah, the little party were able to set off for England after dealing with the business of shutting up the house and arranging for its sale, packing up the contents for shipping back as well as packing their personal belongings and the items they would need for the journey. All this was executed in some haste and in many ways it must have reminded Fanny of that fateful time when she had packed up following Nelson's return to sea in 1801. There is an apocryphal story that Fanny, Frances and the girls made their escape from Paris under cover of darkness, dressed as servants, though quite why was not explained. The originator of that story seems to have muddled the events of the Second Revolution with the First. Fortunately, they were able to get away before the real trouble broke out thus avoiding all the other expatriates who converged on the passport offices seeking the necessary documentation to leave the country. So they missed the fierce battle of 27 July that followed after the police attempted to close down all cafes and reading rooms where people gathered to read liberal papers. As fast as the police moved into one area, newspapers were delivered to others until eventually there was confrontation; mounted police moved in, cannon opened fire and by mid afternoon the city was a blood bath.

Fanny and her family reached the coast, where despite the number of refugees also waiting, they managed to cross the channel to Exmouth. According to *The Exeter Gazette* for 31 July 1830:

> On Friday evening last a French schooner rigged pilot boat arrived at Exmouth with the corpses of Admiral [sic] Nesbit, son of Lady Nelson, who died in Paris the 14th inst of the dropsy and also three of his children who lately died in Paris.

Josiah would have appreciated his rapid promotion. Later father and children were buried in the quiet churchyard at Littleham.

Once the funeral was over and the bereaved females had had time to mourn in private, Fanny decided that what they all needed was a change of air and, for her that panacea, hot sea-bathing. So they went, not to Bath nor to Clifton but to Brighton. Here Fanny took rooms for them at the Sea House Hotel, one of the hotels much favoured by members of the upper classes who did not wish to rent houses for the duration of their stay. Among her fellow guests were the Bishop of Chichester, the Viscountess Dudley and

Ward, and Lady Mary Elliott. Brighton was full of important and titled people taking holidays, enjoying the facilities of the spa and all the social activities of a town graced by the presence of the king himself. William IV and his queen were having a holiday too at the Pavilion. *The Brighton Gazette* faithfully recorded for its readers the comings and goings of all the notable arrivals in the town. The king's itinerary around the area was described, as were the dinner parties he gave. Listed also were those who paid their loyal respects by leaving their names at the Pavilion. This custom allowed His Majesty to know who was in Brighton and to whom he should offer some form of recognition. It is to be assumed that Fanny left her name but whether or not she expected any reaction is not known. It had been some time since Fanny had attended Drawing Rooms in London and in that interval the monarch had changed, not once but twice. George III's son, the Prince of Wales, had acted as Regent for his father before becoming George IV. His reign had been short lived and his heir, his daughter Charlotte, had predeceased him. Thus the throne had passed in 1830 to his brother, William – the same Prince William who had been present at Fanny's wedding. Although Fanny had met him as the Duke of Clarence on several occasions since Nelson's death, she had not been presented to him as king.

When William learned that Fanny was in Brighton, he sent an emissary to the Sea House Hotel on a Saturday at the beginning of September to let Fanny know that the king would call on her on Monday afternoon. *The Brighton Gazette* informed its readers:

> ...about four o'clock on the latter day his Majesty went in his carriage and remained with her Ladyship for three quarters of an hour. We believe that his Majesty, when Duke of Clarence, gave the Viscountess away, at her marriage.

The newspaper also revealed that Fanny's was the last of three visits made by the king that afternoon, he had previously called upon Mrs FitzHerbert and a Mrs Holloway but Fanny's visit merited a greater mention. And no doubt, the king and the viscountess had much to talk about, both being of an age when reminiscences of earlier and happier days were to be relished. For Fanny, this was in many ways her final triumph, without seeking it she had been singled out by the king and was once again brought to the attention of the bel monde many of whom had forgotten her and her history.

She and Frances remained in Brighton for several weeks more. Thereafter her movements are uncertain except that they were all at her home in Harley Street in London in the early months of 1831. Possibly the last letter Fanny wrote to Alexander Davison after a very long gap in their correspondence was in January. Written on black edged mourning paper she asked: 'Is all the business relating to the death of Josiah finished?' Surely after all these years, that wretched Deed of which Davison was a Trustee was still not a problem, yet the doubt is there, for she asked him to say: '...whether it is necessary for Mr Ryder to visit upon you – would you wish to see Mr Marsh.' And then, presumably in answer to some comment Davison had made in his letter to her she referred back to 1801 to the domestic arrangements of her brother-in-law, Maurice: 'I always thought you did not like to know my friend M Nelson's wife and so did Mr Nelson'. Although still able to cope with financial and business matters, that last sentence showed that Fanny was ageing, looking back to the past as if it was within recent memory. Someone else who had aged was Fanny's man Samuel who had been with her for over thirty years as footman and coachman. 'As Samuel is rather deaf I fear he did not hear your message to me.'

It is not certain how long after this Fanny became ill, or indeed what was wrong with her. She had always suffered from rheumatism and chest infections that caused troublesome coughs, so either could have contributed to her final illness. On 18 April Fanny drew up her will. Her life having been plagued either by intestacy or complicated testaments, hers was to be as simple as possible. To her daughter-in-law she left the interest on two instalments of twelve hundred pounds for her life, the principal passing thereafter to her eldest granddaughter. It would appear that Fanny was not at that stage worried that her death was imminent because she added the remark that if she lived long enough to save any more money, then the interest from that too was to go to Frances Nisbet. Simple and direct. In fact too simple; Fanny had forgotten to name her executors, so the following week Lord Bridport and General Egarton were appointed but the codicil lacked the name of the main witness; Ellen Hoye, her maid, who had witnessed the first along with Fanny Francklyn, is described in this second statement as 'under witness'. On 3 May Fanny remembered an old friend in need and wrote a final codicil: 'It is my desire that the Right Honourable Lord Bridport gives one hundred pounds to Miss Locker immediately on my death.' And it was there that Fanny slipped up in her effort to keep things simple. She wrote the date as 'April 3 1831' and then she remembered, or had it pointed out to her that the month was now May, so she crossed through April and substituted May. Three days later on 6 May, with her beloved granddaughters and daughter-in-law at her bedside, Fanny died. But in the midst of their grief, that one little error in Fanny's will resulted in Frances Nisbet, Christiana Morton Herbert and George Delmar all having to appear personally before the Prerogative Court of Canterbury to swear that the handwriting of the substituted word 'May' was indeed that of Fanny. The legal document to cover this is almost twice as long as Fanny's entire will.

But even in death, Fanny was not allowed to pass quietly into oblivion – the Nelson family had to have the last word. Lady Hardy recalled in her *Memoirs*:

Lady Nelson died. I had often seen her during her illness, and as soon as I heard she was dead I called on her daughter-in-law, Mrs Nisbet, who was also a widow and she complained bitterly of the conduct of Lady Bridport

[Charlotte Nelson] who she said had come to the house as soon as she heard of Lady Nelson's death and had carried away two large porcelain vases representing Lord Nelson's battles which had been given to Lady Nelson by Lord Spencer when First Lord of the Admiralty, and she had specially left them to her grand daughters, the children of Capt. Nisbet. She [Mrs Nisbet] asked me, if I was called upon to give testimony to the effect of Lady Nelson's intentions on this subject, if I would do so and as I could conscientiously, I promised I would and so I should, but I believe the vases were restored to Mrs Nisbet for her children.

Fanny's body was taken to Littleham to be interred in the family grave. The funeral, as was customary, was an all-male affair which included her old adversary, the Rector and it was he who, as he had always done, grabbed the attention of the newspapers on the occasion. Perhaps in a form of poetic justice for Lady Bridport's precipitous snatch of the vases, while the Rector was at Fanny's funeral, his London house was burgled.

Whatever eulogies were made about Fanny during the service, none could have had the impact of the tribute Lady Berry made some years later to Sir Nicholas Harris Nicolas when he was researching for his book *The Despatches and Letters of Lord Nelson*. She wrote:

Lord Nelson always bore testimony to the merits of Lady Nelson and declared in parting from her, that he had not one single complaint to make – that in temper, person and mind, she was everything he could wish... I assure you from my personal knowledge, in a long and intimate acquaintance, that Lady Nelson's conduct was not only affectionate, wise and prudent, but admirable throughout her married life...

Sources

Nelson's Letters to His Wife and other documents, 1785–1831 (ed. George P B Naish). This valuable work contains much of the material relevant to this book.

The Davison Letters (Caird Library, National Maritime Museum, Greenwich), DAV/2/1 – 71.

The Monmouth Collection (Nelson Museum, Monmouth): E700; 702; 703; 704; E695; E714/43; 713/7; 724/78; 719/65; 723/76; 722/72; 721/71; 720/61; 718/61; 717/52; 716/50; 715/46; 725/80; 731/105; 727/92; 728/95; 729/97; 730/103; 269a/31; 269/31; 531/2; 333/37; 532.32; 678/1; 726/89.

Houghton Library, Harvard University, Cambridge MA, USA: MS Eng. 196.50: 90; 91; 92; 93.

Log of HMS *Boreas* (National Archives, Kew).

Letters of Harriet Countess Granville (ed. F Leveson Gower).

The Journal of a Lady of Quality (eds E W and C Andrews).

List of Graduates in Medicine in the University of Edinburgh 1705–1860.

Wills: Viscountess Nelson and Bronte; John Richardson Herbert; Revd Edmund Nelson; Maurice Nelson; Josiah Nisbet; Josiah Walter Nisbet; Walter Nisbet; Thomas Williams.

Petition to Dissolve the Marriage of Walter Nisbet and Anne Blomberg, his wife.

Newspapers and magazines: *The Bath Chronicle; The Bath Journal; The Brighton Herald; The Exeter Gazette; The Ipswich Journal; The Ipswich Chronicle; Norwich Mercury; The Sussex Weekly Advertiser; The Times; The Edinburgh Review* (Vol. III).

Bibliography

Andrews, E W and C (eds), *The Journal of a Lady of Quality* (1939) New Haven

Austen, Jane, *Persuasion* (1818) Thomas Dent & Sons, London

_____ *Pride and Prejudice* (1813) Nicholas Vane, London

_____ *Sense and Sensibility* (1811) Nicholas Vane, London

Carr, F B, *Nelson, Nisbet and Nevis (1994)* The Nevis Historical and Conservation Society, Nevis

Coleman, T, *Nelson, the Man and the Legend* (2001) Bloomsbury, London

Cox, M, *The Life and Times of the 12th Earl of Derby* (1974) J A Allen, London

Delaforce, P, *Nelson's First Love,* (1988) Bishopgate Press, London

Edgecombe, R (ed.), *The Diary of Frances, Lady Shelley* (1912) John Murray, London

Eickelmann, C, and Small, D, *Pero – The Life of a Slave in Eighteenth-century Bristol,* (2004) Redcliffe Press, Bristol

Fraser, F, *Beloved Emma, The Life of Emma, Lady Hamilton,* (1986) Weidenfeld & Nicolson, London

Gordon, J, *Nevis, the Queen of the Caribees* (1985) Macmillan Caribbean

_____ *The Little Duchess* (2002) Stanewood Publications, Devon

Gore, J, *Nelson's Hardy and His Wife* (1937) John Murray, London

Grant, N H (ed.), *The Letters of Mary Nisbet, Countess of Elgin* (1926) John Murray, London

Hardwick, M, *Emma – Lady Hamilton* (1969) Cassell, London

Hibbert, C, *Nelson: A Personal History* (1994) Viking, London

Hubbard, V K, *Swords, Ships and Sugar* (1996) Premiere Editions International, Inc. Corvallis, USA

Hunter Blair, P, *The Nelson Boy* (1999) Church Farm Books, Cambridge

Keate, E M, *Nelson's Wife,* (1939) Cassell, London

Leveson Gower, F (ed.), *The Letters of Harriet Countess Granville* (1904) Longman Green, London

Luttrell, B, *The Prim Romantic – A Biography of Ellis Cornelia Knight, 1758–1837* (1965) Chatto & Windus, London

Matcham, M E, *The Nelsons of Burnham Thorpe* (1911) Lane, London

Morriss, R, *Nelson: The Life and Letters of a Hero* (1998) Collins & Brown, London

Naish, G (ed.), *Nelson's Letters to his Wife and other documents* (1958) Routledge & Kegan Paul, London, Navy Records Society

Nicolas, N H (ed.), *Despatches and Letters of Lord Nelson* (1997) Chatham, London

Oman, Carola, *Nelson* (1967) Hodder & Stoughton, London

Pares, R, *A West-India Fortune* (1950) Longman, London

Pocock, T, *Nelson* (1987) Bodley Head, London

_____ *The Women in Nelson's Life* (1999) Andre Deutsch, London

Rawson, G (ed.), *Nelson's Letters* (1960) J M Dent, London

Russell, Jack, *Nelson and the Hamiltons* (1969) Anthony Blond, London

Scarffe, N (ed.), *de La Rochefoucauld: A Frenchman's Year in Britain* (1988) Boydell, London

Southam, B, *Jane Austen and the Navy* (2000) Hambledon, London

Southey, R, *The Life of Horatio Nelson* (1962) J M Dent, London

Trench, Col. (ed.), *The Remains of Mrs Trench* (1862) Parker Sons & Bourne, London

Vincent, E, *Nelson – Love and Fame* (2003) Yale University Press, London

White, Colin (ed.), *The Nelson Encyclopaedia* (2002) Chatham, London

Wright, P (ed.), *Lady Nugent's Journal* (2002) University of West Indies Press

Yorke, P C (ed.), *The Diary of John Baker* (1931) Hutchinson, London

Index